Applied .NET

Applied .NET

Developing People-Oriented Software Using C#

Ronan Sorensen

George Shepherd

John Roberts

Russ Williams

✦✦ Addison-Wesley

Boston   San Francisco   New York
London   Toronto   Sydney   Tokyo   Singapore   Madrid
Mexico City   Munich   Paris   Cape Town   Hong Kong   Montreal   .

The publisher offers discounts on this book when ordered in quantity for special sales. For more information, please contact:

Pearson Education Corporate Sales Division
One Lake Street
Upper Saddle River, NJ 07458
(800) 382-3419
corpsales@pearsontechgroup.com

Visit us on the Web at *www.awl.com/cseng/*

Library of Congress Cataloging-in-Publication Data

Applied .NET : developing people-oriented software using C# / Ronan Sorensen . . . [et al.]
    p. cm.
    ISBN 0-201-73828-7 (alk. paper)
    1. C# (Computer program language)   2. Application software—Development
  I. Sorensen, Ronan

  QA76.73.C154 A67 2002
  005.2'762--dc21   2001045747

Text printed on recycled paper.
1 2 3 4 5 6 7 8 9 10–CRS–05 04 03 02 01
First printing, October 2001

Contents

Preface

Like a storm that has built energy out at sea, the first waves of a new era of computing have begun to pound the "beaches" of software development. The forces behind this storm have been building for some time and as the waves make land, a somewhat unsuspecting industry braces itself and prepares to survive the fury.

Although this is a rather dramatic way to characterize the current state of affairs in the computer industry, it is nonetheless accurate. Never before has so much technology been made available to such a large community of developers in such an integrated and distributed fashion. Just as someone standing on a beach can tell there's a storm approaching, as a developer you can recognize that a change in the industry is underway. Undoubtedly, you're trying to figure out what all this means and how best to prepare yourself. This book is meant to provide a level of understanding that will prepare you not only to survive in this new era of development but to actually thrive. The information here will help you understand the .NET technologies and show you how they all fit together in a way that will enable you to effectively build next-generation solutions. This book conveys these ideas through the development of several .NET applications using C#.

Applied .NET offers a people-oriented perspective on the new forces changing software development and a set of principles that can be applied to building effective Internet software. We use the term *people oriented* to describe the new wave of software that is approaching as it captures the dynamism that stirred up the .NET storm. The origin of this term dates back several years to a book authored by Ronan in 1998— *Inside Microsoft Windows NT Internet Development*. Part I of that book introduced the new paradigm of people-oriented programming and the concepts embodied within this type of software. The second part of the book explained how earlier technologies could be used to develop systems adhering to these principles.

The .NET technologies take such a significant step closer to the goals and ideals first presented in that earlier work that our choice of a subtitle for this book was natural—*Developing People-Oriented Software Using C#*. This serves our desire to present a perspective on how .NET can be applied to build a new and very exciting class of software. Therefore, although this book applies .NET technology, the objective of that application is to create something more transcendent, which is formally referred to as *people-oriented software*.

In the period of time since *Inside Microsoft Windows NT Internet Development* was published, the ideas it presented have matured and sharpened as a result of various discussions among the authors of this current book. Some of those discussions produced more heat than light, but in the end we are all in agreement that the principles laid out in this book are the right ones and that the future will no doubt be people oriented. This became even more evident just recently when Microsoft announced their HailStorm initiative. Any doubts about the people-oriented perspective ended with that announcement. We are entering a new era in which people will not have to be computer oriented to use software—software will be oriented toward how people actually live. Software will be running many everyday devices, and all of them will be connected in unimaginable ways. The core theme running through it all will be how software is embedded within society and oriented to the people who will use it.

From a people-oriented perspective, .NET is a means to an end rather than an end in itself. No doubt, other books will go into more detail in certain areas of .NET than this one does, and they will be very useful in that regard. This book, however, tries to strike a balance between theory and practice so that we can show you not only how to apply .NET but also what you can achieve as a result of that application. As useful as we think the perspectives and principles contained in *Applied .NET* are, we just don't stop there. The book will actually show you how to apply what you've learned by building realistic .NET applications—it takes a practical look forward.

Acknowledgments

The authors, collectively, would like to thank the following people:

- The Addison-Wesley team: Kristin Erickson, Curt Johnson, Chris Kief, Chanda Leary-Coutu, Marilyn Rash, Cathy Comer, Dianne Wood, Karin Hansen, and Mark Bergeron of Publishers' Design; and a special thanks to Stephane Thomas, our fearless editor.
- All our colleagues at Plural for their encouragement, and special thanks to James Watkins and Connie Hughes who assisted with the promotion of this book.
- Miki Bell who provided some of the artwork.
- Sanjay Parthasarathy, Nelson Rossa, Connie Sullivan, and Rodney Miller from Microsoft for their assistance and comments.
- Rob Howard, John McGuire, Greg Hack, Daryl Richter, Don Browning, Maxim Loukianov, and Christophe Nasarre for their technical reviews.

In addition we include the following individual acknowledgments.

First and foremost I would like to thank my wife Irene and my three daughters Mary, Catherine, and Sophia for allowing me to write another book. This time they knew what to expect and so I am particularly grateful that they continue to put up with my ideas and encourage me to write about them. I would also like to thank my extended family in Ireland, America, and Italy from whom I have received faith, hope, and love. Finally, I would like to thank my fellow authors George, John, and Russ for their friendship and for the privilege of writing this book with them.

R.S.

I express my most grateful appreciation to my family, Sandy Daston and Ted Shepherd, for being supportive and gracious while I toiled away on another book. Thanks also to DevelopMentor for being a great training and thinking place for developers. Thanks to Patrick Shepherd for being a great sounding board, participating on the other side of the modern software fence (I kneel toward Redmond while he kneels toward San Jose). Finally, great thanks are due to Ronan Sorensen, John Roberts, and Russ Williams without whose efforts this book would not have been possible.

G.S.

I would like to thank Pete Nash, Mike Cabrera, and Jason Cuplin for their assistance and support. I thank my fellow authors, whom I have had the distinct pleasure of knowing and working with for years. I thank Ronan Sorensen for creating opportunities over the last four years for many fine adventures in software development and publication, including this one. Thanks to Russ Williams for being a continual source of encouragement and inspiration. Thanks to George Shepherd for encouraging me to write back in the early nineties. Working with you all has been the highlight of my software career. Most of all, I wish to thank my wife Sue and my sons Daniel, Luke, and Michael for their patient and understanding support.

J.R.

I would like to start by thanking my family for the sacrifices they made while I worked on this book. The time spent apart, the baseball games missed, the family gatherings I was unable to attend, and my fatigue and distractedness are just some of the things that I have had to ask them to forgive. I thank my children Ryan, Chase, and McKenzie for their understanding and especially my wife Gina who was so supportive and provided me with much-needed encouragement at just the right time. They are a gift from God for which I am eternally grateful. I would also like to thank my co-authors, all of whom I have worked with and greatly admired. It has been an honor to be a part of this book and I thank them for the quality of the contributions they have made. Special thanks go to Ronan who was the point man on this effort. His hard work, leadership, experience, insight, and instinct have shaped the book that you now hold. Finally, I would like to thank my mother and father for their overconfidence in me through the years. It was an offhand conversation with my father in which he described his passion for programming that gave me the "bug," as he called it, for development. That event not only was the beginning of my chosen career, but it also taught me that there really are no *small* conversations with kids. Mom and dad, I love you both very much.

R.W.

While we have made every effort to avoid inaccuracies in this book, some may be uncovered after it is printed. The Web site at *http://www.people-oriented.net* will provide contact details for reporting errors, and it will also list any corrections or updates.

People-Oriented Software

The Internet has brought software to the people. For the first time in history, ordinary people all over the world are using software to connect to each other. This trend will surely continue as Internet connectivity enters the realms of television, radio, telephone, personal digital assistant (PDA) technology, and the automobile. In addition, people's lives are becoming the primary focus of software—either directly through human interaction via Web-user interfaces or indirectly through business-to-business (B2B) communication targeted at serving human needs. The increasing connectivity of the populace through software combined with software's more specialized focus on people is revolutionizing software design.

The software of the past focused on modeling the operation of *things,* which gave rise to the object-oriented movement. Although today people could be viewed as just another collection of objects in an object-oriented world, this approach would be impractical and likely fail. There is simply no plausible way to model the dynamic interactions and forces within our society using object-oriented design. Social interaction involves issues such as the use of freedom, multicultural preferences, mobility, unpredictability, and geographical location, just to name a few. Simply put, society cannot be adequately represented using the abstraction of an object model. The real world of people is radically different from the world of things, as philosopher Karl Wojtyla (better known as Pope John Paul II) pointed out years ago:

> The world in which we live is composed of many objects . . . As an object, a man is "somebody"—and this sets him apart from every other entity in the visible world, which as an object is always only "something." Implicit in this simple,

elementary distinction is the great gulf which separates the world of persons from the world of things.[1]

Because people are singularly exceptional types of objects and their activities are becoming the central focus of software development, a new programming vision is emerging that targets people's complex dynamic interactivity in a more specialized way.

The .NET platform is an early embodiment of this new programming vision that is oriented toward people. It is necessary to understand the elements of this programming vision to fully leverage the capabilities of .NET. In the days when people were migrating from the C language's procedural-oriented programming to the object-oriented programming of the C++ language, it was easy to make the mistake of trying to adopt the new tool without understanding the paradigm shift that it was designed to address. Some mistakenly viewed C++ as just a better version of C instead of as a radically new way to write software. Similarly, today's .NET could mistakenly be viewed as just a better way to build a Web site instead of as an enabling technology for the next generation of the Internet. To prevent this kind of misunderstanding, the rest of this chapter will examine the people-oriented programming paradigm for building the next generations of the Internet and how the paradigm can be implemented with the .NET platform.

What is the Internet evolving into, and how will .NET help? The success of the Internet is tied to the fact that people are social beings. We quickly embrace innovations that facilitate communication, as the success of the printing press, radio, and television demonstrate. The primary need being addressed by the Internet is people's desire to be involved in a community—an online community that is global in scope. The global online community is naturally subdivided into a vast multitude of smaller communities that target specific groups in more personalized ways. The next generation of the Internet, which will evolve using technologies such as .NET, will more completely and seamlessly connect people through economic, social, and cultural interactions.

Building an online community that adequately represents society is a complicated undertaking. Although dramatic improvements in speed and wireless connectivity will be necessary to allow a truly ubiquitous Internet, the greatest challenge engineers face is overcoming inadequate software methodologies. More sophisticated and powerful software tools and techniques are needed to meet the daunting engineering tasks that exist. Once the appropriate methodologies and tools become available, a global online community can emerge out of the somewhat independent initiatives of

---

[1] Karol Wojtyla (Pope John Paul II). *Love and Responsibility*, trans. H.T. Willetts (New York: William Collins Sons, London, and Farrar, Straus and Giroux, 1981), 21. The ethical principles established in *Love and Responsibility* could be applied to the social aspects of the Internet's impact on society at large.

millions of people. Without the right tools, standards, and methodologies, progress will be very slow, and we will make many wrong turns.

THE PEOPLE-ORIENTED PARADIGM

What is the appropriate software methodology needed to transform the World Wide Web into a more globally connected community? Part I of *Inside Microsoft Windows NT Internet Development*[2] introduced a people-oriented programming paradigm to address this question. The people-oriented paradigm focuses on connecting people in more immediate ways through the Internet and on embedding software within the operations of society so that an online community can emerge. Unlike the other paradigm shifts that have already transformed the software industry, such as procedural- and object-oriented programming, people-oriented programming does not focus on the creation of a new programming language, such as Java. Rather, people-oriented programming focuses on leveraging the rich services provided by modern operating systems such as Windows server.

> The Internet revolution represents a dramatic shift in the way society conducts itself, and so it necessarily represents a dramatic shift in the purpose of software—a paradigm shift—from technologies focused on individual computing tasks to technologies focused on social interaction, cultural expression, and information exchange. Essentially, software designed for the Internet will be responsible for building a global community. It will focus on improving the ordinary circumstances of living, enabling people to more effectively accomplish day-to-day activities. Thus you could aptly call this new paradigm *people-oriented programming* . . . While both ActiveX and Java make valuable contributions to Internet development, they are insufficient by themselves to meet the needs of the Internet era. To rapidly build reliable, scalable, distributed software solutions, we need to take ActiveX and Java and embed them in Internet-enabling systems. This is what the Windows NT server platform technologies provide. Windows NT and Microsoft Windows Distributed interNet Applications Architecture (Windows DNA) provide the tools for implementing people-oriented programming.[3]

---

[2] Ronan Sorensen. *Inside Microsoft Windows NT Internet Development* (Redmond, WA: Microsoft Press, 1998), 5. Used with permission.

In December 1999, Pearson PTR, Slashdot.org, Netscape's DevEdge Online, and *Doctor Dobb's Journal* asked readers to nominate the books that have had the biggest impact on computer technologies to date—the books that stand dog-eared next to computers and are ready to tackle the next challenge—the books that stand the test of time and whose value extend into the years to come. *Inside Microsoft Windows NT Internet Development* was ranked fourth in this Best Computer Books of the Twentieth Century contest.

[3] Ronan Sorensen, *Inside Microsoft Windows NT Internet Development*, 10.

This guiding principle, which had its initial implementation in Windows DNA, has achieved more comprehensive expression in Microsoft's next-generation .NET platform. The .NET platform subsumes the rich system services of Windows DNA and extends them to allow for the creation of people-oriented Web services that can be used in an elaborate and personalized way over the Internet. Although Windows DNA focused on satisfying foundational requirements such as Internet connectivity, transactions, asynchronous programming, fault tolerance, security, and scalability, the .NET platform addresses the need for people-oriented Web services. These Web services will allow people to integrate software more seamlessly into their lives. For example, people will be able to view other people's appointment calendars in a standardized way or integrate their business processes between their customers and suppliers. The focus on people has become increasingly important in the software industry during the last few years, and it predates the .NET platform. On March 29, 1999, Microsoft announced that its company had been reinvented. Microsoft intended to encompass a new, broader vision of the empowerment of people through great software—at any time, in any place, and on any device. Bill Gates, Microsoft's Chairman and Chief Software Architect, explained the company's more people-oriented perspective:

> Our original vision of "a computer on every desk and in every home" is still extremely relevant. Looking to the future, our vision is much more expansive. We see a world where people can use any computing device to do whatever they want to do anytime, anywhere. The PC will continue to have a central role in this future, but it will be joined by an incredibly rich variety of digital devices accessing the power of the Internet. We want to give people the power, connectivity, and ability to choose how they want to use computing in their lives.[4]

The .NET platform will facilitate the creation of software that is much more people oriented because it directly enables the implementation of the three concepts embodied within the people-oriented programming paradigm: (1) universalization, (2) collaboration, and (3) translation.

Universalization

Universalization is a model of development which leverages the capabilities of sophisticated universal runtimes that implement universally accepted Internet standards.

The universalization model relies on the runtime to provide system services that are widely applicable to addressing complex software engineering tasks. Although

---

[4] Microsoft press release ("Microsoft Announces Reorganization," 1999): *http://www.microsoft. com/PressPass/features/1999/03-29reorg.asp.*

programming languages such as C or C++ have powerful capabilities and also have runtime libraries, the runtimes proposed for people-oriented programming are many orders of magnitude richer in their capabilities. Instead of concentrating on programming techniques such as encapsulation, polymorphism, or inheritance to write reusable code, people-oriented programming concentrates on reusing the services of ubiquitous runtimes so that code creation can be minimized and the coding effort can be increasingly directed toward developing people-oriented Web services for building an online community.

The focus of programming shifts from the inherent capabilities of a programming language to the inherent capabilities of a runtime. Windows Server is an example of a runtime that implements universal Internet standards and provides very rich features within its component object model (COM+) services layer. The PocketPC is also an example of a runtime that implements universal Internet standards but has scaled down services more suitable for the devices on which it runs. The .NET runtime more eloquently expresses this model, as we will explain later in the chapter.

Collaboration

Collaboration is a model of synergy in which people-oriented Web services cooperate to provide enhanced services.

The collaboration model facilitates much more sophisticated software integration across organizational boundaries. A people-oriented Web service is any application exposing a programmable interface over the Internet, as opposed to a graphical user interface, with the purpose of enabling developers to build an online community. Examples of these Web services in the retail industry include catalogues of products and accessories, billing and payment processing services, and shipping and delivery services. By programmatically binding these Web services together, software developers all over the globe can collaborate to create marketplaces in which the needs of millions of businesses and consumers are identified and matched.

The software engineering challenges of accomplishing this feat are formidable. Directories are needed to identify the available Web services and to describe how developers can integrate other services with them. People need to form a consensus on Web service description contracts for similar types of services to avoid excessive complexity in integrating multiple service providers. Testing and troubleshooting will require easy ways for programmers to collaborate with multiple Web service providers during the development and operational phases.

Translation

Translation is a model of interoperability that addresses conversion of functionality between heterogeneous platforms and between diverse service description contracts.

The translation model provides an approach to creating a virtual uniformity in an environment that is aggressively diverse. Building an online community requires a seamless way for thousands of Web services to talk to each other. This is not an easy task because there are millions of software developers independently building these types of services using diverse technologies. The Internet is a network of heterogeneous infrastructures that run many different operating systems and use incompatible component protocols like distributed component object model (DCOM), Common Object Request Broker Architecture (CORBA), and remote method invocation (RMI).

It is not feasible to migrate all these systems into a common technology. Instead, people-oriented programming concentrates on translation techniques that allow disparate systems to communicate over ubiquitous Internet standards such as the Hypertext Transfer Protocol (HTTP) and the eXtensible Markup Language (XML). People-oriented Web services can be built with any programming language and on any platform. Internally the service may use proprietary protocols to achieve maximum scalability and an external interface can translate back and forth between the proprietary interface and the ubiquitous Internet standard. The translation model has another equally important objective. It is likely that multiple Web service providers will provide the same type of service but use different description contracts that indicate how to programmatically integrate with that type of service. It will be a considerably complex task for the software developer to try to accommodate all these different service description contracts. The model of translation requires tools and techniques to facilitate a way to map all the description contracts into a common format that the consuming system understands.

A .NET APPROACH

The first version of the .NET platform goes a long way to help software engineers build people-oriented systems that facilitate universalization, collaboration, and translation. Although other competing technologies such as Sun ONE could be used instead of .NET to implement these principles—and other new technologies are likely to appear in the future—the purpose of the following analysis is to give a sampling of how .NET facilitates the development of people-oriented software. The rest of this book provides a more comprehensive analysis.

.NET and Universalization

The Internet of the future will be far more ubiquitous and powerful than the Internet of today, with people interacting through natural interfaces. The Internet will be a high-bandwidth, global network transmitting data, voice, and video and connecting billions of computers, telephones, radios, televisions, PDAs, and automobiles all over the globe.

Wireless connectivity will be fast and affordable, potentially displacing landlines as the most predominant means of Internet access. Many new Internet devices will emerge that will hook up home items like refrigerators, doors, windows, air conditioning units, and security systems. Disposable Internet devices will be commonplace, and people will be able to wear them, mail them, and easily replace them. Data will be universally accessible and will usually not be tied to an Internet device. Although security will be enhanced with biometrics, security and privacy will always be difficult issues. Financial transactions using Internet cards will be widespread, and the line between buying online and buying in person will become blurred because the primary distinction between the two will be delivery or pickup. There will be newer, more natural ways of communicating over the Internet. Handwriting recognition, voice recognition, and visual recognition through cameras will allow people to forget that a sophisticated technical infrastructure is enabling them to communicate easily over the Web. Hopefully, software developers will also be able to forget these complexities through the services of universal runtimes and universally accepted Internet standards.

The .NET platform furthers this end through the universal runtime called the Common Language Runtime. This runtime operates on top of the operating system to manage the execution of code and provides services to simplify the development process. Source code that is targeted for the runtime is called *managed code;* the compiler translates it into a Microsoft intermediate language (MSIL) that is independent of the central processing unit (CPU). As the code is being executed, a just-in-time (JIT) compiler converts this MSIL to the CPU-specific code required by the device on which it is running. In theory, this means that software developers can write code for the runtime without having to target each CPU architecture on which it may run. This will become an issue of increasing importance as new Internet devices are built on inexpensive commodity CPUs. Although the .NET runtime will be available for each variation of the Windows operating system, it is also possible that .NET may be ported to other operating systems such as Linux. To enable easier interoperability with alternative universal runtimes on different platforms, the .NET runtime implements inter-machine communication services using universal Internet standards such as HTTP, HTTPS, XML, and the Simple Object Access Protocol (SOAP).

The .NET runtime exposes a unified programming model for many services that are available today through disparate application program interfaces. There are general-purpose libraries, such as the WIN32 application programming interface (API), the Microsoft Foundation Classes (MFC), the Active Template Library (ATL), and WinInet; more specialized libraries, such as DirectX, the Microsoft Telephony application programming interface (TAPI), CrypoAPI; and a whole set of COM interfaces for component services such as transaction processing, queued components, or object pooling that must be learned to develop sophisticated software. The software developer has to absorb many APIs from many sources—some duplicating the same functionality and some targeting different programming languages—to effectively lever-age architectures like Windows DNA. The .NET runtime consolidates most of these APIs under a simpler unified model that abstracts many of the details, especially the interoperable COM underpinnings. In the future, the software developer will be able to focus mostly on the .NET runtime regardless of which programming language is being used. For example, the message queue component in .NET allows easy incor-poration of message-based communication into applications to do tasks such as send-ing and receiving messages, exploring existing queues, or creating and deleting queues. The runtime implementation of HTTP 1.1 frees the developer from complex tasks such as pipelining, chunking, encryption, proxy use, and certificates and authentication mechanisms such as Basic, Kerberos, or Windows NT Challenge/ Response (NTLM).

Many powerful new features that simplify the development process have been incorporated into the .NET runtime. These include cross-language integration through a common type system (CTS), simplified versioning and deployment through the use of assemblies, self-describing components through extensible metadata, easier life-time management through automatic garbage collection, a simplified model for com-ponent interaction, and improved debugging and profiling services.

The .NET runtime introduces a new entity called an *AppDomain* that can greatly facilitate scalability design, a major issue when connecting billions of devices. Normally there is a tug of war between scalability and fault tolerance in the design of high-performance systems. New components are partitioned into different process spaces within an application so that undiscovered bugs do not bring down the entire system through something like a memory access violation. However, cross-process commu-nication can significantly reduce the scalability of an application because of the addi-tional code execution required and the serialization of processors that occurs from memory allocations on the heap during marshalling. In the .NET architecture, managed code is protected from causing many typical faults in the runtime. Any negative con-sequences that may result can also be confined to the offending AppDomain. This allows the software architect to partition code execution into multiple AppDomains within the same process space to avoid expensive cross-process communication. The end result is a much more scalable system that also achieves fault tolerance.

Security is another critical factor determining the evolution of the Internet into a sophisticated online community. People will not connect sensitive business operations to the Web unless they are confident that their transactions will be secure. The .NET runtime provides a code access capability to help address some of these concerns. Mobile code is a big danger because it can come from many sources such as in e-mail attachments or in documents that are downloaded from the Internet. Exploiting known vulnerabilities such as buffer overflows in Internet software applications is another common method of attack. Code access security helps protect computer sys-tems from these kinds of attacks because it allows code to be trusted in varying degrees depending on where the code originates and on its intended purpose. This mechanism does not prevent all mobile code from executing but rather limits what the code is capable of doing. The degree to which this occurs may depend on whether the code has been digitally signed by a trusted source. Code access security can also reduce the risk that other legitimate software can be misused by malicious code using buffer overflows or other exploits. This is accomplished by specifying the set of operations the legitimate code is allowed to perform as well as the set of operations it should never be allowed to perform.

The .NET runtime is an evolving platform that will continue to be enhanced as the needs of the emerging online community expand. One can expect the incorporation of additional features such as natural interfaces in later releases of the universal runtime. These new features will be exposed through the same unified programming model.

.NET and Collaboration

Building a globally connected online community can be a lot easier in theory than in practice. The level of collaboration required is very difficult to achieve, especially given the competing forces active within the different industries that will be involved. However, the existence of the Internet today in its present form demonstrates that it is possible to get a consensus when the opportunities generated through collaboration outweigh the advantages of protecting proprietary gains. What types of desirable applications will be possible in future generations of the Internet?

This is a huge topic, so we will focus only on an e-commerce example. Assume that every product and service has a globally unique identifier. Everything you buy at a shopping mall or supermarket has this identifier encoded on it and it can be scanned through readily available scanners in your home, car, or PDA, all of which are connected to the Internet. Also assume that there are people-oriented Web services that understand your identity and provide you with personal storage. Anytime you buy anything, the item is scanned and your personal inventory is updated. Anytime you consume an item, you scan it and your personal inventory is depleted. After you set the personal preferences for your inventory, automated software agents will be checking periodically on your data to ensure that your house supplies are always replenished. If you are running low on beer, the automated software agent will order more from your local store, which you can pick up next time you drop in. Alternatively the automated agent could search the current prices of this item using its unique identifier and order additional supplies from a less expensive store, which will deliver it to you. Each month your automated agent will produce a report of items it has purchased for you, providing comparative analyses of alternative buying patterns that may be to your advantage. For example, your agent may tell you that if you buy brand X instead of brand Y, you will save a certain amount, or if you stock a two-month supply of product X, you will save money through bulk purchasing. Every month the automated agent will present you with a financial summary of your account and ask for your approval to automatically pay your bills.

Every supplier of products could also have automated agents working on its behalf. By analyzing previous buying patterns, suppliers could predict more accurately the desired inventory levels required for their goods. These could be used to automatically order additional supplies from manufacturers who in turn could rely on automated agents to stock raw materials appropriately. Anytime there are unforeseen events that break traditional buying patterns, adjustments could be quickly made in production, and excess supply could be offered to the automated agents at a discount. The end result is a finely tuned system that minimizes waste and effectively matches supply to demand.

How can .NET help software developers build these kinds of systems? Building these systems is only possible if there are ways to programmatically collaborate the services of multiple companies over the Web. Vast arrays of Web services need to be developed that expose business functionality in well-defined ways. The .NET platform greatly simplifies the creation of these Web services using universally accepted standards. The runtime provides all the necessary plumbing, and development tools—such as Visual Studio.NET—provide wizards that create skeleton Web service applications, which can be enhanced with specific functionality. The .NET platform exposes its functionality through a number of namespaces, a few of which we mention here.

The `System.Web.Services` namespace consists of the classes that enable the user to build and use Web services. Using this functionality can be very easy. For example, to make a method of a public class running inside ASP.NET accessible over the Internet, the user simply adds the `WebMethod` attribute to its definition. The `System.Web.Services.Protocols` namespace consists of the classes that define the protocols used to transmit data across the wire during the communication between Web service clients and the Web service itself. It exposes methods such as `HttpClientRequest` and `HttpServerResponse` and provides the implementation for communicating with a SOAP Web service over HTTP.

The `System.Web.Services.Description` namespace consists of the classes that enable you to publicly describe a Web service via a service description language. Service description contracts are automatically generated when a Web service is created in Visual Studio. A consumer of the Web service uses this contract to learn how to communicate with it—that is, the methods it can call, the input parameters, and the exact format of the potential responses returned. The Web services description language (WSDL) has become the de facto XML Internet standard for describing Web services in this fashion. The `System.Web.Services.Discovery` namespace consists of the classes that allow consumers to locate available Web services. Web service discovery is the process of learning about the existence of available Web services and interrogating them for their description contracts so that users can properly interact with them.

The Universal Discovery, Description, and Integration (UDDI) Project (*http://www.uddi.org*) was created to provide a framework for Web service integration through a distributed directory of Web services. This directory allows the user to locate available Web services within an industry or a particular company. Programmatic registration and discovery of Web services using an assortment of predefined SOAP messages is supported by the .NET platform. The UDDI and WSDL standards emerged out of collaboration between IBM, Microsoft, and Ariba, and more than 30 other software companies also endorse them.

Many Web services will be built through binding and extending other Web services. Some foundationally people-oriented Web services will likely emerge as commodities. A data store Web service could allow people to safely store their information in a universally accessible location. The methods to access this data will have to take into account the speed of the user's Internet connection and allow for offline updates that can be synchronized later. Although the data may be stored as XML, the user should be able to use Microsoft Office applications to view and modify it. An identity Web service will be needed to allow for a single log-on to multiple Internet services. The Microsoft Passport service provides this kind of functionality today. More sophisticated features such as biometrics may be added later. Users will need notification and messaging Web services that push information to people or their software agents, such as stock price updates or news headlines. Online calendar services will also be needed to enable people or agents to collaboratively schedule appointments and meetings. The calendar service should enable users to set permissions that authorize or prohibit access. For example, a user might give access to important clients and deny access for uninvited sales meeting requests. The .NET platform and associated Web services are evolving systems that will always be updating and improving. A dynamic delivery service will likely emerge that will allow users to automatically receive improvements when they occur.

Binding Web services together will present interesting challenges to the software development community. The software development process will need to evolve to encompass the particularities of collaborative development. How do developers test and debug applications that incorporate multiple live systems that they do not control? How is it possible to instrument them with diagnostic information and manage them effectively? How is a denial-of-service scenario that is caused by unexpected circumstances, such as a consumer repeatedly calling a Web service in a tight loop, prevented? How are transactions spanned across multiple Web services so that changes are automatically rolled back if an error occurs? Although the .NET platform is a great first step to facilitating collaborative development, numerous issues still need to be addressed.

.NET and Translation

As of August 2001, the .NET platform was still in the beta version. Although the Internet has connected millions of computers all over the globe, less than a tiny fraction of one percent is running the .NET software. The level of communication between computers on the Web is minimal and is confined mostly to presentation of information and point-and-click buying and selling. Even though standards such as XML, SOAP, WSDL, and UDDI have emerged to facilitate collaborative B2B communication, not many system implementations are currently available.

Today the dominant binding glue of the Internet is still HTML, which has been applied to nonpresentation tasks such as e-commerce. HTML has been a tremendous success because it is easy to implement and acts as a common translation language for the many different types of systems that exist in the wildly heterogeneous Internet environment. Although practically every computer connected to the Internet understands the Internet protocols such as Transmission Control Protocol/Internet Protocol (TCP/IP) and HTTP, these protocols limit the level of communication and collaboration that can occur between them.

One approach to solving this problem would be to get everyone to adopt a common technology or new programming language such as C# that could provide better services. However, this is not realistic given the competing forces active within the software industry, nor is it desirable because it would stifle innovation in the future. A translation approach would allow greater flexibility and freedom of expression.

If the Web is to evolve into a more globally connected online community, new mechanisms of translation are needed that enable richer and more sophisticated software interaction between people. It is not enough to have universally accepted protocols; users also need platforms and tools that simplify their implementation. The .NET platform will help address the translation needs of the online community in two major ways: system interoperability and service contract transformation.

System Interoperability

Although Internet communication is still quite rudimentary, many sophisticated business processes have been computerized. There is already a tremendous amount of software engineering in place that can be used to construct an online community. Most of it is locked within corporations because of the use of proprietary and disparate software protocols. The .NET platform can help companies unlock these rich resources and expose them on the Web. Software developers can build intermediary Web services as translation layers to existing systems and also port some legacy code to .NET. The CTS within the .NET platform facilitates easier code porting through its handling of incompatible generic data types used by different languages, cross-language integration capabilities, and standardized ways of dealing with events, dynamic behaviors, persistence, properties, and exceptions. The .NET implementation of Web services is XML based and can be accessed by any language, component model, or operating system because it is not tied to a particular component technology or object-calling convention. This means that many different companies can independently build Web services that will be able to interoperate without first having to agree on system-level implementation details. If users already have a CORBA- or COM-based system, they can build a .NET Web translation service that wraps its functionality and exposes it on the Web. The .NET architecture uses the simple and extensible SOAP protocol for exchanging information within the heterogeneity of the Internet. SOAP is an XML-based protocol that does not define any application or implementation semantics and can be used in a large variety of systems from asynchronous messaging to remote procedure calls.

Web forms within the .NET platform also simplify the generation of HTML, which serves as a translation mechanism for presentation information. Using Web forms, a user can create Web pages by dragging and dropping rich user interface controls onto a designer and then add code to programmatically bind these components to business layers using any programming language. The .NET platform will translate the desired presentation into pure HTML, which can be understood by browsers on any device and operating system.

Contract Transformation

One of the biggest challenges facing companies who would like to use collaboration to conduct business on the Web will be getting a consensus about industry-specific Web service description contracts. There will be many contracts that serve the same purpose but differ slightly in their format. For example, there could be hundreds of purchase order contract types; without the appropriate translation techniques, programmers could face the nightmarish task of trying to cater to every purchase order contract variation. To simplify these intricacies, users need an easy way to translate disparate Web service contracts into a common format that is expected by the consuming Web service. Fortunately the extensible style language transformation (XSLT) specification addresses this problem in a standardized way. XSLT is a language that transforms XML document types into other XML document types. A transformation expressed in XSLT describes rules for transforming a source tree into a result tree and is achieved by associating patterns with templates. The .NET platform implements the XML document object model (DOM) through classes supported in the `System.Xml` namespace, which also unifies the XML DOM with the data access services provided by ADO.NET. The .NET `System.Xml.Xsl` namespace implements the World Wide Web Consortium (W3C) XSLT specification. The `XslTransform` class can load an XSL style sheet using an `XmlReader` and transform the input data using an `XmlNavigator`.

The capability of the .NET platform to provide easy translation mechanisms for system interoperability and service contract transformation is a huge step forward in the evolution of the Web into a sophisticated online community. We can expect that these capabilities will also emerge in other technologies and platforms so that all Internet systems will be more easily integrated in more powerful ways.

CONCLUSION

The Internet has changed the rules of software development and spurred on the emergence of the people-oriented software paradigm, which aims to transform the Internet into an online community that adequately represents society. Universalization, collaboration, and translation are the three principles proposed in the people-oriented paradigm. The transformation of the Web into a sophisticated online community has begun, and many developers are already building software that engenders the people-oriented characteristic outlined in this chapter. However, today developers are engineering all the plumbing work by hand and are implementing Internet standards on a case-by-case basis. The .NET framework will put in place the tools needed to make software universalization, collaboration, and translation much easier to deliver, thus more effectively transforming the Web into a true, worldwide online community.

Chapter 2

Applied People-Oriented Software

Chapter 1 outlined the three principles of the people-oriented software paradigm and examined how the .NET platform is suited to implement them. The value of a paradigm is that it synthesizes several concepts around a unifying theme. It acts like a filter through which we view reality, determining the points of emphasis and the boundaries of attention. A paradigm helps provide structure and order to what may otherwise appear to be complex, arbitrary, and multifaceted. Understanding a paradigm correctly is important because it provides the model or mental framework for how we think about something.

This chapter examines how the principles of people-oriented programming were applied in the design and development of the InternetBaton Web Collaboration application at *http://www.internetbaton.com*. InternetBaton is a new application and was coded completely from the ground up with the .NET framework.

PEOPLE-ORIENTED DESIGN

The principles behind people-oriented software have evolved with the purpose of transforming the Internet into a global online community. Although bits and bytes are still important, the emphasis shifts toward enabling human connectivity through software and embedding software within the day-to-day operations of society. People orientation does not disregard what preceded it but rather helps it evolve and directs it with a particular focus. The principles of object orientation are assimilated and augmented to focus on a new world where people are the primary "objects" being served, either directly through human interaction or indirectly through business-to-business communication.

Similarly, a people-oriented design methodology should utilize the best of the existing principles of object-oriented design. Good software architecture will always need to be complete and have a coherent vision, leveraging proven successful patterns of design. Comprehensive software architecture and design usually address common themes such as:

> *Fitness of purpose:* Mapping the system correctly to the business requirements of the application in terms of feature set and functionality
>
> *Performance:* Ensuring the system will meet the desired throughput, response time, and execution time metrics in all the various permutations of its use
>
> *Scalability:* Enabling the system to easily accommodate an increase in its performance requirements in terms of throughput or number of concurrent users by scaling up or scaling out
>
> *Security:* Protecting the system from attack and providing sufficient coverage in the areas of authentication, authorization, nonrepudiation, confidentiality, data integrity, and audit trails
>
> *Privacy:* Ensuring the system is compliant with the privacy regulations mandated within the appropriate industry types
>
> *Reliability:* Integrating comprehensive error handling techniques and the transactional principles of atomicity, consistency, isolation, and durability as appropriate
>
> *Availability:* Incorporating fault tolerance into the architecture, perhaps through redundancy or the use of clusters, so that any faults are masked and do not lead to a failure in the system
>
> *Manageability:* Centralizing the administration of the system and providing visibility into its operation through instrumentation and monitoring techniques
>
> *Maintainability:* Anticipating and allowing for easy modifications of the system—in terms of changes to the business requirements or changes arising from technological evolution

People-Types: "Design with Attitude"

To add an additional focus on the new principles of universalization, collaboration, and translation to these existing software design considerations, a people-oriented design concept called *Design Attitudes* is used. Empirically, human factors always seem to affect the successful outcome of software projects. Software architects are obviously people and therefore have dispositions that can influence and shape their designs in positive and negative ways. Attitudes give energy and motivational force to a particular way of thinking. The Design Attitudes methodology seeks to harness this natural human reality by identifying and being attentive to the most beneficial mental perspectives for a given engineering task. To appreciate the benefits of this approach, simply consider the work environment, which clearly reveals that attitudes determine how well people perform. It is also clear that certain attitudes tend to be grouped together and coexist in the same type of person. For example, successful office administrators have a tendency to have an attitude that encourages compliance with policy along with an attitude of eagerness to meeting new demands. The term *People-Type* is used to group a set of attitudes that tend to positively coexist in certain types of people, strengthening and balancing each other. It is the interplay of different attitudes that coexist within a type of person that produces the characteristic behavior of stereotypes.

In a business context, People-Types could be used to identify typical attitudes of people who are successful in meeting the challenges of their profession. For example, certain attitudes and dispositions, such as attention to detail and being meticulous, might prove to be an asset to accountants. In a similar way, People-Types can assist software development architects with identifying which attitudes they should use to successfully accomplish certain engineering tasks. For example, an architect might adopt the outlook of a "Security Guard" People-Type when designing the authentication mechanism of a corporate application. The attitudes of the "Security Guard" People-Type include caution, distrustfulness, and a commitment to providing reliable access to validated users. It is important to note that People-Types are always specific to the problem being solved. A "Security Guard" People-Type would be ill suited for an architect designing a virtual tourist program.

Each People-Type identifies a group of design attitudes. Each particular type can then be used to discuss more clearly and precisely a design outlook. The methodology of Design Attitudes was applied to the principles of people-oriented software, and three distinct People-Types emerged: Miner, Conductor, and Linguist.

Miner

When considering the factors involved in universalization, the "Miner" emerges as the People-Type with the set of design attitudes especially suited to upholding this principle—mining is all about unearthing precious resources. A Miner's outlook could be typified in the following perceptive recommendations:

- Exploit rather than build.
- Invest in discovery.
- Quickly cut losses when discovered resources prove to be inadequate.
- Selectively exploit some hard-to-tap resources through additional investments in technical innovation.

- Recognize that users will eventually want to move on and improve on even the latest technology.

Conductor

When considering the factors involved in collaboration, the "Conductor" emerges as the People-Type with the set of design attitudes especially suited to upholding this principle. A Conductor's outlook could be typified in the following perceptive recommendations:

- Contribute by leading others to perform together in an integrated way.
- Understand that the whole is greater than the sum of the parts.
- Accept the fact that each player needs to depend on others to achieve the desired effect.
- Have substitutes available to replace missing players.
- Frequently rehearse whatever is being conducted, as this is needed to achieve a symphonic performance.

Linguist

When considering the factors involved with translation, the "Linguist" emerges as the People-Type with the set of design attitudes especially suited to upholding this principle. A Linguist's outlook could be typified in the following perceptive recommendations:

- Accept that there will always be diversity of expression.
- Understand that heterogeneity can result in a richer and more erudite environment.
- Focus on the substantive meaning and origin of the expressions.
- Anticipate that new modes of expression will be continually discovered or created.
- Apply the Pareto principle: coverage of 20% of the alternative expressions will satisfy 80% of the needed usage.

These three People-Types can help the software architect to think in new and fresh ways about how to engineer software using the people-oriented model. The recommendations in the People-Types were specifically chosen for their utility in focusing on the important aspects of universalization, collaboration, and translation, and they accentuate the dispositions and outlook appropriate for each principle. However, the characteristics of People-Types, like stereotypes, are not always applicable to every given situation. For example, the Irish stereotypically like to write and enjoy beer. Although these characteristics fit the author of this chapter, who was born and raised in Ireland, many Irish people enjoy neither.

Similarly, there could be a case in which a specific attitude within an appropriate People-Type does not fit a design situation or business requirement. For example, a programmer may choose not to exploit the rich features of a .NET server, such as Commerce Server, because of licensing issues. The point here is that adopting a rigid mentality in the application of all the characteristics of a People-Type is not necessary or helpful. The primary purpose of the appropriate People-Types is to spotlight the best disposition for people-oriented design, as was evident during the design of the InternetBaton application.

NEXT STEPS FOR DESIGN ATTITUDES

The concept of Design Attitudes has only been briefly introduced here for the purposes of discussing the design of the InternetBaton application. A complete discussion of the subject of Design Attitudes could fill an entire book, which would outline the appropriate People-Types for every aspect of design, such as performance, scalability, security, privacy, reliability, availability, manageability, and maintainability.

Imagine how useful a set of People-Types would be if it were developed from interviews with the top architects in the software industry, in which they shared their accumulated wisdom about the design attitudes that have proved to be successful in the different aspects of software construction. Drawing on this material, engineers could then discuss the applicability of the various design attitudes expressed in People-Types to the particular software challenges they need to address.

APPLY THE CONCEPTS: THE INTERNETBATON APPLICATION

The InternetBaton application is a decentralized Web collaboration application that allows people to work together on projects in real time, especially when the collaborators are in different organizations or geographical locations. Effective collaboration requires a mechanism with which people can apply complementary skills to update and improve common factors within a shared space. InternetBaton provides this shared space and manages the complexities of authentication, authorization, concurrent access, and safe edits to the common resources within that space.

InternetBaton Application Features

Although many applications like this may already exist, the InternetBaton application is somewhat different in that the shared resources are not actually stored on the InternetBaton Web server. Instead the InternetBaton application stores virtual uniform resource locators (URLs) to the shared resources. Taking a shared document as an example, let's imagine the authors of this book want to collaborate to write the book's Preface. We would first all agree that the URL to the Preface would be something like *http://www.InternetBaton.com/me@email.com.Book/Preface.bt*. When we accessed this URL, we would be redirected to the most up-to-date version of the Preface, which may be stored anywhere on the Internet. For example, some of us may keep documents on home PCs that are permanently connected to the Internet via a digital subscriber line (DSL), whereas others may keep them on Web servers maintained by various Internet service providers (ISPs). If the most updated version of the Preface were not on my home PC and I wanted to update it, I would type the URL *http://www.InternetBaton. com/me@email.com.Book/Preface.bt* in my browser, and I would be automatically directed to its location.

If the status of the document showed that it had not been checked out, I would be able to check it out and copy it to my shared location on my home PC, which is also permanently connected to the Internet via DSL. After I finished editing the document, I would check it in by updating the virtual URL *http://www.InternetBaton.com/me@ email.com.Book/Preface.bt* to point to my home PC Web server, and the other authors would then be directed to the new version with my updates. You may be asking yourself why I wouldn't simply copy it back to a fellow author's home PC. Well, one reason would be that he does not allow people to upload files to his home PC over the Internet, which helps him prevent someone from planting viruses or Trojan horses on his computer. Another advantage is that his original copy would be saved until he decided to update it with my new version. In addition, if the hard disk of any of our home PCs crashed, we would only lose the changes of one author if that author happened to have the most recent version of the document.

There are other scenarios in which this distributed architecture could be even more advantageous. For example, commercial organizations that work together on shared sensitive documents may want to have complete control over the storage of those documents. They may not want to put the documents out in a shared location managed by an ISP and would prefer to keep them on their own managed Web servers using a Public Key Infrastructure with digital certificates to grant access. InternetBaton can be used to manage the collaboration required between the companies without any of the companies ever having to transfer the actual documents to the InternetBaton Web site. In this way a shared space is provided along with management, notification, and tracking features without ever jeopardizing the actual security of the shared resources. If the authors of this book were paranoid about protecting access to our Preface, we could point the virtual URL *http://www.InternetBaton.com/me@ email.com.Book/Preface.bt* to something like *https://www.a-very-secured-web-server/Book/ Preface*, which could pop up a box requesting a user ID and password that we do not even have to share with the InternetBaton Web site.

Another example in which a distributed storage architecture like InternetBaton is very advantageous is when a person has to collaborate with others who are not known or perhaps not completely trusted. Let's say hundreds of people have volunteered to work for free on a project, such as the translation of a book into numerous languages. The project manager could let the document float around among the volunteers who are updating it. InternetBaton would maintain the current location of the document via the virtual URL, as well as a list of the e-mail addresses and shared locations of all the people who made changes. After periodic intervals, the project manager could update the master copy with the most recent version of the document if the quality of the translation work was good. Otherwise the document could be reset as a previous version and be made available for more translation work. You may be asking why the project manager would not simply store the book document in a location that is accessible to everyone for updating. The project manager may not want to do this because any individual could simply destroy the contents of the document, and all changes would be lost. This would not happen with the distributed InternetBaton application architecture because the users can only make changes to the version they have downloaded to their shared location. If a user destroyed the document at his shared location or pointed the virtual URL to a bogus location, the project manager could simply reset the virtual URL back to a location that was valid.

WHY THE NAME InternetBaton?

The word *baton* has a couple of meanings that are significant for this application. By one definition, a baton is a slender wooden stick used by a conductor to direct an orchestra. In this sense, it is applicable to the Web collaboration application because the virtual URL, like a conductor's baton, is the focal point of everybody's attention, and it is the tool that is used to effectively manage the joint efforts of all the people involved. However, a baton is also a hollow cylinder that is carried by each member of a relay team. It gets passed on from runner to runner. A relay race is a good analogy for the InternetBaton application because each team member only runs a set part of the race and does not run while any other team member is running. The handing over of the baton to the next relay team member means that the next person should carry on the next portion of the race. In the case of the InternetBaton application, only one person at a time can modify a resource. It only becomes available to another member when the virtual URL is handed over to a new location.

Universalization Design: Mining the Runtime

Now that we understand the features of the InternetBaton application, we can move on to issues that came up in its design and development from the perspective of universalization. The Design Attitudes of the Miner People-Type were applied, typified

TABLE 2-1   .NET Resources Used for InternetBaton Implementation

Step	InternetBaton Features	Elements of .NET Framework Used
1	Sign-up page with entry validation	Web application, validation controls, and database inserts
2	Authentication and authorization of users	Authentication and authorization elements of the ASP .NET runtime environment and database query
3	Creation of new Baton projects	Database updates, the DataGrid control, and user controls with custom events
4	Integration of InternetBaton with other Web services	Web service and custom Http Handler
5	Baton synchronization	Asynchronous Web service calls
6	Translations of Baton metadata	eXtensible Markup Language (XML) transforms

in recommendations like "exploit rather than build" and "invest in discovery." It is not hard to imagine the many great resources available for mining within the .NET universal runtime that could help in the implementation of the InternetBaton application (Table 2-1).

Step 1: Sign-Up Page with Entry Validation

The first step is to create a new Web application, which we will call *SignupBaton,* using Visual Studio.NET. This step is a trivial task because a wizard takes care of it for you and produces a file called *WebForm1.aspx* in which you add the elements of the sign-up page. To add labels, buttons, and text boxes, you simply drag them over using the what-you-see-is-what-you-get (WYSIWYG) design support so that you end up with a Web page like the one shown in Figure 2-1.

The code for the page includes the controls and their positioning on the Web page. To conserve space, not all the controls are listed, but you should get the general idea.

```
<%@ Page language="c#" Codebehind="WebForm1.aspx.cs"
   AutoEventWireup="false" Inherits="SignupBaton.WebForm1" %>

<HTML>
 <HEAD>
<meta content="Internet Explorer 5.0" name=vs_targetSchema>
<meta content="Microsoft Visual Studio 7.0" name=GENERATOR>
<meta content=C# name=CODE_LANGUAGE>
   </HEAD>
<body MS_POSITIONING="GridLayout">
```

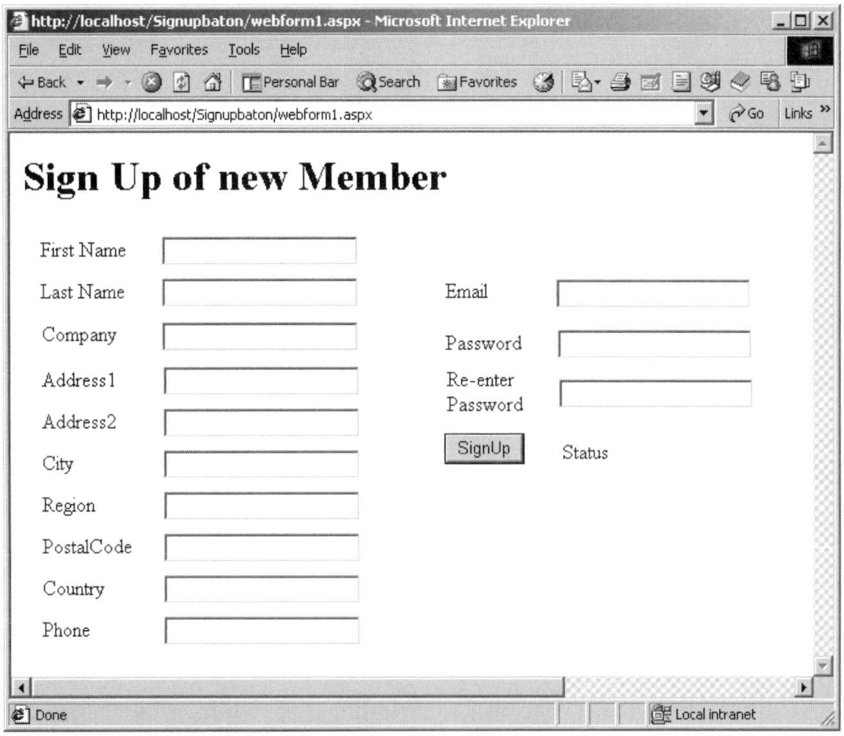

FIGURE 2-1 InternetBaton Sign-Up Page.

```
<H1>Sign Up of new Member</H1>

<form method=post runat="server" ID="Form1">
<asp:button id=SignUp style="Z-INDEX: 124; LEFT: 343px; POSITION: absolute;
   TOP: 231px" runat="server" Text="SignUp"></asp:button>
<asp:textbox id=su_FirstName style="Z-INDEX: 101; LEFT: 120px; POSITION:
   absolute; TOP: 80px" runat="server"></asp:textbox>
<asp:textbox id=su_LastName style="Z-INDEX: 102; LEFT: 120px; POSITION:
   absolute; TOP: 112px" runat="server" NAME="su_LastName"></asp:textbox>
<asp:textbox id="su_Company" style="Z-INDEX: 102; LEFT: 120px; POSITION:
   absolute; TOP: 146px" runat="server" NAME="su_LastName"></asp:textbox>
////more textboxes here
<asp:label id=FirstName style="Z-INDEX: 111; LEFT: 24px; POSITION:
   absolute; TOP: 80px" runat="server">First Name</asp:label>
<asp:label id=LastName style="Z-INDEX: 112; LEFT: 24px; POSITION: absolute;
   TOP: 112px" runat="server">Last Name</asp:label>
<asp:Label id=Company style="Z-INDEX: 127; LEFT: 25px; POSITION: absolute;
   TOP: 145px" runat="server">Company</asp:Label>
//// more labels here
</form>
</body>
</HTML>
```

You will notice that the form is specified to run at the server, and we are using ASP.NET server-side controls for our text boxes, labels, and buttons. At runtime, these server controls automatically generate the appropriate markup language for the consuming client, such as hypertext markup language (HTML) for Web browsers. A great advantage of using ASP.NET server-side controls is that they automatically maintain their state between round trips to the server. No client-side script is required for this, and the control state is not stored on the server either. Instead, ASP.NET stores the state within a hidden form field that is round tripped between requests. For example, if I type my first name in the text box and click Submit, the following hidden field in the HTML page will be returned:

```
<input type="hidden" name="__VIEWSTATE"
    value="dDwxOTg4NzQ2NzI7dDw7bDwxPDE+Oz47bDx0PDtsPDE8Mz47PjtsPHQ8cDxwPGw8V
    GV4dDs+O2w8Um9uYW47Pj47Pjs7Pjs+Pjs+Pjs+IwwsK34NGAPxSCqHnLcz8k3d+Sk=" />
```

This hidden field stores the state of what I entered before I submitted my request. Because the state is stored on a hidden field that gets sent back on every round trip, we do not have to worry about ensuring that the client goes back to the same server within a Web farm to the maintain state across calls. The use of this automatic state management can be disabled if desired. Server-side ASP.NET controls can also detect whether the client browsers can support client scripting and completely avoid round trips to the server for actions like form validation. For example, in the previous sign-up form, we would like to be sure that all the necessary data gets filled in correctly. We could write code that would detect the browser type and send back JavaScript if the client supports it to do it. Alternatively, if the client does not support or has disabled client scripting, the validation would be performed on the server. However, .NET comes with validation controls that simplify all of this for us, so we will use the controls instead of coding this ourselves. To ensure that the first name is filled out, we just need to place the required field validator control on our form and modify the code as follows:

```
<asp:RequiredFieldValidator ID="validFirstName"
controlToValidate="su_FirstName"
errorMessage="You must enter your First Name"
display="static" Runat="server" style="Z-INDEX: 139; LEFT: 289px; POSITION:
    absolute; TOP: 82px">
*</asp:RequiredFieldValidator>
```

To ensure that a password has been entered and then reentered we add a required field validator control and a compare validator control as follows:

```
<asp:RequiredFieldValidator ID="validPassword" Runat="server"
controlToValidate="su_Password"
errorMessage="You must enter your Password"
```

```
    style="Z-INDEX: 140; LEFT: 609px; POSITION: absolute; TOP: 154px"
      width="207px" height="11px" NAME="validPassword">
*</asp:RequiredFieldValidator>

<asp:CompareValidator id="comparePassword" runat="server"
ControlToValidate="su_Password"
ControlToCompare = "su_PasswordAgain"
errorMessage="You must reenter the same password"
style="Z-INDEX: 138; LEFT: 609px; POSITION: absolute; TOP: 191px"
      NAME="comparePassword">
*</asp:CompareValidator>
```

We use the regular expression validator control to ensure that an e-mail address has been entered in the correct format:

```
<asp:RegularExpressionValidator ID="EmailUserIDExpression" Runat="server"
validationExpression=".*@.*\..*"
controlToValidate="su_EmailUserID"
errorMessage="You must use valid characters for your Email User ID"
style="Z-INDEX: 140; LEFT: 611px; POSITION: absolute; TOP: 116px"
      width="309px" height="9px" NAME="EmailUserIDExpression">
*</asp:RegularExpressionValidator>
```

There is also a range validator control that ensures entered values fall with certain ranges, as well as a custom validator control that allows the addition of custom validation logic. Finally, there is a validation summary control, which is used to display the validation errors in summary form for all of the validators on a page:

```
<asp:ValidationSummary ID="validSummarySignUp" Runat="server"
headerText ="Please correct the following"
showSummary="True"
displayMode="BulletList" style="Z-INDEX: 127; LEFT: 357px; POSITION:
      absolute; TOP: 335px"></asp:ValidationSummary>
```

Figure 2-2 shows how the validation summary control notifies me that I forgot to enter my address and mistyped my password when I reentered it.

To finish our form, we need to collect the values after the form has been submitted and write them to a database. To do this we need to capture the Click event of the SignUp button and add code that will write the values to the database. We could tap into the Click event by adding code to the WebForm1.aspx files as follows:

```
<asp:button id=SignUp OnClick="SignUp_Click" style="Z-INDEX: 124; LEFT:
          343px; POSITION: absolute; TOP: 231px" runat="server"
          Text="SignUp"></asp:button>
    <script language="C#" runat=server>
        void SignUp_Click(Object sender, EventArgs e) {
            Result.Text = su_FirstName.Text + " thank you for signing up";
        }
    </script>
```

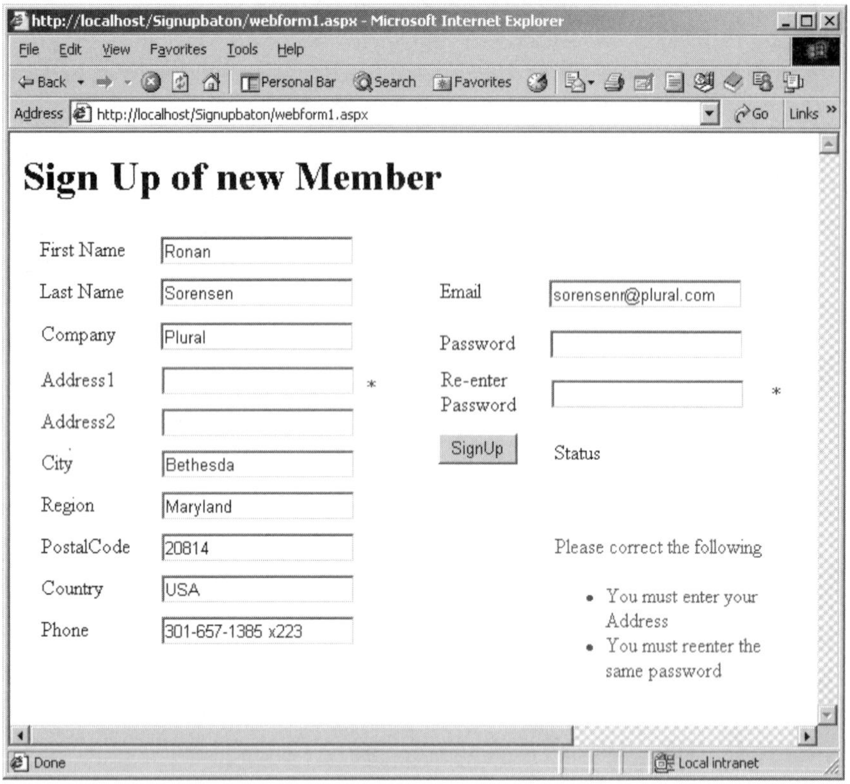

FIGURE 2-2   InternetBaton Validation Summary Control Showing Address and Password Errors.

However, our code might get very difficult to manage if we start adding it to the presentation logic, so .NET provides a much better alternative with the code-behind mechanism. You may have noticed that the first line of WebForm1.aspx has the following line:

```
<%@ Page language="c#" Codebehind="WebForm1.aspx.cs"
   AutoEventWireup="false" Inherits="SignupBaton.WebForm1" %>
```

This specifies that the file WebForm1.aspx.cs will contain the code behind the WebForm1.aspx file to achieve a more clean separation of code from the HTML content. The operations we have done so far using the WYSIWYG editor and control customization have produced the following contents in the WebForm1.aspx.cs file:

```
namespace SignupBaton
{
```

```csharp
using System;
using System.Collections;
using System.ComponentModel;
using System.Data;
using System.Drawing;
using System.Web;
using System.Web.SessionState;
using System.Web.UI;
using System.Web.UI.WebControls;
using System.Web.UI.HtmlControls;

/// <summary>
///         Summary description for WebForm1.
/// </summary>
public class WebForm1 : System.Web.UI.Page
{
    protected System.Web.UI.WebControls.Label Country;
    protected System.Web.UI.WebControls.CompareValidator
                    comparePassword;
    protected System.Web.UI.WebControls.Label PostalCode;
    protected System.Web.UI.WebControls.Label Company;
    protected System.Web.UI.WebControls.TextBox su_Region;
    protected System.Web.UI.WebControls.RequiredFieldValidator
                    validPhone;
    protected System.Web.UI.WebControls.Label Password2;
    protected System.Web.UI.WebControls.TextBox su_Phone;
    protected System.Web.UI.WebControls.TextBox su_Company;
    protected System.Web.UI.WebControls.TextBox su_City;
    protected System.Web.UI.WebControls.TextBox su_Password;
    protected System.Web.UI.WebControls.TextBox su_EmailUserID;
    protected System.Web.UI.WebControls.Button SignUp;
    protected System.Web.UI.WebControls.RequiredFieldValidator
                    validPassword;
    protected System.Web.UI.WebControls.RequiredFieldValidator
                    EmailUserID;
    protected System.Web.UI.WebControls.TextBox su_FirstName;
    protected System.Web.UI.WebControls.RequiredFieldValidator
                    validCountry;
    protected System.Web.UI.WebControls.RequiredFieldValidator
                    validAddress1;
    protected System.Web.UI.WebControls.Label Address1;
    protected System.Web.UI.WebControls.Label Address2;
    protected System.Web.UI.WebControls.Label FirstName;
    protected System.Web.UI.WebControls.TextBox su_Address1;
    protected System.Web.UI.WebControls.RequiredFieldValidator
                    validFirstName;
    protected System.Web.UI.WebControls.TextBox su_Address2;
    protected System.Web.UI.WebControls.RequiredFieldValidator
                    validPostalCode;
    protected System.Web.UI.WebControls.Label LastName;
    protected System.Web.UI.WebControls.TextBox su_Country;
    protected System.Web.UI.WebControls.ValidationSummary
                    validSummarySignUp;
```

```
protected System.Web.UI.WebControls.RequiredFieldValidator
              validCity;
protected System.Web.UI.WebControls.TextBox su_LastName;
protected System.Web.UI.WebControls.Label Result;
protected System.Web.UI.WebControls.RegularExpressionValidator
              EmailUserIDExpression;
protected System.Web.UI.WebControls.Label Phone;
protected System.Web.UI.WebControls.RegularExpressionValidator
              validPhoneExpression;
protected System.Web.UI.WebControls.TextBox su_PasswordAgain;
protected System.Web.UI.WebControls.Label City;
protected System.Web.UI.WebControls.Label Password;
protected System.Web.UI.WebControls.Label Region;
protected System.Web.UI.WebControls.TextBox su_PostalCode;
protected System.Web.UI.WebControls.Label Email;
protected System.Web.UI.WebControls.RequiredFieldValidator
              validLastName;
protected System.Web.UI.WebControls.RequiredFieldValidator
              validRegion;

public WebForm1()
{
    Page.Init += new System.EventHandler(Page_Init);
}
protected void Page_Init(object sender, EventArgs e)
{
    //
    // CODEGEN: This call is required by the ASP.NET Windows
    // Form Designer.
    //
    InitializeComponent();
}

#region Web Form Designer generated code
/// <summary>
///     Required method for Designer support - do not modify
///     the contents of this method with the code editor.
/// </summary>
private void InitializeComponent()
{
    this.SignUp.Click += new System.EventHandler(this.SignUp_
        Click);
    this.Load += new System.EventHandler(this.Page_Load);
}
#endregion
private void Page_Load(object sender, System.EventArgs e)
{
}
protected void SignUp_Click(object sender, System.EventArgs e)
{
}
    }
}
```

You can see that a lot of code has been generated, and a method for `SignUp_Click` has been exposed that will allow us to tap into that event, which was registered in the `InitializeComponent` method. Writing the new member information to a relational database is fairly straightforward because it leverages simple Structured Query Language (SQL) database methods in the `System.Data` and the `System.Data.SqlClient` namespaces. To test our code, we will first need to create a Members table. The .NET SDK installs a developer version of SQL Server for the online samples at `(local)\\NetSDK`. You could create a Members table in the Microsoft Pubs sample database with the following script:

```
if exists (select * from dbo.sysobjects where id =
object_id(N'[dbo].[Members]') and OBJECTPROPERTY(id, N'IsUserTable') = 1)
drop table [dbo].[Members]
GO

CREATE TABLE [dbo].[Members] (
    [FirstName] [nvarchar] (50) NOT NULL ,
    [LastName] [nvarchar] (50) NOT NULL ,
    [Company] [nvarchar] (50) NULL ,
    [Address1] [nvarchar] (50) NOT NULL ,
    [Address2] [nvarchar] (50) NULL ,
    [City] [nvarchar] (50) NOT NULL ,
    [Region] [nvarchar] (50) NOT NULL ,
    [PostalCode] [nvarchar] (50) NOT NULL ,
    [Country] [nvarchar] (50) NOT NULL ,
    [Phone] [nvarchar] (50) NOT NULL ,
    [Password] [nvarchar] (50) NOT NULL ,
    [EmailUserID] [nvarchar] (50) NOT NULL
) ON [PRIMARY]
GO

ALTER TABLE [dbo].[Members] WITH NOCHECK ADD
    CONSTRAINT [PK_Members] PRIMARY KEY NONCLUSTERED
    (
        [EmailUserID]
    ) ON [PRIMARY]
GO
```

Note that in the previous code, we did not pay any attention to the appropriate field sizes and just set everything to 50. The code to write to the Members table is as follows:

```
protected void SignUp_Click(object sender, System.EventArgs e)
{
    if (!Page.IsValid) return;

    SqlCommand SignUpCommand = null;
    SqlConnection SignUpConnection = null;

    try
```

```
{
    SignUpConnection = new SqlConnection("server=(local)\\NetSDK;
                       uid=QSUser;pwd=QSPassword;database=pubs");
    String insertCmd = "insert into Members (FirstName, Lastname,
      Company, Address1, Address2, City, Region, PostalCode, Country,
      Phone, Password, EmailUserID) values (@FirstName, @Lastname,
      @Company, @Address1, @Address2, @City, @Region, @PostalCode,
      @Country, @Phone, @Password, @EmailUserID)";
    SignUpCommand = new SqlCommand(insertCmd, SignUpConnection);

    SignUpCommand.Parameters.Add(new SqlParameter("@FirstName",
                         SqlDbType.NVarChar, 50));
    SignUpCommand.Parameters["@FirstName"].Value = su_FirstName.Text;
    SignUpCommand.Parameters.Add(new SqlParameter("@LastName",
                         SqlDbType.NVarChar, 50));
    SignUpCommand.Parameters["@LastName"].Value = su_LastName.Text;
    SignUpCommand.Parameters.Add(new SqlParameter("@Company",
                         SqlDbType.NVarChar, 50));
    SignUpCommand.Parameters["@Company"].Value = su_Company.Text;
    SignUpCommand.Parameters.Add(new SqlParameter("@Address1",
                         SqlDbType.NVarChar, 50));
    SignUpCommand.Parameters["@Address1"].Value = su_Address1.Text;
    SignUpCommand.Parameters.Add(new SqlParameter("@Address2",
                         SqlDbType.NVarChar, 50));
    SignUpCommand.Parameters["@Address2"].Value = su_Address2.Text;
    SignUpCommand.Parameters.Add(new SqlParameter("@City",
                         SqlDbType.NVarChar, 50));
    SignUpCommand.Parameters["@City"].Value = su_City.Text;
    SignUpCommand.Parameters.Add(new SqlParameter("@Region",
                         SqlDbType.NVarChar, 50));
    SignUpCommand.Parameters["@Region"].Value = su_Region.Text;
    SignUpCommand.Parameters.Add(new SqlParameter("@PostalCode",
                         SqlDbType.NVarChar, 50));
    SignUpCommand.Parameters["@PostalCode"].Value = su_PostalCode.Text;
    SignUpCommand.Parameters.Add(new SqlParameter("@Country",
                         SqlDbType.NVarChar, 50));
    SignUpCommand.Parameters["@Country"].Value = su_Country.Text;
    SignUpCommand.Parameters.Add(new SqlParameter("@Phone",
                         SqlDbType.NVarChar, 50));
    SignUpCommand.Parameters["@Phone"].Value = su_Phone.Text;
    SignUpCommand.Parameters.Add(new SqlParameter("@Password",
                         SqlDbType.NVarChar, 50));
    SignUpCommand.Parameters["@Password"].Value = su_Password.Text;
    SignUpCommand.Parameters.Add(new SqlParameter("@EmailUserID",
                         SqlDbType.NVarChar, 50));
    SignUpCommand.Parameters["@EmailUserID"].Value =
                         su_EmailUserID.Text;

    SignUpCommand.Connection.Open();


    SignUpCommand.ExecuteNonQuery();
    Result.Text = "<b>Thank you for signing up</b><br>";
```

```
    }
    catch (SqlException e1)
    {
        if (e1.Number == EC.AlreadyExists)
            Result.Text = "A record already exists with that email user ID
                            address - please choose another";

        else
            Result.Text = "Could not add record: Error" + e1.Message;

    }
    catch(Exception e1)
    {
        Result.Text = "Could not add record: Error" + e1.Message;
    }
    finally
    {
        try
        {
            if(SignUpCommand != null) SignUpCommand.Connection.Close();
        }
        catch(Exception e1)
        {
            Trace.Write(e1.Message);
            //log error here
        }
    }
}
```

As you can see, the database code is straightforward. The SqlConnection class represents the physical connection to the SQL Server database, and the SqlCommand is used to perform queries, inserts, updates, or deletes. We use the ExecuteNonQuery method of the SqlCommand object because we are not requesting any rows to be returned to us. The return value of this method is the number of rows affected by the command in case of UPDATE, INSERT, and DELETE statements and –1 for anything else.

Step 2: Authentication and Authorization of Users

Access to the InternetBaton Web site always requires that users be authenticated and authorized to view, update, create, or delete Baton projects. Therefore we need to add this capability to our site. Fortunately, with .NET this is also a very easy task to implement. Basic, Digest, and Windows authentication are supported by .NET through its integration with Internet information server (IIS). Support for forms-based authentication and Microsoft Passport is also provided. Forms-based authentication over secure sockets layer (SSL) makes the most sense for InternetBaton since collaborators across organizations boundaries are unlikely to be part of the same network domain and may be using diverse operating system platforms. These organizations may also be using digital certificates to grant access to the actual shared documents on their own servers, and they may not want to duplicate this effort with InternetBaton. To integrate forms-based authentication into InternetBaton, we first create a new Web application called *BatonWeb,* which we will secure. We obviously do not want to secure our existing SignupBaton application since no one would be able to gain access to sign up. Visual Studio.NET provides a wizard to add a new Web form, which we will use to create two new forms called *default.aspx.* and *login.aspx.* Add the line <H1>Welcome to InternetBaton</H1> to default.aspx and <H1>Please Sign-In</H1> to login. aspx. If you compile this application and enter the URL *http://localhost/batonweb/* in your browser, you will get a simple page displaying "Welcome to InternetBaton." Now open the web.config file and replace <authentication mode="None" /> with the following lines:

```
<authentication mode="Forms">
    <forms name=".BATONWEBCOOKIE" loginUrl="login.aspx" protection="all"
                timeout="30" path="/">
    </forms>
</authentication>
<authorization>
    <deny users="?" />
</authorization>
```

Request the URL *http://localhost/batonweb/* again, and you now get redirected to the login.aspx page that displays "Please Sign-In." Having added authentication to the web.config file, this will happen no matter what page you request in the BatonWeb site. If you request the page *http://localhost/batonweb/WebForm1.aspx;* notice that you get redirected to the URL *http://localhost/batonweb/login.aspx?ReturnUrl=http%3a%2f%2flocalhost%2fbatonweb%2fWebForm1.aspx.* This will display the Login page, but .NET remembers the original page you requested in the query string. After users sign in, they will automatically be brought back to the page they originally requested.

Now add a button to the Login page, and add the following code to its click method:

```
protected void Submit_Click(object sender, System.EventArgs e)
{
    FormsAuthentication.RedirectFromLoginPage("me", false);

}
```

You also have to add that you are using the System.Web.Security namespace to the top portion of the login.aspx.cs file in order to successfully compile. Restart your browser, request the URL *http://localhost/batonweb/WebForm1.aspx* again, and then click the new button that you added. You will notice that you are now authenticated and will not have to sign in any more to access pages in the Baton Web site as long as you do not close your browser. All this works through the use of the BATONWEB-COOKIE cookie we specified in the web.config file with the following tag:

```
<forms name=".BATONWEBCOOKIE" loginUrl="login.aspx" protection="all"
timeout="30" path="/">
```

Here we specify that users who do not have the authentication cookie should be redirected to login.aspx. The timeout value in this tag specifies that the cookie expires in 30 minutes. The protection value of *all* specifies to .NET that the cookie should be encrypted as well as validated to make sure that it has not been altered in transit. It is up to our custom code to determine when this cookie should be sent to the client. In the previous example, we authenticated everyone who clicked the button, so we obviously need to modify this code so that it checks against our Members database. We first need to add text boxes allowing the users to enter their names and passwords (Figure 2-3):

You will notice that we have also added a check box asking the users if they want their IDs and passwords to be remembered on their computer (client) after they have closed the browser. This essentially means the cookie persists on the client, which is accomplished by setting the second parameter of the `FormsAuthentication.RedirectFromLoginPage` method to *true*. The code listing for the login.aspx.cs page is as follows:

```
namespace BatonWebLogin
{
    using System;
    using System.Collections;
    using System.ComponentModel;
    using System.Data;
    using System.Drawing;
    using System.Web;
```

FIGURE 2-3   InternetBaton Login Page.

```
using System.Web.SessionState;
using System.Web.UI;
using System.Web.UI.WebControls;
using System.Web.UI.HtmlControls;
using System.Web.Security;
using System.Data.SqlClient;

/// <summary>
///         Summary description for login.
/// </summary>
public class login : System.Web.UI.Page
{
    protected System.Web.UI.WebControls.Label Label2;
    protected System.Web.UI.WebControls.CheckBox Persist;
    protected System.Web.UI.WebControls.TextBox Password;
    protected System.Web.UI.WebControls.TextBox EmailUserID;
    protected System.Web.UI.WebControls.Label Label1;
    protected System.Web.UI.WebControls.Label status;
    protected System.Web.UI.WebControls.RequiredFieldValidator
                    validPassword;
    protected System.Web.UI.WebControls.RegularExpressionValidator
                    EmailUserIDExpression;
    protected System.Web.UI.WebControls.RequiredFieldValidator
                    EmailUserIDvalidator1;
    protected System.Web.UI.WebControls.Button Submit;

    public login()
    {
        Page.Init += new System.EventHandler(Page_Init);
    }

    protected void Page_Init(object sender, EventArgs e)
    {
        //
        // CODEGEN: This call is required by the ASP.NET Windows
        // Form Designer.
        //
        InitializeComponent();
    }

    #region Web Form Designer generated code
    /// <summary>
    ///     Required method for Designer support - do not modify
    ///     the contents of this method with the code editor.
    /// </summary>
    private void InitializeComponent()
    {
        this.Submit.Click += new System.EventHandler(this.Submit_
                        Click);
        this.Load += new System.EventHandler(this.Page_Load);

    }
    #endregion
```

```
private int Authenticate(String user, String pass)
{
    int authenticated = 0;
    SqlCommand SignInCommand = null;
    SqlConnection SignInConnection = null;
    try
    {
        SignInConnection = new SqlConnection("server=(local)\\
                            NetSDK;uid=QSUser;pwd=QSPassword;database
                            =pubs");
        SignInCommand = new SqlCommand("SignIn", SignInConnection);


        SignInCommand.CommandType = CommandType.StoredProcedure;

        SignInCommand.Parameters.Add(new SqlParameter("@Password",
                    SqlDbType.NVarChar, 50));
        SignInCommand.Parameters["@Password"].Value = Password.Text;
        SignInCommand.Parameters.Add(new
                    SqlParameter("@EmailUserID",
                    SqlDbType.NVarChar, 50));
        SignInCommand.Parameters["@EmailUserID"].Value =
                    EmailUserID.Text;

        SqlParameter IsPermitted = new
        SqlParameter("@IsPermitted",SqlDbType.Int);
        IsPermitted.Direction = ParameterDirection.Output;
        SignInCommand.Parameters.Add(IsPermitted);

        SignInCommand.Connection.Open();
        SignInCommand.ExecuteNonQuery();

        if (((int)IsPermitted.Value) == 1) authenticated = 1;

    }
    catch(SqlException e)
    {
        Trace.Write(e.Message);
        //log error here
        authenticated = -1;
    }
    catch(Exception e)
    {
        Trace.Write(e.Message);
        //log error here
        authenticated = -1;
    }
    finally
    {
        try
        {
            if(SignInCommand != null)
                SignInCommand.Connection.Close();
```

```
            }
        catch(Exception e)
        {
            Trace.Write(e.Message);
            //log error here
            authenticated = -1;
        }
    }
    return authenticated;
}

protected void Submit_Click(object sender, System.EventArgs e)
{
    try
    {
        int authenticated = 0;
        authenticated = Authenticate(EmailUserID.Text,
                        Password.Text);
        if ( authenticated == 1)
        {
            status.Text = "Sign-In successful";
            FormsAuthentication.RedirectFromLoginPage(
                        EmailUserID.Text, Persist.Checked);
        }
        else if(authenticated == 0)
        {
            status.Text = "Invalid Credentials: Please try again";

        }
        else
        {
            status.Text = "Error occurred: Please try again";
        }
    }
    catch(Exception e1)
    {
        Trace.Write(e1.Message);
        //log error here
    }
}
private void Page_Load(object sender, System.EventArgs e)
{

}
    }
}
```

The previous code collects the user ID and password and checks to see whether it matches any of the values stored in the Members table. You will notice that in this case, a stored procedure was used to interact with the SQL Server database because it yields better performance. The code for this stored procedure is as follows:

```
CREATE PROCEDURE SignIn
@Password  nvarchar(50),
@EmailUserID  nvarchar(50),
@IsPermitted Int  output
AS
if (select count(*) from Members where EmailUserID= @EmailUserID and
    Password=@Password) = 1
    select @IsPermitted = 1
else
    select @IsPermitted = 0
return
GO
```

Step 3: Creation of New Baton Projects

You have probably seen a pattern in how you can add controls to a page with ASP.NET and program against those controls. We will now explain how we can both create our own custom controls and use a more comprehensive server-side control like the DataGrid provided by ASP.NET. You are undoubtedly already aware of the benefits of modularizing functionality within controls. Our code would get very difficult to maintain if we put everything into large .aspx and .aspx.cs files. Instead, it makes more sense to break up functionality into logical components and create self-standing controls that implement the required methods, properties, and events.

For example, we would like to create one control that allows users to create new projects and one control that allows users to view existing projects. We begin by selecting the add Web user control wizard and naming the controls addproject.ascx and projects.ascx, respectively. Visual Studio.NET will put these files and the code-behind .cs files in the main BatonWeb directory. To simplify the management of these files, create a controls directory with the subdirectories *addproject* and *projects* and move the files there. I had difficulty doing this with the beta version of Visual Studio.NET, so I shut down Visual Studio.NET and edited the BatonWeb.csproj file directly with Notepad. Although this is not a recommended method, it did bring to my attention that the BatonWeb.csproj project file is an XML document with tags for build settings and references in addition to the files included in the project. A shortened version of the XML document that I changed is as follows:

```
<VisualStudioProject>
    <CSHARP
        ProjectType = "Web"
        ProductVersion = "7.0.9148"
        SchemaVersion = "1.0"
    >
        <Build>
            <Settings
                ApplicationIcon = ""
                AssemblyKeyContainerName = ""
                AssemblyName = "BatonWeb"
```

```
            AssemblyOriginatorKeyFile = ""
            DefaultClientScript = "JScript"
            DefaultHTMLPageLayout = "Grid"
            DefaultTargetSchema = "IE50"
            DefaultServerScript = "VBScript"
            DefaultSessionState = "True"
            DelaySign = "false"
            NoStandardLibraries = "false"
            OutputType = "Library"
            RootNamespace = "BatonWeb"
            StartupObject = ""
        >
            <Config
                Name = "Debug"
                AllowUnsafeBlocks = "false"
                BaseAddress = "0"
                CheckForOverflowUnderflow = "false"
                DefineConstants = "DEBUG;TRACE"
                DocumentationFile = ""
                DebugSymbols = "true"
                IncrementalBuild = "false"
                FileAlignment = "4096"
                NoLogo = "true"
                NoOutput = "false"
                Optimize = "false"
                OutputPath = "bin\"
                RemoveIntegerChecks = "false"
                TreatWarningsAsErrors = "false"
                WarningLevel = "4"
            />
            <Config
                Name = "Release"
                .....more here
            />
        </Settings>
        <References>
            <Reference Name = "System" />
            <Reference Name = "System.Drawing" />
            <Reference Name = "System.Data" />
            <Reference Name = "System.Web" />
            <Reference Name = "System.Web.Services" />
            <Reference Name = "System.XML" />
        </References>
    </Build>
    <Files>
        <Include>
            <File
                RelPath = "controls\addproject\addproject.ascx"
                SubType = "UserControl"
                BuildAction = "Content"
            />
            <File
                RelPath = "controls\addproject\addproject.ascx.cs"
```

```
                     DependentUpon = "addproject.ascx"
                     SubType = "ASPXCodeBehind"
                     BuildAction = "Compile"
                 />
                 <File
                     RelPath = "controls\projects\projects.ascx"
                     SubType = "UserControl"
                     BuildAction = "Content"
                 />
                 <File
                     RelPath = "controls\projects\projects.ascx.cs"
                     DependentUpon = "projects.ascx"
                     SubType = "ASPXCodeBehind"
                     BuildAction = "Compile"
                 />
                 ..........more files here
             </Include>
         </Files>
     </CSHARP>
</VisualStudioProject>
```

To complete the InternetBaton Projects page, we need to do the following:

1. Create the Projects table and the stored procedures for adding and retrieving projects.
2. Add the user interface and code-behind for the AddProject control.
3. Add the user interface and code-behind for the Projects control.
4. Add controls to the default page to display projects and tie into the events for the updating, displaying, and hiding of controls at the appropriate times.

1. Create the Projects table and the stored procedures for adding and retrieving projects.

We create the Projects table and the stored procedures for adding a project and querying for projects with the following script:

```
if exists (select * from dbo.sysobjects where id = object_id(N'
    [dbo].[Projects]') and OBJECTPROPERTY(id, N'IsUserTable') = 1)
drop table [dbo].[Projects]
GO

CREATE TABLE [dbo].[Projects] (
    [ProjectID] [nvarchar] (50) NOT NULL ,
    [EmailUserID] [nvarchar] (50) NOT NULL ,
    [AccessType] [nvarchar] (50) NOT NULL ,
    [ShortURL] [nvarchar] (50) NULL
) ON [PRIMARY]
GO

ALTER TABLE [dbo].[Projects] WITH NOCHECK ADD
    CONSTRAINT [PK_Projects] PRIMARY KEY  NONCLUSTERED
```

```
       (
            [ProjectID]
       )   ON [PRIMARY]
GO

CREATE PROCEDURE GetProjects
@EmailUserID  nvarchar(50)
AS
select ProjectID, AccessType, ShortURL from Projects where EmailUserID =
@EmailUserID
GO

CREATE PROCEDURE AddProject
@ProjectID nvarchar(50),
@EmailUserID  nvarchar(50)
AS
declare     @ShortURL nvarchar(50)
select @ShortURL = "None"
declare     @AccessType nvarchar(50)
select @AccessType = "Admin"
insert into Projects Values(
@ProjectID,
@EmailUserID,
@AccessType,
@ShortURL
)
GO
```

2. Add the user interface and code-behind for the AddProject control.

```
<%@ Control Language="c#" AutoEventWireup="false" Codebehind="addproject.
    ascx.cs" Inherits="BatonWebAddProject.AddProject"%>
<DIV>
<table class="tablestyle">
<tr>
    <td bgColor=#aaaadd colSpan=2><b>Add a New Project</b></td></tr>
<tr>
     <td bgColor=white noWrap width=100>Project Name</td>
     <td  bgColor=white align=right>
        <asp:TextBox id=projectname runat="server" width=300
            NAME="projectname"></asp:TextBox>
     </td>
  </tr>
  <tr>
    <td colSpan=2>
        <asp:Button id=AddProjectBtn Text="Add Project" runat="server"
                NAME="AddProjectBtn"></asp:Button>
        <asp:Button id=DoneBtn Text="Done" runat="server"
                NAME="DoneBtn"></asp:Button>
    </td>
  </tr>
  <tr>
```

```
            <td bgColor=#aaaadd colSpan=2 height=10  >
            <asp:Label id=result runat="server" ></asp:Label>
            </td>
      </tr>
      </table>
      </DIV>
```

The previous code for the AddProject.ascx file does not contain the HTML
header, body, and form tags because this control will be positioned with another
form. The code behind this file is as follows:

```
namespace BatonWebAddProject
{
using System;
using System.Data;
using System.Drawing;
using System.Web;
using System.Web.UI.WebControls;
using System.Web.UI.HtmlControls;
using System.Data.SqlClient;
public class EC {public const int AlreadyExists = 2627;}

/// <summary>
///          Summary description for addproject.
/// </summary>
public class AddProject : System.Web.UI.UserControl
{
    protected System.Web.UI.WebControls.TextBox projectname;
    protected System.Web.UI.WebControls.Button AddProjectBtn;
    protected System.Web.UI.WebControls.Button DoneBtn;
    protected System.Web.UI.WebControls.Label result;

    /// <summary>
    public AddProject()
    {
        this.Init += new System.EventHandler(Page_Init);
    }

    public event EventHandler Add;
    public event EventHandler Done;

    protected void OnAdd(EventArgs e)
    {
        Add(this, e);
    }

    protected void OnDone(EventArgs e)
    {
        Done(this, e);
    }
    protected void Page_Init(object sender, EventArgs e)
    {
```

```
        //
        // CODEGEN: This call is required by the ASP.NET Web Form
        // Designer.
        //
        InitializeComponent();
    }

    #region Web Form Designer generated code
    /// <summary>
    ///         Required method for Designer support - do not modify
    ///         the contents of this method with the code editor.
    /// </summary>
    private void InitializeComponent()
    {
        this.AddProjectBtn.Click += new System.EventHandler
                                (this.AddProjectBtn_Click);
        this.DoneBtn.Click += new System.EventHandler(this.DoneBtn_Click);
        this.Load += new System.EventHandler(this.Page_Load);

    }
    #endregion

    private void Page_Load(object sender, System.EventArgs e)
    {

    }
    public void DoneBtn_Click(Object sender, EventArgs E)
    {
        projectname.Text = "";
        OnDone(EventArgs.Empty);
    }

    public void AddProjectBtn_Click(Object sender, EventArgs E)
    {
        if (projectname.Text == "")
        {
            result.Text="<font color=red>You must enter a project
                        name</font>";
            return;
        }
        SqlCommand AddProjectCommand = null;
        SqlConnection AddProjectConnection = null;
        try
        {
            AddProjectConnection = new SqlConnection("server=(local)\\
                                NetSDK;uid=QSUser;pwd=QSPassword;database
                                =pubs");
            AddProjectCommand = new SqlCommand("AddProject",
                            AddProjectConnection);
            projectname.Text = projectname.Text.Trim();
            AddProjectCommand.CommandType = CommandType.StoredProcedure;
            AddProjectCommand.Parameters.Add(new SqlParameter("@ProjectID",
                        SqlDbType.NVarChar, 50));
            string EmailUserID = this.Context.User.Identity.Name;
```

```
            string ProjectID = EmailUserID + "." + projectname.Text;
            AddProjectCommand.Parameters["@ProjectID"].Value = ProjectID;
            AddProjectCommand.Parameters.Add(new
                            SqlParameter("@EmailUserID",
                            SqlDbType.NVarChar, 50));
            AddProjectCommand.Parameters["@EmailUserID"].Value =
                            EmailUserID;
            AddProjectCommand.Connection.Open();
            AddProjectCommand.ExecuteNonQuery();
            result.Text = "<b>Project has been added</b><br>";
            OnAdd(EventArgs.Empty);
        }
        catch (SqlException e1)
        {
            Trace.Write(e1.Message);
            if (e1.Number == EC.AlreadyExists)
                result.Text = "<font color=red>A project already exists
                            with the same name</font>";

            else
                result.Text = "ERROR: Could not add record" + e1.Message;
        }
        catch(Exception e2)
        {
            Trace.Write(e2.Message);
            result.Text = "ERROR: Could not add record";
        }
        finally
        {
            try
            {
                if(AddProjectCommand != null) AddProjectCommand.
                    Connection.Close();
            }
            catch(Exception e3)
            {
                Trace.Write(e3.Message);
                result.Text = "ERROR: Could not add record";
            }
        }
    }
  }
 }
}
```

It is important to notice that we have added two events to this control, which will be fired when a project has been added and when the users click Done. We tie into these events on our default page.

3. Add the user interface and code-behind for the Projects control.

```
<%@ Control Language="c#" AutoEventWireup="false"
Codebehind="projects.ascx.cs" Inherits="BatonWebProjects.Projects"%>
```

```
<DIV>
<table class=tablestyle borderColor=black border=1>
<tr>
<td bgColor=#aaaadd><b>Select Active Project</B>
</td>
<td bgColor=#aaaadd><asp:dropdownlist id=ProjectDropDownList
    NAME="DropDownList1" DataValueField="ProjectID"
    DataTextField="ProjectID" runat="server"></asp:DropDownList>
</td>
</tr>
</table>
<ASP:DATAGRID id=ProjectsDataGrid runat="server" font-names="Verdana"
            Width="532px" BackColor="#CCCCFF" BorderColor="Black"
            CellPadding="3" Font-Name="Verdana" Font-Size="8pt"
            HeaderStyle-BackColor="#aaaadd" AutoGenerateColumns="True">
</ASP:DATAGRID>
</DIV>
```

Probably the most interesting thing about the user interface code for the Projects control is the fact that it is so simple. The DataGrid control is a sophisticated mechanism for displaying and editing tabular data. The ASP.NET QuickStart tutorial included in the .NET SDK goes through the many features of the DataGrid control and is worth reviewing if you plan on using the control. The code behind the Projects control user interface code is as follows:

```
namespace BatonWebProjects
{
using System;
using System.Data;
using System.Drawing;
using System.Web;
using System.Web.UI.WebControls;
using System.Web.UI.HtmlControls;
using System.Data.SqlClient;

/// <summary>
///         Summary description for projects.
/// </summary>
public class Projects : System.Web.UI.UserControl
{
    protected System.Web.UI.WebControls.DataGrid ProjectsDataGrid;
    protected System.Web.UI.WebControls.DropDownList ProjectDropDownList;

    /// <summary>
    public Projects()
    {
        this.Init += new System.EventHandler(Page_Init);
    }

    public void BindGrid()
    {
```

```
        SqlDataAdapter ProjectsCommand = null;
        SqlConnection ProjectsConnection = null;
        try
        {
            ProjectsConnection = new SqlConnection("server=(local)
                              \\NetSDK;uid=QSUser;pwd=QSPassword;database
                              =pubs");
            ProjectsCommand = new SqlDataAdapter("GetProjects",
                          ProjectsConnection);
            ProjectsCommand.SelectCommand.CommandType =
                        CommandType.StoredProcedure;
            string EmailUserID = this.Context.User.Identity.Name;
            ProjectsCommand.SelectCommand.Parameters.Add(new SqlParameter
                            ("@EmailUserID", SqlDbType.NVarChar, 50));
            ProjectsCommand.SelectCommand.Parameters["@EmailUserID"].Value
                        = EmailUserID;

            DataSet ds = new DataSet();
            ProjectsCommand.Fill(ds, "Projects");

            ProjectsDataGrid.DataSource=ds.Tables["Projects"].DefaultView;
            ProjectsDataGrid.DataBind();

            ProjectDropDownList.DataSource=
                            ds.Tables["Projects"].DefaultView;
            ProjectDropDownList.DataBind();
        }
        catch (SqlException e1)
        {
            Trace.Write(e1.Message);
            //log error here
        }
        catch(Exception e2)
        {
            Trace.Write(e2.Message);
            //log error here
        }
    }

    private void Page_Load(object sender, System.EventArgs e)
    {
        if (!Page.IsPostBack)
        {
            BindGrid();
        }
    }

    protected void Page_Init(object sender, EventArgs e)
    {
        //
        // CODEGEN: This call is required by the ASP.NET Web Form
        // Designer.
```

```
    //
    InitializeComponent();
}

#region Web Form Designer generated code
/// <summary>
///          Required method for Designer support - do not modify
///          the contents of this method with the code editor.
/// </summary>
private void InitializeComponent()
{
    this.Load += new System.EventHandler(this.Page_Load);
}
#endregion
    }
}
```

The `BindGrid` method within this code is very interesting because it demonstrates how easy it is to bind data to the DataGrid control and the DropDownList control. You create a DataSet, assign it to the DataSource of the control, and then call `DataBind()`. A DataSet is a powerful, disconnected way to represent data from a data store, and changes to a DataSet can be easily reconciled with the originating data model. The `Page_Load` method is also interesting because it checks to see whether a PostBack is occurring and avoids another binding to the database if it is. This means the DataGrid and DropDownList controls get populated from the database the first time the page is loaded, although this expensive operation does not occur each time form data is posted back by the client.

4. Add controls to the default page to display projects and tie into events for updating, displaying, and hiding controls at the appropriate times.

We now can position our new controls in the user interface code of the InternetBaton default.aspx page by first registering them with the Register tag and then simply adding them like any other ASP.NET control as follows:

```
<%@ Register TagPrefix="Baton" TagName="Projects"
    Src=".\controls\projects\projects.ascx" %>
<%@ Register TagPrefix="Baton" TagName="AddProject"
    Src=".\controls\addproject\addproject.ascx" %>
<%@ Page language="c#" Codebehind="default.aspx.cs" AutoEventWireup="false"
    Inherits="BatonWeb.Cdefault" %>

<html>
  <head>
    <meta name=vs_targetSchema content="Internet Explorer 5.0">
    <meta name="GENERATOR" Content="Microsoft Visual Studio 7.0">
    <meta name="CODE_LANGUAGE" Content="C#">

    <style>
      .buttonstyle
```

```
    {
        font: 8pt verdana;
        background-color:lightblue;
        border-color:black;
        width:130
    }
    .selectstyle
    {
        font: 14pt verdana;
        background-color:lightblue;
        color:purple
    }
    .tablestyle
    {
      cellspacing:0;
      cellpadding:3;
      rules:all;
      bordercolor:black;
      font-size:8pt;
      font-family:Verdana;
      border-collapse:collapse;
      background-color:#ccccff;
      border:1;
      width:532px
    }
  </style>
  </head>
  <body MS_POSITIONING="GridLayout">
    <h2>Welecome to InternetBaton</h2>
    <h3><asp:label id="Welcome" runat="server"></asp:label></h3>
    <form method="post" runat="server">
      <asp:button text="Signout" runat="server" id=SignOut
                    class="buttonstyle"></asp:button>
      <asp:Button id=AddaProject runat="server" Text="Add a project"
                    class="buttonstyle"></asp:Button>
      <Baton:AddProject id="cAddProject"  runat="server" NAME=
                    "cAddProject"/>
      <Baton:Projects id="cProjects"  runat="server" NAME="cProjects"/>
    </form>

  </body>
</html>
```

We defined some styles at the top of this file, and they will be propagated throughout our new controls. The code behind this file is as follows:

```
namespace BatonWeb
{
using System;
using System.Collections;
using System.ComponentModel;
using System.Data;
```

```
using System.Drawing;
using System.Web;
using System.Web.SessionState;
using System.Web.UI;
using System.Web.UI.WebControls;
using System.Web.UI.HtmlControls;
using System.Web.Security;
using BatonWebProjects;
using BatonWebAddProject;

/// <summary>
///         Summary description for Cdefault.
/// </summary>
public class Cdefault : System.Web.UI.Page
{
    protected System.Web.UI.WebControls.Button SignOut;
    protected System.Web.UI.WebControls.Label Welcome;
    protected System.Web.UI.WebControls.Button AddaProject;
    protected BatonWebProjects.Projects cProjects;
    protected BatonWebAddProject.AddProject cAddProject;

    public Cdefault()
    {
        Page.Init += new System.EventHandler(Page_Init);
    }

    protected void Page_Load(object sender, System.EventArgs e)
    {
        // Put user code to initialize the page here
        if (!Page.IsPostBack)
        {
            Welcome.Text = "UserID:   " + User.Identity.Name;
            cAddProject.Visible = false;
        }
    }
    protected void SignOut_Click(object sender, System.EventArgs e)
    {
        FormsAuthentication.SignOut();
        Response.Redirect("default.aspx");
    }
    protected void Page_Init(object sender, EventArgs e)
    {
        //
        // CODEGEN: This call is required by the ASP.NET Windows
        // Form Designer.
        //
        InitializeComponent();
    }

    #region Web Form Designer generated code
    /// <summary>
    ///     Required method for Designer support - do not modify
    ///     the contents of this method with the code editor.
```

```
/// </summary>
private void InitializeComponent()
{
    this.Load += new System.EventHandler(this.Page_Load);
    this.SignOut.Click += new System.EventHandler(this.SignOut_Click);
    this.AddaProject.Click += new System.EventHandler(
                    this.AddaProject_Click);
    this.cAddProject.Add+= new System.EventHandler(
                    this.AddProject_Add);
    this.cAddProject.Done += new System.EventHandler(
                    this.AddProject_Done);
    this.Load += new System.EventHandler(this.Page_Load);
}
#endregion

protected void AddaProject_Click(object sender, System.EventArgs e)
{
    cAddProject.Visible = true;
}
protected void AddProject_Add(object sender, System.EventArgs e)
{
    cProjects.BindGrid();
}
protected void AddProject_Done(object sender, System.EventArgs e)
{
    cAddProject.Visible = false;
}
    }
}
```

The interesting methods in this listing are the ties into the Add and Done events of the AddProject control. These allow us to rebind the Projects control to the database only when a new project has been added in the AddProject control. We therefore avoid unnecessary trips back to the database. Although only the current user has the Admin privileges to add projects in this control, there may be other controls that allow others to modify the database at the same time as the current user. We could occasionally (perhaps once per minute) code trips back to the database to update changes made by others for query operations. All updates, insertions, and deletions should be in real time and perhaps synchronized by an automatic checking out of the record before the change is made.

The SignOut is another interesting method in this listing because it allows the user to remove either durable or session authentication cookies. This step requires a re-authentication for continuous access of InternetBaton from that computer. We identify the current user through the User.Identity.Name property.

The screen shots shown in Figures 2-4 through 2-6 show what the previous code displays when a user logs in to the existing account, adds a new project called *Book,* and then clicks the Done button.

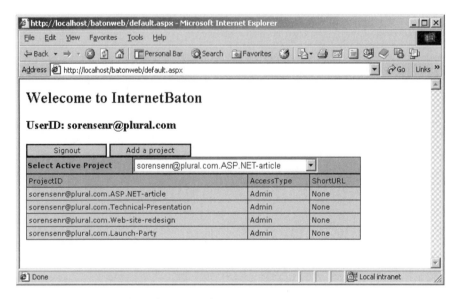

FIGURE 2-4   Page View after User Signs In.

Figure 2-4 shows the view after the user has signed in. Note that I previously added some other projects. (You can ignore the ShortURL field for now. Its purpose is explained in the next section.)

Figure 2-5 shows the view after the user clicks the Add Project button and types in Book. A user could add many different projects by clicking the Add Project button because this control remains visible until the Done button is clicked. The code in default.aspx.cs taps into the custom Add event of the AddProject control and requests a rebind of the DataGrid and DropDownList elements of the Projects control each time a project is added, so they are visible immediately.

Figure 2-6 shows the view after the user clicks the Done button of the AddProject control. The control becomes invisible until the user clicks the Add Project button again.

Adding additional screens to InternetBaton is basically more of the same type of code we have just discussed, so we now move on to Collaboration Design.

Collaboration Design: Conducting the Orchestra

How could we expand upon the capability of the InternetBaton application through collaboration with other Web services? The choices are quite limited today because the technology is new and there are very few Web services currently available. However, there will be great opportunities for collaboration in the future. Let us digress from our application for a moment and consider what these new Web services will offer.

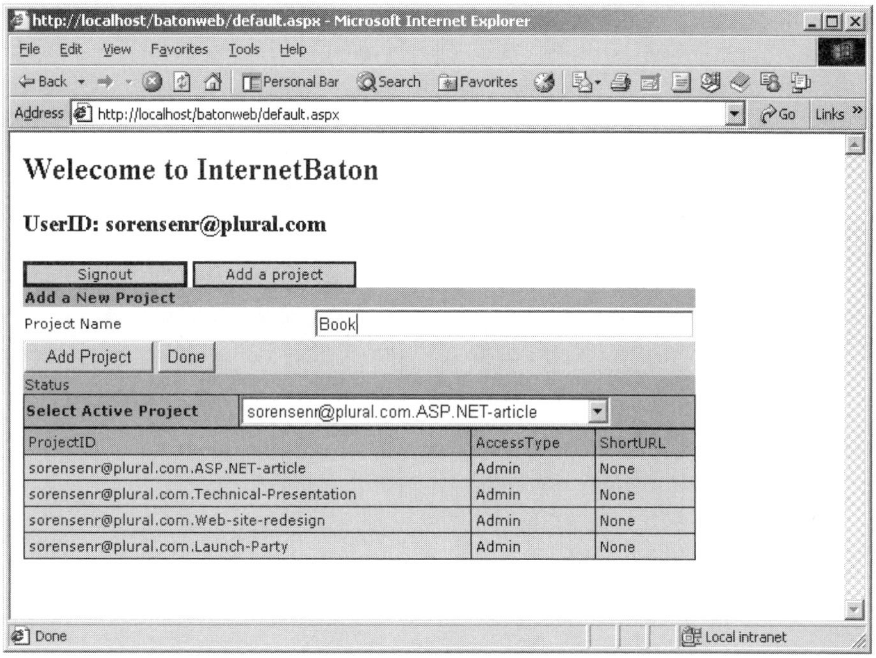

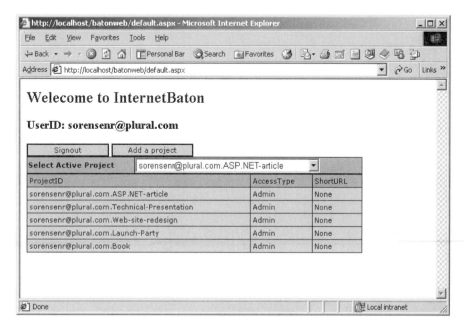

FIGURE 2-5   Page View after User Adds Book Project.

FIGURE 2-6   Page View after User Clicks Done Button.

Microsoft is working on numerous people-oriented Web services projects, code named HailStorm, as their white paper explains.

> As part of the Microsoft .NET initiative, Microsoft is introducing a user-centric architecture and set of XML Web services, code named "HailStorm." Hail-Storm will make it easier to integrate the silos of information that exist today. HailStorm services are oriented around people, instead of around a specific device, application, service, or network.[1]

The white paper goes on to list the following Web services that target an identity, which could be a person or a collection of people who make up an organizational unit such as a team or corporation:

- *myAddress:* Electronic and geographic address for an identity
- *myProfile:* Name, nickname, special dates, picture
- *myContacts:* Electronic contacts (address book)
- *myLocation:* Electronic and geographical location and rendezvous
- *myNotifications:* Notification subscription, management, and routing
- *myInbox:* Items such as e-mail and voice mail, including existing mail systems
- *myCalendar:* Time and task management tools
- *myDocuments:* Raw document storage
- *myApplicationSettings:* Application settings
- *myFavoriteWebSites:* Favorite URLs
- *myWallet:* Items involved in purchases, such as receipts, payment instruments, and coupons
- *myDevices:* Device settings, capabilities
- *myServices:* Provisioned services for an identity
- *myUsage:* Usage report for previous services

These types of Web services will typically be required to facilitate normal every-day interactions between people and companies participating in an online community. More specialized Web services can be orchestrated with these basic services to provide greater capabilities, which will likely be required for business-to-business (B2B) operations. For example, there may be services such as myInvoices, myInventory, myDebtors, or myCreditors. The common characteristic of all these Web services is the notion that they are oriented to an identity (i.e., the person who represents "my"). This identity may be an individual person, but in many cases could be an association of people who have formed a legal identity, such as a corporation or business. A stan-dardized method for identifying individuals or groups of people will be a major fac-

---

[1] Microsoft. "Building User-Centric Experiences: An Introduction to Microsoft HailStorm," March 2001—*http://www.microsoft.com/net/hailstorm.asp.*

tor in shaping the ways that Web services collaborate. The Microsoft Passport service will be a common method of monitoring identity and is central to HailStorm. Passport will tie into many other Web services besides those provided by HailStorm and will likely become a compelling choice for millions of consumers. Sun Microsystems, who is working on an different Web service implementation architecture called Sun ONE, has also stated that knowing the identity of the consumer is a critical factor in creating smart Web services. A Sun alternative to Passport for sharing context about consumers between Web services may also emerge and be widely used. A Sun white paper on Web services states the following:

> Context refers to the things that a Web service needs to know about the service consumer to provide a customized, personalized experience. These things include the identity of the consumer, the location of the consumer, and any privacy constraints associated with the consumer information. . . . Before the vision of transparent, dynamic interaction of widely distributed, heterogeneous Web services can become a reality, this issue of shared context must be solved. . . . The solution can't come from a single vendor. It cannot be proprietary. The solution must be open and interoperable. It must work with any Web service.[2]

The issue of how Web services actually become oriented to the identity of the person or group of people using them is one of the most interesting aspects of how the new people-oriented paradigm will be implemented. It will be much easier to build the sophisticated Web services required by an online community if multiple Web services can easily share context about people in a way that protects privacy and security.

IBM, Microsoft, Sun, and many other vendors agree on the same open standards for Web service interoperability (i.e., SOAP; universal discovery, description, and integration [UDDI]; and Web services description language [WSDL]). However, it is unclear whether the major software vendors will agree about how people's identity and context is shared, managed, protected, and propagated between Web services.

If we narrow our focus to the Microsoft HailStorm set of Web services, how could we use it to enrich the InternetBaton application? This is a situation in which we could apply the design attitudes of the Conductor People-Type, using recommendations such as "accept the fact that each player needs to depend on others to achieve the desired effect," "contribute by leading others to perform together in an integrated way," and "understand that the whole is greater than the sum of the parts."

By integrating HailStorm into InternetBaton, users would not have to log in to any protected areas if they have already logged into a Passport-enabled site. Passport could also be used to specify the other users who are allowed to view or modify the

---

[2] Sun Microsystems. "Sun Open Net Environment (Sun ONE) Software Architecture: An Open Architecture for Interoperable, Smart Web Services"—*http://www.sun.com/software/sunone/wp-arch/*.

documents. The users would not need to specify the shared location of their documents because it could be determined from the myDocuments Web service. The myWallet Web service could be integrated to process payments for using Internet-Baton so that people would not have to enter credit card numbers. By integrating the myNotifications Web service, people could receive an instant message when a document has been checked in or checked out. The myLocation Web service could determine whether this instant message would be sent to a cell phone, personal digital assistant (PDA), or PC. The myInbox Web service could be leveraged to simplify the handling of e-mail or voice mail communication. We could also combine the features of the myCalendar, myContacts, and myNotifications services to schedule online discussions about shared resources such as documents, diagrams, music clips, or videos.

Although these ideas are exciting, we cannot integrate them into the InternetBaton application now because they are not available today. However, InternetBaton does use one very useful Web service that serves as a good example of a collaboration tool. The InternetJump Web site, which you can find at *http://www.internetjump.com*, provides a very useful service to people who have long URLs. For example, if a site has an address such as: *http://www.teztrisp.com/ourusers/~directories/mysite.html*, InternetJump would provide the choice of more than 130 different domain names of much shorter URLs, such as *http://go.quick.to/mysite*.

When anybody uses this shorter URL, the InternetJump service will automatically redirect people to the longer URL. Companies can also offer the InternetJump service as a user-friendly feature to their customers. For example, a delivery company could help customers to track their packages using a nickname instead of a tracking number. A customer called Ed could simply type the URL *http://go.just.to/ed-report*, which would redirect to the URL that follows and indicates where the package is located:

> *http://www.deliverycompany.com/cgibin/tracking?tracknumbers=791127546126&*
> *action=track&language=english&cntry_code=us*

The InternetBaton application also leverages this Web service for simplifying the Baton name. For example, a user who would normally type a URL like *http://www. InternetBaton.com/user@email.com.myproject/adoc.bt* to refer to a shared document could be offered a choice of dozens of shortcuts, such as *http://go.easier.to/adoc*, instead.

It was for this reason that the Projects table had the ShortURL field in the previous section.

Step 4: Integration of InternetBaton with Other Web Services

For the purpose of illustration, we will create a mock URL redirection Web service that mimics the functionality of the InternetJump service. We will be able to programmatically add new shortcuts and URLs to the service using SOAP. We will then implement the URL redirection capability by adding a custom Http Handler to the service. Our test will be to create a shortcut—*http://localhost/IJ/Preface.bt*—that will redirect the user to *http://localhost/WebBaton/myname@email.com.Book/Preface.bt*. To build a skeleton Web service, we will use Visual Studio.NET and call the project *IJ*.

We will create two Web methods accessible using SOAP: AddJump and GetJumpURL. The first will allow us to programmatically add a new shortcut, passing in the shortcut name and the longer URL to which it resolves. The second method allows us to programmatically test whether our shortcut has been added by retrieving the longer URL when the shortcut name is passed in. Because this is just a simulation, we will not be concerned about performance at all. In fact, we will not even use a relational database to store the input data. To cover some new ground, we will use an XML file and a DataSet to manage the list of shortcuts created. Our XML file has the following format:

```xml
<InternetJump>
  <xsd:schema id="InternetJump" targetNamespace="" xmlns=""
      xmlns:xsd="http://www.w3.org/2000/10/XMLSchema"
      xmlns:msdata="urn:schemas-microsoft-com:xml-msdata">
    <xsd:element name="Jumps">
      <xsd:complexType>
        <xsd:all>
          <xsd:element name="Shortcut" minOccurs="0" type="xsd:string"/>
          <xsd:element name="URL" minOccurs="0" type="xsd:string"/>
        </xsd:all>
      </xsd:complexType>
    </xsd:element>
    <xsd:element name="InternetJump" msdata:IsDataSet="true">
      <xsd:complexType>
        <xsd:choice maxOccurs="unbounded">
          <xsd:element ref="Jumps"/>
        </xsd:choice>
      </xsd:complexType>
    </xsd:element>
  </xsd:schema>
  <Jumps>
    <Shortcut>/IJ/contents.bt</Shortcut>
    <URL>http://localhost/WebBaton/myname@email.com.Book/contents.bt</URL>
  </Jumps>
  <Jumps>
    <Shortcut>/IJ/chapter1.bt</Shortcut>
    <URL>http://localhost/WebBaton/myname@email.com.Book/chapter1.bt</URL>
  </Jumps>
  <Jumps>
    <Shortcut>/IJ/chapter2.bt</Shortcut>
    <URL>http://localhost/WebBaton/myname@email.com.Book/chapter2.bt</URL>
  </Jumps>
</InternetJump>
```

The code we need to add for the IJ Web service is as follows:

```
namespace IJ
{
using System;
using System.Collections;
using System.ComponentModel;
using System.Data;
using System.Diagnostics;
using System.Web;
using System.Web.Services;
using System.Threading;
using System.IO;

/// <summary>
///     Summary description for Service1.
/// </summary>
public class Service1 : System.Web.Services.WebService
{
    public Service1()
    {
        //CODEGEN: This call is required by the ASP.NET Web Services
        // Designer
        InitializeComponent();
    }

    #region Component Designer generated code
    /// <summary>
    ///     Required method for Designer support - do not modify
    ///     the contents of this method with the code editor.
    /// </summary>
    private void InitializeComponent()
    {
    }
    #endregion

    /// <summary>
    ///     Clean up any resources being used.
    /// </summary>
    public override void Dispose()
    {
    }

    [WebMethod]
    public bool AddJump(string Shortcut, string URL)
    {
        bool bresult = false;
        Application.Lock();
        try
        {
            DataSet ds = new DataSet();
            FileStream fs = new FileStream(Server.MapPath(
                        "InternetJumpDB.xml"),
            FileMode.Open,FileAccess.Read);
            StreamReader reader = new StreamReader(fs);
```

```
            ds.ReadXml(reader);
            fs.Close();

            DataRow newJump = ds.Tables[0].NewRow();
            newJump["ShortCut"] = Shortcut;
            newJump["URL"] = URL;
            ds.Tables[0].Rows.Add(newJump);
            ds.AcceptChanges();

            fs = new FileStream(Server.MapPath("InternetJumpDB.xml"),
                                FileMode.Create,
            FileAccess.Write|FileAccess.Read);
            StreamWriter writer = new StreamWriter(fs);
            ds.WriteXml(writer);
            writer.Close();
            fs.Close();
            bresult = true;
        }
        catch(Exception e1)
        {
            Trace.Write(e1.Message);
            //log error here
        }
        Application.UnLock();
        return bresult;
    }

    [WebMethod]
    public string GetJumpURL(string Shortcut)
    {
        String cmd = "Shortcut=" + "'" + Shortcut + "'";
        String JumpURL = "Blank";
        Application.Lock();
        try
        {
            DataSet ds = new DataSet();
            FileStream fs = new FileStream(Server.MapPath(
                        "InternetJumpDB.xml"),FileMode.Open,
                        FileAccess.Read);
            StreamReader reader = new StreamReader(fs);
            ds.ReadXml(reader);
            fs.Close();
            DataTable users = ds.Tables[0];
            DataRow[] matches = users.Select(cmd);
            if( matches != null && matches.Length > 0 )
            {
                DataRow row = matches[0];
                JumpURL = (String)row["URL"];
            }
        }
        catch(Exception e1)
        {
            Trace.Write(e1.Message);
```

```
            //log error here
        }
        Application.UnLock();
        return JumpURL;
    }
}
```

You will notice that the method implementations we added open the Internet-JumpDB.xml file and read its contents into a DataSet. We then use the simple methods of the DataSet to operate on this data. If we made changes to the DataSet, it would be very easy to write out the new contents to the XML file again. Note that the previous implementations do not take performance issues into consideration. For example, the use of the `Application.Lock` method provides a simple way to synchronize access to the XML file, but it also has a performance penalty associated with it, since it locks down all global variables in the application. For test purposes, this is acceptable, but you should use a high-performance database such as SQL Server if this design is intended for production use. After we compile the IJ project, we test its programmable interface using the user interface provided by .NET as shown in Figure 2-7.

Presenting the Invoke button adds the new shortcut to the InternetJumpDB.xml file. To do this from the WebBaton project, we would need to add a Web reference to

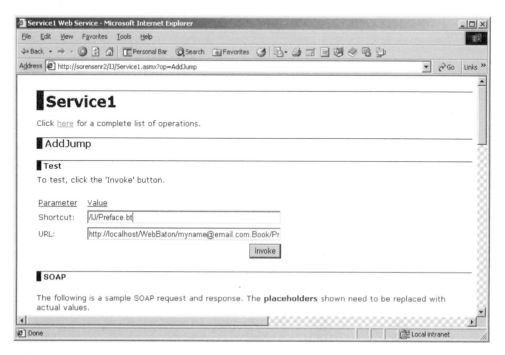

FIGURE 2-7   Testing IJ Project's Programmable Interface.

the IJ project and include its namespace. We would then simply program against the IJ methods as if they were any .NET class.

We now need to actually add the redirection functionality to the IJ service. We do this by creating a customized Http Handler. Http Handlers provide a low-level request/response application program interface (API) that enables the user to service incoming Hypertext Transfer Protocol (HTTP) requests in a customized fashion. Outside of the .NET framework, this type of functionality is usually provided by Internet server API (ISAPI) and common gateway interface (CGI) applications. To create a custom HTTP Handler, the user implements the IHttpHandler interface, which contains the methods IsReusable and ProcessRequest. IsReusable informs the HTTP factory whether the same instance can be used to service multiple requests. The ProcessRequest method is where the customized work is coded and takes an Http-Context instance as a parameter, allowing access to the Request intrinsic and Response intrinsic. The code for the IJ IHttpHandler follows[3]:

```
using System;
using System.Diagnostics;
using System.Web;
using System.Collections;
using System.Collections.Specialized;
using System.Data;
using System.Threading;
using System.IO;

namespace Redirection
{
  // Test InternetJump URL Redirection service
  public class InternetJumpHandler : IHttpHandler
  {
    public void ProcessRequest(HttpContext context)
    {
        string Shortcut = " ";
        string JumpURL = "http://localhost/error.htm";
        context.Application.Lock();
        try
        {
          NameValueCollection ServerVariables;
          ServerVariables= context.Request.ServerVariables;

          for (int i = 0; i < ServerVariables.Count; i++)
          {
          if((string) ServerVariables.GetKey(i) == "URL")
          {
              Shortcut = (string) ServerVariables.Get(i);
```

---

[3] I coded the same application in a previous book using C++ and the Windows Sockets API. The code listing was more than 16 pages, in contrast to one page here. Some things are definitely getting easier.

```
                }
            }

            string cmd = "Shortcut=" + "'" + Shortcut + "'";
            JumpURL = JumpURL + Shortcut;

            DataSet ds = new DataSet();
            FileStream fs = new FileStream(context.Server.MapPath(
                        "InternetJumpDB.xml"),
            FileMode.Open,FileAccess.Read);
            StreamReader reader = new StreamReader(fs);
            ds.ReadXml(reader);
            fs.Close();

            DataTable users = ds.Tables[0];
            DataRow[] matches = users.Select(cmd);
            if( matches != null && matches.Length > 0 )
            {
                    DataRow row = matches[0];
                    JumpURL= (string)row["URL"];
            }
        }
        catch(Exception e1)
        {
            Trace.Write(e1.Message);
            //log error here
        }
        context.Application.UnLock();
        context.Response.Redirect( JumpURL);
        }

    public bool IsReusable
    {
      get { return true; }
    }
  }
}
```

The implementation of the ProcessRequest method retrieves the end portion of
the received URL and then determines whether this shortcut has a matching longer
URL stored in the InternetJumpDB.xml file. If there is a match, the user is redirected
to the longer URL. Because this file is self-standing, we can more easily compile it
using a batch file as follows:

```
csc /t:library /out:..\bin\InternetJumpHandler.dll /r:System.Web.dll
    /r:System.dll InternetJumpHandler.cs
pause
```

The output is InternetJumpHandler.dll, which needs to be located in the bin
directory of the IJ application. We need to add this custom handler to the web.config
file of the IJ application as follows:

```
<httpHandlers>
        <add verb="*" path="*.vb" type="System.Web.HttpNotFoundHandler,
                    System.Web" />
        <add verb="*" path="*.cs" type="System.Web.HttpNotFoundHandler,
                    System.Web" />
        <add verb="*" path="*.vbproj" type="System.Web.
                    HttpNotFoundHandler,System.Web" />
        <add verb="*" path="*.csproj" type="System.Web.
                    HttpNotFoundHandler,System.Web" />
        <add verb="*" path="*.webinfo" type="System.Web.
                    HttpNotFoundHandler,System.Web" />
        <add verb="*" path="*.bt" type="Redirection.InternetJumpHandler,
                    InternetJumpHandler" />
</httpHandlers>
```

By default, resources ending with extensions such as *.vb* or *.cs* have no handler associated with them. This is a security precaution so that they cannot be accessed remotely. Any URL ending with the *.bt* extension is handled by our custom Http Handler. Finally, we need to configure IIS so that it passes any URLs ending in *.bt* to the .NET framework. We do this using the configuration panel of the IIS management tool shown in Figure 2-8. Anyone entering the URL *http://localhost/IJ/Preface.bt* will now be redirected to *http://localhost/WebBaton/myname@email.com.Book/Preface.bt*.

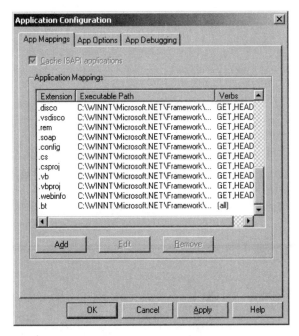

FIGURE 2-8   IIS Configuration Panel.

Translation Design: A Linguist's Delight

The IJ Web service can be integrated into any application on any platform that supports the open Internet standards XML and SOAP. The reason why this type of integration is so easy to implement is that the .NET architecture was designed to support the principle of translation in a very comprehensive way. This translation capability is supported in the areas of system interoperability and service contract transformation. In this section, we examine system interoperability in the context of InternetBaton synchronizing Baton projects with sophisticated clients and service contract transformation and in the context of transforming Baton project metadata files.

Step 5: Baton Synchronization

InternetBaton is a very useful application for sharing resources that people can easily download from remote Web sites. However, imagine a team working on very large files that are more difficult to download, such as those used in multimedia applications. In this type of scenario, it would be beneficial if InternetBaton automatically synchronized the latest version of the files between the collaborators' shared storage areas overnight. For example, imagine that the four authors of this book decided to make a documentary about software development, and each of us was editing content into a set of large movie files. Using InternetBaton, we would agree on virtual URLs, such as *http://www.internetbaton.com/me@email.com.movie/scene1* through *http://www.internetbaton.com/me@email.com.movie/scene15*, to identify the 15 different movie scene files on which we were working. Each night the latest version of these files would be automatically downloaded to each of our home PCs; thus we would all be synchronized to the same versions each morning.

To deliver this feature, we would need to incorporate client-side code into the InternetBaton architecture. This would create complex issues because there could be a multitude of different client devices running on diverse platforms that wish to use this feature. How would we design the InternetBaton application to best support this type of environment? We could apply the design attitudes of the Linguist People-Type, which is characterized by recommendations such as "understand that heterogeneity can result in a richer and more erudite environment," "anticipate that new modes of expression will be continually discovered or created," and "apply the Pareto principle, which states that coverage of 20% of the alternative expressions will satisfy 80% of the needed usage."

A customized client application is one option for providing this type of functionality. People could download the application from the *www.InternetBaton.com* Web site, and a specific version could be developed for each client device and platform. However, this would require a lot of coding that would be time consuming to develop and maintain. Another alternative would be to limit the focus to one popular client platform such as Windows and simply not support others. However, aside from the obvious loss of revenue that would result, this approach has other weaknesses. It does not offer much flexibility for catering to new opportunities that may emerge in the future; any changes would require redeployment of binaries to a multitude of clients.

If we consider the likely clients that will use the new features of InternetBaton and apply the Pareto principle (the 80/20 rule), a more attractive design option emerges. If the objective is to get local access to large files that need to be synchronized overnight, we can safely assume that the majority of clients will be using PCs that are permanently connected to the Internet. In addition, these computers must have a Web server of some kind because the virtual URL redirects people to a location on the client PC.

Therefore we can restrict our focus to interoperating with a profile of client Web servers through extensions such as scripts, CGI, or, even more in the future, SOAP. To ensure maximum flexibility, we can embody in an XML file all the data required for the work that needs to be performed. You may be wondering about the scalability of this approach because it may take a long time for these scripts to finish processing. If the InternetBaton application were to make many calls to clients to process these scripts, it would get tied up waiting for responses. To ensure that this does not happen, the InternetBaton application will call the clients asynchronously.

Our design approach to the new features for InternetBaton is as follows:

1. Restrict support to client Web servers that can support extensions such as script, CGI, or SOAP. (We only focus on SOAP in this example.)
2. Make available on the InternetBaton Web site the implementation of the previous scripts, CGIs, or SOAP methods that can be downloaded to the client.
3. Invoke the client scripts, CGI, or SOAP methods asynchronously so that we do not tie up server threads waiting for a synchronous response.

Chapter 4 provides an InternetBaton client that implements the code for the `DownloadProjectItems` method, so this chapter concentrates on how InternetBaton can call this method asynchronously. To test the differences between our synchronous and asynchronous calls, we have created a sample client Web service that exposes various Web methods. The implementation of each method simulates timely activity by suspending the thread for 10 seconds. For example, in the simplest case of calling `DownloadProjectItems` synchronously, our client method is implemented as follows:

```
[WebMethod( Description = "Starts InternetBaton Synchronization in a
                         synchronous method call." )]
    public void DownloadProjectItems()
    {
        int time = 10000;
        Thread.Sleep(time);
    }
```

To call this method from InternetBaton, we need to add a Web reference to the client Web service in our BatonWeb project and include the generated namespace associated with the Web reference. The actual code to call the method is as follows:

```
protected void SynchronousCall_Click(object sender, System.EventArgs e)
{
    Baton.localhost.Service1 srv = new Baton.localhost.Service1();
    SyncStart.Text = DateTime.Now.ToString();
    srv.DownloadProjectItems();
    SyncEnd.Text = DateTime.Now.ToString();
}
```

You will notice that we have added a few labels, which measure the time it takes to return from the method call. Predictably, in this case it takes 10 seconds. To turn this method into an asynchronous method, we simply set an additional OneWay property as follows:

```
[SoapMethod( OneWay = true )]
[WebMethod( Description = "Starts InternetBaton Synchronization in an
                          asynchronous method call." )]
public void DownloadProjectItemsAsync()
{
    int time = 10000;
    Thread.Sleep(time);
}
```

Setting the OneWay property to *true* causes the Web service to immediately return an HTTP 202 status code just before invoking the Web service method. Consequently the client does not receive an acknowledgement that the server has executed the method successfully. A OneWay method cannot have a return value or any Out parameters. The code to call this method from InternetBaton is as follows:

```
protected void AsynchronousCall_Click(object sender, System.EventArgs e)
{
    Baton.localhost.Service1 srv = new Baton.localhost.Service1();
    AsyncStart.Text = DateTime.Now.ToString();
    srv.DownloadProjectItemsAsync();
    AsyncEnd.Text = DateTime.Now.ToString();
}
```

This time the start and end times are the same because the method returns immediately. There may be cases in which we really do need a Return parameter from an asynchronous method call. This can also be easily accommodated. It is helpful to consider the design pattern the .NET framework uses to implement asynchronous programming. With .NET, it is the caller that decides if a particular call should be asynchronous or synchronous. In fact, no code changes to the method itself are required. However, a Web service may choose to explicitly support asynchronous behavior because it can implement it more efficiently than the general architecture or because it may want to only support asynchronous responses to its callers. Support for asynchronous programming within the .NET framework is included in the following areas:

- File input/output (IO), stream IO, socket IO
- Networking: HTTP, Transmission Control Protocol (TCP)
- Remoting channels: HTTP, TCP
- ASP.NET, ASP.NET Web services
- Messaging message queues over Microsoft Message Queuing (MSMQ) technology
- Delegates

The following code demonstrates an asynchronous call to a method that returns a result:

```
[WebMethod( Description = "Starts InternetBaton Synchronization with a
                          return value" )]
    public int DownloadProjectItemsRet()
    {
        int time = 10000;
        Thread.Sleep(time);
        return time;
    }
```

You will notice that the OneWay property is not set and that this method is coded like any other regular synchronous method. To call this method asynchronously, all the coding takes place on the client as follows:

```
protected void AsynchronousCallAlt_Click(object sender, System.EventArgs e)
{
    Baton.localhost.Service1 srv = new Baton.localhost.Service1();
    AsyncAltStart.Text = DateTime.Now.ToString();
    IAsyncResult result = srv.BeginDownloadProjectItemsRet(null, null);
    AsyncAltEnd.Text = DateTime.Now.ToString();
    // Additional code can go here to perform other tasks while the
    // method is completing.
    //Wait for Async Call to complete
    result.AsyncWaitHandle.WaitOne();
    //Complete the Asynchronous call to Add Web Service method
    int time = srv.EndDownloadProjectItemsRet(result);
    AsyncAltEnd.Text = AsyncAltEnd.Text + " Total time =" + time.ToString();
}
```

Here, notice that the client first calls the BeginDownloadProjectItemsRet method, which returns immediately. The client thread is then free to perform other client-side processing while the server is busy processing the method. After a cer-

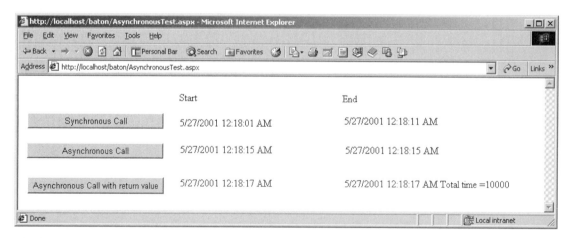

FIGURE 2-9   Results of Synchronous and Asynchronous Call Methods.

tain time, the client checks with the server to determine whether the Web service method has been completed and will wait if it has not. It will then call the method `EndDownloadProjectItemsRet` and receive the return value. The return value in this case is a string, which shows that the method returned immediately after it was first invoked but then took 10 seconds to be completed. Figure 2-9 shows the results of each of the previous methods.

Step 6: Translation of Baton Metadata

Chapter 4 builds a sophisticated client for InternetBaton that implements the method `DownloadProjectItems`. In addition, this client extends the capability of Internet Baton by adding metadata about a Baton project. A client may do this to add new features such as item review and approval. A client may also keep all metadata about Baton items completely on their own managed servers to maintain confidentiality. If a project deals with very sensitive information, then metadata such as a collaborators' notes or approval status could be equally sensitive. If the metadata about a project's Baton is actually another Baton then only the collaborators have access to this information, and it never needs to be stored on the InternetBaton Web server.

At a minimum, InternetBaton needs to store the Baton name, the URL to which it points, and whether the Baton is checked out. An XML representation of a Baton project could be as follows:

```
<?xml version='1.0'?>
<!-- This file represents an InternetBaton project -->
<batonproject>
<baton>
        <batonid>chapter1</batonid>
```

```
        <itemurl>http://www.a-webserver/chapter1</itemurl>
        <status>checked-out</status>
    </baton>
    <baton>
        <batonid>chapter2</batonid>
        <itemurl>http://www.another-webserver/chapter2</itemurl>
        <status>checked-in</status>
    </baton>
    <baton>
        <batonid>chapter3</batonid>
        <itemurl>http://www.yet-another-webserver/chapter3</itemurl>
        <status>checked-out</status>
    </baton>
</batonproject>
```

However, imagine that a client would like to extend this Baton project information with a security field that specifies whether digital certificates are required on col-
laborator sites. The service description contract between InternetBaton and its clients
does not include this field, so the clients need to translate the contract into a new one
that has this additional information. This task can be done totally independently of
InternetBaton and can be implemented easily using an extensible style language
(XSL) style sheet and methods within the .NET framework System.Xml namespace.
For example, a client could create an XSL style sheet as follows:

```
<xsl:stylesheet xmlns:xsl="http://www.w3.org/1999/XSL/Transform"
     version="1.0">
<xsl:template match="/">
<!— This file represents an InternetBaton project with security field
     added—>
<batonproject>
    <xsl:apply-templates/>
</batonproject>
</xsl:template>
    <xsl:template match="batonproject">
    <xsl:apply-templates select="baton"/>
</xsl:template>

<xsl:template match="baton">
    <baton>
        <batonid><xsl:value-of select="batonid"/></batonid>
        <itemurl><xsl:value-of select="itemurl"/></itemurl>
        <status><xsl:value-of select="status"/></status>
        <security>"Digital Certificate"</security>
    </baton>
</xsl:template>
</xsl:stylesheet>
```

This XSL style sheet can be used to transform the InternetBaton project XML file
into a new XML file that contains the new security tag. The following code listing is
an example of how easy it is to translate the InternetBaton service description contract

into a format that the sophisticated client requires, using the previous XSL style sheet and methods in the .NET XML classes:

```
public string TransformBatonMetaData()
{
    String infilename = "C:\\Inetpub\\wwwroot\\ClientWebService
                        \\batonproject.xml";
    String stylesheet = "C:\\Inetpub\\wwwroot\\ClientWebService
                        \\batonsecurity.xsl";
    String outfilename = "C:\\Inetpub\\wwwroot\\ClientWebService
                        \\baton-with-security-field.xml";

    string str = "See new Baton project file at C:\\Inetpub\\wwwroot
                 \\ClientWebService\\baton-with-security-field.xml";
    StreamReader stream = null;
    try
    {
        // create the XslTransform and load the stylesheet
        XslTransform xslt = new XslTransform();
        xslt.Load(stylesheet);

        // load the XML data file
        XmlDocument doc = new XmlDocument();
        doc.Load( infilename );

        // create the XmlTextWriter to output the transform to
        // the new Baton Project file
        XmlTextWriter writer = new XmlTextWriter( outfilename, null );

        DocumentNavigator nav = new DocumentNavigator( doc );

        // transform the file
        xslt.Transform( nav, null, writer );
        writer.Close();

    }
    catch ( Exception e )
    {
        str = e.Message;
        //log error here
    }
    finally
    {
        if ( stream != null )
            stream.Close();
    }
    return str;
}
```

Calling this method produces the following new XML file representation of the InternetBaton project with the additional security tag:

```
<?xml version="1.0"?>
<batonproject>
    <baton>
        <batonid>chapter1</batonid>
        <itemurl>http://www.a-webserver/chapter1</itemurl>
        <status>checked-out</status>
        <security>"Digital Certificate"</security>
    </baton>
    <baton>
        <batonid>chapter2</batonid>
        <itemurl>http://www.another-webserver/chapter2</itemurl>
        <status>checked-in</status>
        <security>"Digital Certificate"</security>
    </baton>
    <baton>
        <batonid>chapter3</batonid>
        <itemurl>http://www.yet-another-webserver/chapter3</itemurl>
        <status>checked-out</status>
        <security>"Digital Certificate"</security>
    </baton>
</batonproject>
```

Although this sample of translation in action may seem very simple, it also demonstrates the power of this model. Clients have great flexibility in adapting and enhancing the functionality of service description contracts without having to coordinate with the service provider. The service provider does not need to facilitate this enhancement or be concerned about changes that could break existing systems.

CONCLUSION

This chapter has shown how the principles of people-oriented software were applied during the creation of a decentralized Web collaboration application, which allows people to work jointly on project resources over the Internet. Although it is evident that the .NET platform is ideally suited for this type of development, it is important to remember that the people-oriented programming paradigm is not tied to any particular system implementation. Ten years from now, we may use an entirely different set of software development tools to build an application such as InternetBaton. However, it is likely that the people-oriented principles of universalization, collaboration, and translation would still be relevant because they reflect generic engineering requirements in designing software for a global online community.

Chapter 3

C#

THIS TIME, IT'S PERSONAL

It has been said that about every ten years, a revolution occurs in the computing industry that elevates application development to a radically simpler level of implementation. The impact and scope of the technology packaged in Microsoft's .NET platform qualifies it as the next computing revolution. This new revolution, as important and exciting as it is, is merely the next step in a continuing journey of application evolution toward something we have been calling *people-oriented software*.

From a development perspective, this evolution has progressed from functions, to objects, to class libraries, to frameworks, to component object models, to systems services, and now to .NET. The scope and impact have incrementally increased with each progression as well. Starting with a scope limited to source code, it progressed to the application, and then past the application to the machine. With object protocols such as distributed component object model (DCOM), remote method invocation (RMI), and CORBA, it moved beyond the machine to the enterprise; now with .NET, it will spread across enterprises to connect customers, business partners, and suppliers.

It is in this broader context of .NET technologies that people-oriented software truly can be appreciated. *People-oriented software* is a term that has been coined to capture the reality of a new and unique class of software—a class of software different enough from the status quo that it requires a distinctive term through which its specific qualities can be expressed. People-oriented software is a class of software that is highly distributed and highly collaborative.

Currently, two primary forces are driving this new class of software:

1. The introduction of a plethora of new personal devices
2. The desire to more closely integrate an enterprise with its partners

For the individual consumer, there will soon be a variety of new devices offering functionality that is largely driven by connectivity and interaction. The software that runs these devices will have a very personal impact on the average individual. For example, the *smart phone* will be a combination cell phone, personal digital assistant (PDA), and Internet device. Applications built for these devices stand to offer a great deal of personal service given the intersection of personal information, handheld capabilities, and the connectivity of the Internet.

For corporations, supply chains will be increasingly integrated, and the marketplace for various commodities will become even more automated. Combine the advantages of this increased integration and automation with the advances we have already made in business-to-consumer (B2C) support, and the result is a much more personalized relationship between the enterprise and its supplier as well as the company and its customers.

It is in this context that the term *people oriented* becomes appropriate to represent and characterize this new integrated and personalized reality. We have devices that allow personalized interactions with people and organizations, many of which provide personalized service to their partners and suppliers. People-oriented software can be viewed as a class of software that can be built using Microsoft .NET. That is, people orientation is an end and Microsoft .NET is a means, and this time when we build software, it's personal!

This brings us to the subject of C#. C# is a language that is very effective for building people-oriented .NET applications, and it's from this perspective that we examine the language in this chapter. Toward that end, C# is viewed from both contemporary and people-oriented perspectives. The chapter concludes with a tour of the C# language, which is designed to provide you with an overall feel for what this language has to offer. The two perspectives combined with the language tour explain how you can most effectively build tomorrow's .NET solutions using C#.

Before we move on, it is worth mentioning that although this may not be the typical way C# is introduced, we feel that this challenging class of software requires an overall perspective more than a myopic understanding of a language. Taking a perspective gives purpose and application for the knowledge learned, whereas a language introduction is simply that—an introduction to the language. Without something to say or a story to tell, knowledge of any language, human or computer, is utterly useless. Our goal is to highlight the most important aspects of C# from the perspective of the key principles of .NET development we have been referring to as people oriented. The next chapter puts this knowledge into practice by applying it in the development of a sample application. Together, these chapters allow you to see these ideas and concepts in action in a tangible way within a realistic context.

WHAT IS C#?

"What is C#?" is a natural and very basic question for which there are many seemingly valid answers. For example, version 0.22 of the C# language specification puts it this way: "C# is a simple, modern, object-oriented, and type-safe programming language derived from C and C++." Anders Hejlsberg, the chief architect of the C# language, describes it as a component-oriented language. Others say it is nothing more than a Java clone that is more a clever response to legal disputes between Microsoft and Sun Microsystems than it is a new language. At the risk of muddying the waters even further, this language also can be viewed from a people-oriented perspective. This perspective is larger in scope than the ones previously mentioned, so a little background may be helpful.

When the C programming language burst on to the scene, its author considered it a better way to write programs for a certain class of systems. At the time, Assembly was the language of choice for writing high-performance systems. The C programming language provided high-level constructs (compared to Assembly), which made writing and debugging programs easier.

As time went on and the class of applications that were being built grew in complexity, it became more and more difficult to build these larger systems. What was needed was a new way of dealing with system complexity. At the time, object-oriented design had emerged as the new choice for dealing with this increasing complexity. There were other benefits that this new design technique offered as well. The notion of software reuse was also a very hot topic. Although this new design technique and its new reuse goals could be achieved using the C programming language, doing so involved following an indirect path. To express the concepts of object-oriented programming required clever coding techniques and conventions (i.e., arrays or structures with function pointers). The lack of these concepts as a formalized part of the language was a hindrance, much like the lack of high-level constructs was in Assembly. For C programmers, the choice of C++ for object-oriented programming was a natural choice. Lean and mean, C++ had all the advantages of C, plus it had the notion of classes that could be used to achieve the goals of object orientation. In fact, "C with Classes" was a very early name for C++.

This brings us to where we are today with the Internet and C#. Just as C became a better alternative to Assembly and C++ became an alternative to C, C# sets out to take its place in this repeating pattern of language evolution. In the same way that each of these languages was designed to better deal with an emerging set of thorny problems for which current languages where not as well suited, C# steps forth as a language that is designed to better deal with issues related to today's Internet development. C++ was a natural choice for C programmers who wanted to develop object-oriented programs. In a similar way, C# is a natural choice for developers who want to develop Internet-class applications. The point is that each new language has a different focus, and it was within that context that the language became a better choice.

Each of these languages chose to address the problems of the day by directly representing concepts that were not effectively addressed by their predecessors. C introduced features such as functions, primitive types, and structs. C++ introduced classes, enums, and overloaded operators. C# introduces direct support for, among other things, the concept of attributes, component orientation, and seamless integration of a specialized common language runtime.

Therefore yet another way to answer the question "What is C#?" is that it is a language that stands ready to address the sticky problems involved in people-oriented software. You could use a traditional language to develop people-oriented software and still be successful, but it would be like choosing C to tackle a complex application that would be better served by the richness that is available in C++.

WHAT'S SO SPECIAL ABOUT C#?

To fully explain what makes C# so special, we need to examine C# from two different perspectives. First, we examine C# to see how well it stacks up against the needs of contemporary development. Second, we view C# in terms of how well it meets the new challenges of people-oriented software.

Contemporary Perspective

What does C# offer the contemporary programmer? The answer to this question is undoubtedly somewhat subjective, but elegance, object orientation, and component orientation are important characteristics of this new language and a significant benefit for the serious programmer. Let us take a look at each of these important characteristics individually.

It's Elegant

Elegance is an abstract term that is often used to describe a programming language. Although a precise programming definition may not exist, there is a common understanding that is captured quite nicely by a quote from the French aviator, adventurer, and author, Antoine de Saint-Exupéry, who said, "A designer knows he has achieved perfection not when there is nothing left to add, but when there is nothing left to take away." This emphasis on simplicity and a canonical set of features is a hallmark of elegance and it characterizes the choices that the C# designer made when considering which language features to add. Several other descriptions, such as refined, polished, lucid, clear and to the point, and an absence of things offensive, also characterize these choices.

What is so elegant about C#? First of all, C# is derived from C++, which has long been known for its economy of syntax and expressiveness, each of which is a form of elegance. C# borrowed most of its operators, keywords, and statements directly from C++ and has kept a number of useful language features such as structs, enums, and operator overloading.

Elegance is also about simplifying and making things easier. As elegant as C++ is, there are aspects of it that are complicated, confusing, and sometimes even problematic. In the spirit of simplicity, the designers of C# decided not to incorporate several very notable C++ language features. For example, multiple inheritance and programmer-managed memory allocation were considered a hindrance rather than a blessing, so single inheritance and garbage collection have replaced them in C#. Header files were considered a feature that spread the nature of application elements over several files. As a result, the need for header files has been eliminated, and they do not exist in C#. Instead, everything can be centrally located and self-contained—a simplification that is helpful when it comes to embedding C# code in other environments, such as active server pages (ASP).

C++ was not the only language to provide inspiration for the design of C#. Java, Modula 2, C, and Smalltalk also contributed ideas to C#'s elegance. It is worth noting here that C# started with a clean slate. Its designers did not have to make compromises for the sake of backward compatibility with an existing language, which allowed them to incorporate the best ideas of several languages. For example, Smalltalk and Java contributed the idea of a singly rooted class hierarchy in which everything is derived from a class called *object*. This conformity enhances elegance by allowing all types to be treated the same way regardless of whether they are intrinsic or user defined.

Other simplifications that add to the elegance of C# include:

- The elimination of interface description language (IDL) files and the use of globally unique identifiers (GUIDs) as well as general COM plumbing
- A simplified notion of iterations that extends to all intrinsic types
- User-defined types
- Support for self-documentation code that can be understood by the compiler to automatically generate documentation directly from the source code

It's Object Oriented

C# is an object-oriented language. The merits of object orientation are accepted as a general truth in contemporary development and the principles of object-oriented development are now accepted axioms. As you would expect with an object-oriented language, C# provides user-defined types, classes, inheritance, and polymorphism.

Programmers need to be able to create new user-defined data types to make their solutions more understandable and to extend the available base types. They need to use classes as a basic means of program structure and abstraction to model real-world concepts as directly as possible. They need to use inheritance to model the types of relationships inherent in a problem space. Inheritance gives rise to polymorphism that can be applied in building as generic a solution as possible , which allows a common set of operations to be applied to a diverse set of types. This reduces the complexity of code by eliminating similar but essentially redundant solutions that really only differ in type but not semantics.[1]

It's Component Oriented

Other than object orientation itself, no other single concept has had such a significant impact on the practice of building modern software systems than has the concept of the software component. Given the enormous importance of components in contemporary development, you would expect any new language worth its salt to provide comprehensive component support. This was clearly an extremely important goal for C#'s chief architect, Anders Hejlsberg. In fact, in a wonderful interview with Hejlsberg done by O'Reilly editor John Osborn at the Microsoft Professional Developers Conference (July 2001), the interviewer made this observation:

> You [Anders] gave an introduction to C# recently, and the first bullet on the first slide said, "The first component-oriented language in the C/C++ family."

In the same interview, Anders summed up the formal language support for components and its priority in the language design:

> . . . one of our key design goals was to make the C# language component oriented—to add to the language itself all of the concepts that you need when you write components. Concepts such as *properties, methods, events, attributes,* and *documentation* are all first-class language constructs. The work that we've done with attributes—a feature used to add typed, extensible metadata to any object—is completely new and innovative. I haven't seen it in any other pro-

---

[1] This is an area in which genericity can be of significant benefit. Anders Hejlsberg has been quoted as saying that this is something that will be part of C# in the future. In fact, it will be part of any .NET language since it will be supported in the .NET runtime. He makes a compelling argument as to why it should be in the runtime and not in the language and what the benefits would be. The designers wanted to make it part of the runtime of the initial release but could not get it done in time. They have designed for it and its implications even affect the design of the IL! There is a working lab version of the .NET runtime that supports generics and it was used to make sure that they would not need to rewrite the entire runtime to support genericity when the time is right.

gramming language. And C# is the first language to incorporate eXtensible Markup Language (XML) comment tags that can be used by the compiler to generate readable documentation directly from source code.

In this chapter, we discuss each of these language constructs, and in Chapter 4 we put those concepts into action in the process of building a people-oriented application.

A BLAST FROM THE PAST

The notion of software components is not a new idea. Surprisingly, this concept dates as far back as 1968, when the first NATO Software Engineering Conference was held. Doug McIlroy presented a truly visionary paper in which he proposed that software should be assembled from prefabricated components. Imagine that! It was quite a radical idea in those days and one that was clearly ahead of its time. The following are a few quotes from that paper to give you a flavor of how prophetic it actually was.

> . . . but certain ideas from industrial technique I claim are relevant. The idea of subassemblies carries over directly and is well exploited. The idea of interchangeable parts corresponds roughly to our term *modular* and is fitfully respected . . .

> I would like to see components become a dignified branch of software engineering . . .

> What I have just asked for is simply industrialism, with programming terms substituted for some of the more mechanically oriented terms appropriate to mass production. I think there are considerable areas of software ready, if not overdue, for this approach.

This man was ahead of his time! Although other portions of the paper show that he could only see his vision through darkened glasses that were limited by the state of software development in the late 1960s, it is clear that he understood both the role and utility of today's modern component. It would not be until some 25 years later that the concept of components became mainstream.

C#'s support for components allows both the production and the consumption of software components to seemingly be a very natural part of programming in C#, which is one direct benefit of formalizing the concept of components in the language. With the semantics of each construct well defined, the compiler is able to assist in the process of importing and exposing components and provide a level of abstraction to hide all the messy plumbing that is necessary for COM. The common language run-time (CLR) plays a very important role in all of this.

Although a full discussion of the merits and benefits of component orientation is outside the scope of this book, the ability of components to provide a simple and uniform model for development can be readily understood even by those new to the concept. Components are the very building blocks of modern systems and they are the basis of such a variety of critically important properties that help deal with complexity. Factors such as binary independence, language independence, location transparency, platform independence, and version independence are all a function of the power of component technology.[2] The decision to treat components as first-class citizens with all the rights and privileges of other language constructs is something that truly sets C# apart from other languages.

People-Oriented Perspective

Considering the C# language from a people-oriented perspective involves focusing on how the principles of people-oriented software can be expressed in the C# programming language.

C# and Universalization

The power of universalization in C# is leveraged through its seamless access to the CLR. As was demonstrated in Chapter 1, the .NET platform provides a very capable universal runtime that contains many components essential to building people-oriented software. The CLR contains the building blocks from which this new class of software will be built. The CLR is C#'s universalization story, and a full discussion of the CLR and all its wonders is presented in Chapters 5 and 6.

C# and Collaboration

The concept of collaboration in C# is the notion of Web services. Web services expose functionality on the Internet. Developers incorporate this exposed functionality in their applications and use it as a building block. In a Web service model, new applications can be a blend of custom code and an amalgamation of other existing Web services. These other Web services may be organic to the organization or exposed services of other organizations. Software service applications (applications built

---

[2] Given the power and utility of component technology, it is not surprising that Microsoft is exposing more and more of Windows itself through components.

from Web services), are a symphony of collaboration orchestrated by the application architect. Once complete, the software service application itself can become yet another Web service ready to take its place in the circle of life—consuming and being consumed.

C# and Translation

From a people-oriented perspective, translation is reflected in C#'s use of attributes and its access to certain common runtime functionality. C# attributes are a means of creating metadata. Metadata is an important people-oriented language feature because it allows development environments and other programming tools to more easily support people-oriented goals such as translation; universal discovery, description, and integration (UDDI); and the expression of Web services. The declarative nature of attributes allows them to express what something means, not how it is implemented, which is a requirement in a world that will be connecting various systems from different platforms. You are introduced to attributes in this chapter, and in Chapter 4 you see attributes in action when they are applied in building a C# application.

WEB SERVICES: "ENTERPRISES WITHOUT WALLS"

A decade ago, when components were introduced to the mainstream programming public, the phrase "software without walls" was coined to communicate the degree of freedom that components offered. Before CORBA and COM, the wonders and inherent potential of every application were held hostage behind a wall called the executable. There was no way to reach inside the executable and use its features individually. Back then, we built monolithic applications. The only way to benefit from them was to run the applications in their entirety. If you were writing a new application and wanted to leverage some functionality from another application, you were out of luck. The functionality was trapped because software had walls.

In the same way that the Berlin wall came down, so too did the software wall. Using components, a developer writing a word processor could leverage functionality from a spreadsheet application and a spreadsheet developer could incorporate word processing functionality. This was possible because the designer of both applications exposed inherent functionality as components so that others could leverage them. Exposing applications as components allowed others to peer over the wall that used to separate producer from consumer and host from client. In addition to simply exposing individual components, an application could expose an entire object hierarchy or application architecture. Conceptually, this is similar to exposing the

---

application's architecture to an x-ray machine, which allows any client to manipulate that application toward an effective end—a basic motivation behind scripting languages.

The concept of software without walls did not just eliminate the barriers that exist on a single execution platform. Using distributed component technology such as DCOM and CORBA, components have allowed machine barriers to be torn down as well. Components have become location independent so that developers can just as easily use a remote component as they can a local component. Developers have free reign over the entire enterprise, no matter how many machines are involved or how geographically dispersed it is.

What if I don't want to stop there? What if I want to integrate across enterprises and connect to my supplier's system, which has entirely different hardware and software run by a totally separate company? If DCOM and CORBA allow software integration and interaction across the machines of my enterprise, surely they should work between my servers and those of my suppliers! Well, not so fast. As it turns out, there are a host of reasons, although technically feasible, that neither the DCOM nor the CORBA approach has made much headway in this area. Although there may be disagreement about what those reasons are, one thing is clear. There aren't the numbers of DCOM or CORBA applications that would suggest that either would be the technology of choice for building these types of distributed applications. If this is true, then we still have walls—only this time the walls may be a lack of unified acceptance.

What we need is something that would allow an enterprise to expose functionality in a way that gets around the problems inherent in other existing approaches. Web services are the answer. Web services allow an enterprise to expose business services and business process in a way that they can be consumed by both business partners and consumers, regardless of language or platform differences.

The net effect of Web services is Enterpises Without Walls.

LANGUAGE TOUR

This section provides a tour of the C# language, and its purpose is twofold:

1. To provide an outlet for the energies of those who want to jump right in
2. To convey the flavor of the language by highlighting significant language features in an organized way

The intent is not to explain every aspect of the examples but rather to provide an over-all understanding without the distraction of detail.

The Basics

It is a time-honored tradition—nay, an outright obligation—to begin a discussion of any language that uses curly braces with the "hello world" example. To keep from being ostracized and demonstrate what the minimal C# program looks like, we present what may be the most redundant program ever written.

```
using System;
class Hello
{
    static void Main()
    {
        Console.WriteLine("hello, world");
    }
}
```

If you are a C++ programmer, this syntax looks very familiar. In C#, as in C++, statement blocks are grouped using curly braces, and individual statements are terminated using semicolons. When this program runs, it simply displays the text "hello, world". The following analysis highlights the important aspects of this example:

- The using System; statement introduces the System namespace. Namespaces are used to organize class libraries by allowing elements to be grouped together in a logical fashion. The System namespace is a collection of elements from the Microsoft .NET framework class library that all relate to system-level functionality. The effect of this statement is that all the elements of the System namespace are made available for direct use in that source file. This allows an abbreviated syntax to be used and the statement Console.WriteLine("hello, world"); can then be written rather than the fully qualified System.Console.WriteLine("hello, world"); statement that would otherwise be required.
- The class Hello statement both declares and defines the class Hello. C# does not separate the concept of *declaration*, which is used to establish an element's existence, and the concept of *definition*, which is used to specify the code associated with that element. All of this is done in a single file and as a result there is no need for things like header files.
- The statement static void Main() defines the main entry point in the program. The main entry point for a C# program is always a method called

`Main`. In this example, `Main` is a member of the `Hello` class and when the program is started, this method is hunted down by the execution environment and then invoked. There are a few more things to say about the `Main` method, but we will get to that later.

- The `Console.WriteLine("hello, world");` statement causes `"hello, world"` to be displayed. The `Console` class is part of the CLR and is shared by all .NET applications regardless of language and can be used to write text that is visible when the program is run from the command line.

C# source code is stored in files that use a `.cs` file extension. Typically, C# applications will involve many separate source files that get compiled together into an executable. To create the Hello World program, we could store the source in a file named Hello.cs and compile it into an executable called `Hello.exe` by entering the following on the command line: `csc Hello.cs`.

Program Structure

Generally speaking, C# programs are structured as a collection of source files that contain one or more type definitions that are members of some namespace. The programming logic in a C# application is contained in either a class or a struct. Having the entire program expressed by objects and the elimination of global functions is a bit of a departure for the C++ programmer.

Namespaces

As we mentioned previously, namespaces are used to organize program elements in a logical fashion. Whereas files are used to physically structure the source code, namespaces logically structure the compiled result. If the compiled result is a class library, then the namespace organizes the classes and types that are part of that library in a way that will be meaningful to the library consumer. If the compiled result is an application, then the namespace can be used to organize the subsystems of the application. If you use the concept of a package[3] in your application design, then this approach to using the namespace is a way to reflect that design concept in implementation.

---

[3] UML has the concept of a package and it can be used to help decompose systems into smaller areas of concern. Typically, you want to group together things that are interdependent into a single package and minimize cross-package dependencies. This approach helps to limit the impact of change to as small a scope as possible. If this method of decomposition is carried over into implementation, then the result of the elements placed in a namespace can be a very logical organization of the subsystems of the applications as well.

The members of a namespace are the types and nested namespaces declared with the namespace block. Member types can be classes, structs, interfaces, enums, and delegates. A nested namespace is simply a namespace declared inside another namespace definition. In the following example, the class A and the namespace L2 are both members of the L1 namespace, but the class G is not.

```
public class G {}       // Not a member of L1 namespace
namespace L1 {          // Start of L1 namespace definition
    public class A {} // Member since it's defined inside namespace

    namespace L2 {      // Nested namespace member
            // L2's members would be declared in here
    }
}
```

Both G and L1 are actually part of the global namespace, which is defined as all the namespaces and types without an enclosing namespace.

Every member of a namespace must have a unique name because namespaces are used to uniquely identify program elements. Namespaces are hierarchical, and a period (".") is used to identify members within a namespace following the pattern of Namespace.MemberName. Two identically named types can coexist within one program if each is in a different namespace. In the following example, L1's class A is distinct from L2's class A:

```
namespace L1 {
    public class A {}     // L1's class A
}

namespace L2 {
    public class A {} // OK since it's in a different namespace
}
```

Declarations referred to each would look like the following:

```
L1.A FromL1; // This A is from L1's namespace
L2.A FromL2; // This A is from L2's namespace
```

Namespace members can have an access modifier that is either public or internal. If no accessibility is specified then the default is internal. The public access modifier means that other programs can see the type; internal means the type is hidden so that only application code can access it. In the following example, G is visible to other programs, but H would be hidden and inaccessible because its access defaults to internal.

```
public class G {}      // Access modifier is public so other programs
                       // can see class G
namespace L1 {
```

```
class H {}          // No access modifier specified, no other programs
                    // can see class H
}
```

Namespaces can span several different source files. There is no need to put all the members of a namespace into a single file. Repeating the same namespace directive in each file instructs the compiler to collect all the members under that particular namespace.

The following is a look at a more detailed example of a namespace:

```
public class G {}      // In global namespace since no enclosing namespace
namespace L1           // First-order namespace
{
    public class A {} // Must be public for access outside of namespace

    namespace L2       // Nested namespace
    {
        public class Foo {}
    }
}
namespace L1.L2        // Shorthand syntax that in this case continues L1.L2
{
    public class Bar {}
}
```

In the previous example, the L1.L2 declaration is split in two parts, yet Foo and Bar are still members of the same namespace. The various namespace members are accessed as follows:

```
class LongHand
{
    G aG;               // No qualifier needed - G was declared in global
                        // namespace
    L1.A aA;            // A comes from the L1 namespace
    L1.L2.Foo aFoo;     // Foo is from the nested namespace L1.L2
    L1.L2.Bar aBar;     // Bar is from continuation of L1.L2 namespace
}
```

Because all this nesting can be tedious to type and cumbersome to read, we can use the using directive to introduce all the members of a namespace into the current scope so that we don't have to fully qualify them anymore. The following is what the code to access the members would look like using this directive:

```
using L1;          // Introduce all of L1's members into the current scope
using L1.L2;       // Need this since the using directive is not recursive
class ShortHand
{
    G aG;
```

```
        A aA;        // First using directive allows this unqualified name
        Foo aFoo;    // Second using directive allows these unqualified names
        Bar aBar;
}
```

Assemblies

Assemblies are the physical packaging of a C# application that results from compilation. Assemblies come in two different forms: application and library. Applications, as you might expect, must have a main entry point, can run standalone, and have a file extension of *.exe*. Libraries do not have a main entry point and cannot run standalone; rather, they are meant to be included as part of some larger standalone application. Libraries have a file extension of *.dll*.

Assemblies not only contain the code to implement the types they contain, but also contain metadata for those types. This is an important change in the way things are packaged on the Windows platform. We take a closer look at this and what it means in Chapter 5.

Variables

Variables are named storage areas that can contain specific types of values. Variables are a very basic concept in any language and in terms of a concept, variables do not require much of a discussion. However, there are several issues related to variables that are important to understand. For instance, which different kinds of variables can you have? What are the semantics of each kind of variable? How do variables get initialized? You cannot effectively write C# programs without knowing the answers to these questions.

There are three different kinds of variables in C#: local variables, fields, and parameters. Fields come in two forms: class variable and instance variable.[4] Parameters have four different forms: value parameter, reference parameter, out parameter, and parameter array. To eliminate a very common programming error, C# has eliminated the possibility of an uninitialized variable. If the programmer does not initialize a variable, then the compiler provides a default value or flags as an error any attempt to use an uninitialized variable. The code that follows provides an example of each kind of C# variable and highlights some important issues. By examining the code and reading the brief explanation, you should get a good basic understanding of the key issues.

---

[4] C# calls class variables and instance variables *fields* to distinguish them from the concept of properties which we will soon discuss.

```
using System;

class Variables
{
    // Example of static fields (a.k.a. class variables or static variables)
    static int S1 = 123;   // Initialized to 123 upon entry to static constructor
    static int HVar;       // This variable will be hidden from scope inside Main()

    // Example of instance fields (aka instance variables)
    int InstanceVar;       // Accessed through object instance
    int InitedIVar = 15;   // Initialized to 15 at object creation

    static void Main()
    {
        // Example of local variables
        int LVar;                  // Simple local variable declaration
        //int Bad = LVar;          // Error — Must be assigned before using it
        int ILVar = 1;             // Initialized when statement executes
        int HVar = 20;             // This local variable hides the HVar class
                                   // variable
        int Mult1, Mult2 = 100;    // Multiple declarations allowed

        Console.WriteLine("Local HVar={0}, Hidden HVar={1}", HVar, Variables.HVar);

        Console.WriteLine("Before PTest: ILVar={0}, Mult2={1}", ILVar, Mult2);

        // Example of variables as formal parameters
        PTest(ILVar, ref Mult2, out LVar, ILVar, Mult2);

        Console.WriteLine("After PTest: ILVar={0}, Mult2={1}, LVar={2}",
                                 ILVar, Mult2, LVar);
    }

    static void PTest(int IOnly, ref int IO, out int OOnly,
                      params object[] PArray)
    {
        IOnly += 5;  // In only — assignment won't affect caller's value
        IO += 5;     // In and out — assignment changes caller's value
        OOnly = 5;   // Out only — assignment changes caller's value

        Console.WriteLine("Inside PTest: IOnly={0}, IO={1}, OOnly={2}",
                                 IOnly, IO, OOnly);

        // Iterate through variable number of arguments contained in PArray
        for (int i=0; i < PArray.Length; i++)
        {
            Console.WriteLine("Inside PTest: PArray[{0}]={1}", i,
                              PArray[i].ToString());
        }
    }
}
```

The output of this program is:

```
Local HVar=20, Hidden HVar=0
Before PTest: ILVar=1, Mult2=100
Inside PTest: IOnly=6, IO=105, OOnly=5
Inside PTest: PArray[0]=1
Inside PTest: PArray[1]=100
After PTest: ILVar=1, Mult2=105, LVar=5
```

In the previous example, `S1` and `HVar` are class variables because they are declared within the scope of the class with the `static` modifier. The value of a class variable is shared across every instance of the class, so change through one instance is seen by all instances. Access to class variables does not require an instance and takes the general form of `Class.ClassVariable`. Class variables get initialized only once when the class is first loaded and are assigned a default value appropriate to their type unless overridden by an initial value specified in their declaration. When the class loads, `S1` is assigned the value `123` and `HVar` will be assigned `0`, which is the default value for `int`.

`InstanceVar` and `InitedIVar` are instance variables because they are declared within the scope of the class without the `static` modifier. The value of an instance variable is unique for each instance of the class, so change through one instance only affects that one instance. Access to instance variables requires an instance of the class and takes the general form of `Instance.InstanceVariable`. Instance variables get initialized when the class is instantiated and are assigned a default value appropriate to its type unless overridden by an initial value specified in its declaration. When the class loads, `InstanceVar` will be defaulted to `0` and `InitedIVar` will be assigned the value `15`.

`LVar`, `ILVar`, `HVar`, `Mult1`, and `Mult2` are all local variables because they are declared within the scope of a method. Access to local variables is only allowed in the body of the method.[5] Unlike fields, local variables do not have default values and must be assigned a value before they can be used. This assignment can be an initial value specified in the declaration, as in `int ILVar = 1`, or later in the body of the code. The declaration `int Bad = LVar;` would cause a compilation error because `LVar` is being used before it has been assigned a value. Local variables hide a field declaration if the type and name are the same, which is the case in the local declaration `int HVar = 20;`. The hidden field is not lost within the scope of the method, but it requires the use of a qualified name to get at its value, such as `Console.WriteLine("Local HVar={0}, Hidden HVar={1}", HVar, Variables.HVar);`. `Variables.HVar` is used here to refer to the class variable. Multiple declarations make it easy to declare several variables on the same line. The declaration `int Mult1, Mult2 = 100;` is equivalent to `int Mult1; int Mult2 = 100;`.

---

[5] Indexers and properties can also contain local variables since both are a form of method.

The PTest method shows all the various kinds of parameters. IOnly is an "in only" type of parameter and is referred to as a *value parameter*. Changes to value parameters do not affect the value the caller passed in. IO is an "in and out" parameter and is referred to as a *Reference parameter*. The caller's value passed through a reference parameter is available to the method, and assignments made to that parameter affect the value the caller passed in. OOnly is an "out only" parameter and is referred to as an *Out parameter*. Out parameters are used to return a value to the caller and must be assigned a value before the method returns or the compiler flags it as an error. The console.writeline() statements are meant to illustrate all this by using a *before, in,* and *after* look at these issues.

Parameters declared as params hold a varying number of arguments of a given type and are referred to as *parameter arrays*. In our example, we declared the parameter array to be of type object from which all C# types are derived. This allows any number and any kind of object to be passed to a method. The for loop simply prints a string version of the value passed. Cool, huh?

Expressions

Table 3-1 is taken directly from the C# language specification and summarizes the C# operators,[6] listing them in order of precedence from highest to lowest. Because this is just a language tour, we only briefly introduce the more commonly used operators. It is important to get a feel for these operators because they are frequently used and are mentioned in other examples in this book. When you get serious about using C#, it would be a good idea to get a complete understanding of all the C# operators by referring to the language specification.

The new Operator

The new operator is used to create an instance of a given type. If you have programmed in an object-oriented language before, then this concept is nothing new. There is, however, one aspect of the C# approach to instantiation that is different. In C#, invoking the new operator does not always imply a dynamic allocation of memory. For example, value types require no dynamic allocation or additional memory beyond what is associated with the type needed. As is common with other object-oriented languages, the new operator results in an invocation of a constructor. If we assume that T is a class, then the following code causes three primary events to occur:

```
T t = new T();
```

---

[6] For the most part, these operators are the same as the ones found in C++. The C++ programmer will find a few new operators (e.g., typeof, checked, unchecked, and is) and a few that are missing (e.g., -> and ::).

TABLE 3-1   C# Operators

Category	Operators
Primary	`(x)   x.y   f(x)   a[x]   x++   x--   new` `typeof   sizeof   checked   unchecked`
Unary	`+   -   !   ~   ++x   --x   (T)x`
Multiplicative	`*   /   %`
Additive	`+   -`
Shift	`<<   >>`
Relational	`<   >   <=   >=   is`
Equality	`==   !=`
Logical AND	`&`
Logical XOR	`^`
Logical OR	`|`
Conditional AND	`&&`
Conditional OR	`||`
Conditional	`?:`
Assignment	`=   *=   /=   %=   +=   -=   <<=   >>=   &=   ^=   |=`

First, memory is dynamically allocated to hold an instance of class T. Second, the reference variable t is assigned a value that points to the newly created object. Third, the constructor for T is called to initialize the instance of t. Value and reference types as well as constructors are discussed in more detail a little later on.

The Increment and Decrement Operators

When applied to C#'s numerical types, the increment and decrement operators add 1 or subtract 1, respectively. The following code shows the various forms of these operators.

```
int i = 0;
int j;

j = ++i;     // j and i equal 1 because i was incremented BEFORE being
             // returned
j = i++;     // j equals 1 and i equals 2 because i was incremented AFTER
             // being returned
j = --i;     // j and i equal 1 because i was decremented BEFORE being
             // returned
```

TABLE 3-2   Arithmetic, Relational, and Conditional Operators

Operator	Meaning
*	Multiplied by
/	Divided by
%	Remainder (modulo)
+	Plus (addition)
−	Minus (subtraction)
<	Less than
>	Greater than
<=	Less than or equal to
>=	Greater than or equal to
==	Equal to
!=	Not equal to

```
j = i--;     // j equals 1 and i equals 0 because i was decremented AFTER
             // being returned
```

As this code shows, the ++ and -- operators can either precede or follow an identifier. The important thing to understand is *when* the value gets incremented or decremented. When the operator *precedes* the identifier, the value is incremented or decremented *before* it is returned. When the operator *follows* the identifier, the value is incremented or decremented *after* the value is returned.

The Arithmetic, Relational, and Conditional Operators

Although the operators in Table 3-2 have standard meanings, the syntax might be new to you. We provide the table for clarification.

The Assignment Operators

Beyond the normal assignment operator =, which is used to assign a value or reference to a variable, there are also what are known as the *short cut* assignment operators. The arithmetic operators, for example, can each be combined with the assignment operator to form a short cut, such as *=, /=, %=, +=, and --=. The general form of usage for these operators is A <op>= B; which is a short cut for A = A <op> B; where <op> is one of the arithmetic, logical, or shift operators. So, for example, A += B; is equivalent to A = A + B; with the effect being that the value of A and B get added together and the result is assigned to A.

The Conditional Operator

The conditional operator returns one of two values pending the outcome of a conditional test. The syntax takes the form of A ? B : C;, where A is a condition and B and C are expressions. If A evaluates to true, then the result of the expression B is returned as the result of the operator. If A evaluates to false, then the result of the expression C is returned as the result of the operator. For example, in the following code, R equals 20 because the condition of A < 0 was false, and the expression B * 2 was returned rather than the value of B:

```
int R, A = 15, B = 10;
R = A < 0 ? B : B * 2;
```

Statements

Table 3-3 was adapted from the statement table found in the C# language specification (see next three pages). This adaptation of the table lists several of the more common C# statements and provides an example of their use. This brief introduction to the statements gets you up to speed in a hurry and prepares you for the next chapter, but it does not provide exhaustive coverage.

Local Constants

Local constant declarations are variables containing values that cannot be changed (i.e., cannot be on the left-hand side of an assignment statement). Constants must be values that can be computed at compile time. They receive their initial and immutable value in the declaration itself, meaning that they can only be assigned a programming constant (e.g., 15 or "Some String") or some other constant variable or a combination of both. The example given in Table 3-3 shows two local constants, pi and r, being used to print out the area of a circle. The following example shows some other important aspects of local constants.

```
void F(int A) {
    const int B = A * 2;   // Compile error! Value of 'A' is not known at
                           // compile time
    const int C = 15;      // Fine, '15' is a constant expression
    const int D = C * 2;   // Fine since 'C' is a constant variable and '2'
                           // is a programming constant
    D = C;                 // Compile error!  You can't change the value
                           // of a constant
}
```

The constant B is in error because A is a parameter, and the value of a parameter can never be known at compile time. Parameters are just one example of variables whose values cannot be known at compile time and therefore cannot be used in constant declarations. The constant D, on the other hand, is fine because the expression C * 2 can be fully computed at compile time.

TABLE 3-3   Common C# Statements

Statement	Example
| Local constant declarations | ```csharp
static void Main() {
    const float pi = 3.14;
    const int r = 123;
    Console.WriteLine(pi * r * r);
}
``` |
| expression statements | ```csharp
static int F(int a, int b) {
    return a + b;
}
static void Main() {
    F(1, 2);  // Expression statement
}
``` |
| if statements | ```csharp
static void Main(string[] args) {
    if (args.Length == 0)
        Console.WriteLine("No args");
    else
        Console.WriteLine("Args");
}
``` |
| switch statements | ```csharp
static void Main(string[] args) {
    switch (args.Length) {
        case 0:
            Console.WriteLine("No args");
            break;
        case 1:
            Console.WriteLine("One arg ");
            break;
        default:
            int n = args.Length;
            Console.WriteLine("{0} args", n);
            break;
    }
}
``` |
| while statements | ```csharp
static void Main(string[] args) {
    int i = 0;
    while (i < args.length) {
        Console.WriteLine(args[i]);
        i++;
    }
}
``` |
```

TABLE 3-3 *(Continued)*

Statement	Example
| do statements | ```
static void Main() {
    string s;
    do { s = Console.ReadLine(); }
    while (s != "Exit");
}
``` |
| for statements | ```
static void Main(string[] args) {
    for (int i = 0; i < args.length; i++)
        Console.WriteLine(args[i]);
}
``` |
| foreach statements | ```
static void Main(string[] args) {
    foreach (string s in args)
        Console.WriteLine(s);
}
``` |
| Labeled statements and goto statements | ```
static void Main(string[] args) {
    if (args.Length == 0)
        goto done:
    Console.WriteLine(args.Length);

done:
    Console.WriteLine("Done");
}
``` |
| break statements | ```
static void Main(string[] args) {
    int i = 0;
    while (true) {
        if (i > args.Length)
            break;
        Console.WriteLine(args[i++]);
    }
}
``` |
| continue statements | ```
static void Main(string[] args) {
    int i = 0;
    while (true) {
        Console.WriteLine(args[i++]);
        if (i > args.Length)
            continue;
        break;
    }
}
``` |

continued

TABLE 3-3   Common C# Statements *(Continued)*

Statement	Example

`return` statements	```static int F(int a, int b) {```
	 ``` return a + b;```
	 ```}```
	 ```static void Main() {```
	 ``` Console.WriteLine(F(1, 2));```
	 ``` return;```
	 ```}```

`throw` statements and `try` statements	```static int F(int a, int b) {```
	 ``` if (b == 0)```
	 ``` throw new Exception("Divide by zero");```
	 ``` return a / b;```
	 ```}```
	 ```static void Main() {```
	 ``` try {```
	 ``` Console.WriteLine(F(5, 0));```
	 ``` }```
	 ``` catch(Exception e) {```
	 ``` Console.WriteLine("Error");```
	 ``` }```
	 ```}```

`lock` statements	```static void Main() {```
	 ``` A a = …```
	 ``` lock(a) {```
	 ``` a.P = a.P + 1;```
	 ``` }```
	 ```}```

Expression Statements

Expression statements do not really have much of a story other than the fact that they evaluate expressions and have side effects. A method invocation and an assignment statement are both examples of expression statements that have a side effect (i.e., have a purpose beyond just the expression itself). In the example given in Table 3-3, `F(1, 2);` is an example of an expression statement. An invalid expression statement would result if we were to add the statement `c + d;` at the end our previous example, which shows the important aspects of local variables. An expression statement that merely adds two constants is an example of a statement that does not have a side effect or purpose beyond the statement itself. It would be flagged as a compilation error, which is a good thing because it is useless to spend precious cycles on that type of statement.

Selection Statements

There are two kinds of selection statements in C#: `if` and `switch`. Both allow alternative blocks of code to be executed based on the outcome of a condition.

The `if` Statement

The `if` statement allows conditional branching in your code. It consists of a conditional test, a `then` statement, and an `else` statement. If the condition evaluates to `true`, then the statement that follows the condition is executed. If the condition is `false`, then the `else` portion of the statement is executed. If either the `then` or the `else` portion of the statement involves two or more statements then a statement block (i.e., a statement enclosed in curly braces) is required. In the example given in Table 3-3, the `Console.WriteLine("No args");` statement would be executed if the conditional test (`args.Length == 0`) is `true`; otherwise the statement `Console.WriteLine("Args");` is executed.

The `switch` Statement

The `switch` statement tests whether an expression matches one of a list of possible choices. There are three main parts to the statement: *switch expression, candidate values,* and *switch statement list*. The example given in Table 3-3 shows an integer-based `switch` expression and is a typical `switch` statement. In C#, strings can also be used as a `switch` expression. Following is an example of how the `switch` statement works using a string case:

```
const string S = "VERSION 3";
bool IsMatch = false;
switch (S.ToLower())
{
    case "version 1":
        IsMatch = true;
        break;
    case "version 2":
        IsMatch = true;
        break;
    case "version 3":
        IsMatch = true;
        break;
    default:
        IsMatch = false;
        break;
}
```

The expression `S.ToLower()` is the switch expression in this example, the `case` labels are the candidate values, and following each is a switch statement list. The switch expression is evaluated, and the result is checked against each candidate value. If there is a match, then the switch statement list following the matching `case` label is executed. In our example, `IsMatch` will be `true` because the `S.ToLower()` expression converted the string `"VERSION 3"` to lower case (because matching is case sensitive) for a uniform test that then matched the case `"version 3"`.

The last statement in a `switch` statement list is always a `break;`. If the `break;` statement is not found, the compiler flags it as an error. Once the `break;` statement is reached, control passes to the end of the `switch` and bypasses all other cases.

The switch expression can be any of the following types: `sbyte`, `byte`, `short`, `ushort`, `int`, `uint`, `long`, `ulong`, `char`, `string`, or an enum type. If it is not one of these types then it must be able to be converted to one of these types unambiguously.

You can case fold several case labels together to provide a common switch statement list that needs to be shared by multiple *candidate values*. For example, the following `switch` statement is functionally equivalent to the previous one presented:

```
const string S = "VERSION 3";
bool IsMatch = false;
switch (S.ToLower())
{
    case "version 1":
    case "version 2":
    case "version 3":
        IsMatch = true;
        break;
    default:
        IsMatch = false;
        break;
}
```

If no match is found for the switch expression, then control passes to the `default:` label and its statement block is executed.

Iteration Statements

There are four kinds of iteration statements in C#: `while`, `do while`, `for`, and `foreach`. Each continues to allow a statement block to be repeatedly executed until a given condition is no longer `true`.

The `while` and `do while` Statements

Both the `while` and the `do while` statements operate in essentially the same way, with the chief difference being where the loop condition is tested. The `while` loop tests the condition at the beginning of the loop, and the example given in Table 3-3 shows a loop that prints out command-line arguments until the expression (`i < args.length`) evaluates to `false`. The `do while` tests the condition at the end of the loop and the example given in Table 3-3 shows a loop that reads from the command line until the expression (`s != "Exit"`) evaluates to `false`.

The `for` *Statement*

The `for` statement is a looping construct that standardizes where common loop control-type code is placed. Code that loops tends to follow a general pattern involving initialization, testing, and loop counter maintenance. Therefore the `for` loop tries to standardize all this with a loop that looks like this: `for (<init>; <test>; <update>) { <statement block> }`. The `<init>` portion is code that initializes loop control variables and is only executed once when the loop is entered. The `<test>` portion is code that specifies the loop condition and is tested before each iteration. The `<update>` portion is code that updates loop control variables so that they can reflect the fact that an iteration has taken place. The `<update>` portion is executed after every iteration of the loop. Finally, the `<statement block>` is the body of the loop and is executed at every iteration of the loop.

In the example given in Table 3-3, `int i = 0;` is the `<init>` portion of the loop, test `i < args.length;` is the `<test>` portion of the loop, `i++` is the `<update>` portion of the loop, and `Console.WriteLine(args[i]);` is the `<statement>` portion of the loop. All together, the `for` loop given in the table is functionally equivalent to the previous `while` loop example from the same table. Looking at them both, you can see that the `for` loop tends to be more compact and readable.

The `foreach` *Statement*

C# has formalized the notion of enumeration with the `foreach` statement. Its general form is `foreach (<element type> <element variable> in <collection> ) <statement block>`. Here is how it works. For each element in `<collection>`, an assignment is made to `<element variable>`. Then the `<statement block>` is entered, and `<element variable>` always holds a valid `<collection>` element that is next in line to be processed. The type of `<collection>` and `<element variable>` should be compatible, and that type must be reflected in the `<element type>` portion of the statement. The example given in Table 3-3 is functionally equivalent to that of the `for` and `while` loops we saw in this same table. In the case of the `foreach` example, because the `args` variable is an array of strings and because arrays can be treated as collections, this code also prints out all the command-line arguments. You can see that this may even be a more compact and cleaner alternative to both the `for` and `while` loops.

The C# concept of enumeration extends to various types such as strings, arrays, user-defined types, and even appropriately implemented COM objects. These can all be used in a `foreach` statement even though they are fundamentally different.

Jump Statements

There are five kinds of jump statements in C#: `goto`, `break`, `continue`, `return`, and `throw`. Each of these statements transfers control to another part of the program in slightly different ways.

The goto *Statement*

The goto statement simply transfers control to the label specified as the target of the goto statement. In the example given in the table, the goto done; statement transfers control to the done: label. Much is made of the evils of using goto statements in programming, so use this statement with great care and prudence. Quite often there are alternative ways to achieve the same effect without using a goto statement, and these alternatives can be just as efficient without the downsides of the go-to approach.

The break *Statement*

The break statement is used to bail out of switch, while, do, for, and foreach statements, and control is transferred to the statement following whatever has enclosed the break statement. In the example given in the table, the break; statement transfers control to the statement following the while (true) statement, thus exiting the while loop. We already saw how this worked in the case of switch statements.

The continue *Statement*

The continue statement is used to stop the current iteration of a loop and start a new iteration if the condition for the loop is still true. In the example given in the table, the continue; statement transfers control back to the while (true) test as long as if (i > args.Length) evaluates to true. The continue statement applies to while, do, for, and foreach statements. If it appears in any other context, it causes a compilation error.

The return *Statement*

The return statement returns control to the caller who invoked the method that contains the return statement. The return statement conforms to the return type of the method. That is, if the method specifies a value to return, then the return statement must return a value that is convertible to the type specified. If there is no return type specified (i.e., the return type is void), then the return statement cannot return a value. In the example given in the table, the return; statement transfers control back to the execution environment that called the main() method of the application. Because main was defined as void, the return statement does not supply a return argument.

The throw *Statement*

The throw statement is generally used to indicate that an error has occurred and execution of the current method must be abandoned. This is not to say that it can't be used as a general means to transfer control, but conventional wisdom says that this is a bad practice fraught with peril. It is generally a good idea to stick with just using the throw statement for catastrophic errors. The throw statement works in tandem with the try/ catch pair to form an approach to error handling, which is the subject of a full section later in this chapter. In the example given in the table on page 94, the throw new Exception("Divide by zero"); statement transfers control to the catch (Exception e) statement because it is the nearest enclosing try/catch block.

The lock *Statement*

C# provides formal language support with the lock statement for the notion of thread control. Those of you with experience in multithreaded programming have almost certainly rolled your own utility classes around synchronization primitives such as critical sections so that entering the critical section and exiting it is sure to happen. Well, this is just what the lock statement offers. In the example given in Table 3-3, the a.P = a.P + 1; statement only executes if the lock(a) statement successfully achieved a mutually exclusive lock.

Types

Like other contemporary languages, C# offers both a variety of predefined types and the ability to create user-defined types. The predefined types cover the standard types that programmers have come to expect like characters, strings, integers, Booleans, and floating point types. Whether predefined or user-defined, C# divides its types into one of two categories: value or reference.

Value Types

A defining characteristic of value types is that variables of value types are said to directly contain their data, and each holds a private copy. This means that assignments produce a copy of the value rather than share the same value between two variables. Integers are value types, and in the following example, A is assigned the literal value of 15 and then is assigned to B.

```
using System;
public class ValueTypeExample
{
    public static void Main() {
        int A;
        int B;

        A = 15;    // Assign a literal value of 15
        B = A;     // B gets a copy of A's value (not a reference to it)
        A = 20;    // Changes A's value, but not B's
        System.Console.WriteLine("A: {0}, B: {1}", A, B);
    }
}
```

At this point, both A and B hold separate copies of the value 15 so when A is assigned the value 20, the value in B is unaffected as is shown by the following program output:

```
A: 20, B: 15
```

Adapted from the language specification, Table 3-4 lists all the predefined value types and shows how to assign them a literal value.

In addition to these predefined value types, C# allows for user-defined value types through the use of `struct` and `enum` declarations. In fact, C#'s predefined types

TABLE 3-4   Value Types and Their Literal Values

Type	Description	Example
sbyte	8-bit signed integral type	sbyte val = 12;
short	16-bit signed integral type	short val = 12;
int	32-bit signed integral type	int val = 12;
long	64-bit signed integral type	long val1 = 12; long val2 = 34L;
byte	8-bit unsigned integral type	byte val1 = 12; byte val2 = 34U;
ushort	16-bit unsigned integral type	ushort val1 = 12; ushort val2 = 34U;
uint	32-bit unsigned integral type	uint val1 = 12; uint val2 = 34U;

ulong	64-bit unsigned integral type	ulong val1 = 12;
		ulong val2 = 34U;
		ulong val3 = 56L;
		ulong val4 = 78UL;

float	Single-precision floating point type	float val = 1.23F;
double	Double-precision floating point type	double val1 = 1.23; double val2 = 4.56D;
bool	Boolean type; a bool value is either true or false	bool val1 = true; bool val2 = false;
char	Character type; a char value is a Unicode character	char val = 'h';
decimal	Precise decimal type with 28 significant digits	decimal val = 1.23M;

are really language keywords that refer to system-defined `struct` definitions that are found in the CLR and simply act as shorthand for the corresponding definition. This is an important point because it means that the programmer can extend the primitive types. The effect is something that Microsoft refers to as *No type lockout*. Only those types expressed as either a struct or an enum have the value semantics we have just described.

Reference Types

The defining characteristic of reference types is that they store references to their data, which take the form of object instances. Variables of reference types either are `null` or refer to an instance of a class, interface, array, or delegate type. Instances of reference types are created using the `new` operator.[7] Unlike value types, assignment of reference types causes two or more reference type variables to refer to the same object instance. Changes in one reference variable would therefore be visible to the other reference variables that refer to that same object instance. Reference types with a value of `null` do not currently reference any object instance. The following example shows two reference type variables: `ARef` and `BRef`.

```
using System;

public class A
{
    public int D;
}

public class ReferenceTypeExample
{
    public static void Main()
    {
        A ARef;     // Reference to an A class (reference not yet set)
        A BRef;     // Reference to an A class (reference not yet set)

        ARef.D = 0;       // Error! Use of unassigned local variable
        ARef = new A();   // Create an instance of A and assign reference
                          // to it
        BRef = new A();   // Create separate instance of A and assign
                          // reference to it

        ARef.D = 100;     // Set the first instance's D value
        BRef.D = 200;     // Set the second instance's D value
```

---

[7] In contrast to most other languages, C#'s new operator does not always imply a dynamic allocation! For example, the new operator can be applied to a value type and no dynamic allocation will occur. Instead, variables of value types are simply made ready for use (i.e., initialized by their constructors) when the new operator is applied and no additional memory beyond the variables in which they reside is necessary or allocated.

```
System.Console.WriteLine("Separate Instances==> ARef's D: {0},
                               BRef's D: {1}", ARef.D, BRef.D);

BRef = ARef;      // Set both references to refer to the same
                  // object instance
BRef.D = 300;     // Change D's value through what is now a shared
                  // reference

System.Console.WriteLine("Shared Reference==> ARef's D: {0}, BRef's
                               D: {1}", ARef.D, BRef.D);

ARef = null;      // Set reference to point to nothing
BRef = null;      // Set reference to point to nothing
    }
}
```

The first assignment is an error because ARef is a reference and not a local instance of the class A. This generally comes as a surprise to C++ programmers, who are used to being able to declare local class instances. Next we see both ARef and BRef being set to two separate instances of the A class. Because they are separate instances, the assignment of 100 to ARef and 200 to BRef is totally separate, as the first Write-Line() demonstrates. The assignment BRef = ARef; causes both ARef and BRef to refer to the same instance (the first instance created). The instance that BRef previously referred to (the second instance that was created) is now unreferenced and is a candidate for garbage collection. Because ARef and BRef both refer to the same object instance, the effects of the assignment BRef.D = 300; can be seen through either reference, as is demonstrated by the second WriteLine(). Finally, ARef and BRef are set to refer to nothing through the assignment of null. Now the other instance of A becomes a candidate for garbage collection.

The output of this program follows:

```
Separate Instances==> ARef's D: 100, BRef's D: 200
Shared Reference==> ARef's D: 300, BRef's D: 300
```

Adapted from the language specification, Table 3-5 lists all the predefined reference types and shows how to assign them a literal value.

TABLE 3-5   Predefined Reference Types and Their Literal Values

Type	Description	Example
object	The ultimate base type of all other types	object o = null;
string	String type; a string is a sequence of Unicode characters	string s = "hello";

The `string` class is a C# primitive for handling character strings. As we mentioned previously, all the primitives types are shorthand for actual CLR elements, and the `string` type maps to the `System.String` class. This class is a sealed class, which means that other classes are not allowed to derive from it. This class has many useful methods and overloaded operators that allow it to be intuitively used in `string` expressions. For example, you can index it with the [ ] expression, concatenate it using a + expression, and check for equality using == and != expressions. The following example shows each of these operators in action:

```
using System;
public class StringExample
{
    public static void Main()
    {
        string A = "A,B,C,";
        string B = "D,E";
        string C = "A,B,C,D,E";
        int IntVariable = 100;
        string NullString = null;

        System.Console.WriteLine("A[4]: \"{0}\"", A[4]);
        System.Console.WriteLine("A: \"{0}\", B: \"{1}\", C: \"{2}\"", A,
                        B, C);
        System.Console.WriteLine("A + B: \"{0}\"", A + B);
        System.Console.WriteLine("A + B == C: {0}, A != C: {1}",
                        A + B == C, A != C);
        System.Console.WriteLine("A + IntVariable: \"{0}\",
                        IntVariable + A: \"{1}\"",
                        A + IntVariable, IntVariable + A);
        System.Console.WriteLine("A + NullString: \"{0}\"", A +
                        NullString);
    }
}
```

Not much commentary is needed because the code speaks for itself. You may notice something new in the format string around the first substitution indicator. It's a \" and is called the *quote character*. The quote says to interpret the next quotation mark as part of the output string rather than as part of the format string, a step that is necessary to actually print the quotation mark (") character. The string equality operators perform a case-sensitive comparison of the character values. Strings are considered equivalent if they are both `null` or have the same number of characters and each character matches. Even nonstring values and `null` values can appear in the concatenation expressions. Any nonstring value has its `ToString()` method called. `ToString()` is a method of the `object` class, which we discuss next.

The output of this program follows:

```
A[4]: "C"
A: "A,B,C,", B: "D,E", C: "A,B,C,D,E"
A + B: "A,B,C,D,E"
A + B == C: True, A != C: True
A + IntVariable: "A,B,C,100", IntVariable + A: "100A,B,C,"
A + NullString: "A,B,C,"
```

Array Types

As you would expect, C# support the concepts of arrays that are both single dimensional and multidimensional. All the elements of an array must conform to the type of the array. Individual elements are accessed by an index that is in the range of 0 and *N*–1, where *N* is the declared size of the array. Indexing outside the bounds of an array causes a runtime exception. Because arrays are reference types, their declarations only set aside space for the reference and not the actual array itself.

C# arrays can be either *rectangular*, meaning all its rows are the same size, or *jagged*, meaning its rows may be different sizes. Rectangular arrays have consistent dimensions, so printing out this type of array always results in an orderly block with a straight right edge. Jagged arrays, on the other hand, print out in a disorderly fashion, and the right edge can be very ragged.

The element type and shape of an array (i.e., jagged or rectangular and its dimensions) are part of its type, but the size (i.e., the length of each of its dimensions) is not. An array's size is a function of its creation or initialization expression. In the following example, the variable SDim is the typical single-dimensional array.

```
using System;
public class ArrayExample
{
    public static void Main()
    {
        int[] SDim;        // Typical single-dimensional array
        int[,] MDim2;      // "rectangular" 2-dimensional array of int
        int[][] MDimJ2;    // "jagged" array of (array of (array of int))

        // Instantiate and initialize single-dimensional array
        SDim = new int[]
        {    // Unbounded # of initializer elements
            1, 2, 3, 4, 5, 6, 7, 8, 9
        };

        // Instantiate and initialize multidimensional "rectangular"
        // array
        MDim2 = new int[,]
        {    // Unbounded # of initializer rows but they must be uniform
            {1, 2, 3},
            {4, 5, 6},
            {7, 8, 9}
        };
```

```
// Instantiate and initialize multidimensional "Jagged" array
MDimJ2 = new int[][]
{       // Unbounded # of initializer rows but they need not be
        // uniform
    new int[2] {1, 2},
    new int[4] {3, 4, 5, 6},
    new int[3] {7, 8, 9}
};

System.Console.Write("\nSingle dimensional array\n");
foreach (int i in SDim)
{
    System.Console.Write("{0} ",i);
}

System.Console.Write("\n\nMultidimensional \"rectangular\"
        array\n");
for (int i = 0; i < 3; i++)
{
    for (int j = 0; j < 3; j++)
    {
        System.Console.Write("{0} ",MDim2[i,j]);
    }
    System.Console.WriteLine();
}

System.Console.Write("\nMultidimensional \"Jagged\" array\n");
foreach (int[] i in MDimJ2)
{
    foreach (int j in i)
    {
        System.Console.Write("{0} ",j);
    }
    System.Console.WriteLine();
}
    }
}
```

MDim2 is a two-dimensional regular array, and MDimJ2 is a two-dimensional jagged array. Following the declarations, we see the syntax for initializing each type of array. It's at this point in the code that the actual dimension is determined. Alternatively, these arrays could have gotten their dimensions from a dynamic initialization expression. For example, MDim2's creation could have looked like Mdim2 = new int[3,5] for an array that was three rows of five elements. While we are on the topic of initialization, we should also mention that there is a shorthand for array initialization. The expression int[ ] a1 = new int[ ] {1,2,3} can be shortened to int[ ] a1 = {1,2,3}.

Following the array initialization are the looping constructs that print out each array. Each one requires a slightly different approach to printing out the array. The first loop is straightforward and simply iterates through each element and prints out its value. The second loop requires two loops: an outer and inner loop. The outer loop iterates over each row in the array while the inner loops iterates through each of the row's elements. The third loop has an outer and inner loop as well, but because it is an array of arrays, its inner loop can be a `foreach` construct, which tends to be easier to write and a bit easier on the eyes as well.

The output of this program follows:

```
Single dimensional array
1 2 3 4 5 6 7 8 9

Multidimensional "rectangular" array
1 2 3
4 5 6
7 8 9

Multidimensional "Jagged" array
1 2
3 4 5 6
7 8 9
```

The object Type

C# was designed in the tradition of "pure" object-oriented languages such as SmallTalk and Java, in which a single class, named `object`, is defined as the base class from which all other classes are either directly or indirectly derived. Thus this mother of all objects provides type unity because every type in C# is an object whose ancestry can be traced back to `object`. Even language literals can be treated as an `object` type that allows the expressions `15.ToString()` and `"How Long Am I".Length` to return the appropriate values.

Type Harmony

At this point, you have learned the difference between value and reference types and you understand that local variables that are value types live on the stack and reference types are heap based and garbage collected. All this leads to a very interesting question. What happens if I mix the two types in an assignment? Will the garbage collector try to free a stack-allocated variable, or can a local value type accidentally free a managed reference? The answer, thankfully, is *no*. The designers of the language have already figured this out and come up with a solution that deals with this issue seamlessly.

The solution is called *boxing*, and it involves taking a value type and putting it inside an object box, hence the name. Now that the value is safely encapsulated inside this object box, it has all the benefits available to objects and thus type harmony is achieved. The "box" to which we are referring is a conceptual one. The C# language sees to it that a value wrapper is automatically generated. The value is then copied to this value wrapper, which we can think of as the box object. In fact, if we were to ask this box object what its type was at runtime using the is operator, the response would be the value type and not some reference to a language-generated value wrapper.

Not surprisingly, there is an unboxing conversion that can turn a boxed value back into a value type. Although the syntax is identical, unboxing should not be confused with type conversion. When an object is unboxed, the language actually checks to make sure that the object instance is a boxed value of the given type before it copies the value out. A type conversion, on the other hand, does not perform this type of check so instead of copying a value, the result still refers to the original value. The following example demonstrates this:

```
public static void Main()
{
    int a = 100;
    object o = a;      // Value type gets boxed and o is a reference to
                       // the box
    int b = (int) o;   // Reference to box is unboxed

    if (o is int)
        Console.WriteLine("It's an int");
    else
        Console.WriteLine("It's something else");

    o = 50;            // Assigning 50 to box does not affect a and b

    Console.WriteLine("a: {0}, o: {1}, b: {2}", a, o, b);
}
```

The expression object o = a; causes a box object to be created, and a reference to that object is assigned to the reference variable o. Next, the expression int b = (int) o; causes the boxed object to be unboxed. The conditional verifies that the type of the boxed object is int and not object. To demonstrate that boxing involves the duplication of boxed values, 50 is assigned to the variable o. Console.WriteLine() is a statement that shows that each of these is a separate value.

The output of this program follows:

```
It's an int
a: 100, o: 50, b: 100
```

Classes

By and large, C# programs are expressed in terms of class declarations, so understanding this language construct is critically important. Up to this point we have seen classes being used but we have not discussed them in any kind of detail. These classes are very basic examples, and they were always secondary to the actual topics of interest. This section examines classes in more detail and gives coding examples for clarification.

Inheritance

C# provides single inheritance, which can be used to extend the functionality of a class by adding new methods or overriding existing base class methods using polymorphism. Overridden methods are referred to as either *virtual* or *abstract* methods that have been given a new implementation in a derived class. Virtual methods are declared with the `virtual` keyword and overridden using the keyword `override`. Abstract methods are declared with the `abstract` keyword and overridden using the keyword `override`. Classes that contain abstract methods or derived classes that choose not to implement all virtual methods cannot be instantiated but may be used to reference an instance of a concrete derived class. The name of the base class to derive from follows the class name, and a colon separates the two.

The following example shows that when the base class is used to refer to a derived class (as a result of the reference assignment `Base B = D;`), the most derived method is invoked.

```
using System;
abstract public class Base          // Declares Base class to be abstract
{
    abstract public string A();     // No method body allowed on abstract methods

    virtual public string B()       // This implementation is used if not overridden
    {
        return "Base B()";
    }

    virtual public string C()       // This implementation is used if not overridden
    {
        return "Base C()";
    }
}

    public class Derived : Base      // The class Derived is being derived from Base
    {
        override public string A()   // Override A so we can instantiate Derived
        {
            return "Derived A()";
        }
        override public string B()   // Override B so this implementation is used
        {
            return "Derived B()";
        }
    }
}

public class InheritenceExample
```

```
{
    public static void Main()
    {
        Derived D = new Derived();
        Base B = D;                         // Let's access D through B's eyes

        System.Console.WriteLine("B.A() returns \"{0}\"", B.A());
        System.Console.WriteLine("B.B() returns \"{0}\"", B.B());
        System.Console.WriteLine("B.C() returns \"{0}\"", B.C());
    }
}
```

B.A() refers to Derived.A() because it was abstract and this is the only implementation. B.B() refers to Derived.B() because it is the most derived method. B.C() refers to Base.C() because Derived chose not to supply an implementation of the virtual method.

The output of this program follows:

```
B.A() returns "Derived A()"
B.B() returns "Derived B()"
B.C() returns "Base C()"
```

Members

Classes are made up of members, which can be constants, fields, methods, properties, events, indexers, operators, constructors, destructors, static constructors, and nested-type declarations, as well as the members of any derived class. Classes can be made up of various types of members, which define the behavior of the class.

Member name or signature conflicts that result from inheritance can be gracefully addressed by using the new modifier in the declaration. When there is a conflict the derived name or signature will hide in the one found in the base class. Now although it is not a compile error to hide a method, if you use the new modifier it tells the reader that you intended to hide the member and the compiler warning will go away.

Members of a class can be static (with the exception of const members), and their semantics are the same as those for static variables. You can specify the level of accessibility of each class member as either public, protected, internal, protected internal, or private. Table 3-6 lists the meaning of each member access modifier.

It is necessary to show code from two different programs (Program 1 and Program 2) to fully understand member access restrictions.

From Program 1:

```
public class AccessExample
{
    public int A;
    protected int B;
```

TABLE 3-6   Member Access Modifiers

Accessibility	Meaning
public	No access restrictions
protected	Access granted to containing class and any class derived from the containing class
internal	Access limited to code within the program that includes the containing class
protected internal	Internal access granted to code within the program that includes the containing class; protected access granted to code outside the program
private	Access limited to the containing type
readonly	Only applies to field members; cannot assign field a new value after its initialization; can combine modifier with the other modifiers in this list

```
    protected internal int C;
    private int D;
    internal int E;
    public readonly int F = 123;

    public void TestAccess()
    {
        A = 10; // OK since a class always has access to all its immediate members
        B = 20; // OK since a class always has access to all its immediate members
        C = 30; // OK since a class always has access to all its immediate members
        D = 40; // OK since a class always has access to all its immediate members
        E = 50; // OK since a class always has access to all its immediate members
    }
}

public class ProgramClient
{
    public void TestAccess()
    {
        AccessExample Y = new AccessExample();
        Y.A = 10; // OK since there aren't any access restrictions on public members
        Y.B = 20; // Error - can't access B since its protected
        Y.C = 30; // OK since it uses the internal aspect of protected internal access
        Y.D = 40; // Error - can't access D since it's private
        Y.E = 50; // OK since any code with Program 1 can access internal members
    }
}
```

```
public class ProgramDescendent : AccessExample
{
    public new int F; // Hide F member in AccessExample

    public new void TestAccess()
    {
        A = 10; // OK since there aren't any access restrictions on public members
        B = 20; // OK since derived classes get access to protected members
        C = 30; // OK since it can use either aspect of protected internal access
        D = 40; // Error - can't access D since it's private
        E = 50; // OK since any code with Program 1 can access internal members
        F = 60; // OK since the new keyword hid the base class's F member
    }
}
```

From Program 2:

```
public class ForeignDescendent : AccessExample
{
    public new void TestAccess ()
    {
        A = 10; // OK since there aren't any access restrictions on public members
        B = 20; // OK since derived classes get access to protected members
        C = 30; // OK since it uses the protected aspect of protected internal access
        D = 40; // Error - can't access D since it's private
        E = 50; // Error - can't access E since it's internal
    }
}

public class ForeignClient
{
    public void TestAccess()
    {
        AccessExample X = new AccessExample();
        X.A = 10; // OK since there aren't any access restrictions on public members
        X.B = 20; // Error - can't access B since it's protected
        X.C = 30; // Error - can't access C since it's protected internal
        X.D = 40; // Error - can't access D since it's private
        X.E = 50; // Error - can't access E since it's internal
        X.F = 60; // Error - can't assign a value to a readonly member
    }
}
```

The core of this example is the AccessExample class, which shows every possible access modifier through the declaration of several integer members. The comments in the code explain why access is either granted or denied in the given context.

Constructors

Constructors are special methods that initialize classes when they are instantiated or first loaded. Constructors are optional and if one is not specified, then an empty one with no arguments is supplied by the compiler. There are two types of constructors in C#: instance constructors and static constructors.

Instance constructors are automatically called each time an object instance is created using the C# new operator. Instance constructors can take arguments that can be used to parametrically provide important initialization state.

Static constructors are class-level initialization routines that get called once when the class gets loaded. Static constructors cannot take parameters nor do they have accessibility modifiers, and the programmer cannot call them explicitly.

Placing an access modifier on a constructor limits who can create an instance of a given class. The example shows how to declare instance, static, public, and private constructors.

```
class ConstructorExample
{
    private ConstructorExample Shadow;

    // Static constructor - called when class is loaded
    static ConstructorExample() {}
    // Instance constructor - called each time class is instantiated
    public ConstructorExample() {}
    // Private instance constructor with args - called
    private ConstructorExample(string Trusted) {}
    // Public instance constructor with args
    public ConstructorExample(int State)
    {
        // Use private constructor to set trust level
        if (State == 1)
            Shadow = new ConstructorExample("Yes");
        else
            Shadow = new ConstructorExample("No");
    }
}

class ConstructorClient
{
    public void TestConstrcution()
    {
        ConstructorExample X;

        // Invokes instance constructor
        X = new ConstructorExample();
        // Error - clients not allowed to instantiate using private
        // constructor
        X = new ConstructorExample("Yes");
        // Invokes the constructor that takes an int
        X = new ConstructorExample(100);      }
}
```

Notice there is no return type needed for a constructor and that it uses the name of the class as its method name.

Destructors

Destructors are automatically called just before the object is destroyed and provide an opportunity to do whatever is appropriate before the instance is destroyed. Destructors cannot take arguments nor do they have access modifiers, and the programmer cannot explicitly call them. Declaring a destructor is as simple as creating a method using the class name prefixed by the "~" character. Following is an example of what this looks like:

```
class DestructorExample
{
    ~DestructorExample() {}
}
```

If you are not accustomed to working with a language that implements garbage collection, then there is something that you should know. C# destructors only get called when the garbage collector sees fit to free the object. That is, you never know exactly when the destructor will be called, and it is possible that it may not get called at all! This fact changes what you typically do in a destructor. You may have been accustomed to freeing up memory or other resources in the destructor in languages such as C++, but you do not want to code C# that way because you cannot be sure when or if the destructor will get called. This is not as bad as it seems if what you typically did in the destructor was free things you previously allocated, because now the garbage collector does that automatically. That leaves the matter of how to deal with freeing up other nonobject resources such as a database connection or file handle. This is when the `Finalize()` and `Dispose()` methods come into play.

To deal with freeing up finite resources, you need both an explicit and an implicit way to release things. The implicit approach involves the `Finalize()` method, which is automatically called by the garbage collector when the object is no longer being referenced. The explicit way to release object resources involves the `IDisposable()` interface. Classes with resources that need to be freed should implement the `IDisposable` interface so that the `Dispose()` method can be called by a client when it is determined that the object will no longer be used. With a little care, both of these methods can be written to share a single method that actually frees up the resources, allowing this code to only live in one spot. The following coding pattern is taken from the documentation that came with the beta release of the .NET framework software development kit. It shows how both of these approaches to freeing resources can be coded.

```
class ResourceWrapper : IDisposable
{
    private IntPrt handle; //pointer to an external resource
    private OtherResource otherRes; //other resource you happen to use
    private bool disposed = false;

    public ResourceWrapper () {
```

```
        handle = //allocate on the unmanaged side
        otherRes = new OtherResource ( . . . );
    }

//free your own state
  private void freeState () {
      if (!disposed) {
          CloseHandle (handle);
          dispose = true;
      }
  }

  //Free your own state, call dispose on all state you hold, and take
  //yourself off the Finalization queue.
  public void Dispose () {
      freeState ();
      OtherRes.Dispose();
      GC.SuppressFinalization(this);

  }

  //Free your own state (NOT other state you hold) and give your
  //parent a chance to finalize.
  public void Finalize (){
      freeState();
      Base.Finalize();
  }

//When ever you do something with this class, check to see if the
//state is disposed, if so, throw this exception.
public void DoStuff () {
      if (disposed)  {
          throw ObjectDisposedException ("ResWrapper");
      }
  }
}
```

Methods and Method Overloading

Methods are the member functions that define a class's behavior and functionality. At this point, we have already seen and used several methods and learned a lot about them as a consequence of discussing other topics. For example, as a class member, methods can have access restrictions applied to them, a topic we mentioned previously when we discussed member access. When we discussed inheritance, we learned that methods can be virtual or abstract and discussed the semantics. When we discussed variables, we explained the various types of parameters that methods can have, as well as their semantics.

Just like local variables, methods can also be declared as instance methods (the typical case) or static methods. As with local variables, a static method is a class method rather than an instance method, and it can be called without a reference to an instance of the class. In fact, it is a compile error to attempt to call a static method using a reference to an instance of the class, which is pretty aggravating, actually!

C# allows overloading, which means that several methods can share the same name as long as they have different signatures. Besides the method name, signatures are considered different if they vary in the number or type of their arguments or in the modifiers used in the signature. The return type is not considered when determining whether two signatures differ.

The following example shows several overloaded methods and a static method. The code comments reinforce the points we made in the methods discussion.

```
using System;
public class Methods
{
    // Class method S()
    static public string S()
    {
        return "Static";
    }
    // First method named OverLoaded
    public string Overloaded(int A)
    {
        return "public string OverLoaded(int A)";
    }
    // Same # of args but the ref modifier makes it different enough to
    overload public string Overloaded(ref int A)
    {
        return "public string OverLoaded()";
    }
    // Varied the # of args so it's a new overloaded signature
    public string Overloaded(ref int A, int B)
    {
        return "public string OverLoaded()";
    }
    // Varied the type of args so it's a new overloaded signature
    public string Overloaded(ref int A, string B)
    {
        return "public string OverLoaded()";
    }
    // Error!  Just changing the return type does not change the signature
    public int Overloaded(ref int A, string B)
    {
        return 15;
    }
}

public class MethodExample
{
    public static void Main()
    {
        Methods     A = new Methods();
```

```
        string      B;
        int         C = 100;

        // Compiler selects OverLoaded(ref int A, string B)
        // as match of call signature
        B = A.Overloaded(ref C, "Test");
        // Error!  Can't use instance reference, must use typename instead
        B = A.S();
        // OK since we used typename to access it through the class
        B = Methods.S();
    }
}
```

Properties

Properties are special class members that exist to provide access to the state of an object or class. From the client's perspective, properties look just like fields, and the syntax for accessing them is the same. The difference shows up in the property declaration.

Properties simulate a field through special methods that get and set the value of the property. In this way, properties provide formal and guarded access to member variables. Properties can even be used to return a computed value when the syntax would lead a client to believe it is a field value. When a C# class with properties is exposed as a component, the formalization provides the basis for automatic generation of an object binding that formally exposes the properties. In the following example, the members B and C are property values.

```
using System;

public class MyClass
{
    // Declare a field
    public int A;
    public int D;

    // Declare a property (notice it is read-only)
    public string B
    {
        get
        {
            if (A > 50)
                return "Big";
            else
                return "Small";
        }
    }

    // Declare a property with both a get and a set
    public int C
    {
```

```
        get
        {
            return D * 2;
        }

        set
        {
            D = value / 2;
        }
    }
}

public class FieldsAndPropertiesExample
{
    public static void Main()
    {
        MyClass C = new MyClass();

        C.A = 200;          // Assign a value to the field
        //C.B = "Small";// Error!  B is read-only since no set method
        C.C = 100;          // Assign a value to a property
        Console.WriteLine("C.A: {0}, C.B: {1}, C.C: {2}", C.A, C.B, C.C);
    }
}
```

Property values have two special methods: get() and set(). The get() method is used when the property's value is required. The set() method is used when the property's value needs to be set. The set() method makes use of a special value variable, which represents the value to assign to the property. Considering the Main() method, the C.A = 200; expression demonstrates the normal assignment to a field member. The C.B = "Small"; expression causes a compilation error because there is no set method defined for the property. The B property is an example of a calculated value: the typical property that just returns the value of a member. The expression C.C = 100; assigns a value to a property. As you can see, the syntax is no different than the assignment to the field variable A that was done a few lines before.

The output of this program follows:

```
C.A: 200, C.B: Big, C.C: 100
```

Operators

Operators allow objects to be used naturally in expression statements and permit the programmer to use semantics appropriate for a given class. Operators must be static methods and must be public. The following example shows how the addition operator can be overloaded to create a very natural mathematical expression with a user-defined class.

```
using System;
```

```csharp
public class MyClass
{
    public int A;

    public MyClass(int InitialA)
    {
        A = InitialA;
    }

    public static int operator+(MyClass L, MyClass R)
    {
        return L.A + R.A;
    }
}

public class OperatorExample
{
    public static void Main()
    {
        MyClass C = new MyClass(10);
        MyClass D = new MyClass(20);

        Console.WriteLine("C.A: {0}, D.A: {1}, C + D: {2}", C.A, D.A, C + D);
    }
}
```

The output of this program follows:

```
C.A: 10, D.A: 20, C + D: 30
```

Events

Events are class members that provide outgoing messages to notify clients of object-specific events. Clients who want to be notified of these object events simply use the += and -= operators to subscribe and unsubscribe to the desired events.

The following example shows how an event source can notify several event handlers about the occurrence of an event.

```csharp
using System;

// Define what the delegates should look like for this event source
public delegate void EventHandler();

public class EventSource
{
    // Define an event member
    public event EventHandler Done;

    public void Fire()
    {
        // Assume that we determined that an event occurred and it's
```

```csharp
        // time to notify the subscribers
        Done.DynamicInvoke(null);
    }

    public void Subscribe(EventHandler H)
    {
        // Add an event handler for Source's Done event
        Done += H;
    }

    public void Unsubscribe(EventHandler Handler)
    {
        // Remove Handler as an event handler for Source's Done event
        Done -= Handler;
    }
}

public class Subscriber
{
    int Instance;
    Subscriber(int InstanceID)
    {
        Instance = InstanceID;
    }

    public void On_Done()
    {
        Console.WriteLine("Instance {0} received the done event",
                          Instance);
    }

    static void Main()
    {
        EventSource Example = new EventSource();
        Subscriber S1 = new Subscriber(1);
        Subscriber S2 = new Subscriber(2);
        Subscriber S3 = new Subscriber(3);
        EventHandler H1 = new EventHandler(S1.On_Done);
        EventHandler H2 = new EventHandler(S2.On_Done);
        EventHandler H3 = new EventHandler(S3.On_Done);

        // Add three handlers for the Done event
        Example.Subscribe(H1);
        Example.Subscribe(H2);
        Example.Subscribe(H3);

        Console.WriteLine("Notify all existing handlers:");
        // Publish the Done event to any existing handlers
        Example.Fire();

        // Remove the second handler
        Example.Unsubscribe(H2);

        Console.WriteLine("Notify the handlers that are still left:");
```

```
            // Only the first and third handlers are still receiving events
            Example.Fire();
    }
}
```

C#'s event handling makes use of something called a *delegate*. A delegate encapsulates the concept of a method. The result is somewhat like a type-safe, object-oriented function pointer. The declaration `public delegate void EventHandler();` establishes the type and signature of the delegates that will be used for a given event source (which is `Done()` in this example). The delegate in this example does not take any arguments, but if it did they would have been specified in this declaration.

The `EventSource` class has an event member named `Done`, a `Fire()` method that informs the existing event handlers of an event, and two utility methods for adding and removing event handlers. The `public event EventHandler Done;` declaration specifies that the class member is an event that notifies `EventHandler` delegates when things are `Done`. Look at the code for these methods to see how to work with the event class.

The `Main()` method shows how all this comes together. First, the event source is created, followed by the creation of the event subscribers and then of the event handlers themselves. The `Subscribe()` method then is called to add each handler to the event source. Now that there are handlers ready to receive event notifications, the `Fire()` method is invoked, which causes all three event handlers to be notified. The `Unsubscribe()` method shows how a specific handler can be removed for the list of handlers so that it no longer receives events. The last `Fire()` method confirms that only the first and third handlers are still receiving events.

The output for this program follows:

```
Notify all existing handlers:
Instance 1 received the done event
Instance 2 received the done event
Instance 3 received the done event
Notify the handlers that are still left:
Instance 1 received the done event
Instance 3 received the done event
```

Indexers

Indexers allow array-like access to an object. Used appropriately, indexers can allow sequential or direct access to object state. In the following example, the first thing you notice is that the declaration of an indexer looks a bit strange:

```
using System;
public class Indexed
{
    int[] A1 = {1,2,3};
    int[] A2 = {4,5};
```

```csharp
       int[] A3 = {6,7,8};

   public int this[int index]
   {
         get
         {
             if (index >= 0 && index < 3)
                 return A1[index];
             else if (index >= 3 && index < 5)
                 return A2[index - A1.Length];
             else if (index >= 5 && index < 8)
                 return A3[index - A1.Length - A2.Length];
             else
                 throw new Exception("Index out of range");
         }
         set
         {
             if (index >= 0 && index < 3)
                 A1[index] = value;
             else if (index >= 3 && index < 5)
                 A2[index - A1.Length] = value;
             else if (index >= 5 && index < 8)
                 A3[index - A1.Length - A2.Length] = value;
             else
                 throw new Exception("Index out of range");
         }
     }
   }

   public class IndexerExample
   {
       static void Main()
       {
           Indexed Ndx = new Indexed();

           Console.WriteLine("Getting values from an indexed object");
           for (int i=0; i < 8; i++)
           {
               Console.WriteLine("Ndx[{0}]: {1}", i, Ndx[i]);
           }
           // Double every value
           for (int i=0; i < 8; i++)
           {
               Ndx[i] *= 2;
           }
           Console.WriteLine("\nAfter setting values in an indexed object");
           for (int i=0; i < 8; i++)
           {
               Console.WriteLine("Ndx[{0}]: {1}", i, Ndx[i]);
           }
       }
   }
```

The `public int this[int index]` declaration specifies that this object supports an integer index that returns that an integer value. In this example, three arrays are used to show how the object can create the illusion of a contiguous array, while in reality the index spans all three arrays. Just as with properties, the special variable `value` is used in the `set()` method to represent the value being assigned to the position indicated by the specified index.

The output of this application follows:

```
Getting values from an indexed object
Ndx[0]: 1
Ndx[1]: 2
Ndx[2]: 3
Ndx[3]: 4
Ndx[4]: 5
Ndx[5]: 6
Ndx[6]: 7
Ndx[7]: 8

After setting values in an indexed object
Ndx[0]: 2
Ndx[1]: 4
Ndx[2]: 6
Ndx[3]: 8
Ndx[4]: 10
Ndx[5]: 12
Ndx[6]: 14
Ndx[7]: 16
```

Interfaces

Interfaces are described in the C# language specification as "contracts." Just as contracts are used to specify compliance in a legal matter, interfaces define programmatic compliance. An interface is a specification of a set of methods, properties, indexers, and events that must be implemented if a class wants to advertise its support for a particular interface. In fact, interfaces are not permitted to include method implementations or declare fields.

Although C# does not support multiple inheritance, it does permit a class to implement more than one interface, which can be confusing at first because both appear to use the same syntax. Specifying multiple interfaces allows a class to support more than one contract and in effect provide multiple views to clients. Software that integrates through the use of interfaces rather than class types tends to be more resilient to change and more extensible.

The following example shows several important points about interfaces in C#:

```
using System;

public delegate void EventHandler();
```

```
public interface I1
{
    int this[int Index] { get; set; }
    void A(int value);
}

public interface I2
{
    event EventHandler E;
    string B { get; set; }
}

public interface I3: I2
{
    void C();
}

public class Implementer : I1, I3
{
    EventHandler Handler;

    public Implementer()
    {
        Handler = new EventHandler(On_E);
    }

    public void On_E() { /* Handler Implementation goes here */ }

    int I1.this[int Index]
    {
        get
        {
            /* Indexer get implementation goes here */
            return Index;
        }
        set
        {
            /* Indexer set implementation goes here */
        }
    }

    public void A(int value) { /* A's implementation goes here */ }
    void I3.C() { /* C's implementation goes here */ }

    public event EventHandler E
    {
        get
        {
            /* E's get implementation goes here */
            return Handler;
        }
        set
```

```
        {
            /* E's set implementation goes here */
        }
    }

    string I2.B
    {
        get
        {
            /* B's get implementation goes here */
            return "Something";
        }
        set
        {
            /* B's set implementation goes here */
        }
    }
}

public class InterfaceExample
{
    static void Main()
    {
        Implementer X = new Implementer();
        X.A(15);    // No problem to call I1.A()
        //I.C();    // Error!  C() is an explicit interface method
        I3 I = X;   // Get a reference to the I3 interface
        I.C();      // OK since C() is being called through its interface
    }
}
```

The interfaces I1, I2, and I3 show how to specify interface methods, properties, indexers, and events as interface members. The interface I3 shows an example of interface inheritance.

The Implementer class shows how to implement all the required interface members. The class inherits from both I1 and I3 and because I3 inherits from I2, the Implementer class is required to implement the members of all three interfaces. There are two ways to implement a member of an interface. A member can be implemented as public, which means that it can be called directly from an instance of the implementing class (Implementer in this example). A() and E are examples of a public implementation of an interface member. Alternatively, an interface can be implemented as an explicit interface member, which means that it can only be invoked through a reference to its interface. The indexer, C, and B are examples.

The code for the Main() method shows an example of calling the implemented public interface method A(). The I.C() call had to be commented out because it causes a compilation error since C() is an explicit interface member. The statement I3 I = X; shows how to get the I3 interface from the Implementer instance so that the I.C() invocation can be made legally.

Struct

C#'s use of structs can be a bit confusing for the uninitiated. At first glance, they appear to look and act just like a class. In fact structs can implement interfaces and can have the same kinds of members as classes, although they do not support inheritance. The obvious question is "Why have both?" The answer is that one is a reference type and the other is a value type. Remember that reference types require dynamic allocation and object management by the garbage collector, whereas value types require neither. As it turns out, classes are reference types, and structs are value types. For small objects, structs are the way to go because they are more efficient. In fact, most of the predefined types defined in C# are merely shorthand for a corresponding element in the CLR. For example, `double` is shorthand for `System.Double`. In reality, they can be viewed as intrinsic struct definitions that have corresponding reserved keywords in the language. From a pure type perspective, these predefined structs are no different than ones that you or I could create. In fact, this was an intentional language design decision that allows programmers to create user-defined "primitives" that have all the advantages of the ones predefined by the language.

You might be wondering why we do not just make everything a struct. Well, the answer is that the efficiency of the struct type disappears for objects larger than 16 bytes because of the overhead related to pass-by-value semantics of value arguments. In fact, improper usage (structs of 16 bytes or more) can actually make programs slower!

The following example shows a struct with two members: `A` and `F()`.

```
using System;
struct SomeStruct
{
    public int A;
    public void F(int W)
    {
        A = W;
    }
}

public class StructureExample
{
    static void Main()
    {
        SomeStruct S1;
        SomeStruct S2;

        S1.A = 15;
        S1.F(20);
        S2 = new SomeStruct();
    }
}
```

The main routine shows how to declare a struct and demonstrates that you can use it immediately without first dynamically allocating it. Structs are value types and are ready to go as soon as they are declared. It is interesting to note that the statement S2 = new SomeStruct(); does not result in a heap allocation. Although there is an allocation, it is on the stack and not the heap.

Enum

Enums can be used to introduce a new type that defines a set of related symbolic constants. Variables of an enumerated type can only be set to one of the symbolic constants listed in the type definition. Enums are commonly used when there is a reasonably small set of possible values for an enumeration, and the use of that enumeration makes the code easier to read. The following example shows an enumeration for the days of the week.

```
enum DayOfWeek
{
    Monday,
    Tuesday,
    Wednesday,
    Thursday,
    Friday,
    Saturday,
    Sunday
}

public class EnumerationExample
{
    static void Main()
    {
        DayOfWeek C;

        C = DayOfWeek.Friday;
    }
}
```

The Main() method shows how to assign a value to a variable of that enumeration type. Notice that a qualified name is required to make an assignment to this variable.

Attributes

Attributes allow programmers to add their own metadata information to their class definitions. This information is then compiled into an assembly and becomes available to anyone or any third-party tool that might be able to take advantage of it. Using attributes, writing code to search for components within an assembly that have certain characteristics is a rather simple operation. This is something that will undoubtedly have a significant impact on development tools and component-oriented development. Imagine how much more support your development environment could provide if it had a better understanding of what it was looking at. For example, if your development tool defines several attributes for you to use in your code, then the sky is the limit. In fact, this is exactly how Visual Studio.NET gets the information it needs to create a Web service out of your C# components. As we discuss in Chapter 4, attaching the [WebMethod] attribute to a method informs Visual Studio.NET that it should be exposed as part of the Web service.

This example was taken from the ManagedSynergy application (see Chapter 4).

```
[WebMethod]
public void VersionChanged(string ProjectID, string BatonID)
{
    // Implementation removed for clarity's sake
}
```

It shows the [WebMethod] attribute in action and identifies the VersionChanged method as a method that needs to be exposed as a Web service.

Exceptions

As we discussed briefly in the section on C# statements, exceptions generally indicate that an error has occurred and execution of the current operation must be abandoned. To signal that an exception has occurred, an instance of a class type derived from System.Exception is thrown using the throw statement. To handle an exception, the catch statement is used. Exceptions can be either application defined or systems defined, but in either case the catch statement is used to handle the error. The following example shows various forms of exception handling:

```
using System;

public class UserDefinedException : System.Exception
{
    public UserDefinedException(string M) : base(M)
    {
    }
}

class ExceptionTester
{
    public void A()
    {
        try
        {
            B();
        }
```

```
        catch (System.DivideByZeroException e)
        {
            Console.WriteLine("Not called — exception was changed to user
                              defined");
        }
        catch (UserDefinedException e)
        {
            Console.WriteLine("Caught user defined exception: {0}",
                              e.Message);
            Console.WriteLine("Stack Trace: \n{0}", e.StackTrace);
            throw new System.OutOfMemoryException();
        }
        catch (System.OutOfMemoryException e)
        {
            Console.WriteLine("This exception does not happen in this
                              test");
        }
    }

    public void B()
    {
        try
        {
            int X;

            C();
        }
        catch (System.DivideByZeroException e)
        {
            Console.WriteLine("Caught divide by zero exception");
            throw new UserDefinedException("Re-throw a user defined
                                           exception");
        }
    }

    public void C()
    {
        try
        {
            int X;
            int Y = 0;

            X = 100 / Y;
        }
        catch (System.OutOfMemoryException e)
        {
            Console.WriteLine("This exception does not happen in this
                              test");
        }
        finally
        {
            Console.WriteLine("Gets called no matter how C() is exited");
        }
```

```
        }
    }

    public class ExceptionExample
    {
        static void Main()
        {
            ExceptionTester Test = new ExceptionTester();

            try
            {
                Test.A();
            }
            catch
            {
                Console.WriteLine("General catchall caught some kind of
                                  exception");
            }
        }
    }
```

In this example, we have created a situation in which one method calls another until we have a deep enough call stack to show various things about exception handling. As you can see, Main() calls A(), which calls B(), which calls C(), and then we throw our way back out to Main().

The C() method demonstrates that we can test for very specific exceptions in catch blocks. The System.OutOfMemoryException exception does not occur in this test, so this specific exception is skipped over and never caught. The finally block, on the other hand, is always executed no matter how the method is exited. Therefore even though a "divide by zero" exception occurs, the finally block executes, as is shown in the application output.

The B() method catches the "divide by zero" error and shows how to change the exception object and rethrow an exception object that has a context-specific exception message.

The A() method demonstrates that the exception has been changed because the divide by zero method is not caught. Instead, the user-defined exception is caught and it shows how to write out a stack trace, which can be very helpful when debugging applications. The stack trace also confirms that the exception object has changed because it traces to B() rather than all the way to C(), where the original exception occurred. The last thing that A's catch handler does is to rethrow a predefined exception.

The Main() method shows how to write a general catch handler that will catch any exception that is thrown. Notice that this construct does not provide an exception object to the catch handler. Alternatively, we could have written an equivalent general catch handler like the following:

```
catch (System.Exception e)
{
    Console.WriteLine("General catchall caught: {0}", e.Message);
}
```

The output to this program would look like the following:

```
Gets called no matter how C() is exited
Caught divide by zero exception
Caught user defined exception: Re-throw a user-defined exception
Stack Trace:
    at ConsoleApplication1.ExceptionTester.B() in
c:\consoleapplication1\class1.cs:line 49
    at ConsoleApplication1.ExceptionTester.A() in
c:\consoleapplication1\class1.cs:line 18
General catchall caught some kind of exception
```

CONCLUSION

In this chapter, we have considered the C# language from both contemporary and people-oriented perspectives. The contemporary perspective allowed us to understand the strength of this language in terms of features that are required to build the current systems. The people-oriented perspective helped us understand how this language can be used to build an important class of software that is the focus of Microsoft's .NET technology. We ended the chapter with a language tour that highlighted the important features of the C# language, which included short programming examples of each feature in action. Chapter 4 shows us how to apply what we have learned in this chapter to build a people-oriented application called *ManagedSynergy*.

Applied C#

Chapter 3 discussed the merits of C# and gave a tour of the language that included small coding examples to explain specific language details. This chapter has a broader focus and shows you how all those isolated language constructs can be woven together to produce the new and exciting class of software we call *people-oriented software*. We have chosen an example application that demonstrates what is likely to be a very common development scenario—an application is built to seamlessly integrate with complementary Web services of another application. In keeping with the spirit of our book's title, *Applied .NET*, the following list highlights a variety of different aspects of .NET development that are demonstrated in this chapter:

1. Producing a Web service
2. Invoking a Web service
3. Using server-side controls and events
4. Implementing field validation using active server page (ASP) .NET validation controls
5. Implementing an ASP.NET custom control
6. Performing object serialization over the Internet
7. Using various common language runtime (CLR) classes
8. Applying .NET exception handling

MANAGEDSYNERGY

In Chapter 2, we introduced the InternetBaton application, which allows people to collaborate on a shared resource in a decentralized fashion over the Internet. In this chapter, we create a new application called *ManagedSynergy* that makes use of the services provided by InternetBaton to create a decentralized document management system.

The Vision

ManagedSynergy is an application that combines document management features such as approval workflow with the distributed project folder capabilities of InternetBaton. The result is a document management system that does not require a centralized document server. This approach would be ideal for collaborative projects in which funds are tight and the participants have no real organizational relationship (which makes it tough to find shared servers to use). Charity work and certain Internet development projects are good examples in which this model would work well. In both cases the work being done is a labor of love but nonetheless needs to be done right with document management. The ultimate goal of this application is to provide an inexpensive means for people to practice managed collaboration in hopes that the end result is greater than the sum of the individual efforts.

The Functionality

The core concept in ManagedSynergy is the notion of a shared project file, which, not surprisingly, contains project items, each of which represents a shared InternetBaton resource. The focus of the application centers on manipulating the project file. Using ManagedSynergy, you can add and delete project items, check items in and out, view an item and its properties, and review an author's changes and either approve them or request that revisions be made. Checking an item out means that other authors participating in the shared project are not allowed to modify the item until it is checked back in. This is more a change management feature than it is version control because there is no notion of version history in this application.

Here is how it all works. When an author wants to make a change to the content of a project item, the first step is to check the item out so that others know it is being worked on. At this point, displaying the properties for that item would show that its revision status is *checked out* and its approval status is *in revision*. The author makes whatever modifications are needed and checks the item back in. At this point the revision status changes to *checked in* and the approval status (assuming that the review feature was enabled for this project) changes to *in review*. Each reviewer can look over the changes that were made and submit a brief review along with an indication of whether the changes were approved or further revisions are necessary. When all the reviewers have finished reviewing the changes, the approval status changes to either *approved* or *revise* depending on the verdict of each of the reviews. The changes are considered approved if all the reviewers agree to approve them; otherwise, the changes are rejected and revisions are required. To make things simple, all reviews are cleared each time changes are checked back in.

ManagedSynergy does not have its own administration facilities. Instead it uses those provided by InternetBaton. When project administrators want to set up a new shared project, they select the ManagedSynergy administration option, which takes them to the InternetBaton application where the project can be set up and participants can be identified. Once the project is set up, the users are no longer aware that they are using InternetBaton because its exposed Web services are programmatically accessed to seamlessly integrate the two applications. That is, when an item is added to the ManagedSynergy, it is also added behind the scenes to InternetBaton. The same holds true for checking out an item—it is reflected in both applications. When ManagedSynergy's view option is selected, the browser simply points to the Internet-Baton link, and the shared item is displayed.

Things are a little different when an item is reviewed. InternetBaton does not have the concept of reviewing items or establishing an approval process. This functionality resides solely in ManagedSynergy, and it is the added value this application brings to the table. In essence, what this application has done is to seamlessly extend the project file supported by InternetBaton and other than the administration angle, the user is truly unaware of which features ManagedSynergy provides and which features are provided by InternetBaton.

An interesting aspect of this application is that integration with InternetBaton is not just one way. ManagedSynergy operates in a multiuser environment in which several project participants may be working on their project items concurrently. Therefore it is necessary for project status to be dynamically updated as it changes. Because all project-related activity is mirrored to this Web service, InternetBaton becomes a natural choice for the central location from which to replicate out project changes to the other active project participants. This means that in addition to consuming Web services, ManagedSynergy will also expose Web services so that InternetBaton can call them to cause replication to occur. Another useful feature made possible as a result of exposing Web services is a synchronization feature that allows quite large files to be automatically updated overnight.

The Design

Chapter 2 introduced the concept of People-Types and how they could be used to help focus a developer's attention in the areas that are most important for people-oriented software. We continue with that approach in this chapter as we examine how the ManagedSynergy application addresses the primary forces that shape people-oriented software: universalization, collaboration, and translation. Because the process of using people-types involves stepping back and taking a look at how these forces factor into the design of an application, it may be helpful to first provide a concise list of this application's features.

Universalization

Now that we know what features the ManagedSynergy application provides, we can discuss those aspects of the design that resulted from taking a "miner's" perspective and determining how much of the functionality could be achieved through universalization. Universalization is ultimately concerned with identifying what existing resources can be utilized and applied in the design and implementation of an application. We consider the features in Table 4-1 one at a time to understand how all this worked.

When we looked into the issue of a shared project file, we discovered that what was needed was the ability to save the current state of the project to disk. Further, we decided that if we could get the object that held the project data to serialize itself, we could have it write itself to disk and then later read itself back in with very little effort on our part. (In this context, laziness is a good thing.) Our miner-focused investigation determined that all this could be accomplished using .NET serialization.

Another interesting wrinkle related to object serialization was the fact that the project file itself needed to be a Baton item just like project items. Taking this approach, the project file could be easily shared between the participants. It would also ensure that the contents would always be accurate (because everyone would point to the same project files no matter where the current version was). Given this requirement,

TABLE 4-1   Features of ManagedSynergy

Feature	Description
Shared decentralized projects and files	Allows files to be collaboratively developed by geographically distant participants without the need for a centralized document server
Check-in, check-out, version status	Allows files to be safely modified in a multiuser environment
Document approval, publication, document status	Allows management of changes to documents
Offline document replication	Allows the decentralized files to be replicated to each participant's machine overnight
Real-time version and document status	Allows status changes to be reflected in every active (running) instance of the ManagedSynergy client

being able to serialize the project file over the Internet became a very desirable option and as it turned out, the CLR classes directly supported serialization over the Internet as well. We discuss serialization when we expand on ManagedSynergy's implementation later in this chapter.

When we thought about the issue of checking project items in and out, we found that one of the things that was needed was field validation. During the process of checking an item back in, the author needs to fill out a form that includes a check-in comment for others to refer to before they conduct their review. Because this comment is so important, ensuring that it was filled out became a requirement. Service-side controls provided field validation—just what the doctor ordered. As we thought about the other forms involved in the application, field validation was applicable in those instances as well, so once again our miner's perspective paid off.

Also in the area of forms management there was the desire to manage form control events in a familiar manner. ASP .NET and Visual Studio offer an event model that most programmers have already become accustomed to in Visual Basic and C++, so selecting this approach was an easy choice.

In terms of document publication, we had to make the movement of files from working directories to public directories automatic so that the users would not have to keep track of the details and to ensure that the copy took place when it should. It is not until the project items are copies to this public location (along with some necessary Baton collaboration) that they are visible to other participants.

As it turns out, offline document replication had very similar requirements to those of document publication in that files need to be copied from one place to another. Using the CLR's `File` and `Directory` classes made designing and implementing both of these application features a snap.

Throughout the design and implementation, we constantly had to deal with the unexpected. How would we deal with things not working because of external factors such as a full disk or a lack of proper file permissions? Our miner's perspective resulted in adopting .NET exception handling. (Okay. It was not that noteworthy or courageous a decision, but it was a decision born out of a miner's spirit and so I mention it here). Using this type of exception handling, we will even be able to receive exceptions thrown by the InternetBaton Web service, yet another application that we are calling over the Internet!

Collaboration

Collaboration affects how your application interacts with other applications and services to accomplish its goals. Continuing with the technique we learned in Chapter 2, we adopted a "conductor" perspective to help focus our attention on collaborative aspects of the application. In ManagedSynergy, collaboration is required to accomplish a seamless integration of InternetBaton functionality as well as support dynamic project status updates and offline document replication.

Integrating with InternetBaton involves calling its Web services to add, delete, view, check in, or check out project items. Each of these actions has an effect on the shared state of the project file as well as an effect on the state held in the InternetBaton application. For most of these actions, the general order of events is as follows:

1. Check out the project file from InternetBaton.
2. Deserialize the contents of that project file (just in case it changed since we started our session).
3. Apply the intended action (e.g., add, delete) to the project object.
4. Save the project object to disk using serialization, and copy the project file to its shared location.
5. Forward the action to InternetBaton, if appropriate.
6. Check back in the project file, thus making the change public.

In the scenario just described, ManagedSynergy takes an active role in the integration of the two applications. In contrast, implementing dynamic project status updates and offline document replication involves a passive approach (with respect to ManagedSynergy) in which the ManagedSynergy application itself is used as a Web service by the InternetBaton application. When a project item is checked in or out, the resulting status changes are sent to each of the participant's Web servers. Any participant who is currently using the application is dynamically notified of the change. Similarly, when InternetBaton has been instructed to perform offline document replication and it is time to perform the task, each participant's Web service is invoked and instructed to update the contents of each of the project items.

The new Web services capability provided by the .NET platform makes this kind of synergy very straightforward. Thinking about software as services has several positive implications and is something that will be one of the more important technologies being developed.

Translation

Translation is all about how identical concepts that may be dissimilar in form can be used in a heterogeneous environment. The translation story for ManagedSynergy is limited to the use of Web services. Web services in .NET are implemented using Simple Object Access Protocol (SOAP) technology; therefore any client that can speak SOAP can be a client of this application. InternetBaton could be ported to another operating system and the dynamic status notification would still work, as would the offline replication and the remaining interactions between the two applications. The point is that Web services allow clients to translate a SOAP request into a correct response no matter what kind of implementation was chosen for that client. This perspective shows that translation is of no small consequence.

The Implementation

Although this application's complexity is not on par with the software that launches the space shuttle, there is a reasonable amount of functionality in the Managed-Synergy application. What is surprising is that using .NET and our people-oriented techniques makes this implementation a rather simple one. In Chapter 3 we presented .NET as a revolution that elevates application development to a radically simpler level of implementation. Reviewing this application implementation should lend credibility to that statement. Developing in .NET is a pleasure, and your intuition about how things *should* operate is exactly how they *do* operate.

Before we get into the details of the implementation, we are going to discuss the application's main screen. Figure 4-1 is a screen shot of the Project.aspx page, the page on which the users spend the bulk of their time. Listed in the action bar are the various steps we outlined earlier in this chapter. Each of these actions originates from this

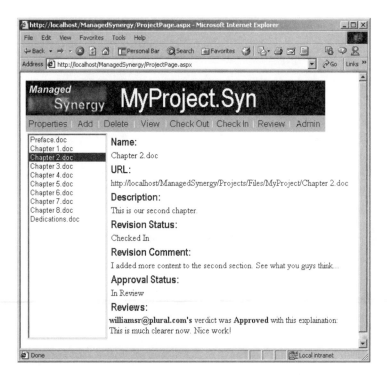

FIGURE 4-1   Project Page (Main Screen) for ManagedSynergy.

page and returns back to it once completed. On the left-hand side of the page is the project item list (in this case, the chapters of a book that is being collaboratively developed). To the right of the project item list are the property details of selected items (in this case, Chapter 2.doc).

Probably the easiest way to examine this implementation is to describe a scenario that weaves through all the various actions that could be taken by a user. This will give us a basis for discussion as well as provide complete coverage of the various aspects of the implementation that need to be examined. The following list describes the various scenarios and the order in which we will cover each one:

1. Opening an existing project
2. Creating a new project
3. Adding a project item
4. Deleting a project item
5. Checking out an item
6. Viewing a project item
7. Checking in an item
8. Reviewing an item
9. Viewing an item's properties
10. Invoking administration services

Opening an Existing Project

We begin by discussing the steps involved in logging a user in to the application. Figure 4-2 shows the Start.aspx page, which users complete so that they can log in. The user ID is an e-mail address, and the project uniform resource locater (URL) must be linked to an InternetBaton resource that identifies the project file. If the project file does not exist, then users are alerted and asked if they want to create a new project file.

We mentioned previously that server-side controls and field validation played a role in this implementation. The ASP .NET code for this page shows an example of both. Because all the other ASP .NET pages in this application involve the very same processes, we only need to discuss one example to explain how the presentation of this works. As pointed out in Chapter 2, ASP .NET introduces a way to cleanly separate the presentation code from the "code behind" the form. Therefore every form you see in this application has a presentation file (identified by an *.aspx* extension) and a "code-behind" file (identified by a *.cs* extension). We use the term *code behind* because this is how the relationship between the two files is specified in the hypertext markup language (HTML) file.

The following only includes the relevant portion of Start.aspx that shows server-side controls and field validation in action. (The complete source for this entire application can be found on this book's Web site.)

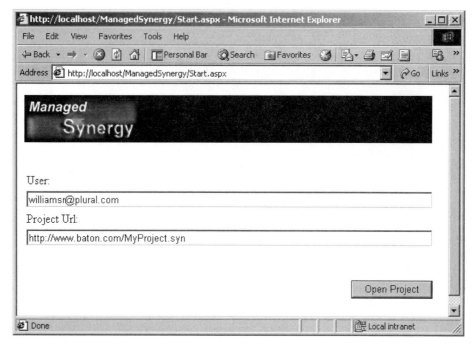

FIGURE 4-2   Start Page for ManagedSynergy.

```
<asp:TextBox id=m_UserTB runat="server" ></asp:TextBox>
<asp:TextBox id=m_ProjectUrlTB runat="server" ></asp:TextBox>
<asp:Button id=m_OpenProjectButton runat="server"
    Text="Open Project"></asp:Button>
<asp:requiredfieldvalidator id=m_UserValidator runat="server"
    controlToValidate="m_UserTB"
    errorMessage="Must enter your email address as your user name." />
<asp:requiredfieldvalidator id=m_ProjectFileValidator runat="server"
    controlToValidate="m_ProjectUrlTB"
    errorMessage="Must enter Baton project URL." />
<asp:validationsummary id=m_StartPageValidSummary runat="Server"
    headertext="Form errors exist:" />
```

This listing shows an example of the `<asp:TextBox>` and `<asp:Button>` server-side controls. The first text box control is for the user ID, and the second one is for the project URL. The `id` attribute specifies the name of the member variable that represents these controls in the code behind this form. Not surprisingly, the `<asp:button>` control is the Open Project button. Each of the text boxes has its own `<asp:requiredfieldvalidator>`, which is the field validation control. (See Chapter 2 for a full explanation of validation controls.)

Now we can discuss the code behind this form. The following is code from the Start.cs file, which was specified as this form's `Codebehind` attribute.

```csharp
namespace ManagedSynergy
{
  using System;
  using System.IO;
  using System.Collections;
  using System.ComponentModel;
  using System.Data;
  using System.Drawing;
  using System.Web;
  using System.Web.SessionState;
  using System.Web.UI;
  using System.Web.UI.WebControls;
  using System.Web.UI.HtmlControls;
  using System.Runtime.Serialization.Formatters.Binary;

  public class Start : System.Web.UI.Page
  {
    protected System.Web.UI.WebControls.ValidationSummary
        m_StartPageValidSummary;
    protected System.Web.UI.WebControls.RequiredFieldValidator
        m_ProjectFileValidator;
    protected System.Web.UI.WebControls.RequiredFieldValidator
        m_UserValidator;
    protected System.Web.UI.WebControls.Label m_ExceptionMsg;
    protected System.Web.UI.WebControls.Button m_OpenProjectButton;
    protected System.Web.UI.WebControls.TextBox m_ProjectUrlTB;
    protected System.Web.UI.WebControls.TextBox m_UserTB;

    public Start()
    {
      Page.Init += new System.EventHandler(Page_Init);
    }

    protected void Page_Load(object sender, EventArgs e)
    {
      if (!IsPostBack)
      {
        //
        // Evals true first time browser hits the page
        //
      }
    }

    protected void Page_Init(object sender, EventArgs e)
    {
      //
      // CODEGEN: This call is required by the ASP+ Windows Form Designer.
      //
      InitializeComponent();
    }
```

```
/// <summary>
///     Required method for Designer support - do not modify
///     the contents of this method with the code editor.
/// </summary>
private void InitializeComponent()
{
  m_OpenProjectButton.Click += new
      System.EventHandler (this.OpenProjectButton_Click);
  this.Load += new System.EventHandler (this.Page_Load);
}

public void OpenProjectButton_Click (object sender, System.EventArgs e)
{
  // Save the user ID in the Application object for use later
  Page.Application.Contents["User"] = m_UserTB.Text;
  Page.Application.Contents["ProjectUrl"] = m_ProjectUrlTB.Text;

  // Create a baton object so we can access the InternetBaton
  // Web service
  ManagedSynergy.localhost.Baton Baton = new
      ManagedSynergy.localhost.Baton();

  // A Baton query for the existence of the project specified in
  // the m_ProjectUrlTB field
  if (Baton.ProjectExists(m_UserTB.Text,
      Project.UrlToName(m_ProjectUrlTB.Text)))
  {
    try
    {
      // Create a project object that points to the shared
      // project file.
      Project Proj = new Project();

      // Load data from the shared project file ProjectUrl
      Project.Load(ref Proj, m_UserTB.Text, m_ProjectUrlTB.Text);

      // Make project data available to other pages
      Page.Application.Contents["Project"] = Proj;

      // Point browser to project page
      Response.Redirect("ProjectPage.aspx");
    }
      catch (System.Runtime.Serialization.SerializationException)
      {
      m_ExceptionMsg.Text = "Could not load project file. The Baton
          server may be down or the project file may be corrupt or an
          incompatible format.";
      }
  }
  else
  {
    // Project does not exist so let's see if the user wants to create
```

```
        // a new one
        Response.Redirect("ConfirmCreate.aspx?ProjectUrl=" +
            m_ProjectUrlTB.Text);
      }
    }
  }
}
```

As with the previous presentation code, we will not take the time to explain every aspect of this listing. Instead we highlight those sections that show .NET in action, as well as those aspects that are necessary for understanding the rest of the application.

The first thing that you should note is the control member declarations:

```
protected System.Web.UI.WebControls.ValidationSummary
        m_StartPageValidSummary;
protected System.Web.UI.WebControls.RequiredFieldValidator
        m_ProjectFileValidator;
protected System.Web.UI.WebControls.RequiredFieldValidator
        m_UserValidator;
protected System.Web.UI.WebControls.Label m_ExceptionMsg;
protected System.Web.UI.WebControls.Button m_OpenProjectButton;
protected System.Web.UI.WebControls.TextBox m_ProjectUrlTB;
protected System.Web.UI.WebControls.TextBox m_UserTB;
```

Each of these corresponds to the IDs that were specified in the previous presentation code. If you are using Visual Studio.NET, then members are automatically added to your code-behind class.

If you skip down to the `InitializeComponent()` class, you can see how the event handling is specified in .NET. There is only one event in which we are interested in this form, so the code ends up looking like the listing that follows. The control `m_OpenProjectButton` has its event handler set in the `OpenProjectButton_Click()` method:

```
private void InitializeComponent()
{
   m_OpenProjectButton.Click += new
        System.EventHandler (this.OpenProjectButton_Click);
   this.Load += new System.EventHandler (this.Page_Load);
}
```

The last thing to discuss in this file is the `OpenProjectButton_Click()` method itself. Clicking the Open Project button on the start page invokes this method. The first thing this code does is save the user's ID and the project URL in the application object:

```
// Save the user ID in the Application object for use later
Page.Application.Contents["User"] = m_UserTB.Text;
Page.Application.Contents["ProjectUrl"] = m_ProjectUrlTB.Text;
```

The application object operates just as it did in ASP, and assigning it values makes the values available to other pages in the application. We use the application object rather than the session object because we need to get at these values in the Web service code, which has a different session instance. The code behind the various forms in this application also makes use of the values stored in the application object.

Next we use the InternetBaton Web service to determine whether this project already exists:

```
// A Baton query for the existence of the project specified in
// the m_ProjectUrlTB field
if (Baton.ProjectExists(m_UserTB.Text,
    Project.UrlToName(m_ProjectUrlTB.Text)))
```

If the project does not exist, we ask the users if they want to create a project. If the project does exist, then we load the project over the Internet using InternetBaton to get the most up-to-date project file:

```
// Load data from the shared project file ProjectUrl
Project.Load(ref Proj, m_UserTB.Text, m_ProjectUrlTB.Text);

// Make project data available to other pages
Page.Application.Contents["Project"] = Proj;

// Point browser to project page
Response.Redirect("ProjectPage.aspx");
```

After loading the project, we again use the application object to save a reference to the project object, which now holds all the most current project data. Finally, we use the ASP .NET response object to point the browser to the main application page we showed previously.

While we are here, we can take a look at the code that loaded the project data from an InternetBaton resource accessed over the Internet. The `Load()` method is a member of the project class that is located in the `Project.cs` file. The project class and the other classes in this file encapsulate and abstract the notion of a ManagedSynergy project. This allows the code behind the forms in this application and the methods that are used as Web services to cleanly call project-related primitives. Without these classes, the implementation of a project would be spread around various places in the application, and the methods of these classes would have to be redundantly coded "in-line" every time the functionality was needed. With the encapsulated approach the code is centralized, so fixing an error only requires the user to make a change in one place rather than search the application looking for the various other places that might also need to be changed. As we discuss this implementation, keep in mind that architecturally the forms and the Web service exist for the purpose of connecting clients to the functionality encapsulated in the project classes.

Turning our attention to the `Project.Load()` method, you will notice that we used a static method for this code. We chose to use a static method because we had a chicken-or-egg type of problem; it seemed safer to pass in the object rather than assign the deserialized object to the `this` reference. That is, the alternative would have involved invoking the `Load()` method on an object instance, and inside that method we would have needed to point the `this` reference to the new object.

```
public static void Load(ref Project Project, string UserName,
                        string ProjectUrl)
{
    // Create a Web-based stream gives access to the project file
    // over the Internet
    WebRequest Request = WebRequest.Create("http://<IB>"
        + Project.UrlToName(ProjectUrl));
    Stream ProjStream = Request.GetResponse().GetResponseStream();

    try
    {
      // Create the formatter
      BinaryFormatter ProjFormatter = new BinaryFormatter();
      // Load the project file from the Web-based stream. This always
      // causes the most current project file to be loaded.
      Project = (Project) ProjFormatter.Deserialize(ProjStream);
    }
    finally
    {
      ProjStream.Close();
    }
}
```

The `WebRequest` class shown here is provided by the .NET framework. This class can be used to treat a uniform resource identifier (URI) as a `stream`, which is exactly what the `BinaryFormatter` requires for deserialization. Once the stream is established, the binary formatter can be used to deserialize the `Project` object and assign the resulting value to the reference argument that was passed to the method. This code is a good example of the power and simplicity of the .NET framework.

Creating a New Project

When creating a new project, we assume that the project URL specified by the user points to a project file that does not yet exist. We want to ask users whether they want to create a new project. (Who knows? They may have mistyped the URL and do not intend to create a new project.) If the users decide to create a new project, their browser will point to the CreateProject.aspx page shown in Figure 4-3.

Although we said previously that each page is so similar we only need to examine the startup page, there is one detail in this presentation code worth revisiting. This page makes use of the `<asp:regularexpressionvalidator>` regular expression field validator. The following is how this is defined in CreateProject.aspx:

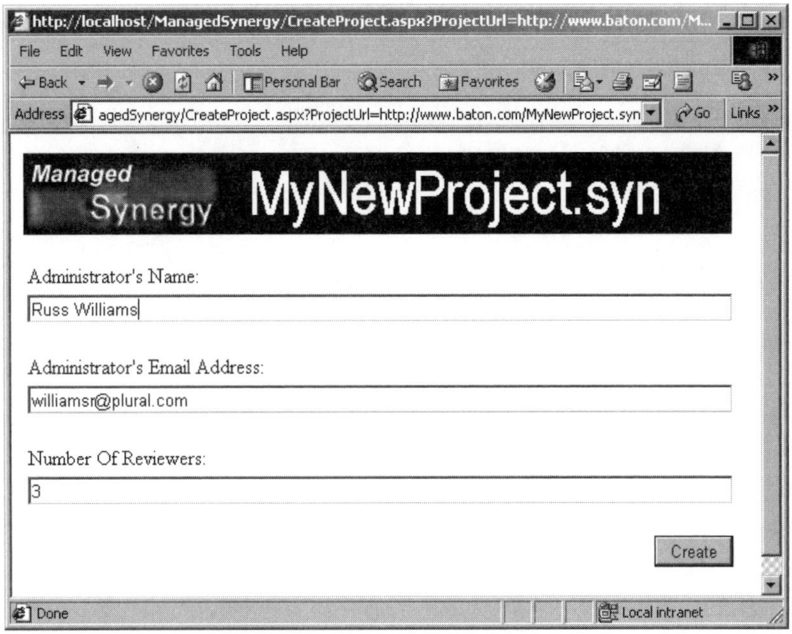

FIGURE 4-3 Create Project Page for ManagedSynergy.

```
<asp:regularexpressionvalidator id=m_DigitNumOfReviewersValidator
    runat="server" controlToValidate="m_NumOfReviewersTB"
    errorMessage="Number of reviewers must be a numeric value"
    display="none" validationexpression="[0-9]*"/>
```

The regular expression validator ensures that the characters entered in a field on a form match a pattern (i.e., the regular expression). We used this validation control to make sure that the value for the number of reviewers is a numeric value. We already discussed each of the attributes used in this definition, and the ones shown here have the same meaning. What is new here is the `validationexpression` attribute. This attribute defines the regular expression that should be used to validate the field. We specified the regular expression `"[0-9]*"`, which says that the input must be zero or more digits and nothing else. Because you can set more than one validator on a given field, we were able to add an `<asp:requiredfieldvalidator>` for the same field to catch a case in which nothing at all is entered in the field (which would have been valid if we had used `<asp:regularexpressionvalidator>` only).

The following is the code behind this page. Many of the standard steps are repeated in this listing:

```
namespace ManagedSynergy
{
    using System;
```

```csharp
using System.Collections;
using System.ComponentModel;
using System.Data;
using System.Drawing;
using System.Web;
using System.Web.SessionState;
using System.Web.UI;
using System.Web.UI.WebControls;
using System.Web.UI.HtmlControls;

    public class CreateProject : System.Web.UI.Page
    {
    protected System.Web.UI.WebControls.Label m_ExceptionMessage;
    protected System.Web.UI.WebControls.ValidationSummary
          m_CreateProjectValidSummary;
    protected System.Web.UI.WebControls.RegularExpressionValidator
          m_DigitNumOfReviewersValidator;
    protected System.Web.UI.WebControls.RequiredFieldValidator
          m_RequiredNumOfReviewersValidator;
    protected System.Web.UI.WebControls.RequiredFieldValidator
          m_AdminEmailValidator;
    protected System.Web.UI.WebControls.RequiredFieldValidator
          m_AdminNameValidator;
    protected System.Web.UI.WebControls.Button m_CreateButton;
    protected System.Web.UI.WebControls.TextBox m_NumOfReviewersTB;
    protected System.Web.UI.WebControls.TextBox m_AdminEmailTB;
    protected System.Web.UI.WebControls.TextBox m_AdminNameTB;
    protected System.Web.UI.WebControls.Label m_ProjectLabel;
    private static string s_ProjectUrl;

    public CreateProject()
    {
       Page.Init += new System.EventHandler(Page_Init);
    }

    protected void Page_Load(object sender, EventArgs e)
    {
       if (!IsPostBack)
       {
          // Save this for later
          s_ProjectUrl = Page.Request.QueryString["ProjectUrl"];

          // Set the form heading
          m_ProjectLabel.Text = Project.UrlToName(s_ProjectUrl);

          // Give default values to the fields
          m_AdminEmailTB.Text =
             (string)Page.Application.Contents["User"];
          m_NumOfReviewersTB.Text = "0";    // Default to no approval
       }
    }

    protected void Page_Init(object sender, EventArgs e)
```

```
        {
            //
            // CODEGEN: This call is required by the ASP+ Windows Form
            // Designer.
            //
            InitializeComponent ();
        }

        /// <summary>
        ///     Required method for Designer support - do not modify
        ///     the contents of this method with the code editor.
        /// </summary>
        private void InitializeComponent ()
        {
            m_CreateButton.Click += new System.EventHandler
                    (this.CreateButton_Click);
            this.Load += new System.EventHandler (this.Page_Load);
        }

        public void CreateButton_Click (object sender, System.EventArgs arg)
        {
            Project Proj;
            string UserID = (string)Page.Application.Contents["User"];
            string ProjectUrl =
                (string)Page.Application.Contents["ProjectUrl"];

            try
            {
                Proj = new Project(UserID, ProjectUrl,
                    Page.MapPath("Projects"), m_AdminNameTB.Text,
                            m_AdminEmailTB.Text,
                    Convert.ToInt32(m_NumOfReviewersTB.Text));

                // Store project in Application object for other pages to use
                Page.Application.Contents["Project"] = Proj;

                // Add the newly create project file to InternetBaton
                Proj.AddProjectToBaton();

                // Point the browser to the project page
                Response.Redirect("ProjectPage.aspx");
            }
            catch (Exception e)
            {
                m_ExceptionMessage.Text = "Error: \"" + e + "\\";
            }
        }
    }
}
```

There are a lot more server-side controls in this code than there were in the previous page but other than that there is nothing new. There is, however, something new in the implementation of the `Page_Load()` method. Previously, we did not have any work that needed to be done in this framework method, which gets invoked every time the page is loaded. The code in the following conditional, on the other hand, is only executed the first time the browser hits this page:

```
if (!IsPostBack)
{
    // Save this for later
    s_ProjectUrl = Page.Request.QueryString["ProjectUrl"];

    // Set the form heading
    m_ProjectLabel.Text = Project.UrlToName(s_ProjectUrl);

    // Give default values to the fields
    m_AdminEmailTB.Text = (string)Page.Application.Contents["User"];
    m_NumOfReviewersTB.Text = "0";    // Default to no approval desired
}
```

The first two lines of code set the label in the page's display heading, and the second two set default values for the form fields.

This brings us to `CreateButton_Click()`, which is the last method in this file and the method that is invoked when the Create button is clicked. The first two methods get the values that we saved in the application object when the user first logged in to the application. The remaining code in this method (the code inside the `try` block) creates a new project object by passing on its initial values, adds a link to the newly created project to InternetBaton, and finally, points the browser to the ProjectPage.aspx so that the user can start adding items. We discuss the exception handling itself when we take a look at adding items to the project.

As we did previously, let's take a look at another `Project` method before we move on. The purpose of the `AddProjectToBaton()` method is to add a link that points this newly created project file to InernetBaton.

When we thought about the design of the ManagedSynergy application, our focus was on adding some approval workflow to document revision. Using Internet-Baton was a logical choice for sharing the user's document, and on top of that we would add the approval workflow. Then we had to figure out how to share the ManagedSynergy project file itself, which is when we came up with the idea that we could use an InternetBaton resource. This would solve the problem of managing the changes to the project file, as well as sharing the result.

Therefore in this implementation the project file itself is not a link that the user adds but instead is an internal link that the application manages behind the scenes. From the user's perspective, the project file somehow gets magically shared. In reality, there is no magic at all. It is yet another example of collaboration in action. Let's see how all this gets done.

```
public void AddProjectToBaton()
{
```

```
ManagedSynergy.localhost.Baton Baton = new
   ManagedSynergy.localhost.Baton();

// Save the project data to the shared directory
Save();

// Add yourself to InternetBaton which will initially point
// participants to this new added project
Baton.Add(UserID, this.Name, this.Name);
}
```

As you can see, there is not a lot of code required in this method either. First, the project data is saved to disk in the shared directory. Saving to the shared directory allows others to access it as InternetBaton redirects their Web request to this server. Once the file is safely saved to disk, the only thing left is to add a link to this newly created project file to InternetBaton.

The story here is not complete until we factor in the `Project.Save()` method.

```
public void Save()
{
   // Create the directory if it does not already exist
   if (!Directory.Exists(m_ProjectPath))
      Directory.CreateDirectory(m_ProjectPath);

   // Creates a project if one does not exist or updates its contents
   // if project does exist
      FileStream ProjectStream = (FileStream)File.Create(m_ProjectPath +
         "\\" + Name);

   // Create a serializer that will know how to persist
   BinaryFormatter Serializer = new BinaryFormatter();

   // Persist the state of the project to the project file
   Serializer.Serialize(ProjectStream, this);

   // Free the file handle since there is no telling when, or even if, GC
   // will get around to it.
   ProjectStream.Close();
}
```

The `Save()` method starts by ensuring that the shared project directory exists. The code creates the specified directory and any missing directories in between the root and the specified directory:

```
Directory.CreateDirectory(m_ProjectPath);
```

This shared directory lives in the virtual path of the ManagedSynergy Web site so that it is accessible for the redirection of requests by InternetBaton. Next, a file stream is created so that it can be passed to the serializer. The serializer uses the meta information associated with the object itself to write out the state of the object in a way that allows it to be read back in. This serialization is the format of our project file. When these steps are complete, the only thing left to do is to close the file stream, which frees up the file handle. Notice that we need to explicitly close the stream rather than depend on it being freed when the object is destroyed. This task is typically carried out by the garbage collector, which is not even guaranteed to run during an application session.

At this point, we know how this application opens existing project files or creates new ones. Next, we examine how the user adds items to this project.

Adding a Project Item

When adding a project item, we assume that the user has already created a project and is ready to add an item to that project. The screen shot in Figure 4-4 shows the Add page. As you can see, the user specifies the display name for the new item, the URL of the shared document, and a brief description of the shared document. Jumping right to the code behind this form, we have the following:

```
namespace ManagedSynergy
{
    using System;
    using System.Collections;
    using System.ComponentModel;
    using System.Data;
    using System.Drawing;
```

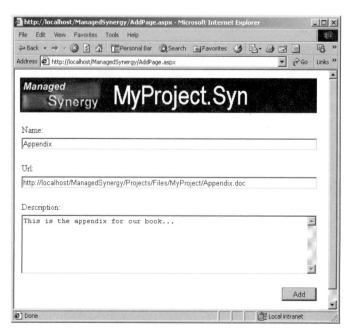

FIGURE 4-4   Add Page for ManagedSynergy.

```csharp
using System.Web;
using System.Web.SessionState;
using System.Web.UI;
using System.Web.UI.WebControls;
using System.Web.UI.HtmlControls;
using System.Runtime.Serialization.Formatters.Binary;
using System.IO;

public class AddForm : System.Web.UI.Page
{
    protected System.Web.UI.WebControls.RequiredFieldValidator
        m_UrlValidator;
    protected System.Web.UI.WebControls.RequiredFieldValidator
        m_NameValidator;
    protected System.Web.UI.WebControls.Label m_ExceptionMessage;
    protected System.Web.UI.WebControls.ValidationSummary
        m_AddItemValidSummary;
    protected System.Web.UI.WebControls.RequiredFieldValidator
        m_DescriptionValidator;
    protected System.Web.UI.WebControls.Button m_AddButton;
    protected System.Web.UI.WebControls.TextBox m_DescriptionTB;
    protected System.Web.UI.WebControls.TextBox m_UrlTB;
    protected System.Web.UI.WebControls.TextBox m_NameTB;
    protected System.Web.UI.WebControls.Label m_ProjectLabel;

    public AddForm()
    {
        Page.Init += new System.EventHandler(Page_Init);
    }

    protected void Page_Load(object sender, EventArgs e)
    {
        if (!IsPostBack)
        {
            // Get the project data stored in the Application object
            Project Proj = (Project)Page.Application.Contents["Project"];
            // Set the project name in the page heading
            m_ProjectLabel.Text = Proj.Name;
        }
    }

    protected void Page_Init(object sender, EventArgs e)
    {
        //
        // CODEGEN: This call is required by the ASP+ Windows Form
        // Designer.
        //
        InitializeComponent();
    }

    /// <summary>
    ///     Required method for Designer support - do not modify
    ///     the contents of this method with the code editor.
```

```
   /// </summary>
   private void InitializeComponent()
   {
      m_AddButton.Click += new System.EventHandler
         (this.AddButton_Click);
      this.Load += new System.EventHandler (this.Page_Load);
   }

   public void AddButton_Click (object sender, System.EventArgs arg)
   {
      // Retrieve project data that was saved in the Application object
      Project Proj = (Project)Page.Application.Contents["Project"];

      try
      {
         // Add this new project item to the project
         Proj.AddItem(m_NameTB.Text, m_UrlTB.Text,
            m_DescriptionTB.Text);

         // Point browser to the project page
         Response.Redirect("ProjectPage.aspx");
      }
      catch (System.Exception e)
      {
         string UserID = (string)Page.Application.Contents["User"];
         string ProjectUrl =
            (string)Page.Application.Contents["ProjectUrl"];

         // Re-load the project data since it may be out of sync
         Project.Load(ref Proj, UserID, ProjectUrl);

         // Display a message on the form informing user about error
         m_ExceptionMessage.Text = e.Message;
      }
   }
}
}
```

The only item we need to discuss in this listing is the AddButton_Click() method. Once the user fills out the form and then clicks the Add button, the AddButton_Click() method is invoked. The first thing that happens is that the project object is retrieved from the application object. The code inside the try block adds the new item to the project and then returns to the project page.

Looking once more in the Project.cs source file reveals the following code from the Project.AddItem() method:

```
public void AddItem(string ItemName, string ItemUrl, string Description)
{
   ManagedSynergy.localhost.Baton Baton = new
   ManagedSynergy.localhost.Baton();
```

```
// Check out the project file so we can add an item
CheckOut();

try
{
    // Create a new item to add to project
    ProjectItem Item = new ProjectItem(this, ItemName, ItemUrl,
    Description, InitialApprovalStatus, "[Initial Check In]", 0);

    // Add item to Baton
    Baton.Add(UserID, this.Name, ItemName);

    // Add the item to project
    m_ProjectItems.Add(Item);

    // Save the project data to the project file (in effect updating it)
    Save();

    // Check in the project file which will point the other users to
    // the project file we just modified. All in all, project file is //
    // not kept locked all that long.
    CheckIn();
}
catch
{
    // Since we were unsuccessful in our attempt to take this action
    // we need to undo the check out we did for the project
    UndoCheckOut();

    // Re-throw so that others can perform exception handling
    throw new Exception("Could not add item to \"" + m_ProjectPath +
        Name + "\". The disk may be full or ...");
}
}
```

After creating the InternetBaton object, this code calls the `Project.CheckOut()` method, which checks out the project file. This step is necessary because adding an item to the project changes the state of the project file, requiring us to first check it out. We then create a new item based on the values passed to the `AddItem()` method. After creating the new item, we add it to InternetBaton using the Web service method `Baton.Add()`. We add the newly created object to the `m_ProjectItems` array, save the project file to its shared location, and then check the project file back in using the `Project.CheckIn()` method.

We need to mention a couple of things. First, we chose the `ArrayList` as the type for the `m_ProjectItems` member of the project class because it acts like an array but has a dynamic quality that allows it to grow as new elements are added. Therefore we got the best qualities of an array without the usual drawback of worrying about whether the array is big enough.

Second, we need to discuss exception handling. The first thing we do is check out the project file, and the last thing we do is check it back in. What if something happens before we are able to check the project file back in? For example, if the disk were full and the Save() method caused an exception, we would skip checking in the project and the other participants would not be able to access the project file because it would still be locked. The try/catch block is used to solve this dilemma. If anything causes an exception after the point at which the project file is checked out, then the catch block will catch the exception and undo the check-out. The catch block also rethrows the exception with an associated specialized message. If we do not rethrow the exception then our catch handler would have totally handled it, and the caller would be unaware of the problem. In this application, the exception rethrow is caught by the presentation code, and a proper message (based on the error message we set) can be shown to the user. Take a look at the AddButton_Click() method in the previous listing to examine the catch handler that would catch the rethrow. This same exception handling pattern is also used in several other project methods.

Deleting a Project Item

When deleting a project item, we assume that the user has already created a project, added items to the project, and now wants to delete an item from the project. To delete an item from a project, the user must select it from the project items list box and select "Delete" on the action bar.

The code for deleting an item is so similar to the code used for adding an item that it would be of little value to repeat here. The only real difference is that the code deletes an item instead of adding it. You can find the source to both AddPage.cs and DeletePage.cs on this book's Web site if you would like to compare these files for yourself.

Checking out an Item

When checking out an item, we assume that the user has already created a project, added items to the project, and now wants to check out an item so that it can be modified. To check an item out, users must first select it from the project items list box and then select "Check Out" on the action bar. After users confirm that they want to check the item out, the ProjectItem.CheckOut() method is called:

```
public void CheckOut()
{
    ManagedSynergy.localhost.Baton Baton = new
    ManagedSynergy.localhost.Baton();

    // We need to check out the project file before we change its
    // state by checking out a project item
    m_Project.CheckOut();
```

```
try
{
   // Make this item reflect a checked out state
   ReflectCheckedOutState();

   // Save the project data to the project file (in effect updating it)
   m_Project.Save();

   // Check out the project item
   Baton.CheckOut(m_Project.UserID, m_Project.Name, this.Name);

   // Check in the project file
   m_Project.CheckIn();
}
catch
{
   // Since we were unsuccessful in our attempt to take this action
   // we need to undo the check out we did for the project
   m_Project.UndoCheckOut();

   // Re-throw so that others can perform exception handling
   throw new Exception("Could not check item out of \"" +
   m_Project.ProjectPath + Name +
      "\". The disk may be full or the project file has be deleted.");
}
}
```

Keep in mind that this method is part of the `ProjectItem` class, and in a sense it is the item attempting to check itself out. Once again, the code begins with the obligatory checking out of the project file. Checking out a file changes the state of a project item to reflect the fact that it is being revised and does not yet have a check-in comment. These changes are encapsulated in the `ProjectItem.ReflectCheckedOutState()` method:

```
private void ReflectCheckedOutState()
{
   // Checking out a file always puts it in the "in Revision" state
   m_AStatus = ApprovalStatus.InRevision;

   // Reset check in comments and set it to "To Be Determined"
   m_CheckInComment = "[TBD]";
}
```

Once the state has been updated, the project object is saved to disk, after which the check-out request is made to InternetBaton. If all this goes well, the last thing to do is check the project file back in.

During the design of this method, we had to consider the possibility that the desired file may have already been checked out by someone else. If it has, the checkout fails and causes an exception that takes us back to the check-out form, where the error is reported. The problem is that the state of the project will have already been written out to disk. Our solution to this dilemma was to have the exception handler that reports the error also roll back the project file by reloading it from InternetBaton using deserialization over the Internet. The code in the ConfirmCheckOut.aspx file looks like the following:

```csharp
public void OKButton_Click (object sender, System.EventArgs arg)
{
    // Retrieve project that was saved in the Application object
    Project Proj = (Project)Page.Application.Contents["Project"];
    // Get the project item that corresponds to index pass to this page
    ProjectItem Item = (ProjectItem)Proj.ProjectItems[s_ItemIndex];

    try
    {
        // Check out the specified item
        Item.CheckOut();

        // Point browser to the project page
        Response.Redirect("ProjectPage.aspx");
    }
    catch (System.Exception e)
    {
        string UserID = (string)Page.Application.Contents["User"];
        string ProjectUrl = (string)Page.Application.Contents[
                          "ProjectUrl"];

        // Re-load the project data since it may have become out of sync
        Project.Load(ref Proj, UserID, ProjectUrl);

        m_ExceptionMessage.Text = e.Message;
    }
}
```

As you can see, the `catch` block first reloads the project object and then displays an error message that explains what happened.

Viewing a Project Item

When viewing a project item, we assume that the user has already created a project, added items to the project, and now wants to view an item's contents. To view an item from a project, the user must select it from the project items list box and then select "View" on the action bar. After a user requests to view an item, the browser points to the URL associated with the item.

When we thought about how a user could download documents to work on them, we decided that it could be accomplished by selecting the Save As option in the browser. Having first checked out an item, the user could view the item and then choose the Save As option to save the document to a personal work directory. The idea is that this file in the user's work directory is the one that would later be checked back in. As we find out in the next scenario, the check-in process causes the file to be copied to the shared project directory and makes the changes public when Internet-Baton is notified of the check-in.

The following is the code behind the "View" callback:

```
public void ViewButton_Click (object sender, System.EventArgs e)
{
    if (m_ProjectListBox.SelectedIndex >= 0)
    {
        // Get the project data and the selected project item
        Project Proj = (Project)Page.Application.Contents["Project"];
        ProjectItem ProjItem = (ProjectItem)Proj.ProjectItems[
                            m_ProjectListBox.SelectedIndex];

        // Point browser to the shared project item. This is not to be
        // confused with a local version of the same file, if one even
        // exists. This will view the most current version of this
        // file on whichever machine is currently holding it.
        Response.Redirect(ProjItem.ItemUrl);
    }
    else
        // Complain to user
        m_DetailCWC.Text =
            "You must select a project item before you try to view it";
}
```

This code begins by ensuring that an item has been selected before retrieving the project data. Using the index from the list (which corresponds to the index of the correct item in the project's item array), the selected item is retrieved. At this point, we simply use the `ItemUrl` property to point the browser to the item in question. We merely pass it as the argument to the `Response.Redirect()` method.

Checking in an Item

When checking in an item, we assume that the user has previously checked out a project item and now wants to check that item back in. To check in an item, the user first selects it from the project items list box and then selects "Check In" on the action bar. The screen shot in Figure 4-5 shows the check-in page. To check an item in, the user needs to specify the local file that contains the author's changes and enter a brief comment explaining the changes that were made. The file being checked back in is the same one that was downloaded using the Save As option in the check-out scenario and has presumably been modified in some way. When a file is checked back in, one of the behind–the-scenes activities involves publishing the new version of the document by copying it to a standard shared location that is a subdirectory in the application's virtual root.

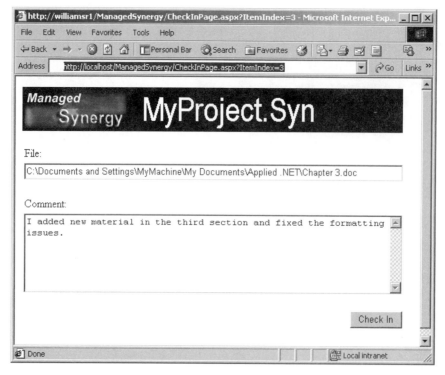

FIGURE 4-5   Check-In Page for ManagedSynergy.

The code behind this page fits the same pattern we covered previously when discussing similar types of requests. Once the user selects "Check In" from the action bar, the `ProjectItem.CheckIn()` method is called:

```
// Checks in project item
public void CheckIn(string LocalPath, string CheckInComment)
{
   ManagedSynergy.localhost.Baton Baton = new
   ManagedSynergy.localhost.Baton();

   // We need to check out the project file before we change its
   // state by checking in a project item
   m_Project.CheckOut();

   try
   {
      // Make this item reflect a checked in state
      ReflectCheckedInState(CheckInComment);

      // Save the project data to the project file (in effect updating it)
      m_Project.Save();
```

```
        // Publish the local item in the project directory in its shared
        // location
        Publish(LocalPath);

        // Check in the project item
        Baton.CheckIn(m_Project.UserID, m_Project.Name, this.Name);

        // Check in the project file
        m_Project.CheckIn();
    }
    catch
    {
        // Since we were unsuccessful in our attempt to take this action
        // we need to undo the check out we did for the project
        m_Project.UndoCheckOut();

        // Re-throw so that others can perform exception handling
        throw new Exception("Could not check item in to \"" +
        m_Project.ProjectPath + Name + "\". The disk may be full or the
        project file has been deleted or is read-only.");
    }
}
```

Two aspects of this method that need to be discussed are `ReflectCheckedIn-State()` and `Publish()`. Checking in a file changes the state of a project item in various ways. These changes are encapsulated in the `ProjectItem.ReflectChecked InState()` method, which contains the following lines of code:

```
private void ReflectCheckedInState(string CheckInComment)
{
    // Set the initial approval status for items in this project
    m_AStatus = m_Project.InitialApprovalStatus;

    // Reset the number of reviews for this change
    m_NumberOfReviews = 0;

    // Record the check in comments that the author made
    m_CheckInComment = CheckInComment;

    // Get rid of reviews from last document revision and start freah
    // with this new change
    m_ReviewItems.Clear();
}
```

Checking in an item requires that the approval status be reset to an initial approval status. This initial approval status is different depending on whether there are reviewers involved. For example, if there are no reviewers, then the status is automatically "Approved." On the other hand, if there are reviewers involved, then the status is "In Review." All of this is taken care of in the `ProjectItem.Initial ApprovalStatus` property. This is an example in which a property is not actually the value of a member variable but instead is a calculated value. You would never know it by looking at the line of code that sets the status though.

The other steps that need to be followed to properly set the state on a checked-in item are resetting the number of reviews to zero, assigning the check-in comment, and clearing out all the old reviews.

We mentioned that publishing a change to a project item requires it to be copied to its shared directory. The following code shows how the `ProjectItem.Publish()` method accomplishes this task:

```
private void Publish(string LocalItemPath)
{
    try
    {
        // If necessary, create the shared directory to hold project files
        if (!Directory.Exists(m_Project.ProjectItemsPath))
           Directory.CreateDirectory(m_Project.ProjectItemsPath);

        // Copy file to its shared location
        File.Copy(LocalItemPath, m_Project.ProjectItemsPath + "\\"
           + Name, true);
    }
    catch
    {
        // Specialize the exception and re-throw it
        throw new Exception("\"" + LocalItemPath + "\" could not be published
        to the following shared location: \"" + m_Project.ProjectItemsPath +
        "\". Make sure the file path you specified above is correct and the
        disk is not full and that you have the correct permissions.");
    }
}
```

This code uses the project name to create a directory, if one does not exist, in the shared directory (which is in the virtual root of this application). This shared directory was revealed to InternetBaton when we first added the item. The static `File.Copy()` method is used to actually copy the file.

Reviewing an Item

When reviewing an item, we assume that the user has already created a project, added items to that project, and made changes to an item—and now a reviewer wants to submit a review of those changes. To submit a review, the user must first select the item from the project items list box and then select "Review" on the action bar. The screen shot in Figure 4-6 shows the review page. Reviewing an item involves entering a brief review that is based on the reviewer's assessment of the most recent changes. The reviewer specifies a good or bad verdict using the dropdown control on the form.

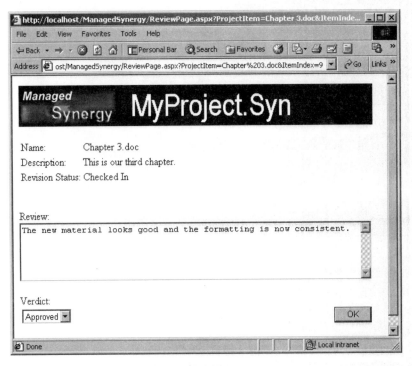

FIGURE 4-6   Review Page for ManagedSynergy.

The code behind this page is found in the ReviewPage.aspx file. It is so similar to patterns we have already discussed that reviewing this code would not broaden your understanding of applied .NET. Therefore we have included the code without any discussion.

When the user clicks the OK button, the following code is invoked:

```
public void OKButton_Click (object sender, System.EventArgs arg)
{
    // Get the user name that was stored in the Application object
    string User = (string)Page.Application.Contents["User"];
    ApprovalStatus Verdict;
    // Get the project data that was stored in the Application object
    Project Proj = (Project)Page.Application.Contents["Project"];

    try
    {
        // Record the verdict of the review
        if (m_VerdictDDL.SelectedItem.Text ==
            EnumToString.AStatusToString(ApprovalStatus.Approved))
            Verdict = ApprovalStatus.Approved;
        else
```

```
            Verdict = ApprovalStatus.Revise;

        ReviewItem Review = new ReviewItem(User, m_ReviewTB.Text, Verdict);

        // Add the review to the project
        s_ProjectItem.AddReview(Review);

        // Point your browser to the project page
        Response.Redirect("ProjectPage.aspx");
    }
    catch (System.Exception e)
    {
        string UserID = (string)Page.Application.Contents["User"];
        string ProjectUrl = (string)Page.Application.Contents["ProjectUrl"];

        // Re-load the project data since it may have become out of sync
        Project.Load(ref Proj, UserID, ProjectUrl);

        // Display a message on the form that informs the user about error
        m_ExceptionMessage.Text = e.Message;
    }
}
```

The code that submits the review looks like the following:

```
public void AddReview(ReviewItem Review)
{
    // We need to check out the project file before we change its
    // state by adding a review for this item
    m_Project.CheckOut();

    try
    {
        // Add review to the review item object array
        m_ReviewItems.Add(Review);

        // Account for addition of review
        m_NumberOfReviews++;

        // Determine the approval status of this item.
        DetermineApprovalStatus();

        // Save the project data to the project file (in effect updating it)
        m_Project.Save();

        // Check in the project file
        m_Project.CheckIn();
    }
    catch
    {
        // Since we were unsuccessful in our attempt to take this action
        // we need to undo the check out we did for the project
        m_Project.UndoCheckOut();
```

```
        // Re-throw so that others can perform exception handling
        throw new Exception("Could not add a review ... ");
    }
}
```

Viewing an Item's Properties

When viewing an item's properties, we assume that the user has already created a project, added items to that project, and now wants to see the various properties for an item. To view an item's properties, the user must first select it from the project items list box and then select "Properties" on the action bar. The screen shot in Figure 4-7 shows the properties page. The properties for an item are shown to the right of the project items list box.

When implementing this function, we decided that a custom control would work quite nicely for displaying an item's properties. We needed the ability to dynamically create HTML so that each request to display an item's properties could be uniquely handled. This was especially important because the number of reviews is arbitrary. The code behind this form is as follows:

```
public void PropertiesButton_Click (object sender, System.EventArgs e)
{
```

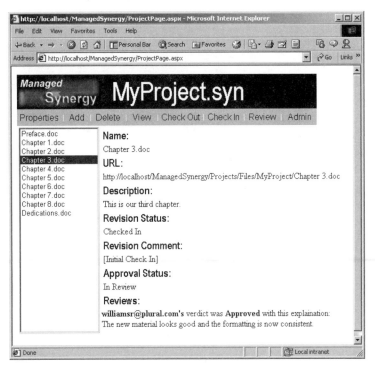

FIGURE 4-7   Properties Page for ManagedSynergy.

```
    ManagedSynergy.localhost.Baton Baton = new
    ManagedSynergy.localhost.Baton();
    string DetailFormat = "<table><tr><td><b  style=\"FONT-SIZE: 14pt;
FONT-FAMILY: 'Arial
Narrow'\">Name:</b></td></tr><tr><td>{0}</td></tr><tr><td><b  style=\"FONT-
SIZE: 14pt; FONT-FAMILY: 'Arial Narrow'\">URL:</b></td></tr><tr><td>{1}
</td></tr><tr><td><b  style=\"FONT-SIZE: 14pt; FONT-FAMILY: 'Arial
Narrow'\">Description:</b></td></tr><tr><td>{2}</td></tr><tr><td><b  style=
\"FONT-SIZE: 14pt; FONT-FAMILY: 'Arial Narrow'\">Revision Status:</b>
</td></tr><tr><td>{3}</td></tr><tr><td><b  style=\"FONT-SIZE: 14pt; FONT-
FAMILY: 'Arial Narrow'\">Revision Comment:</b></td></tr><tr><td>{4}</td>
</tr><tr><td><b  style=\"FONT-SIZE: 14pt; FONT-FAMILY: 'Arial Narrow'
\">Approval Status:</b></td></tr><tr><td>{5}</td></tr><tr><td><b  style=
\"FONT-SIZE: 14pt; FONT-FAMILY: 'Arial Narrow'\">Reviews:</b></td></tr>
</table>";
    string Detail;

    if (m_ProjectListBox.SelectedIndex >= 0)
    {
    // Get the user name that was stored in the Application object
    string User = (string)Page.Application.Contents["User"];
    // Get the project data and the selected project item
    Project Proj = (Project)Page.Application.Contents["Project"];
    ProjectItem ProjItem =
        (ProjectItem)Proj.ProjectItems[m_ProjectListBox.SelectedIndex];
    RevisionStatus RStatus = (Baton.IsCheckedIn(User, Proj.Name,
        ProjItem.Name)) ? RevisionStatus.CheckedIn :
        RevisionStatus.CheckedOut;

// Load up the objects that will provide the values for the
format string object[] FormatArgs =
    {ProjItem.Name,ProjItem.ItemUrl,ProjItem.Description,EnumToString.
    RStatusToString(RStatus),ProjItem.CheckInComment,EnumToString.AStatusTo
    String(ProjItem.AStatus)};

        // Create the dynamic property details for this item
        Detail = String.Format(DetailFormat, FormatArgs);

        // Add the item reviews to the end of the details string
        for each (ReviewItem R in ProjItem.ReviewItems)
            Detail += "<b>" + R.Reviewer + "'s</b> verdict was <b>" +
                EnumToString.AStatusToString(R.Verdict) + "</b> with this
                explaination:<br>" + R.Review + "<br><br>";

        // Assign the property details to our custom control so it can
        // be rendered.
        m_DetailCWC.Text = Detail;
    }
    else
        // Complain to user
        m_DetailCWC.Text = "You must select a project ... ";
}
```

This code uses string formatting to fill in the placeholders that were placed in the properties HTML. The placeholders are the {N} elements found in the HTML, where N is the number corresponding to the formatting argument that is to be substituted (much like a printf() statement in C or C++). Once the placeholders have been filled in, then the reviews are appended to the HTML string we are building by looping through all the reviews and adding them one at a time. Finally, we take the resulting HTML string and assign it to the Text property of the custom control we created.

The following is the complete implementation of the custom control:

```
[DefaultProperty("Text"),
    ShowInToolbox(true),
    ToolboxData("<{0}:ItemDetail runat=server></{0}:ItemDetail>")]
public class ItemDetail : System.Web.UI.WebControls.WebControl
{
    private string text;

    [Bindable(true),
        Category("Appearance"),
        DefaultValue(""),
        Persistable(PersistableSupport.Declarative)]
    public string Text
    {
        get
        {
            return text;
        }

        set
        {
            text = value;
        }
    }

    protected override void Render(HtmlTextWriter output)
    {
        output.Write(Text);
    }
}
```

That is all there is to implementing a custom control. We added the Text property to make it easy for clients to associate the HTML they want to be displayed as the value of this control, but the only real requirement is that you have a Render() method with the right signature. This method is called, and it does whatever it needs to with the HtmlTextWriter argument. In our case, we just wrote out the Text property we were given.

The other aspect to this custom control is how to use it in HTML. The following is a snippet from the PropertyPage.aspx file.

```
<%@ Register TagPrefix="AC4" NameSpace="ManagedSynergy"
Assembly="ManagedSynergy" %>
[Other unrelated HTML omitted...]
<AC4:ITEMDETAIL id=m_DetailCWC runat="server"></AC4:ITEMDETAIL>
```

As you can see, the formatting for custom control is exactly like the formatting for any standard server-side control. You specify a tag prefix followed by the class name and an ID.

Invoking Administration Services

When invoking administration services, we assume that the user has already created a project and wants to perform some InternetBaton administration activities, such as adding a user to the project. The user merely selects "Admin" on the action bar, which causes the browser to point to the InternetBaton application. The code for this task is simple:

```
public void AdminButton_Click (object sender, System.EventArgs e)
{
    // Point browser to the Baton Web site for any admin tasks
    // like adding users, creating projects, etc.
        Response.Redirect("http://www.InternetBaton.com/AdminPage.aspx");
}
```

Dynamic Status Updates and Overnight Project Replication

As we mentioned previously, ManagedSynergy exposes Web services in addition to its application functionality. These Web services allow the state of the project to be dynamically updated, as well as allow off-hours project synchronization. As was mentioned in Chapter 2 regarding dynamic status updates, InternetBaton calls on the Web service method `VersionChanged()`; it is up to the Web service to reconcile itself with the new state of the project. For off-hours project synchronization, InternetBaton calls the Web service method `DownloadProjectItems()`, and it is up to the Web service to download each of the items in the project. Following is a look at the `VersionChanged()` Web service method:

```
[WebMethod]
public void VersionChanged(string ProjectID, string BatonID)
{
    string UserID = (string)Application.Contents["User"];
    Project Proj = new Project();

    // Reload project object since something has changed
    Project.Load(ref Proj, UserID, Proj.ProjectUrl);

    // Overwrite old copy with updated project object
    Application.Contents["Project"] = Proj;
}
```

Because Web services were introduced in Chapter 2, we do not elaborate on them here other than to follow up on a Chapter 3 topic. In that chapter, we discussed the fact that the C# language supports the concept of attributes as a means to express declarative information. The [WebMethod] attribute is a good example of how beneficial attributes can be. This attribute makes it possible to create the right kind of "plumbing" to properly use the method as a Web service. Chapter 2 also explained another use of attributes when it demonstrated how easy it is to implement asynchronous Web service calls with the addition of the [SoapMethod(OneWay = true)] attribute. Attributes will surely play a significant role in .NET development as a declarative way of having significant service provided for you.

The code for the VersionChanged() method leverages an application primitive we have already discussed—the Project.Load() method. Using the Load() method in this context causes the current state of the project file to be loaded into a project object, which then overwrites the outdated object.

The DownloadProjectItems() Web service method is merely a pass-through to Project.DownloadProjectItems(), the method that does the real work.

```
[WebMethod]
public void DownloadProjectItems(string ProjectID, string EmailUserID)
{
    // Download entire project
    Project.DownloadProectItems(ProjectID, EmailUserID);
}
```

The Project.DownloadProjectItems() looks like this:

```
public static void DownloadProjectItems(string ProjectID, string
EmailUserID)
{
    Project Proj = new Project();
    Project.Load(ref Proj, EmailUserID, ProjectID);
    foreach(ProjectItem Item in Proj.ProjectItems)
        Item.Download();
}
```

Once again we see another method making use of Project.Load() to initialize a project object with the most current project state. Previously we mentioned that one of the benefits of the approach we took with the project class was that the methods could be cleanly called; the equivalent functionality was not redundantly coded "inline." This was clearly the case with the Load() method, which confirms the wisdom of our design choice.

Let's get back to the DownloadProjectItems() method. Once the project is loaded, the code loops through each of the project items and asks each one to download itself by calling the ProjectItem.Download() method that follows:

```csharp
public void Download()
{
    WebRequest Request;
    FileStream LocalFile = null;
    Stream ItemStream = null;
    int BufferSize = 1024;
    Byte[] Buffer = new Byte[BufferSize];
    int BytesRead;

    try
    {
        // Request HTTP access to project item
        Request = WebRequest.Create(m_ItemUrl);

        // If necessary, create the shared directory to hold project files
        if (!Directory.Exists(m_Project.ProjectItemsPath))
            Directory.CreateDirectory(m_Project.ProjectItemsPath);

        // Get the Web-based stream so we can download the file
        ItemStream = Request.GetResponse().GetResponseStream();
        // Create local file that will hold downloaded project item
        LocalFile = new FileStream(m_Project.ProjectItemsPath + "\\"
            + m_Name, FileMode.Create, FileAccess.Write);

        // Read from download file and write to local file until copied
        BytesRead = ItemStream.Read(Buffer, 0, BufferSize);
        while (BytesRead != 0)
        {
            LocalFile.Write(Buffer,0,BytesRead);
            BytesRead = ItemStream.Read(Buffer, 0, BufferSize);
        }
    }
    finally
    {
        // Close these streams no matter how the thread of control
        // leaves this method
        if (ItemStream != null)
            ItemStream.Close();

        if (LocalFile != null)
        {
            // Flush any remaining data to disk
            LocalFile.Flush();
            LocalFile.Close();
        }
    }
}
```

This code is similar to the code used to load the project over the Internet. We use the WebRequest class to create a stream that can be used to access the contents of project items. After creating a directory to hold the downloaded items, a File stream is used to open a local file in write mode so that the contents of the project item can be copied. To copy the project item, the code simply reads from the downloaded stream and writes to the local stream until the entire file has been copied. We have used the `finally` construct because the file handles used by these streams need to be freed, no matter how this method is exited. Even if the code in the `try` block throws an exception, the code in the `finally` block is still executed.

CONCLUSION

In this chapter, we have taken a look at a people-oriented application and how Microsoft's .NET technology can be applied to the problem of decentralized collaboration that requires simple approval workflow. We showed once again how People-Types can be an effective way to focus our attention on design and implementation so that the three key principles of Internet development are effectively addressed. Discussing the application provided an opportunity to see the following .NET technology in action:

- Web services
- Server-side controls and events
- Field validation
- ASP .NET custom controls
- Object serialization
- .NET's Internet classes
- Various CLR classes
- .NET exception handling

ManagedSynergy is an excellent example of what we can accomplish using this new style of Web development. When you think of how we have leveraged the powers of abstraction in the past with object-oriented designs, and then you think about the new levels of abstraction that are possible with the CLR and Web services, it is easy to get truly excited about the future of software development. In fact, if you have not yet had the urge to tell complete strangers, regardless of their computer knowledge, about how cool all this is, chances are that you will.

Chapter

5

The Common Language Runtime

The first chapters of this book discussed the new territory being entered by software today. Over the years, we experienced massive changes in the computing world as its focus shifted from mainframes to client-server computing to three-tier and multitier computing. The mid 1990s were characterized by the huge boom in Internet development, with advancements on both the Web server and the Web client sides. Today, we stand at the forefront of a new wave in computing: people-oriented software.

As introduced in the first chapter, three principles characterize the people-oriented software movement: universalization, translation, and collaboration. The entire history of software development (especially within the last decade) has incorporated hints of each of the characteristics. For example, Sun Microsystems took a stab at incorporating *universalization* with the development of Java. The mantra of the typical Java developer during the mid 1990s was "write once—run anywhere." The idea was for operating system platforms supporting Java to be able to run a standard Virtual Machine (VM). Java source code would be translated into byte codes, shipped to a machine, and then run through the Java VM.

The people-oriented software principle of *translation* involves translating functionality between a variety of platforms and between diverse service description contracts. Although different platforms supported different distribution models (most notably the distributed component object model [DCOM] from Microsoft and Common Object Request Broker Architecture [CORBA]), many enterprise shops wanted to be able to bridge the two. Bridge products between DCOM and CORBA offered a translation of functionality between the object models.

Finally, examples of *collaboration* exist within systems such as the Microsoft transaction server (MTS), in which several singular components collaborate within a transaction to produce a result for the client.

Although we can cite examples of each of these principles in practice within the software industry, never before have they all worked together in a unified manner. The Microsoft .NET platform represents a formal embodiment of these principles.

Within the world of .NET, the common language runtime (CLR) is going to play a huge part in the universalization aspect of people-oriented software. This chapter covers the CLR, the problems it solves, and how it works. We start by discussing the evolution of components within Windows and identifying some of the problems solved by each step in the evolution of its component architecture: static libraries, dynamic linking, and the component object model (COM). It turns out that each evolutionary step introduced some new issues as well. We address those issues, as well as how the .NET CLR manages to solve them. In the process, we discuss the Common Type System (CTS), .NET's deployment mechanism, and the system library provided by the runtime.

PEOPLE-ORIENTED TRIVIA

Although the term *people oriented* has been presented in this book as a new term for describing Internet software, it actually dates back to 1997. The earliest submission of the new term to describe Internet software and the justification for choosing it is summarized as follows:

> This term should include the concepts of structured programming, object-oriented programming, and distributed computing but also capture what is particular about the Internet. The definition should be rooted in the new radical use of computers being applied to the Internet. If communication is the hallmark of this new era, why not describe the new paradigm as communication-oriented programming? This has two defects. First, communication is an action, and object-oriented programming has already demonstrated that it is more natural to develop software based on objects than procedures. Second, the essence of the Internet is more than communication; it is oriented to many different aspects of human life: education, financial transactions, entertainment, and cultural expression. The term people-oriented programming aptly describes what the Internet offers, and it is descriptive of the paradigm shift to transform a computing device into a spectacular interactive medium . . . It is helpful when the definition of something points to the purpose of that thing. The term people-oriented programming alludes to the purpose of Internet software development. We started this chapter by asking what the purpose of software is. The

> answer is somewhat elusive, as software is an artificial entity that has no end in itself. Unlike natural things, software has no inner laws or innate tendency to become anything. It is purely a tool for our human ends and therefore will be oriented towards what people choose for it. Ordinary non-technical people will be the predominate users of the Internet, and most of the software developed for this medium will be directed to theirs needs. (Sorensen, 1997)[1]

WINDOWS AND COMPONENTS

One of the most important evolutionary steps within software development has been the enabling of component architectures. The idea behind component-based software is simple. It's hard to get *everything* in a single program right at once. Therefore instead of trying to nail everything down simultaneously, component-based architectures enable dynamic composition and evolution of software, allowing you to isolate the pieces and making it much easier to debug and manage the application as a whole.

This section details the evolution of components within the history of PC software. Exploring the evolution of PC software helps set the stage for examining .NET's CLR. Then we take an in-depth look at the .NET runtime—the heart of the .NET platform.

Static Libraries

If you step back in time to the early 1980s, you may remember that most software applications were deployed as single executable programs. This was especially true for DOS applications. Lotus 1-2-3, WordPerfect, and dBASE III are all great examples of the monolithic architectures common to the era. In those days, if you wanted to share code among applications, the only way to do that was to write some procedures and gather them into a library.

Static linking serves as a great beginning for breaking applications into smaller chunks from a source code perspective. Unfortunately, the finished product of the static linking process is still a single executable application, which introduces a couple of interesting issues.

To get a good picture of the issues involved in static linking, imagine inventing some piece of software so compelling that a huge contingent of software developers wants to use it. To deploy your library, you make your software available as either some source code or a binary file that client application developers can link into their

---

[1] Sorensen, R., "The Internet Challenge," 1997. Used with permission.

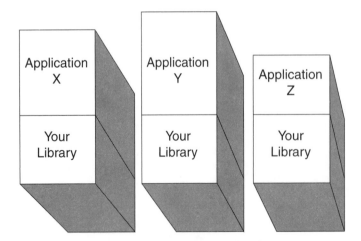

FIGURE 5-1   Your Library Statically Linked to Several Client Applications.

own applications. In either case, the library code is glued onto the end of the client application. Figure 5-1 shows your library statically linked to several client applications.

The first issue with static linking is that linking large libraries to client applications tends to bloat applications, chewing up valuable disk space and runtime memory. This may not be as much of an issue these days, as the price of disks continues to plummet. However, runtime memory is still at a premium these days, and any ways to help conserve memory at runtime are always welcome. The second more insidious issue is the fact that if a library has a bug, gluing it to the client application forces the entire application to be rebuilt and redeployed to fix the bug. The way around these issues is through dynamic linking.

Dynamic Link Libraries

Windows (and earlier OS/2) introduced dynamic linking to the PC software arena. Rather than gluing an entire library onto the end of a client application (as static linking does), dynamic linking uses a single copy of a library available on disk. That library is loaded on demand at runtime by the client applications. If there is already a copy of the library loaded, Windows simply maps the code pages into the client's memory space. At any rate, only one copy of the dynamic link library (DLL) remains loaded at runtime. Figure 5-2 shows your library dynamically linked to several client applications.

DLLs are simply binary files containing loadable, executable code (and perhaps some Windows resources such as icons or cursors). DLLs export their entry points via an export table included as part of the DLL header. With static linking, client appli-

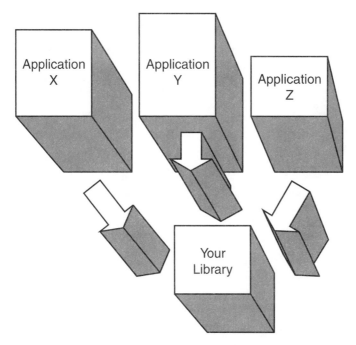

FIGURE 5-2 Your Library Dynamically Linked to Several Client Applications.

cations and libraries depend on the compiler and linker to resolve the function addresses between the client application and the library during the link step of the compiling process. With dynamic linking, clients defer resolving the library addresses until load time (or even later—until runtime). Windows supports two forms of dynamic linking: implicit linking and explicit linking.

Implicit Linking

One of the byproducts of building a DLL is a small binary file named the *import library*. For example, if you build a library named `yourlib.dll` and explicitly export one or more functions (using either a module definition file or the `__declspec (dllexport)` compiler special declaration), a file named `yourlib.lib` will emerge from the build process. This file (`yourlib.lib`) is the import library corresponding to `yourlib.dll`.

Client applications use the import library in much the same way they would use a statically linked library file. However, whereas a statically linked library contains both the actual library code and information required by the linker to resolve the addresses in the library, an import library contains only the information required by the linker to resolve library addresses—a table including a list of the functions exported by the DLL. The DLL contains the executable code and a table of function

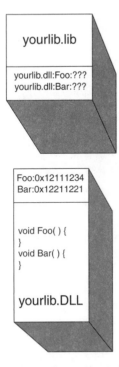

yourlib.lib

yourlib.dll:Foo:???
yourlib.dll:Bar:???

Foo:0x12111234
Bar:0x12211221

void Foo( ) {
}
void Bar( ) {
}

yourlib.DLL

FIGURE 5-3   The Relationship between a DLL and Its Import Library.

name/address pairs. Figure 5-3 shows the relationship between a DLL and its import library.

Notice that `yourlib.dll` contains the executable code and a table listing the entry points and the address of each function within the DLL. The file `yourlib.lib` includes simply a table listing the entry points of `yourlib.dll` and a blank space to hold the address of the function.

The primary job of an import library is to make the linker happy. During linking, the linker only wants to know that a function is available. When linking to a static library, the linker looks at information within the library and fixes up the address at link time. Of course, the linker is actually gluing a copy of the static library to the end of the application at the same time. An import library is kind of like a promissory note. It promises that the function will be available in the *future*. When linking to an import library, the linker looks at the export table within the library and inserts a little bit of fix-up code for each function exported by the DLL. When the client application finally runs, the first code that is executed by the application is the set of address fix-ups stipulated by the import DLL. Figure 5-4 shows several client applications implicitly linking to your library.

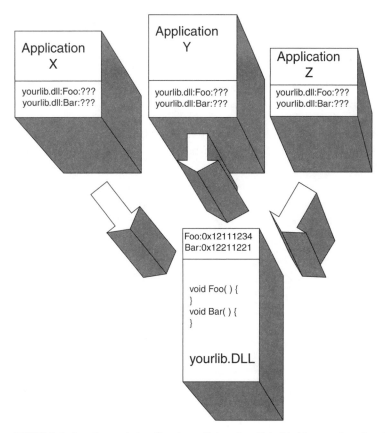

FIGURE 5-4 Several Applications Using Implicit Linking to Resolve Addresses.

Notice that Application X, Application Y, and Application Z all have import libraries attached to them. The address slots in the client applications are filled up at runtime when the client applications begin executing.

The upside to implicit linking is that it is extremely convenient. From the developer's point of view, using an import library is no different than using a statically linked library. The resulting executable code shrinks dramatically in size (because the linker is not adding a copy of the entire library to the application). In addition, resource consumption is greatly reduced because only one copy of the library remains loaded in memory at runtime.

The downside of implicit linking is twofold. First, the resulting application takes a little longer to load as the startup code executes the address fix-ups into the DLL. The second (and more serious) downside to implicit linking is that the resulting application expects the entire functionality described by the import library to be available. If the DLL is missing from the executable path or one of the entry points is missing from the DLL itself, the entire application stops loading and Windows displays a very rude and hard-to-read error message. The alternative to implicit linking used to fix this issue is explicit linking.

Explicit Linking

With explicit linking, the burden of fixing up addresses is on the client developer. Rather than tacking an import library onto the end of an application, resulting in the linker adding code to fix up the addresses, explicit linking involves resolving the individual entry point addresses by explicitly calling functions within the Win32 application program interface (API). The functions required to manage DLLs by hand include LoadLibrary, FreeLibrary, and GetProcAddress. The following listing shows the Win32 API for loading a DLL:

```
HINSTANCE LoadLibrary(LPCTSTR szFileName);
BOOL      FreeLibrary(HINSTANCE hinstDLL);
FARPROC GetProcAddress( HMODULE hinstDLL,
                        LPCSTR szSymbolName );
```

Loading a library and resolving the addresses within are fairly straightforward. You just call LoadLibrary to get a handle to the loaded library, call GetProcAddress to find the address of the function you want to call, and finally free the library when you are done with it. FreeLibrary decrements the reference count on the library, sweeping it from memory if there are no more references to it. The following shows explicitly loading yourlib.dll and calling the function Foo within the library:

```
typedef int (WINAPI * PFNFOO)();
void CallFoo()
{
  HINSTANCE hInst;
  hInst = LoadLibrary(__TEXT("yourlib.dll"));
  if( hInst ) {
    PFNFOO pfnFoo;
    PfnFoo = (PFNFOO)GetProcAddress(hInst, "Foo");
    if (pfnFoo) {
      pfnFoo();
    }
    FreeLibrary(hInst);
  }
}
```

The only thing that may strike you as odd about this code is the typedef preceding the function CallFoo. Addresses coming back from GetProcAddress are of type FARPROC—they do not have any shape to them. The typedef gives shape to the address coming back from GetProcAddress so that the compiler knows how to set up the stack before jumping the address in the DLL. The rest of the code simply

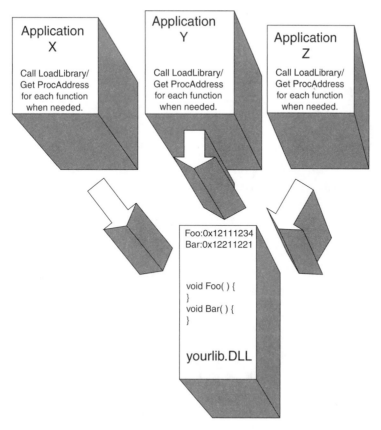

FIGURE 5-5 Several Client Applications Linking to `yourlib.dll`.

loads the DLL, finds the address of the symbol Foo, and jumps to that function. Figure 5-5 shows several client applications explicitly linking to `yourlib.dll`.

The upside to explicit linking is the amount of control you get. Notice that Foo is only called when the DLL loads successfully *and* the symbol is found. Remember that with implicit linking, *all* imported functions have to be resolved before the application will even finish loading. If any DLLs are missing from the path or any of the entry points are missing, Windows displays an unfriendly message and halts the loading process. Explicitly linking the DLL affords greater control—an application encountering a missing symbol can degrade gracefully rather than refusing to load at all. In addition to catching missing entry points, explicitly loading the DLL lets the client application choose the path of the DLL rather than rely on the system execution path to pick the DLL.

Of course, the downside to explicit linking is the coding overhead involved. The client code has to acquire each entry point—that is a lot of code for the developer to write.

Upsides and Downsides

The advantage of using DLLs is that they help enable component development. Just pack the functionality you want to share between applications into a DLL, and clients are able to link to the DLL at loadtime/runtime. This reduces resource consumption and allows components to be updated in the field . . . in theory, that is.

One of the main problems with plain-vanilla DLLs is simply getting everybody to agree on the shape of the boundary between the client and the DLL—that is, the function signatures of the exported functions. When the set of exported DLL functions is fairly stable or atomic deployment of your entire system is an option (or both), DLLs in and of themselves work great. (Most of Windows itself is several atomically deployed DLLs—USER32.DLL, GDI32.dll, KERNEL32.dll, and so on. And the function signatures remain stable.)

Regardless, when you want to fix your system by slipping in a new DLL, both the client and the object need to agree on the names *and* signatures of the functions. This information is usually included as part of a C header file—nowhere else. Obviously, managing DLLs is a bit trickier when clients and DLLs link implicitly (because of the all-or-nothing nature of implicit linking). However, the versioning problem is still present. If a DLL decides to change the signature of a function (by adding a parameter, for example) and the client application is not recompiled, the client application will probably face an untimely death. Another scenario is that an older version of a popular library may be copied over a newer one, resulting in some sort of function mismatch between the client and the DLL.

The bottom line is that one of the most important means of developing software these days is by dynamically composing it, and DLLs by themselves will not cut it. Clients and DLLs need to agree on what the stack frame looks like at the boundary between the client and the DLL, and there is no formal way to manage these boundary crossings with raw DLLs and entry points. That is, the notion of *typing* is absent from the DLL loading process. This is one of the reasons behind using COM—the component object model.

COM Tries to Fix It

This is how life works: Once you solve a problem, life thumbs its nose at you and lobs a bigger problem at you. If you have been living in the Microsoft world, you have probably spent the last seven or eight years working to understand COM—for many of us, learning COM was a bigger hurdle than learning C++.

DLLs provide a wonderful means of loading executable code and resources on demand. DLLs bring with them the promise of dynamically composeable software. The idea is that you can have a very small core application and swap parts (component DLLs) in and out at will.

As we explained previously, DLLs consist of some executable code with a bunch of entry points. The client and the object need to agree on the signatures of these functions. The minute a client or a DLL changes its mind about what the signature (or signatures) of an entry point looks like, the poor client application has to pay the price—usually in the form of a program crash (and most likely during an important trade show demonstration). This mismatch can happen for any number of reasons, including changes in the client or DLL source code, the copying of different versions of DLL over existing working ones, and having the wrong DLL loaded unknowingly through the environment executable path variable. Remember, the signatures are usually available only through a C header file—they don't come bundled with the DLL and are not available at runtime.

There is just no effective means of developing client and raw DLL code independently. The fundamental problem is that although DLL interfaces are expressed in a typed language, the actual entry point in the import library is not typed. The entry point is just a name in the import library. The successful linkage between the client and the DLL depends on both parties agreeing to the stack frame (defined by the DLL's function signatures), and for a long time there were no formal rules about how to make sure this agreement happens.

COM tries to fix the DLL issue by introducing the discipline of *interface-based programming*. COM is Microsoft's sanctioned brand of interface-based programming. The fundamental point to interface-based programming is that separating interfaces from implementations is a good thing and keeping the interface constant is an even better thing. Of course, this is something they teach in Computer Science 101. If you hold constant the interface to a piece of code, you should be able to change the implementation as much as you please without causing the client code to break.

The interface to a plain-vanilla DLL is simply a bunch of entry points defined in a header file. If the function signatures between the client and the DLL change for some reason, the result is usually a program crash. Interface-based programming, and specifically COM, go a long way towards fixing this situation by adding shape and consistency to DLL entry points. Although plain-vanilla DLL loading is based on an ad-hoc linking protocol, interface-based programming turns DLL loading into a typed operation; code is loaded based on type, and that type is an interface.

COM Interfaces

One of the most important things COM brings to the table is a formal separation between interfaces and implementations. Traditional C++ classes usually combine interfaces and implementations. COM formalizes the distinction between interfaces and implementations. COM clients never talk to COM objects directly. They talk to COM objects only through predefined interfaces.

COM interfaces are function table prototypes describing the functionality of an object. COM interfaces define a contract between a COM object and its clients. In C++, COM interfaces are conveniently defined as pure abstract base classes. They are meant to define single orthogonal units of functionality.

For example, a developer may define two interfaces to describe the drawing and storing behavior of an object. Neither the drawing nor the storing functionality necessarily arise together. However, it is useful for a single object to expose both types of functionality. Therefore rather than piling the functionality into a single class and forcing the client to accept the terms and conditions of programming to an entire class exposing both types of functionality, COM separates the different functionality into separate interfaces. The drawing and the storing interfaces represent the problem domain functionality.

Of course, separating functionality into separate interfaces implies the need to be able to jump from one interface to another. In addition to the regular problem domain functionality, the COM object supports two fundamental areas of functionality: object lifetime management and interface management. This functionality is part of the COM infrastructure, and COM itself includes an interface defining this functionality. IUnknown is the name of this interface, and it has three functions: QueryInterface, AddRef, and Release.

```
struct IUnknown {
  virtual HRESULT __stdcall QueryInterface(
                    const IID& riid, void **ppv) = 0;
  virtual ULONG __stdcall AddRef( ) = 0;
  virtual ULONG __stdcall Release( ) = 0;
};
```

Please forgive the people who named this interface IUnknown. We have heard various reasons for this core interface's name, and the best reason we have heard so far is that "you do not know anything about the object before you start working with it."

The trick to understanding IUnknown is that (1) every COM object implements this functionality and (2) this functionality is made available through every COM interface. The first part is easy. All the COM code you see includes code to handle QueryInterface, AddRef, and Release. The second part implies that every COM interface you will ever see will start off with these three functions. Another way to phrase this is that every COM interface derives from IUnknown, as IDraw and IStore do here:

```
struct IDraw : IUnknown {
  virtual HRESULT __stdcall Render() = 0;
};
```

```
struct IStore : IUnknown {
  virtual HRESULT __stdcall Persist(IMedium* pMedium) = 0;
};
```

Let's start off with reference counting.

Reference Counting

When working in a single source-code style environment where there is usually only one reference to an object in memory, creation and dispose operators (such as *new* and *delete*) in C++ are sufficient for managing object lifetimes. These mechanisms are usually compiler and source-code dependent. COM uses API functions to create objects. Object lifetime management (i.e., determining when to delete the object) is usually handled using reference counting. The reference count is manipulated by AddRef and Release (which are part of every interface). A COM object knows it is alive as long as its reference count is greater than zero. When clients are done with interfaces, they call Release through the interface pointer, usually decrementing the object's reference count. When an object's reference count is zero, the object often self-destructs. Note that the client should call Release for every new reference it acquires. Although many objects use the reference count to manage their lifetimes, there are some objects that do not. That detail remains hidden from the client.

Acquiring Interfaces

The second area of functionality necessary for COM objects to work involves providing a way for clients to garner multiple interfaces. Remember that COM classes usually implement several orthogonal interfaces (as in the previous example of a COM object implementing both drawing and storing interfaces). Rather than being forced to accept all the interfaces it provides up front, COM clients must explicitly request interfaces. This occurs through the other IUnknown function, QueryInterface. QueryInterface allows clients to arbitrarily widen the connection to an object, introducing a flexibility and robustness not available with traditional development tools like classic C++.

In a distributed environment, it is important to avoid naming collisions. That is, when inventing an interface with a human-readable, name such as IDraw, it's quite likely that someone else may already have invented a different interface with the same name. To avoid the conflict, COM uses globally unique identifiers (GUIDs) to name interfaces. GUIDs are 128-bit numbers guaranteed to be unique when generated properly (that is, when generated on a computer using a working network card). GUIDs include IUnknown's GUID and GUIDs for IDraw and IStore:

```
{00000000-0000-0000-C000-000000000046} // IID_IUnknown
{ED9C9F8E-ED94-4c99-A48D-C26AC6B7B25D} // IID_IDraw
{F3DC1013-C7A8-4bba-A208-F9641176D302} // IID_IStore
```

GUIDs are useful when acquiring new interfaces through `QueryInterface`. Following is a bit of code showing how some COM client code might use `QueryInterface` to widen its connection to the drawing/storing object:

```
void DrawAndStore(
    IUnknown* punk,
    IMedium* pMedium) {

  IDraw* pDraw;
  HRESULT hr;
  hr = pUnknown->QueryInterface(
      IID_IDraw,
      (void**)&pDraw);
  if (hr == S_OK) {
    pDraw->Render();

    IStore* pStore;
    hr = pDraw->QueryInterface(
        IID_IStore,
        (void**)&pStore);
    if (hr == S_OK) {
      pStore->Persist(pMedium);
      pStore->Release();
      pRender->Release();
    }
  }
}
```

From the client's point of view, all that is known is the signatures to the `IUnknown`, `IDraw`, and `IStore` interfaces. Given an `IUnknown` pointer, the client can widen its connection to the object arbitrarily by calling `QueryInterface`. In contrast to a C++ class, which often implements only one interface, a single COM object may implement several interfaces. In fact, a full-blown ActiveX control may implement up to 21 of these interfaces.

Let's take a look at COM objects living on the other side of the interface.

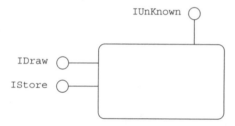

FIGURE 5-6   Lollipop Diagram of a COM Object Implementing `IDraw` and `IStore`.

COM Objects

COM objects are bodies of code that have been loaded into memory and implement COM interfaces sharing a common IUnknown pointer. COM provides a well-defined way (QueryInterface) to access interfaces via the ubiquitous COM interface IUnknown.

Within system design notations, COM objects are often notated using the "lollipop diagram" (Figure 5-6). The following listing shows the code for a typical COM object in C++:

```cpp
class DrawAndStore: public IDraw , public IStore {

    ULONG m_cRef;

    public:
    DrawAndStore() : m_cRef(0) {}

    // IUnknown methods
    STDMETHODIMP QueryInterface(REFIID riid, void **ppv) {
      if (riid == IID_IDraw)
         *ppv = static_case<IDraw*>(this);
      else if (riid == IID_IStore)
         *ppv = static_cast<IStore*>(this);
      else if (riid == IID_IUnknown)
         *ppv = static_cast<IDraw*>(this);
      else {
         *ppv = 0;
         return E_NOINTERFACE;
      }

      reinterpret_cast<IUnknown*>(*ppv)->AddRef();
      return S_OK;
    }

    STDMETHODIMP_(ULONG) AddRef(void) {++m_cRef;}
    STDMETHODIMP_(ULONG) Release(void) {
      LONG r = --m_cRef;
      if (r == 0)
         delete this;

      return r;
    }
    // IDraw methods
    STDMETHODIMP Render() {
       // Render Here...
    }

    // IStore methods
    STDMETHODIMP Store(IMedium* pMedium) {
       // Store to a medium...
    }
};
```

The drawing and storing object in the previous listing inherits from `IDraw` and `IStore`. Both interfaces share common signatures for `IUnknown`, so `QueryInterface`, `AddRef`, and `Release` are all shared by the same running instance. `QueryInterface` provides a switching mechanism that works by examining the interface request (identified by a GUID) and casting the `this` pointer to the various pure abstract base classes, thereby yielding the correct `vptr`.

COM Classes and Class Objects

COM objects obviously need to live somewhere—they live inside COM servers and are activated using COM class objects. For example, consider the following C++ code:

```
class DrawAndStore {
public:
    DrawAndStore() {
        // Initialize State
    }
    ~DrawAndStore() {
        // Clean up
    }
    void Render() {
        // Do some drawing
    }
    void Store(char* pszFileName) {
        // do some storing...
    }
};

void UseDrawAndStore() {
    DrawAndStore* pDrawAndStore;
    pDrawAndStore = new CDrawAndStore;

    // Work with drawing and storing

    delete pDrawAndStore;
}
```

In the previous code, the C++ class is the `DrawAndStore` class. Operator new creates new *instances* of the class. COM classes work the same way semantically. That is, the COM class object represents the *class of objects*. Most class objects implement the interface named `IClassFactory`. For this reason, much of the popular COM literature uses the term *class factory* interchangeably with *class object*.

Just as interfaces are named using GUIDS, so are COM classes. COM classes are implemented using class objects. For example, imagine a COM server composed of three COM classes. That server would also contain three class objects—one for each kind of COM class in the server.

Class objects generally serve two purposes. First, COM class objects usually implement the activation interface named `IClassFactory`. Clients usually end up using the `IClassFactory` interface to create instances of COM classes. The second purpose for COM class objects is to serve as the static data area for a COM class. The nature of the class object is that it is global and static on a single machine. A COM class's class object lifetime begins before the lifetime and extends beyond the life of the COM object it represents. This makes the class object the ideal place to store static data or implement a static interface (similar to the static modifier in C++).

Loading COM Dynamic Link Libraries

Loading a regular DLL means finding it by name, loading it, and fixing up the entry points—while praying that the client and the DLL agree on the signatures of the entry points. COM brings type to the loader. Loading a COM DLL and accessing the code inside mean first getting to the class object, then asking the class object to create an instance of the object. The API function for loading the class object is named `CoGet-ClassObject`. Following is the signature:

```
STDAPI CoGetClassObject(
   REFCLSID rclsid,     // Name of the class object
   DWORD dwClsCtx,      // Context (in/out proc, remote
   COSERVERINFO* pSI,   // Pointer to remote machine
   REFIID riid,         // Name of interface to retrieve
   LPVOID * ppv         // Indirect pointer to the interface
);

interface IClassFactory : IUnknown {
   // create a new com object
   HRESULT CreateInstance([in] IUnknown *pUnkOuter,
                          [in] REFIID riid,
      [out,retval,iid_is(riid)] void **ppv);

   // hold component code in memory
   HRESULT LockServer([in] BOOL bLock);
}
```

`CoGetClassObject` uses the class ID (CLSID) to find the name of the DLL in the registry. `CoGetClassObject` loads the DLL and searches the DLL exports for a well-known entry point named `DllGetClassObject`. (If the DLL does not export `DllGetClassObject`, it cannot play in the COM game.) `DllGetClassObject` returns the requested interface pointer (the one attached to the class object) to the client. This is usually a pointer to `IClassFactory`. Then the client can use `IClass-Factory::CreateInstance` to manufacture an instance of the COM object. Following is a bit of client code using `CoGetClassObject` and `IClassFactory` to acquire a pointer to some COM code.

```
void UseDrawAndStore() {
   IDraw* pDraw= 0;
   IStore* pStore= 0;
```

```
        IClassFactory *pcf = 0;

        // ask SCM to load class code for Draw and Store
        HRESULT hr;
        hr = CoGetClassObject(CLSID_DrawAndStore,
                             CLSCTX_ALL, 0,
                             IID_IClassFactory,
                          (void**)&pcf);

    if (SUCCEEDED(hr)) {
       // ask class code to create new class instance
       hr = pcf->CreateInstance(0,
                             IID_IDraw,
                             (void**)&pDraw);
       if (SUCCEEDED(hr)) {
          hr = pDraw->QueryInterface(IID_IStore,
                                    (void**)&pStore);
          // use drawing and storing interface pointers
          }
          pcf->Release();
    }

}
```

CoGetClassObject/IClassFactory::CreateInstance takes several round trips to get going. Therefore there is a shortcut—CoCreateInstance function. CoCreateInstance fetches the class object and uses IClassFactory:: CreateInstance to create an instance of the object and return the requested interface pointer. Following is the signature for CoCreateInstance, followed by a bit of client code using CoCreateInstance to create an instance of the DrawAndStore object.

```
HRESULT CoCreateInstance(
   [in] const CLSID& rclsid, // which class?
   [in] IUnknown *pUnkOuter, // used in aggregation
   [in] DWORD dwClsCtx,      // locality?
   [in] REFIID riid,         // which interface?
   [out, iid_is(riid)] void **ppv // put it here!
);

void UseDrawAndStore() {
   IProgrammer* pProg = 0;
   // ask COM to load class code and create instance
   HRESULT hr = CoCreateInstance(CLSID_DrawAndStore,
                              0, CLSCTX_ALL,
                              IID_IDraw,
                              (void**)&pStore);
   if (SUCCEEDED(hr)) {
      // Use pDraw
      pDraw->Release();
   }
}
```

Interface Description Language and Type Information

It is hard to know quite where to start when trying to explain COM. We started by discussing interfaces individually, progressed to COM objects, and finally moved on to COM classes and instantiation. The world of COM is all about defining boundaries between components. These components can be written in any language, so there needs to be a way of connecting these binaries produced by different languages. Because of this, COM centers itself around the interface description language (IDL). COM developers usually start a project by defining interfaces and COM classes through IDL.

When trying to understand IDL, the most important thing is to pay attention to that middle initial: the *D*. IDL is a purely *descriptive, declarative* language. IDL is a bit similar to C in syntax. It has curly braces and allows you to define structures and typedefs in IDL. In addition to its C-like syntax, IDL brings the notion of *attributes* to interface and structure definition. IDL code is littered with keywords surrounded by square brackets. For example, take a look at the following IDL code for defining the IDraw and IStore interfaces and a COM class implementing the interfaces.

```
// DrawStorelib.idl
import "oaidl.idl";
import "StoreDefs.idl";

[
  helpstring("IDraw interface"),
  object,
  uuid(ED9C9F8E-ED94-4c99-A48D-C26AC6B7B25D)
]
interface IDraw : IUnknown  {
  HRESULT Draw();
}

[
  helpstring("IStoreinterface"),
  object,
  uuid(F3DC1013-C7A8-4bba-A208-F9641176D302)
]
interface IStore : IUnknown  {
  HRESULT Store([in]IMedium* pMedium);
}

library DrawStoreSvr {
  importlib("stdole2.tlb");
  importlib("hisstuff.dll");
    [ uuid(03C20B33-C942-11d1-926D-006008026FEA) ]
    coclass DrawAndStore
    {
      [default] interface IDraw;
      interface IStore;
    }
}
```

This bit of IDL code defines the IDraw and IStore interfaces in completely unambiguous terms. In addition, note that the interface definitions in the IDL code are where the interfaces and their GUIDs are associated for the first time. Preceding each interface definition is a set of square braces with the attributes pertaining to the interface (which is where IID_IDraw and IID_IStore come from). The interface definitions can even give the directions of the parameters! Finally, note the IDL keywords *library* and *coclass*. The coclass keyword tells the IDL compiler to include a type definition for a COM class named DrawAndStore (which is where CLSID_DrawAndStore comes from). The library keyword tells the IDL compiler to emit a type library containing the types defined within the IDL.

The reason for such explicit detail within the IDL file is that anyone who wants to use the interfaces uses its definitions to make sure the call stack is set up correctly before jumping to a function. In fact, the call may be made between processes or even between machines, and the remoting layer needs to literally pick up the call stack from one machine and move it to the other machine.

IDL code is fed through the IDL compiler named MIDL.EXE. The results of compiling the IDL code are several files. In this case, the files are DRAWSTORE.TLB, DRAWSTORE_I.C, and DRAWSTORE.H. The file DRAWSTORE.TLB (the type library) is the binary version of the type definitions. The type library is usually used by such tools as Visual Basic (so you can use COM-type definitions within your Visual Basic application) and by the remoting layer (to build proxy-stub pairs). The GUIDs defined within the IDL code come out in the file named DRAWSTORE_I.C. Finally, DRAWSTORE.H includes the interface definitions in pure virtual abstract base classes suitable for both COM implementations and clients written in C++. Then type libraries are usually attached to the DLL as a resource, so the DLL becomes self-describing.

COM+

In the year 2000, Microsoft introduced a technology named *COM+ 1.0*. COM+ took all the good ideas from MTS and made it part of the operating system. COM+ layers on services through proxies (and other means). Rather than having to write all sorts of boilerplate code to serialize calls into your objects or make security happen, objects are configured to include these services at deployment time.

For example, rather than sprinkling your code with calls to system primitives (such as EnterCriticalSection and LeaveCriticalSection) to serialize access to data within objects, you can involve your object in a COM+ *activity*. In this case, COM+ serializes calls into your object. It is easy to create deadlock race conditions in a multithreaded environment. Pushing the serialization code down into the runtime makes such problems less likely to occur. In addition, COM+ activities are reentrant, which is not possible with normal Win32 critical sections.

In Win32 programming, there are certain types of code that have *thread affinity*, meaning that certain code can only run on a single thread and cannot be switched. A great example of this kind of code is the standard Win32 window message loop. The same code that called `CreateWindowEx` *must* run the `GetMessage/Dispatch-Message` loop. COM+ *apartments* provide the runtime service of segregating code with thread affinity from code not requiring thread affinity. COM+ layers transactions and security (and other services) in a similar fashion.

What Is Right in COM?

COM goes a long way toward making distributed computing a reality. In fact, many enterprises have built their core systems using COM. The reason COM works so well in so many cases is multifaceted.

The first reason helping COM succeed is the emphasis on interfaces. Inherent in the act of separating the interface from the implementation is a decoupling of clients from the objects serving them. This decoupling encourages component architectures, allowing separate parties to develop software independently of each other.

Loading DLLs using standard Win32 API calls is an ad-hoc procedure. A client loads the DLL by path name and searches for DLL entry points by a human-readable name. The client then has to hope that the header file it is using defines function signatures the same way the DLL does. If there is a mismatch for any reason, the client is going to set up the stack the wrong way. COM loads services by named type. The name is the GUID, and the type is the interface definitions. In COM, you call `CoCreateInstance`, pass in the GUID representing the type (the interface ID)—where it lives (the class ID)—and you get an instance of the type. Not only that, you can widen your connection at runtime and get even more types. Therefore in COM, `LoadLibrary/GetProcAddress` is replaced by the single function `CoCreateInstance` and well-defined extensible interfaces to the code in the DLL. In a nutshell, COM introduced the notion of type into the DLL loading mechanism.

Finally, COM adds the notion of *type information*. COM DLLs usually include a type library advertising the types (data types and interface types) and implementations (class IDs) contained within. Type libraries are very useful for tool sets like Visual Basic and the Microsoft Visual C++ `#import` directive. In addition, the COM+ runtime layer depends on type information to set up the proxy-stub pairs at runtime.

COM has been used to devise a huge variety of useful architectures—all the way from ActiveX controls to transaction servicing. With all this good stuff, who would ever ask for more? As it turns out, there are a couple of deficiencies within COM. Let's discuss them.

What Is Wrong in COM?

COM's deficiencies include a few niggling details and a whopping deficiency. The first issue is that the names of the COM DLLs and accompanying configuration information all go into the registry, leading to an overburdened registry. Perhaps you've heard this running joke: "You know what the registry is don't you? It's this thing in Windows that decays." Information goes into the registry—and it usually stays there.

The second problem with COM is that it requires everyone to follow its rules, including the rule to never change an interface once it has been published, as well as the rule to release interface pointers when you are done with them. In Visual Basic, there is no problem because the runtime makes resource management automatic. However, some people still do not follow the rules.

Probably the biggest problems in COM reside in the way type information works. First on the list is the issue of COM's disparate type system. Everybody is supposed to agree on the type boundaries introduced by interfaces, but it turns out there really are three distinct type systems for COM developers. If you program in C++ and you expect your clients to be mostly C++ clients, then you can do pretty much anything you want as long as it can be described in IDL (including sending a linked list across the wire to another machine). However, introducing target clients written in Visual Basic into the picture reduces the data types you can send back and forth. Then if you feel the urge to include Web pages and scripting clients, you have to back down your data type selection a bit more and include only those types that fit in a VARIANT. Ultimately, the type information in the type library does not completely match up to the type information within the IDL. In addition, you cannot get information about imported types, the type library does not provide any information about internal types, and there is no way to find out the dependencies within a COM DLL.

At the end of the day, COM programming is still about loading DLLs and defining the boundary between the client and the object. Although COM improves the situation by introducing type into the loader, the boundary between the client and the loader is based on the type library format, which is fundamentally broken (as described previously). In addition, certain programming environments (C++ in particular) are prone to memory leaks. The goal underlying the CLR is to fix these issues.

ENTER THE COMMON LANGUAGE RUNTIME

With the goal of fixing COM's problems, developers began work on what was to become the .NET runtime back in the late 1990s. From 1997 to the present, the .NET platform has gone through a number of name changes, including *COR* and *COM+*. You may remember Mary Kirtland's articles in *Microsoft Developer Network Magazine* (back when it was called *Microsoft Systems Journal*) during the fall of 1997. The articles discussed the new COM+ platform that would be coming from Microsoft. These articles promised a new universal runtime engine, better type information, and services layered on top of your objects. Although the final feature just listed (layering of services) ended up within the release of COM+ in Windows 2000, the former two features are only now emerging. Microsoft calls the universal runtime and the better type information the *common language runtime.*

The CLR takes several good ideas from existing component technologies and rolls them into a single component technology. For example, the CLR features the language tolerance of COM and CORBA, the runtime type model of Java, and the extensibility model of MTS and COM+ with the notion of Web services based on SOAP and eXtensible Markup Language (XML) inherent throughout the whole runtime.

Just as COM added the notion of type to the loader, the CLR component loader is based on type. In this vein, the CLR requires component boundaries to be defined in terms of type definitions, much as COM and Java do. However, the CLR goes one step further by employing a pervasive type system.

A Pervasive Type System

COM was all about defining component boundaries. A scheme for defining boundaries was necessary in the early 1990s when there were no formal rules for doing so. By contrast, the CLR is all about blurring the boundaries between components. To that end, the CLR is based on a pervasive type system. This means that the CLR enforces a common managed type system for all programming languages. Systems running under the CLR all agree on what types look like, and there is no difference between intracomponent and intercomponent types. The type system is singly rooted (in a class named `System.Object`). The closest COM got to this is `IUnknown` and `VARIANT`s.

At DevelopMentor, they have a saying: "COM is Love." COM lets different parties integrate software because it sets up rules about what the boundaries are supposed to look like between components. C++ and Visual Basic components may exhibit runtime behaviors different from each other, but when it comes to integrating the software, they can look past their differences and agree on the component boundaries.

If COM is love, then the CLR and CTS represent Brahman. The type system in the CLR suffuses all components running within it and is woven into the runtime. Integrating components using the CLR is easy because of the pervasive type system that permeates both the runtime and your component code. The CLR simply makes the boundaries disappear! Everybody agrees on what the types are so that the CLR does not have the same boundary type issues associated with normal COM.

The biggest advantage of the CLR's pervasive type system is that *everything* is known at runtime. (This is largely accomplished through the manifest, which we discuss shortly). Nothing escapes the watchful eye of the runtime. The CLR makes all aspects of a type definition available at both development time and runtime. This is needed for the runtime to function properly, because the runtime is responsible for activities such as allocating and deallocating memory, laying out objects in memory, and controlling access to code and resources. Types that are loaded and handled by the CLR are called *managed types* because all aspects of their creation and execution are managed by the runtime.

Types Are Fundamental

When it comes to programming the CLR, type is everything. Types are the fundamental unit of design, implementation, and execution under the CLR. In classical programming languages such as C++, types include primitives such as `int`, `long`, and `char`. You can also make up your own types using the `typedef` statement or by defining structures and classes. When defining type within the context of C++, you are telling the compiler about the shape of the call stack when jumping from one routine to another.

Because the CLR is all about mixing *binary* software, the CLR goes one step further in extending the notion of type. CLR types belong to the runtime; they are not isolated within the context of a particular language (C++) or runtime (Visual Basic). Like types in C++ and classic Visual Basic, CLR types package related code into reusable abstractions. CLR types are bound by the rules of the Common Type System (CTS).

The Common Type System

By clearly and unequivocally defining types within the context of a *common* runtime (rather than a language or specific runtime like Visual Basic), .NET becomes a framework enabling cross-language integration, type safety, and high-performance executable code. The CTS is object oriented and defines rules for various language implementations to follow. By enforcing languages to follow these rules, .NET guarantees interoperability between components written in different languages. One of the most important distinctions here is that type commonality is being designed into the system up front rather than after the fact (which is what happened in the development of COM).

Types within the CTS derive from a system-defined type named `System.Object`. `System.Object` provides some fundamental services useful to both the runtime and developers. Some of the more useful functions hanging off `System.Object` include `Equals`, `GetType`, `ToString`, `Finalize`, and `MemberwiseClone`. Whenever you have an instance of any CLR type, you may call these functions to get information about the instance or to operate on the instance. `Equals` is an overloaded member that determines whether two instance references refer to the same instance. `GetType` returns the type of an instance at runtime. `ToString` returns a string representing the type of the instance. `Finalize` tells the object to free up resources and perform other cleanup operations before being swept away by the garbage collector. Finally, MemberwiseClone is like the copy constructor in C++, performing a deep copy of an instance of a CLR type.

The CTS defines several types, including value types, enumerations, classes, interfaces, delegates, and arrays. Following is a rundown of each of these types.

Value Types

The fundamental property distinguishing value types is that they are copied when they are passed around as arguments. .NET's CLR supports two kinds of value types: built-in value types and user-defined value types.

Classic languages such as C, C++, and Visual Basic include various built-in value types such as integers and floating point numbers. The .NET CLR's built-in value types include these primitives scoped within the system namespace. For example, the system defines System.Int32 and System.Boolean. These correspond to the primitive data types used by the classic programming languages like C++ and Visual Basic. For example, System.Int32 is really a four-byte integer.

Classic languages such as C++ let you compose your own value (and reference) types. .NET's CLR also supports user-defined value types. These types derive from System.ValueType. For example, imagine you wanted to define a value type representing Cartesian coordinates with two integers. By defining it as a value type, the CLR can pass it around by value efficiently.

Value types can be instantiated, passed as parameters, stored as local variables, or stored in a field of another value type or object. Value types do not have the overhead associated with storing an instance of a class, and they do not require constructors.

.NET is very efficient at storing and managing value types—even user-defined value types. You may call methods on instances of a .NET value type, including the virtual methods defined on the System.Object and System.ValueType classes, as well as any methods defined on the value type itself.

Enumerations

Enumerations are a special form of value type, inheriting from System.Enum and supplying alternate names for the values of an underlying primitive type. Enumeration types are composed of a name, an underlying type, and a set of fields. The underlying type must be one of the built-in signed or unsigned integer types (such as Byte, Int32, or UInt64).

Great examples of enumerations include days of the week, months of the year, and suits in a card deck. Using enumerations provides a level of type safety and code readability above and beyond using primitive types. For example, in classic C-style programming, you might assign the values 1 through 12 to represent the months of the year. However, when you use the numbers, you have to keep track of which number represents which month. If you want to use the numbers to index an array, you have a one-off issue. Enumerations get rid of these problems.

You can create an instance of an enumeration and call the System.Enum methods, as well as any methods defined on the enumeration's underlying type. The functions of System.Enum include Format, GetNames, GetUnderlyingType, GetValues, IsDefined, Parse, and ToObject.

Classes

Classes glue together methods and data, and objects are instantiated from classes at runtime. As with the notion of *class* in normal object-oriented programming systems, the .NET class defines the operations (methods) that may be performed on the state of the object (its fields). .NET classes can include both definition and implementation, and they can have one or more members that have no implementation.

.NET's CLR borrows from modern programming paradigms such as Java to extend the standard notion of a class. For example, .NET classes may be *sealed*, in which case no additional classes may be derived from them. They may also implement interfaces, much like C++ classes implement COM interfaces. They may be abstract, meaning they may not be instantiated. .NET classes may inherit from other base classes, bringing in the implementation and virtual functions of the base classes. Finally, .NET classes may or may not be exported out of the assembly in which they live.

Delegates

If you are a C++ developer who has been working with Windows for a while, you have dealt with function pointers. In the .NET runtime, delegates serve a similar purpose. When defining function pointer types in C++, you describe a call stack that the compiler understands. This way, you can have various sections of your code calling back and forth between each other.

Delegates are type-safe, secure, managed objects that point to other valid .NET CLR objects. A delegate defines a method signature, which can reference any method with a matching signature. However, delegates are different than C++ function pointers in that they can reference all styles of methods on classes and objects: static, virtual, and instance methods. Delegates are usually most useful for event handling and callbacks within the .NET framework. Each instance of a delegate can forward a call to one or more methods that take those parameters and return the same type.

Delegates include an invocation list, which is a linked list of methods that are executed when the delegate is invoked. The .NET delegates inherit from System.Delegate and therefore acquire several useful member functions including Combine and

`Remove` for managing invocation lists, and `DynamicInvoke` for late-binding, as well as the standard type functions such as `ToString`, `Equals`, and `GetType`.

Arrays

In C, arrays are just blocks of memory. C++ and the standard template library provide useful templates for vectors (arrays) and lists and add type safety to array-based memory access. Visual Basic defines arrays—even multidimensional arrays. .NET has arrays as well, and its arrays are types (as is everything else in .NET). A .NET array type is defined using the array's element types, number of dimensions in the array, and upper and lower bounds. If you have worked with COM's `SafeArrays`, you are familiar with these concepts. Arrays are homogenous and may hold only elements of a single type.

Just as the other types within the runtime derive from system types, the .NET array types inherit from `System.Array` and provide sophisticated functionality for .NET arrays. This functionality includes allocating an array based on size and lower bound information, indexing an array to read and write a value, computing the address of an element of an array (a managed pointer), and querying for the rank, bounds, and total number of values stored in an array.

Interfaces

The most important notion introduced by COM was that of the *interface*. .NET fully supports interfaces. Interfaces can have static members and nested types, as well as abstract methods, virtual methods, properties, and events. Any class implementing an interface must supply definitions for the abstract members declared in the interface. An interface can require that any implementing class must also implement one or more other interfaces.

Pointers

The .NET runtime supports three kinds of pointers: managed pointers, unmanaged pointers, and unmanaged function pointers. The CLR generates managed pointers as needed. For example, the CLR generates managed pointers to types as it passes them back and forth as references. Of the three, only managed pointers are compliant with the common language specification (CLS). Unmanaged pointers are there for backwards compatibility (i.e., for unmanaged C++). (Although backwards compatibility was not a major goal for C#, it was a major goal for .NET and especially for managed C++.) Unmanaged pointers are just addresses in memory. They may refer to objects in the runtime, but the value of a pointer type may not be treated like a CLR object. For example, you cannot determine a data type from a pointer to that type.

Pointers that are useful within the CLR are those used for reading and writing raw data. In fact, reading from and writing to locations referenced by a pointer are the two type-safe operations you may perform on pointer types.

Value versus Reference

The CTS supports value types and reference types. If you have worked with either C++ or Visual Basic, you are probably familiar with the distinction. Instances of value types are stored simply using their values. For example, a pair of coordinates would be stored as two numbers. Value types can be built in (implemented by the runtime), user defined, or enumerations. Reference types represent layers of indirection pointing to value types. Instances of reference types refer to the value's location. In a nutshell, value types are formatted memory, whereas reference types point to CLR objects. C# and Visual Basic primitives types (e.g., longs, shorts, floats), structs, and enums are value types; C# and Visual Basic classes are reference types.

The Common Language Specification

The .NET framework defines a pervasive type system that permeates all executable code running under the CLR. Remember that one of the key goals of .NET is to provide a high degree of interoperability between components—no matter what languages are used to write the components. To support this interoperability, the .NET framework defines the CLS. The CLS defines how languages interact with the runtime. It is basically a set of rules defining the behavior of externally visible items. Remember that the CLR breaks down the barriers between binary components. When execution crosses between binary components, the runtime wants to think both components behave the same in terms of stack setup, return value types, and so forth. These externally visible types include those types visible outside of their own assemblies and members of those types marked with public, family, or family-or-assembly accessibility. As a developer, using the `System.CLSCompilantAttribute` when describing types gives you control over whether to mark items as CLS compliant.

Boxing

You can see there is a fundamental difference between value types and reference types. There is a need from time to time to convert value types to reference types and then back to value types, a process known as *boxing*. Value types are simply formatted memory and are not real CLR objects until they become boxed. Imagine running across a function call that takes a reference type and the caller holds only a value type. You may box the object, which clones the object and creates a reference to it. Then you may pass the object reference. Boxed objects may be copied back into the instance as well. This is called *unboxing*.

How Types Map to C#

We just gave you a rundown of the type system. In Chapters 3 and 4, you got a pretty good look at C# in detail. Very briefly, here is how C# relates to the CLR. Within C#, everything must be within the scope of a type. These types include classes, modules, interfaces, structures, and enumerations. C# lets you control the visibility of your types as either private or public. Anything you want to be accessible from the outside must be defined as public.

Types include simple value types such as integers and floating point members. In addition, C# types may be composed from other types. Composite C# types are made up of members. These member declarations include fields, methods, constructors, and properties. Like the types themselves, members may be public or private.

Fields

Within a type definition, a field is a uniquely named (within the type definition) member that becomes associated with storage at runtime. Fields are used to hold values of a given type. Every field in a class must have a unique name. When the CLR instantiates a type at runtime, it considers all the fields to know how much memory to allocate. Because each field is also of a CLR type, the runtime knows everything about it. Type fields are initialized to zero, null, or false (unless an explicit value is provided as part of the field declaration or writes constructor code to initialize the field to something else). The fields of an object are accessed using the dot (".") operator against an object variable or the name of a class.

Methods

Methods are defined by signatures and have code associated with them; they represent operations that may be performed on instances of that type. A method may return a typed value. Method signatures may contain typed parameters as well as a typed return value.

Properties

Properties are special methods that simulate public fields. Like fields, properties have unique names and are of a specific CLR type. Properties are defined by implementing a get block, a set block, or both. Properties can be defined as ReadOnly or WriteOnly, and they can take parameters.

Good class and structure design often calls for encapsulating data members. CLR properties provide the illusion of public fields while simultaneously maintaining encapsulation. Another reason to use properties is that they allow you to intercept access to data programmatically to do such things as data validation.

Constructors

If you have worked with C++ before, you are certainly familiar with constructors. Constructors are special methods designed to initialize fields. As with C++, C# constructors are executed automatically by the CLR whenever the new operator is called to instantiate a class.

There are two different kinds of constructors. Those used to initialize objects are called *instance constructors.* Note that instance constructors are also commonly just called *constructors.* The *shared constructor* or *class constructor* is a second kind of constructor used to initialize the shared fields of a class. We start by examining the design and use of instance constructors.

For a class to be creatable, it must have at least one accessible instance constructor. Classes may have more than one instance constructor, and instance constructors can be parameterized and overloaded for flexibility. Also like C++, C# classes may have a default constructor—a nonparameterized instance constructor that is called in the absence of parameters.

In addition to instance constructors, a class may contain a shared constructor that executes once per class. In C#, these are known as static constructors.

You may have noticed the mysterious absence of destructors within the CLR and C#. We address this when we discuss garbage collection. For now, let's take a look at where .NET code lives: inside *assemblies.*

Assemblies

Over the last fifteen years, classically trained Windows developers have compiled much of their code into DLLs. As we discussed previously, DLLs are simply bundles of executable code with some entry points. By the mid 1990s, most developers began packaging executable code into DLLs exposing COM objects. These days, .NET developers compile their code into *assemblies.*

Assemblies are the .NET way to package and distribute executable code. Technically, an assembly is a collection of type definitions. Type definitions include code encapsulated within classes, enumerations, user-defined types, and so forth. Assemblies may also contain resources, such as bitmaps, JPEG files, and resource files).

Assemblies represent the fundamental unit of deployment and include code that the runtime executes. To be executed by the runtime, code must live within an assembly. When you compile source code into an assembly, it is compiled into a portable executable (PE) file (DLL or EXE or both)—a module. Assemblies (the logical unit of deployment) may consist of one or more modules (the physical unit of deployment). Assemblies may have only one entry point: DllMain, WinMain, or Main.

Assemblies form the CLR's type boundary. Every type within .NET must appear in an assembly somewhere. The types we have discussed already (such as System.Object and System.ValueType) are contained within the framework core assemblies. Type names within the CLR are identified by two parts: the name of the assembly and the name of the type. In this way, assemblies form a type boundary. Because every type name includes the name of the assembly in which it resides, a type within the scope of one assembly is not the same as a type loaded in the scope of another assembly—even if it shares the same name.

Assemblies also represent version control within .NET. The assembly is the smallest versionable unit in the CLR. When you create a version of an assembly, everything within the assembly becomes versioned. The assembly's manifest describes the version dependencies you specify for any dependent assemblies.

Assemblies and Modules

For a long time within Windows programming, there was a one-to-one correspondence between physical DLLs and the actual deployable code. MTS introduced packages, or the logical DLL. One or more DLLs were tied together as a single deployable unit called a *package*. MTS's deployment unit then became the package, and that notion carried forth in Windows 2000. .NET also supports the notion of a logical (separate from physical) deployment unit.

A module is an executable file containing code and type definitions, and assemblies comprise one or more modules. The assembly linker al.exe can link multiple modules and create the manifest

The Manifest

One of the main contributions COM makes to Windows programming is the addition of type information. Adding type information to a DLL or executable makes the module self-describing, enabling both tools and runtime environments to know and understand the contents of the module. For example, Visual Basic and Visual Studio used type information to drive Intellisense—the feature of the tools that gave hints about method calls. The MTS and COM+ runtimes use type information to manufacture proxy-stubs on the fly.

.NET includes the same facility, but the type information is called the *manifest*. An assembly's manifest is a top-level directory for the assembly, detailing the contents (e.g., code, types) of the assembly. Manifests are integral to .NET development. They arise from the simple act of compiling CLR-compliant source code. Note that this is different from how COM/COM+ development works. With COM/COM+, type information arises out of the IDL though a separate compile step.

One of the main problems with COM is that there is no way to tell whether one DLL depends on another. In standard Windows programming, the developer tool named DEPENDS.EXE examines the import list of an EXE file and can tell you about the module's dependencies. There is no way to simply look at a COM DLL and figure out the dependencies. .NET manifests do include the dependencies of assemblies. When loading an assembly, the CLR loader makes sure all required assemblies may be loaded before executing the code.

Private versus Public Assemblies

The .NET runtime supports both public and private assemblies. When you build an assembly, it is usually intended for use by a single application. The idea is that to deploy an application, you should be able to pick up the entire contents of a directory and XCOPY the contents to a new directory or machine. This means that the components of an application basically live together. In other words, most assemblies are private assemblies.

The directory containing the application is referred to as the *AppBase* directory of that application. The private assemblies for a particular application go into the App-Base directory or a subdirectory of it. At runtime, assembly references are completed by a component named the *Assembly Resolver*. The Assembly Resolver locates an assembly when given an assembly reference.

In standard Windows programming, a reference to a DLL is simply its physical name. In COM programming, clients refer to classes rather than to the DLL. In .NET, the way to locate code is through an assembly reference. A complete assembly reference specifies the assembly name, version, culture, and originator. If an application is using the complete assembly reference, the runtime uses that information to find the assembly. This is known as a *public assembly.*

Private assemblies do not have the originator and version specifications. The Assembly Resolver locates a private assembly using a process called *probing.* The runtime first looks in the AppBase directory and then in a subdirectory under App-Base with the same name as the assembly, checking within the culture subdirectory if it is not found immediately. The runtime searches for DLLs first and EXEs second. The runtime stops searching after finding the first match.

Probing is the default assembly search mechanism. In addition, you may specify further assembly locations using an application's configuration file. For example, an EXE file named FOO.EXE would have a configuration file named FOO.CONFIG. ASP.NET applications have a configuration file named WEB.CONFIG.

Therefore whereas most assemblies are private, some assemblies are public or shared. In terms of physical structure, private and shared assemblies are similar. For example, both public and private assemblies may be either single-module or multi-module assemblies. Both types include a manifest and exist within PE files (DLL or EXEs). However, public and private assemblies do have a few important differences.

Shared assemblies must be visible across the entire machine or even on the network. They are more akin to the current software approach that uses DLLs (COM or otherwise). Although private assemblies may be used by only one application, shared assemblies may be used by multiple applications on the machine. Private assemblies are not deployed beyond the application's directory hierarchy, whereas shared assemblies are. Because shared assemblies must be visible beyond the bounds of their own directories, they must be named uniquely. In COM, we solved this problem using GUIDs—those long, 128-bit numbers. The CLR uses a different approach called *strong naming.*

A CLR assembly name consists of four parts: a simple text name, a version number, culture information, and a public key and "strong name." A strong name is based on a pair of keys—one public and one private. The unique name of an assembly is the conjunction of the text name and the public key. We discuss strong naming in more detail in Chapter 6.

.NET Versioning

One of the main goals of the .NET platform is to get rid of "DLL Hell," as Microsoft calls it. That is, .NET should support the simplest installation and uninstallation procedure: picking up the entire contents of a directory and moving it (like using XCOPY with the /s option). All the components of an application generally reside within the same vicinity on a machine's hard drive. Installation pretty much means picking up a directory and its subdirectories and moving the components where you want them. Uninstalling means removing the application directory and its subdirectories. No more bit rot in the registry. Toward this end, .NET encourages reducing dependencies on shared components, which is why there is such an emphasis on private assemblies.

Still, there are times when sharing a component makes sense, which is why there are shared assemblies. However, shared code introduces the possibility of one application updating the code independently of other applications; this is the point at which "DLL Hell" ensues. With standard DLL-style programming, upgrading a DLL produces an incompatibility between the new version and the old version of the DLL. COM tried to fix this by enforcing rules regarding interface-based programming. COM worked for the most part, but sometimes not everyone followed the rules. Therefore .NET proposed another solution, which was to keep all the old versions of components.

The CLR runtime enables multiple versions of a shared assembly to reside on the same machine. The assembly may be used concurrently on the same machine and even in the same process. Assembly references used by client code contain the version number of the assembly the client expects to see. The runtime includes the version number when binding to a shared assembly. Rather than hoping that a DLL is compatible by name, .NET builds the version number into the name of the DLL. Clients latch onto a specific DLL by binding to a specific version number.

Life within the Common Language Runtime

Traditional Windows applications have been compiled down to native Intel code. .NET and the CLR add an intermediate step: intermediate language (IL). .NET applications are complied down to IL and then turned into native code before executing. Because the CLR is a complete execution engine, your programming language must translate its constructs into instructions the CLR can understand. This applies to type definitions as well as simple instructions.

The CLR provides a family of runtime libraries that provide a language-neutral way to write Web programs, database access programs, XML programs, and Windows programs. Most of these libraries reside in MSCORLIB, the core system library that virtually every CLR-based program relies on. In .NET programming, the idea is to write code to the system libraries rather than to an operating-system–specific API (like the Windows API).

With the addition of IL, a whole new breed of compilers is needed for the languages targeting the CLR. As long as the compiler turns source code into IL, it does not matter which programming language or environment you use. The CLR instruction set, or IL, was designed to support a wide range of programming languages. The CLR's execution engine (MSCOREE) compiles the IL into machine code before its execution. This process is called *just-in-time compiling,* or "JITting."

Intermediate Language and Just-in-Time Compiling

Standard Windows development entails compiling source code into native executable code understood by the platform (most often an Intel box). When building applications in .NET, compiling .NET CLS source code turns it into IL. IL code is finally turned into executable native code at deployment or runtime, thus adding one more layer of indirection between the human-created source code and the eventual chip the code is to run on. As when any layer of indirection is introduced in the system, this IL adds a certain amount of flexibility and power to the .NET platform.

Remember that one of the most insidious problems in standard Windows programming is the notion that code may be type safe within specific modules, but the boundaries between the components were a free-for-all. IL brings the advantage of ensuring that *all* code can be verified by the CLR during the final JIT compilation down to machine code. The CLR verifies code to make sure that code does not access memory directly or perform some other nefarious deeds that might harm the application. Standard native machine code exposes many openings to attack. Adding IL between the source code and the final native code allows a higher degree of protection than having pure native code applications around.

Using IL inherently decouples your EXEs and DLLs from the operating system. Decoupling the EXEs and DLLs from any specific operating system or hardware platform introduces the notion of real platform independence. Right now, there is a version of the CLR that runs on Windows 2000, Windows NT, and Windows 98. By using IL, Microsoft retains the possibility of deploying the runtime on other platforms that are *not* running Windows, or *not* running the Intel processors.

.NET Garbage Collection

One of the good ideas .NET borrows from runtime engines such as Java's is the notion of garbage collection. If you are a C++ developer, you are probably accustomed to the power of being able to allocate dynamically as much memory as you need whenever you need it. You are probably also well aware of the issues involved with dynamic memory allocation, most of which are centered on memory overruns and memory leaks. In the .NET environment, you allocate objects and then simply forget about them because the system cleans up after you! It performs what is known as *garbage collection*.

During the course of a typical program, that program allocates memory from the heap for various purposes. In addition to dynamically allocated memory, other pieces of heap memory are allocated and references to them maintained for various reasons. Allocation items include storage for static members, global objects, local variables and parameters, object pointers, and even central processing unit (CPU) registers that may contain pointers to objects. The listed items are called an application's *roots*. The garbage collector has to watch this entire show and understand which pieces of memory may be freed; it starts with the application's roots.

The JIT compiler knows about references to an application's roots, builds this list, and with the CLR maintains it as the program executes. The list of roots becomes the starting point the garbage collector uses to figure out which memory portions may be freed. Basically, if an object is unreachable from one of the application roots, the runtime classifies the object (and memory) as garbage. As long as the only party allocating the memory directly is the runtime, the runtime can guarantee that the application no longer has any means of referencing it.

Garbage collection occurs in three particular instances: when an allocation fails, during calls to the GC.Collect method, or at otherwise regular intervals. When it is time to collect garbage within a process (because of one of the reasons listed previously), the CLR suspends all threads within the process. Obviously, it is not beneficial for the runtime to continue allocating memory or otherwise access memory while garbage collection is occurring.

There are several safepoints during which threads in the CLR may be suspended. Threads in the CLR can only be suspended when they have reached a safepoint. A safepoint is a location in code where the runtime has the opportunity to safely suspend a thread. Threads are not randomly suspended. Instead, suspended threads are taken over by the runtime. When a thread suspension request is made (for example, during garbage collection), the thread waits for a safepoint in the execution when it can replace the return address on the stack with an address in the runtime. The function then returns to the CLR instead of the original caller. The runtime suspends that thread. When the suspended threads resume after collection, the threads are returned to the original calling program, and nobody is aware a suspension occurred.

Once the threads are suspended, the garbage collector starts with application roots that were described and traverses the object graphs within the system. The runtime makes the assumption that everything not reachable from the application's roots is garbage. It then builds a list of objects visited during the traversal, classifying them as nongarbage (because they may be reached from the roots). The runtime uses this list for a couple of reasons. First, to make sure performance is efficient, the list keeps the garbage collector from revisiting objects during traversals. Second, if any objects contain cyclical references, the list is a way of breaking that cycle (otherwise the garbage collector might end up in an infinite loop).

After traversing the object graphs and building the nongarbage list, the garbage collector makes a linear heapwalk, pushing nongarbage objects towards the bottom of the heap to make room at the top. After the heap has been walked and the objects pushed to the bottom of the heap, the runtime resumes the threads. The garbage collector updates any references to nongarbage objects (if they have been moved). Objects are unaware of any relocations once the threads resume.

For the most part, all this memory allocation and deallocation happens behind the scenes, and you do not have to worry too much about it. Even if you deeply nested references, the garbage collector takes good care of you and you can live the Visual Basic lifestyle—not worrying about managing your object references and being able to go home to your family on time. With managed system memory, the need for traditional destructors diminishes. In C++, destructors are used for cleaning up your objects when they are deleted, which usually involves deleting memory and cleaning up other references held by objects. However, although formal destructors have disappeared with the CLR (because the CLR manages references to memory now), you may find you need to clean up your objects before the garbage collector claims them. A good example of this scenario is cleaning up objects that may hold references to unmanaged resources. Therefore the CLR supports *finalization*.

Finalization

For objects needing notification that they are about to be physically deleted by the system, the runtime and garbage collection mechanisms provide a method for alerting objects right before they are reclaimed. If you have objects that want to be notified before the runtime physically deletes them, you may override the virtual `Finalize` method (a method from the `System.Object` class). Whenever the collector classifies an object as garbage, the runtime invokes the object's `Finalize` method before hustling the memory back to the heap.

There are a couple of rules and caveats about using finalization. The first is that calls to finalize should be chained up the hierarchy; they are not chained automatically. Second, you do not need to override `Finalize` if the object holds only references to other managed objects. The CLR is smart enough to track the references down correctly. Finalization is really there to help classes hold things like file references or other unmanaged resources.

C# includes destructor syntax that lets you add destructors to your classes. C# destructors manage finalization for you.

If you can get around using finalization you should, because finalization slows both allocations and garbage collections. Whenever the garbage collector finds an object with `Finalize`, the collector records the reference for consultation during collection, thereby slowing the allocation. The garbage collector has to check the finalization list and wait until `Finalize` is called to release the memory, thereby slowing collections.

Finally, you have no guarantee about when (or even if) `Finalize` will be called on your object, which means strange things may happen. For example, objects embedded within another object may be finalized before the containing object. (If you are a C++ developer, this is something you do not expect.).

Threading and the Common Language Runtime

Windows NT introduced the notion of preemptive multitasking to the Windows platform. Windows developers have come to depend heavily on this feature, and the CLR would be an incomplete platform if it were missing the preemptive multitasking feature. Fortunately, the CLR provides a straightforward way to create and manage multiple threads of execution.

Within the normal raw Windows platforms (NT, 95/98, 2000, and XP), threads are the scheduling units. That is, a thread is the smallest unit of execution that may be scheduled by the underlying operating system. Every EXE assembly that is running gets one thread automatically, and you may create more as needed. The CLR includes types for starting, stopping, and suspending threads. (See Chapter 6 for examples of threading and synchronization.)

AppDomains

In standard Windows development, the basic execution and resource boundary is the process. EXE processes start up with a single thread. Processes maintain their own heaps and other resources, and Windows processes define a boundary for types and security. Within the CLR, AppDomains serve this function.

There are still physical processes at runtime, but the *AppDomain* serves to define a logical process space. Just as assemblies serve as the logical (rather than physical) deployment model (in which there is not necessarily a one-to-one relationship between assemblies and modules), a process may host separate AppDomains to form separate fault-tolerance boundaries within a single process. You get many of the same advantages of putting your code into a separate process without the overhead of a process. AppDomains are cheaper than operating system processes, and threads can switch AppDomains much more quickly than they can switch between processes.

Interoperability

Microsoft sometimes seems like a big juggernaut that keeps on moving. One lesson Microsoft has learned is to support older legacy code bases. For example, one of the reasons Windows has succeeded is because it has always fully supported older applications. Keeping the old code running is very important. Companies are not going to go out and rewrite all their code, so getting new code to work with older code is an extremely important feature of .NET. .NET provides three basic mechanisms to facilitate interoperability between new code and old code, including Platform Invoke and two utilities for converting back and forth between CLR metadata and COM type libraries.

Platform Invoke

"In the beginning there was Windows. And Windows begat dynamic linking." As we discussed previously, client applications need a way to load library code dynamically and get to the entry points. In Windows, these functions are LoadLibrary and GetProcAddress. If you find yourself needing to call entry points within a specific legacy DLL, Platform Invoke (P/Invoke) is the way to go. P/Invoke is part of the `System.Runtime.InteropServices` namespace.

The idea behind P/Invoke is that the CLR will call `LoadLibrary/GetProc Address` automatically for you when you mark them correctly. C# syntax allows you to mark methods in various ways. One of the attributes you may use to mark methods is the `DllImport` attribute. (Visual Basic.NET's `Declare` statement serves the same purpose within Visual Basic.NET). To get P/Invoke working within your C# code, declare the DLL entry points as static external members within your class. Just make sure the signatures you use to declare the imported methods match their real signatures. When the CLR encounters a call to one of the imported methods, the CLR calls `LoadLibrary` for you.

The `DllImport` attribute allows you to control the entire loading process. For example, you may specify the calling convention, you may alias the method so that it has a different name from the real DLL function within your program, and you may control the character set the function uses.

TLBEXP and TLBIMP

Sometimes it is important to be able to call back and forth between COM code and CLR code. For example, you may find yourself with a legacy COM class that you want to call from the CLR, or you may want to call a CLR class from some existing COM code. For these reasons, the .NET framework provides two utilities: TLBIMP and TLBEXP. TLBIMP converts a COM type library to CLR metadata (which is what you find in the manifest). TLBEXP converts CLR metadata to a type library. These utilities are fairly straightforward to use, and we discuss an example in Chapter 6.

CONCLUSION

The computer industry is a real celebration of the impermanence of all things (except change). For years, as Windows developers we were concerned with building desktop applications and back-end systems using object-oriented programming techniques. Eventually, we caught the buzz of the Internet, but the component models we were using were woefully inadequate for widespread distribution through this medium. The game changed. Now we are more concerned with building a global community using people-oriented software.

As a Windows developer, you are probably accustomed to building separate DLLs, hoping that end users have the correct version of the DLL installed and that everybody is using COM correctly. The .NET framework changes everything.

In this chapter, we discussed the .NET runtime environment. The .NET runtime—the common language runtime—takes many of the best ideas from component software development over the last twenty years and rolls them into one package.

First, the .NET platform is based on the CLR. In the past, getting software to interoperate was a matter of getting clients and objects to agree upon the boundary between the client and the object. The CLR enables software to interoperate by breaking down the boundaries. The biggest problems between software components written in different languages included getting everyone to agree on the shape of the types involved and who cleans everything up. With the .NET CLR, these problems simply vanish because (1) software must comply with the CTS to execute under the runtime, and (2) the runtime takes care of cleaning everything up.

The CLR ships with a set of libraries based on the CLR. No more worrying about whether to use the Microsoft Foundation Library (MFC) , Visual Basic, or the Active Template Library (ATL)—each of which have their own peculiarities in their runtime behaviors. Every component now simply lives under the martial law of the CLR, and everybody is happy.

By basing the CLR on IL, the .NET runtime eliminates dependencies on any specific hardware platform. This is helpful for Microsoft developers because the world's processing systems are getting more and more diverse. For the last few years, we have been lulled into the feeling that as long as we write for the dominant desktop platform (any operating starting with a *W*—i.e., Windows 95, Windows 98, Windows NT, Windows 2000, or Windows XP), we will have a safe career path. However, the hardware companies have come up with some compelling reasons to use other platforms such as palmtop computers and Internet phones. In a nutshell, there are going to be literally millions of other devices out there that do not use the Windows operating system. Regardless, they are going to be part of the game, and we should write software that works on these platforms. By not forcing the final executable to work on an Intel box, .NET widens by a huge margin the available devices on which software runs. (We discuss this in depth when we address ASP.NET in Chapters 7 and 8.)

In Chapter 6, we discuss developing software that runs effectively under the CLR, as well as some of the issues you may encounter as a .NET developer.

Applied Runtime

.NET is many things, including ASP.NET, C#, Visual Basic.NET, and Simple Object Access Protocol (SOAP). At the heart of it all is the common language runtime (CLR). As we discussed in the last chapter, building .NET software is all about creating types that live under the CLR. There are a variety of ways you can talk to the CLR, including C#, managed C++, and Visual Basic.NET. The CLR also represents a language-independent base class library and ASP.NET.

In this chapter, we discuss the process of building and working with .NET assemblies, both dynamic link libraries (DLLs) and EXEs, using C# and Visual Studio. We look at such things as how to use the compiler, how to develop and use types in C#, and what goes into the manifest. Along the way, we explain how to interact with the runtime and how the .NET runtime fits in with people-oriented software.

BUILDING ASSEMBLIES AND APPLICATIONS

When it comes to building .NET software (which means building and combining assemblies), there are a couple of ways to build and compile assemblies—through the command-line compiler or through Visual Studio.NET. Each one has advantages and disadvantages depending on your development environment and culture.

The Command Line

The first approach to building and compiling assemblies is through the command line. The Microsoft compilers have all been available through the command line for years, and the .NET toolset is no different. The C# compiler is named CSC.EXE, the Visual Basic compiler is named VBC.EXE, and the C++ compiler (with managed extensions) is named CL.EXE.

The basic command line for building a single-module assembly with C# looks like this:

```
csc /t:library MyLibrary.cs
```

The C# compiler looks at the incoming command line, sees the input file named MYLIBRARY.CS, and compiles the file using the switches it finds. The most common switch is the /t switch, which informs the compiler about the type of target to build. There are four options: /t:library, /t:exe, /t:module, and /t:winexe. The /t:library switch builds a DLL, complete with the manifest (that is, a .NET assembly). The /t:exe switch builds a console executable while /t:winexe switch builds a Windows executable (with a windowing interface and message loop). To build a module without the assembly manifest, use the /t:module switch. Use this option when you want to build an assembly out of several modules. The default target is an executable, so if you try to build a library and leave out the /t:library switch, the compiler produces an error.

The other important command-line argument—the /r: command line—is the one that tells the compiler which other assemblies to bring in. If you go back and peruse some of the C# code throughout this book, you will not find a single #include statement. In traditional C and C++ code, header files were often used to bring in definitions and types defined outside the program. For example, WINDOWS.H (along with the other subordinate include files) provides all the definitions required for normal Windows development. .NET does not need to include files because all the type definitions are included within the manifests of the assemblies you are using.

For example, if you had some type definitions inside MYLIBRARY.DLL that you wanted to use within a final executable named CLIENT.EXE, you would simply include the MYLIBRARY assembly using the /r: command line. The C# source code does not need to include any definitions because all the definitions are included within the manifest for MYLIBRARY. Following is the command line to build a normal console executable named CLIENT.EXE:

```
csc /t:exe /r:MyLibrary.dll client.cs
```

In addition to building assemblies and executables wholesale, the command-line compiler has facilities for building multimodule assemblies using the assembly linker. For example, if you had a multiple module that you wanted to include in a single assembly, the assembly linker would build the assembly for you and put the assembly's manifest in the file you specified. Following are the command lines for building a multimodule assembly:

```
csc /t:module /r:system.dll moduleA.cs
csc /t:module /r:System.dll moduleB.cs
al /out:MultiModuleAssembly.dll moduleA.netmodule moduleB.netmodule
csc /t:exe /r:MultiModuleAssembly.dll client.cs
```

The /t:module command-line switch tells the C# compiler to build modules out of the source files MODULEA.CS and MODULEB.CS. The /t:module command-line parameter causes the compiler to place netmodule as the default extension. The assembly linker takes the modules and combines them into an assembly named MULTIMODULEASSEMBLY.DLL, which contains the manifest. Then the compiler can use the assembly normally—that is, the compiler can read the metadata out of the manifest.

There are many other command-line switches for controlling output directories, optimizations, debugging information, and so forth. They are well documented within the .NET software development kit (SDK). Search for "C# command-line switches" in Visual Studio help.

Makefiles

In addition, any good command-line environment will have a makefile utility, which analyzes dependencies and compiles only those modules that are out of date. .NET makefiles pretty much follow the classic Microsoft makefile structure as shown here.

```
all: client.exe
 client.exe : client.cs MyLibrary.dll
 csc /t:exe /r:MyLibrary.dll client.cs
MyLibrary.dll : MyLibrary.cs
  csc.exe /t:library MyLibrary.cs
```

The keyword all specifies the final executable named CLIENT.EXE and its dependencies. Notice that the makefile specifies that CLIENT.EXE depends on files named CLIENT.CS and MYLIBRARY.DLL. Building the complete project means running NMAKE.EXE on the makefile. NMAKE looks at the dependencies specified by CLIENT.EXE and makes sure they are updated. If MYLIBRARY.DLL is not updated, NMAKE looks up the rule for MYLIBRARY.DLL that says MYLIBRARY.DLL depends on a file named MYLIBRARY.CS. The command line to execute for MYLIBRARY.DLL says to run the C# compiler and build a DLL from the source file named MYLIBRARY.CS. Once the DLL is updated, NMAKE looks up the rule for CLIENT.EXE, which says to run the C# compiler to build CLIENT.EXE.

Makefiles are useful for large projects containing multiple assemblies and client executables. For example, if you are managing a huge project and would like to perform builds overnight, the easiest thing to do is to set up the compiling and linking rules in a makefile and run NMAKE overnight. The alternative to using the command line is to build projects using Visual Studio.NET.

BUILDING PROJECTS USING VISUAL STUDIO.NET

The other way to build assemblies and applications is through Visual Studio.NET. Visual Studio.NET provides an entire development environment rolled into one package. Until now, Visual C++ and Visual Basic lived as separate entities, and the only way to bridge applications written using these two environments was by using the component object model (COM). However, now that everybody is living under the same roof these days (because we all believe in the CLR), it makes sense to roll all the development options into one development environment. In addition, working from an integrated environment such as Visual Studio.NET provides a common ground for developers in terms of managing projects.

Like Visual Basic and Visual C++ before it, Visual Studio.NET includes Wizard code generators to get you started quickly. Visual Studio.NET builds project directories for you and populates them with boilerplate source code and configuration files that Visual Studio understands. The environment is fairly flexible, and it is easy to add new source code and resources to your project. The downside of Visual Studio.NET is that the Wizards do not produce standard makefiles, so it is harder to manage command-line compiling of projects created using the Wizards.

Other books discuss using the Visual Studio.NET environment and driving the Wizards well. For the most part, developing a new application involves starting a new project. The environment includes numerous Wizards, including the following:

- Visual Basic.NET and C# versions of Windows forms applications
- Visual Basic.NET and C# versions of component libraries
- Visual Basic.NET and C# versions of Windows control libraries
- Visual Basic.NET and C# versions of WebForm applications
- Visual Basic.NET and C# versions of Web control libraries
- Visual Basic.NET and C# versions of console applications
- Visual Basic.NET and C# versions of Web services
- Visual Basic.NET and C# versions of Windows services
- All the Microsoft Foundation Classes (MFC) and Active Template Library (ATL) Wizards from earlier versions of Visual C++
- Managed C++ applications
- Managed C++ component libraries
- Managed C++ Web services
- ATL server projects (including Web services)

Visual Studio.NET also includes Wizards for creating installation packages, CAB files, and database projects.

EXAMINING THE MANIFEST

The result of all this compiling and building is eventually some binary code. For the last fifteen years, the result of compiling and linking Windows application source code has been native Intel binaries. Remember that .NET adds another layer of indirection, compiling source code into intermediate language (IL). The .NET platform SDK includes a useful tool named *intermediate language disassembler,* or ILDASM.

Using ILDASM

To examine assemblies, we discuss an assembly named TYPETEST.DLL. TYPETEST includes various types—some structures and classes, an interface, and some enumerations. Remember that building an assembly results in a file containing some binary code and a manifest. ILDASM shows both pieces. The following listing shows the source code for the assembly, including all the types. Figure 6-1 shows ILDASM viewing the TYPETEST assembly.

```
namespace TypeTest {
    using System;

    public enum MonthType {
        January, February,
        March, April,
        May, June,
        July, August,
        September, October,
        November, December
    }
    public enum DayType {
        Monday, Tuesday,
        Wednesday, Thursday,
        Friday, Saturday,
        Sunday
    }

    public struct Appointment {
        public Appointment(MonthType month,
                           DayType day) {
            this.month = month;
            this.day = day;
            Console.WriteLine("Calling Constructor");
        }

        public void AMethod(MonthType month) {
            Console.WriteLine("Calling AMethod");
        }

        public MonthType month;
```

```
      public DayType day;
   };

   public interface IFibbonaci {
      int Fibbonaci(int x);
   };

   public class SomeClass {
      public SomeClass() {
      }

      public int Method1() {
         return 42;
      }

      public int AddTwo(int x, int y) {
         return x + y;
      }
   };
}
```

There are two parts to the assembly: the manifest and some binary code. ILDASM lets you look at an assembly's manifest. Notice the numbers at the bottom. This assembly is in its first iteration. The numbers shown at the bottom of ILDASM change as the assembly evolves. Popping open the manifest node reveals this view of TYPE-TEST (Figure 6-2).

Notice that ILDASM shows the types contained within the assembly. The assembly defines a namespace TYPETEST and all the members scoped within the namespace TYPETEST. There is a value class named Appointment, enumerations named MonthType and DayType, a class named SomeClass, and an interface named IFibonacci. Figure 6-3 shows details about the type Appointment.

FIGURE 6-1   ILDASM Peering into the TYPETEST Assembly.

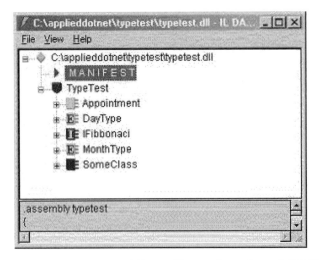

FIGURE 6-2 TYPETEST's Manifest as Seen through ILDASM.

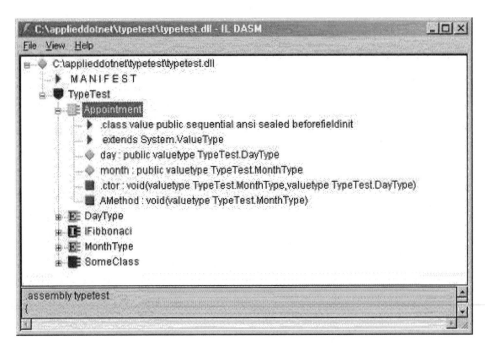

FIGURE 6-3 Appointment Structure as Seen through ILDASM.

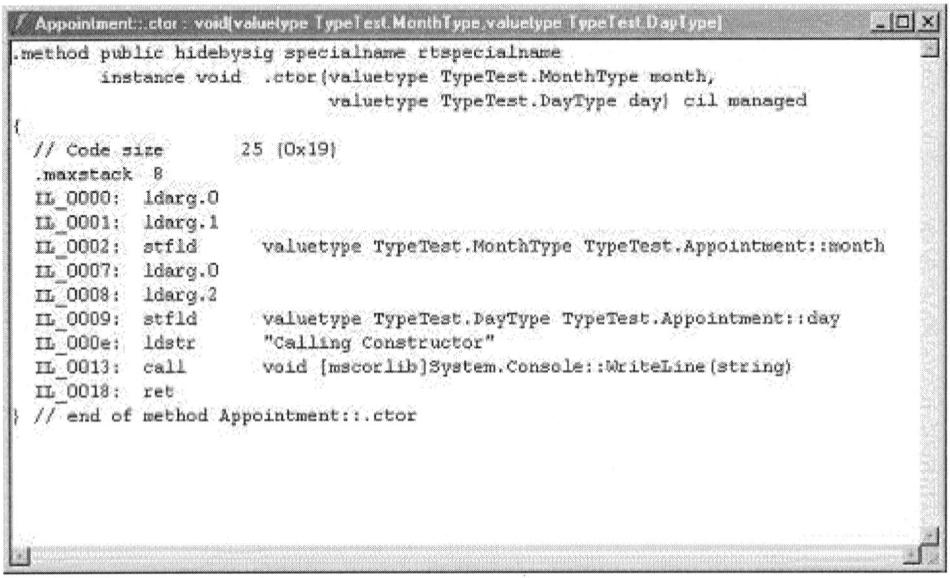


```
.method public hidebysig specialname rtspecialname
        instance void  .ctor(valuetype TypeTest.MonthType month,
                             valuetype TypeTest.DayType day) cil managed
{
  // Code size       25 (0x19)
  .maxstack  8
  IL_0000:  ldarg.0
  IL_0001:  ldarg.1
  IL_0002:  stfld      valuetype TypeTest.MonthType TypeTest.Appointment::month
  IL_0007:  ldarg.0
  IL_0008:  ldarg.2
  IL_0009:  stfld      valuetype TypeTest.DayType TypeTest.Appointment::day
  IL_000e:  ldstr      "Calling Constructor"
  IL_0013:  call       void [mscorlib]System.Console::WriteLine(string)
  IL_0018:  ret
} // end of method Appointment::.ctor
```

FIGURE 6-4 IL Disassembly for `Appointment`'s Constructor.

ILDASM shows that `Appointment` extends `System.ValueType` and has a parameterized constructor and a method named `AMethod`. `Appointment` also has a couple of member variables: a month (of type `MonthType`) and a day (of type `DayType`). Double-clicking on `Appointment`'s constructor yields the IL disassembly shown in Figure 6-4.

Notice the completeness of this assembly's description. The metadata included for this assembly is better than the metadata for COM's type libraries. Nothing is left to the imagination. ILDASM can peer into the assembly and see everything it needs to know about the types contained within. Development environments (such as Visual Studio.NET) can use this information to aid developers in understanding the contents of binary software, and the runtime can use it to help the types in TYPETEST to interoperate with other types within other assemblies.

Now let's take a look at that version number and discuss how .NET handles binary versioning.

DEPLOYMENT AND VERSIONING

At the July 2000 Professional Developers Conference (PDC), Microsoft made quite a noisy declaration that the current method for deploying DLLs was just no good, and they emphasized the phrase "DLL Hell." For many applications, this is an apt description. How many times have you had a program crash because someone put the wrong version of a DLL in your executable path or took one out of your executable path? Even COM does not work completely because not everyone follows the rules of interface versioning. In other words, interfaces should not change—new ones should be created and renamed with a new GUID. In addition, machines using COM frequently face issues such as bloated registries. How do we get out of DLL Hell? The philosophy behind .NET is that you should think carefully about sharing components and do so only whenever necessary. In other words, keep applications and their DLLs as close together as possible. In a nutshell, when you install an application, just pick up the whole directory structure and move it somewhere else—lock, stock, and barrel—whether using File Transfer Protocol (FTP), XCOPY, or some other mechanism.

As it turns out, there is a little more involved, but XCOPY is the general idea. For the most part, .NET applications include a collection of assemblies that are closely related yet loosely coupled. When you build applications using assemblies, the command line you might use looks something like this:

```
csc /t:exe /r:MyLibrary /r:CommonLib /r:YourLib client.cs
```

The resulting client depends on three different assemblies: `MyLibrary`, `CommonLib`, and `YourLib`. The question is, how does the client know that it is connecting to the correct version of the DLL when it is deployed? The answer is that the version information embedded within the assembly becomes embedded within the client application. The current version of TYPETEST is 0.0.0.0. Notice that this version of the client was built using version 0:0:0:0 of TYPETEST, as shown by ILDASM in Figure 6-5. In addition, notice that the TYPETEST client also depends on version 1.0.2411.0 of MSCORLIB.

It turns out that the version information is just one of four components that the CLR uses to identify assemblies. These four components include the simple name of the assembly (usually the file name), the version of the assembly (major version, minor version, build number, and revision number), culture information (language and region), and originator information identifying the developer of the assembly. The only absolutely necessary component is the name of the assembly. The version, the culture information, and the originator are optional. However, these other components are extremely useful for versioning assemblies.

By default, the version number of an assembly is 0.0.0.0. You can set this version number explicitly using an attribute in the source code as follows:

```
using System.Reflection;
[assembly:AssemblyVersionAttribute("1.2.1.*")]
```

If the assembly is built from separate modules, you may set the version using the assembly linker.

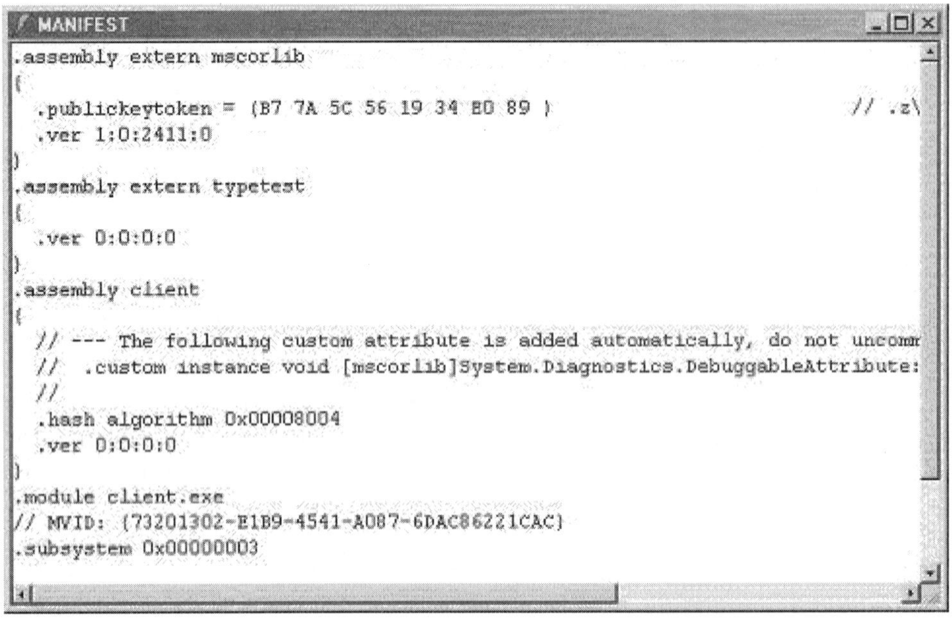

```
/ MANIFEST                                                        _ |□| x|
.assembly extern mscorlib
{
  .publickeytoken = (B7 7A 5C 56 19 34 B0 89 )          // .z\
  .ver 1:0:2411:0
}
.assembly extern typetest
{
  .ver 0:0:0:0
}
.assembly client
{
  // --- The following custom attribute is added automatically, do not uncomm
  //   .custom instance void [mscorlib]System.Diagnostics.DebuggableAttribute:
  //
  .hash algorithm 0x00008004
  .ver 0:0:0:0
}
.module client.exe
// MVID: {73201302-E1B9-4541-A087-6DAC86221CAC}
.subsystem 0x00000003
```

FIGURE 6-5   Client of the TYPETEST Assembly as Seen through ILDASM.

When versioning assemblies, the major number is mandatory. You may leave the other fields out, and they will be assumed to be zero. Once you define the major version, you also have the option of defining the minor version. Once you define the minor version, you may define the build field using an asterisk (*). An asterisk appearing in the build number causes the compiler to base the build number on the number of days elapsed since February 1, 2000. This way, the build number is unique each day.

The culture and language information for an assembly is specified by a structure, CultureInfo, embedded within the assembly. The CultureInfo identifies the spoken language and country code for which an assembly has been designed. You can add culture and language information to an assembly using the AssemblyCulture-Attribute, just as you can specify the version number. Following is the code used to apply the attribute:

```
using System.Reflection;
[assembly:AssemblyCultureAttribute("en-US")]
```

The AssemblyCultureAttribute takes the two-part string representing the language for which the assembly is intended. The second part identifies the region in which the language assembly is to be used. The previous code specifies that the assembly is intended for English-speaking users in the continental United States. Culture identifiers are intended for use within localized resource assemblies. Assemblies containing executable code should not have culture identifiers. They compile, but the compiler forbids their use in client code.

The originator attribute identifies the developer of the component using a digital signature. When you are about to ship or deploy your assembly, you sign the assembly. The public key used to sign the assembly is unique to each developer. The signature is made up of two parts: a public key and a private key, which are based on well-established algorithms.

A digital signing tool—called SN.EXE—comes with the .NET SDK for creating strong names. (A "strong name" is so called because it is the name that identifies an assembly as yours—even if there are other assemblies around with the same name.) SN is a command-line–driven tool that provides you with a digital signature in a file. The command line to run SN.EXE follows:

```
sn -k mykey.snk
```

Running SN.EXE (with the -k option) generates a new signature and places it in a file (MYKEY.SNK in this case). Then you can use the file to sign your assembly by applying the `AssemblyKeyFileAttribute` as follows:

```
using System.Reflection;
[assembly:AssemblyKeyFileAttribute("mysignature.snk")]
```

Applying this attribute to your assembly causes the compiler to embed the public key in the assembly (which you can see in the manifest). The compiler also computes a hash of the file containing the assembly manifest, signs the hash with the private key to create the digital signature of the file, and then stores the signature within the file containing the assembly manifest. The assembly's simple name (usually the file name) and the public key form the strong name of the assembly.

Figure 6-6 shows ILDASM's view of the TYPETEST component after applying the digital signature to it. Be careful with the file generated by SN.EXE because it contains your (or your organization's) private key and should be kept safe to ensure the security of your components. Signed components (with strong names) are meant to be shared (rather than private).

Global Cache

The general idea when developing .NET applications is to keep the components and applications as close to each other as possible. Deploying the application usually means picking up an entire application directory structure and dropping it on a new machine—no more globally unique identifiers (GUIDs), no more funny indirection through the registry, no weird executable path error, and (hopefully) a goodbye to DLL Hell.

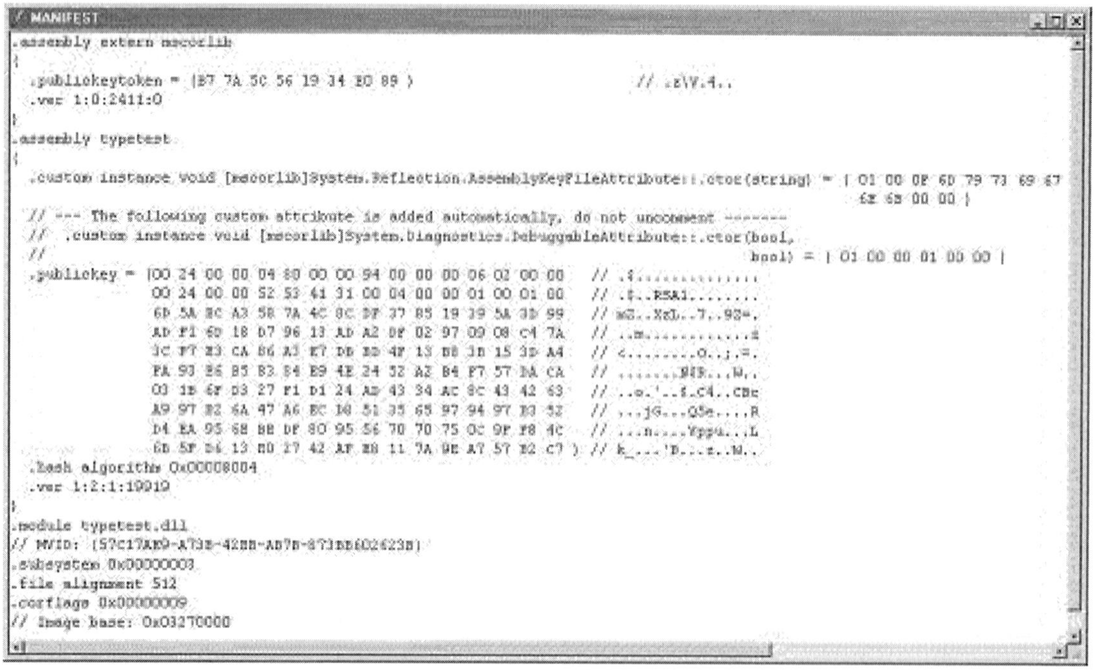

```
MANIFEST
.assembly extern mscorlib
{
  .publickeytoken = (B7 7A 5C 56 19 34 E0 89 )                         // .z\V.4..
  .ver 1:0:2411:0
}
.assembly typetest
{
  .custom instance void [mscorlib]System.Reflection.AssemblyKeyFileAttribute::.ctor(string) = ( 01 00 0F 6D 79 73 69 67
                                                                                              6E 6B 00 00 )
  // --- The following custom attribute is added automatically, do not uncomment -------
  //  .custom instance void [mscorlib]System.Diagnostics.DebuggableAttribute::.ctor(bool,
  //                                                                                  bool) = ( 01 00 00 01 00 00 )
  .publickey = (00 24 00 00 04 80 00 00 94 00 00 00 06 02 00 00   // .$..............
                00 24 00 00 52 53 41 31 00 04 00 00 01 00 01 00   // .$..RSA1........
                6D 5A EC A3 58 7A 4C 8C DF 37 85 19 39 5A 3D 99   // mZ..XzL..7..9Z=.
                AD F1 6D 18 D7 96 13 AD A2 DF 02 97 09 08 C4 7A   // ..m............z
                3C F7 E3 CA 86 A3 E7 DB ED 4F 13 B8 3B 15 3D A4   // <........O..;.=.
                FA 93 E6 B5 B3 E4 E9 4E 24 52 A2 B4 F7 57 DA CA   // .......N$R...W..
                03 1B 6F D3 27 F1 D1 24 AD 43 34 AC 8C 43 42 63   // ..o.'..$.C4..CBc
                A9 97 E2 6A 47 A6 EC D0 51 35 65 97 94 97 B3 52   // ...jG...Q5e....R
                D4 EA 95 68 BE DF 80 95 56 70 70 75 0C 9F F8 4C   // ...h....Vppu...L
                6B 5F D6 13 D0 27 42 AF E8 11 7A 9E A7 57 E2 C7 ) // k_...'B...z..W..
  .hash algorithm 0x00008004
  .ver 1:2:1:19919
}
.module typetest.dll
// MVID: {57C17AE9-A73E-42EE-AB7B-873BB602623B}
.subsystem 0x00000003
.file alignment 512
.corflags 0x00000009
// Image base: 0x03270000
```

FIGURE 6-6 ILDASM's View of TYPETEST Component after Being Signed.

Although private assemblies are the norm within .NET development, there are occasions when it is useful to write a shared component. For this purpose, it is important to be able to distinguish your assemblies from others that may have the same name. In COM, we tried to do this with GUIDs. The .NET solution is to sign your assembly and then place it within the global cache. The global assembly cache is a systemwide code cache for storing assemblies (even if they share the same name). The same-name scenario could occur if someone invented an assembly with the same name as your assembly or when your assembly evolved—it would have the same name but a different version number.

The global assembly cache actually consists of two caches—the temporary download cache and the permanent global assembly cache. Sharing an assembly means more than simply copying the assembly to the cache. You need to place an assembly into the global assembly cache. When an assembly is in the global assembly cache, it is visible to all applications. By keeping all the global assemblies in the same place, component loading is optimized because there is only one place the CLR needs to look to find global shared components. If the CLR cannot find an assembly using a strong name, the CLR looks in the global cache.

The .NET SDK ships with a command-line tool named GACUTIL, which places an assembly in the global assembly cache. GACUTIL uninstalls shared assemblies, as well.

Loading Assemblies and Versioning

When the CLR needs to load an assembly, it must resolve which assembly to load. Resolving an assembly reference involves a number of steps, a process called *probing*. These steps represent a set of heuristics used to locate the assembly based on its name, version, and culture.

During compile and build time, static references to the required assemblies are recorded in the manifest of the assembly being compiled. If the reference is a dynamic reference, it is constructed on the fly as a result of calling an API-like `System.Reflection.Assembly.Load`. An assembly reference contains the name, version, culture, and public key token (if one exists) of the requested assembly. This is information the runtime needs to locate the assembly. Following is the algorithm used by the CLR for finding an assembly:

- The CLR checks the configuration files, including the application, publisher policy, and machine policy configuration files (i.e., the WHATEVERTHE-APPLICATIONISNAMED.CONFIG file, the publisher's policy configuration file in the global cache, and the "MACHINE.CONFIG" file). The application configuration file modifies the loading process for assemblies and is used to specify other probing locations. The application's configuration file name is the executable's base name with a CONFIG extension. The configuration file is simply an extensible markup language (XML) file describing the binding process. The following listing shows the syntax of a configuration file defining alternative probe paths for the TYPETEST client:

```
<Configuration>
 <AppDomain PrivatePath="bin;custom"/>
</Configuration>
```

  A publisher policy is a file located in the global assembly cache containing assembly redirection settings. Vendors producing shared assemblies can broadcast the availability of a newer version of an assembly by including a publisher policy with the upgraded assembly.

  Finally, the machine configuration file includes settings that apply for the entire machine.
- The runtime checks whether the assembly name has been bound already and uses the previously loaded assembly if that is the case.
- If the assembly needs to be loaded (because it is not already loaded), the runtime checks the global assembly cache. If the assembly is found there, the runtime uses this assembly.

- If the assembly is not found in the global cache, the runtime probes for the assembly. If the configuration and publisher information previously listed does not affect the original reference *and* if the bind request was created using the `Assembly.LoadFrom` method, the runtime checks for the following location hints:
    1. If the runtime finds a CodeBase in the configuration files, it checks only this location. If this fails, the runtime fails the binding request.
    2. The CLR probes for the assembly. The probing algorithm looks in the application base directory, in a subdirectory of the application base directory with the same name as the assembly, and then looks in the culture directory of the application base directory. Failing the previous binding algorithm, the CLR probes the same directories under the application base\binpath directory.

If the runtime fails to bind the assembly, the information is written to a log file that may be read through the Assembly Binding Log Viewer (`Fuslogvw.exe`). In addition, there is no version checking for assemblies without strong names.

More on Configuration Files

As with the current Windows programming paradigm, your job in .NET programming is to build assemblies against which client code runs. What happens when a new version of an assembly is deployed? The most common scenario is that the client should use the newer (and presumably better version). This was the assumption made in COM—that DLLs automatically progressed in fitness and robustness. Unfortunately, a new version sometimes introduces new bugs, so you want client code to stick to the older version. This is why the CLR goes to such great lengths to include versioning in the assembly architecture. Configuration files are the way to tell the CLR to load particular assemblies on behalf of client code.

As described previously, when probing for shared assemblies the application uses a configuration file to search for the correct version. The following listing is a configuration file containing two version policies. The configuration file is used to map versions so the runtime loads the correct one.

The `<BindingPolicy>` tag indicates the section of the configuration file containing the version maps. Sandwiched between the `<BindingPolicy>` and the `</BindingPolicy>` tags is the `<BindingRedir>` tag. The `<BindingRedir>` tag tells the CLR that binding requests for one version be redirected to another version. You may also include an asterisk for the original version to ask the CLR to map all requests to a specific assembly.

```
<?xml version="1.0" ?>
<Configuration>
```

```
<BindingPolicy>
  <BindingRedir
    Name="TYPETEST"
    Originator="1234567890123456"
    Version="1.2.3.4" VersionNew="1.3.0.0"
    UseLatestBuildRevision="no"
  />
</BindingPolicy>
</Configuration>\
```

GARBAGE COLLECTION

In the last chapter, we got a good look at how the CLR manages garbage collection. The system periodically examines all the memory that's been allocated from the managed heap. When the garbage collector finds an object that's no longer referenced, it returns the memory used by the object back to the heap whence it came.

Effects

The side effect of garbage collection is the absence of destructors within CLR classes and the fact that you never really know when (or even if) your object is cleaned up. The C# syntax provides for a destructor independently of the runtime. C#'s destructor simply overrides `Finalize` and calls the base class's version of `Finalize`—the standard CLR cleanup mechanism. It is not a problem if your object contains only references to other managed types (from the managed heap, of course). The runtime cleans up those references. However, if your object holds a reference to something other than an object on the managed heap, there is an issue. For example, if your object holds a connection to a Structured Query Language (SQL) database, you should be sure it gets cleaned up when it is no longer needed. Then it becomes necessary to implement some sort of deterministic finalization. If you are using unmanaged resources, you should make sure your object (and its constituents) does disappear completely by ensuring that a destructor-like mechanism is called on your object to clean up any unmanaged references it might be holding.

Deterministic Finalization

If you want deterministic finalization to happen, it is mostly your responsibility as a programmer. There is a finalization mechanism available for CLR classes. That is, you may override the `Finalize` method on your class and hope the runtime cleans up your object. It turns out that `Finalize` may never be called, so you should not rely on that mechanism to clean up expensive or unmanaged resources held by your object. The way around this is to place some method on your class that clients may call to clean up your object when they are done with it. The usual name for this method is Dispose. The CLR defines an interface named IDisposable that defines the method Dispose for you if you inherit from it. The following listing shows the IDisposable interface, a class inheriting from it, and some client code using the class:

```csharp
namespace System {
  public interface IDisposable {
    void Dispose();
  }
}

public class FinalizeTest {
    public class DisposeOfMe : IDisposable {
        public DisposeOfMe() {
            // do expensive stuff—perhaps
            //   SQL connection or unmanaged
            //   resource
            Console.WriteLine("Constructing");
        }
        public void UseMe() {
            Console.WriteLine("Thanks for using me");
        }
        private void TearDown() {
            Console.WriteLine("Tearing down the resources");
        }
        public void Dispose() {
            TearDown();
            System.GC.SuppressFinalize(this);
        }
        ~DisposeOfMe() {
            Console.WriteLine("Destructor is called");
            TearDown();
        }
    }

    public static void Main() {
        Console.WriteLine("Finalize Client");
        DisposeOfMe dispofme = new DisposeOfMe();
        DisposeOfMe dispofme2 = new DisposeOfMe();
        dispofme.UseMe();
        dispofme.Dispose();
    }
}
```

Following is the output of the previous program:

```
Finalize Client
Constructing
Constructing
Thanks for using me
```

```
Tearing down the resources
Destructor is called
Tearing down the resources
```

When `DisposeOfMe` is constructed, it sets up some expensive or unmanaged resources. Notice that the first instance of `DisposeOfMe` is manually deleted—the client calls `Dispose` explicitly. The reference to the second instance is deleted normally when it goes out of scope, and the destructor (`Finalize` method) is called by the run-time *eventually*. This is a short program, so holding on to an expensive resource is not a big deal. In a larger program, it might be a huge deal. Notice the destructor (`Finalize` method) cleans up the resources. Notice that `Dispose` cleans up the resources and then invokes the garbage collector to get rid of the object. `Dispose` prevents the garbage collector from calling the class's destructor twice.

The advantage of garbage collection is that it largely frees the client from having to worry about troublesome resource management issues. If you are a C++ developer, how many times have you forgotten to delete a reference (which often becomes a major source for anomalous bugs and memory leaks)? In 95 percent of the cases, standard garbage collection gets rid of any resource leaks. However, there are times when you need to clean up an object yourself—specifically when your object holds onto unmanaged resources. Deterministic finalization is the standard way to make that happen. However, notice that deterministic finalization puts the onus back on the client to free the object.

THREADING AND THE CLR

No modern operating system would be complete without some sort of preemptive multitasking. With clock speeds continually going up, any platform these days is going to have tons of spare cycles that could be put to better use. This is true of .NET, and the CLR supports preemptive multitasking and the ability to run multiple threads within a single application. This feature is useful in numerous scenarios. A background thread is often the best way to process lengthy operations. For example, inserting a lengthy operation to handle a user interface event (such as the `MouseDown` event) freezes the user interface—which is a great time to use a thread. Certain other designs benefit from concurrent operation. For instance, you might use separate reader and writer threads to process buffers of data. The .NET framework fully supports multithreading. Let's start by discussing the .NET way to create threads.

Creating Threads

Creating threads within a CLR-based program is pretty straightforward. In fact, creating threads is a great example of using delegates. In standard Win32 programming, the way to create threads is through the application program interface (API) function

CreateThread. You declare a thread function with a very specific signature, pass a pointer to the function using the CreateThread API, and voila—your process space starts scheduling the thread.

   The CLR includes a class, System.Threading.Thread, that takes the place of the Win32 CreateThread, function. To start a thread within the CLR, you write a class with a static or nonstatic function you would like to dispatch as another thread. To launch the method as a thread, create an instance of the Thread class and the method to be threaded within the constructor. Then call the Thread instance's Start method. The following listing shows using delegates to start threads:

```
using System;
using System.IO;
using System.Threading;

public class Threading {
    public class ThreadMe  {
        public ThreadMe() {
            Console.WriteLine("Constructing");
        }
        public void NonStaticThreadProc() {
            for(int i = 0; i < 5; i++) {
                String str = "Running NonStaticThreadProc " + i;
                Console.WriteLine(str);
            }
            Console.WriteLine();
            Console.WriteLine();
        }
        static public void StaticThreadProc() {
            for(int i = 0; i < 5; i++) {
                String str = "Running StaticThreadProc " + i;
                Console.WriteLine(str);
            }
            Console.WriteLine();
            Console.WriteLine();
        }
        public void StartThreads() {
            Console.WriteLine("Starting Thread1");
            ThreadStart tsNonStatic;
            ThreadStart tsStatic;
            tsNonStatic = new ThreadStart(this.NonStaticThreadProc);
            tsStatic = new ThreadStart(ThreadMe.StaticThreadProc);
            Thread thread1 = new Thread(tsNonStatic);
            Thread thread2 = new Thread(tsNonStatic);
            thread1.Start();
            thread2.Start();
            Thread thread3 = new Thread(tsStatic);
            Thread thread4 = new Thread(tsStatic);
            thread3.Start();
            thread4.Start();
        }
```

```
   }
   public static void Main() {
      Console.WriteLine("Threading Client");
      ThreadMe threadMe = new ThreadMe();
      threadMe.StartThreads();
   }
}
```

Of course, whenever you work with a system that manages multiple threads, there is a good possibility of data contention. The way to manage data contention is by using various synchronization techniques.

Synchronization

The idea behind synchronization is to allow code to run only when it is safe (usually when no other threads are accessing shared data). Threads must agree to wait while other threads that may access the data are running. The CLR provides a class named Monitor for synchronizing threads.

In one way, using the CLR's Monitor class is very much like using a Win32 CriticalSection in your class. Win32 critical sections worked by passing an opaque CriticalSection structure around, and client threads would wait to enter it. As long as no other thread was holding the CriticalSection, that thread got a chance to run. Monitor (and its Enter and Exit functions) is like using a lock manager that places objectwide locks on CLR objects. It is like giving your class a CriticalSection structure and calling EnterCriticalSection on every method entrance and LeaveCriticalSection on every method exit.

The CLR's Monitor class may not be instantiated. To use it, you merely call its methods, which include Exit, Enter, Pulse, PulseAll, TryEnter, and Wait. Threads call Enter and TryEnter to ask the Monitor for a lock. Exit releases the lock. Threads call Wait to block a thread. Finally, Pulse awakens a single waiting thread and PulseAll awakens all waiting threads. If you have a simple object whose state you need to protect, Monitor's Enter and Exit functions by themselves work well. Following is the signature for Monitor.Enter:

```
public static void Enter(Object obj);
```

Calling Enter and passing a CLR object as the parameter causes the calling thread block if another thread holds a lock on the object. Calls to Enter and Exit must be balanced. Following is the signature for Monitor.Exit:

```
public static void Exit(Object obj);
```

Exit releases the monitor's lock on an object. The next waiting thread is unblocked and allowed to proceed (provided the current thread has balanced calls to

Monitor.Exit with Monitor.Enter). The following shows code using Monitor.Enter and Monitor.Exit:

```
using System;
using System.IO;
using System.Threading;
public class Threading {
    public class ThreadMe  {
    String strSharedState;
        public void ThreadProc1() {
            for(int i = 0; i < 10; i++) {
                Monitor.Enter(this);
                strSharedState =
                  "ThreadProc1 iteration " + i + "  locked...";
                Console.WriteLine(strSharedState);
                Thread.Sleep(1000);
                Monitor.Exit(this);
                Console.WriteLine("Unlocked");
                Thread.Sleep(500);
            }
            Console.WriteLine();
            Console.WriteLine();
        }
        public void ThreadProc2() {
            for(int i = 0; i < 10; i++) {
                Monitor.Enter(this);
                String strSharedState =
                    "ThreadProc2 iteration " + i + "  locked...";
                Console.WriteLine(strSharedState);
                Thread.Sleep(500);
                Monitor.Exit(this);
                Console.WriteLine("Unlocked");
                Thread.Sleep(500);
            }
            Console.WriteLine();
            Console.WriteLine();
        }
        public void StartThreads() {
            ThreadStart ts1, ts2;
            ts1 = new ThreadStart(this.ThreadProc1);
            ts2 = new ThreadStart(this.ThreadProc2);
            Thread thread1 = new Thread(ts1);
            Thread thread2 = new Thread(ts2);
            Console.WriteLine("Starting Thread1");
            thread1.Start();
            Console.WriteLine("Starting Thread2");
            thread2.Start();
        }
    }

    public static void Main() {
        Console.WriteLine("Threading Client");
        ThreadMe threadMe = new ThreadMe();
```

```
        threadMe.StartThreads();
    }
}
```

The previous example shows a single class named `Threading` that includes a couple of threaded methods that manipulate a string member variable. The string member is visible to both methods, and so it should be protected. `ThreadProc1` and `ThreadProc2` both call `Monitor.Enter` before trying to access the data and call `Monitor.Exit` after accessing the data. Notice that the argument for `Enter` and `Exit` is this. Calling `Enter` places a lock on the object, meaning no other threads (besides the one that called `Enter`) may invoke methods on the object. Calling `Exit` releases the lock.

In addition to behaving like a `CriticalSection` using the `Monitor.Enter` and `Monitor.Exit` calls, `Monitor` can act like an event signaling mechanism in much the same way as Win32 events. The methods expressing this functionality include `Pulse`, `PulseAll`, and `Wait`.

Following are the signatures for `Pulse` and `PulseAll`:

```
public static void Pulse(Object obj);
public static void PulseAll(Object obj);
```

`Pulse` sends a notification for a single waiting object. `PulseAll` sends a notification to all waiting objects. Waiting objects are those objects that have called `Monitor.Wait`.

`Monitor.Wait` has several overloaded versions:

```
public static bool Wait(Object obj);
```

This version waits (perhaps forever) for notification from the object (via `Pulse`/`PulseAll`). That is, the object needs to call back to the runtime at some point via a call to `Pulse` or `PulseAll`.

```
public static bool Wait(Object obj, int millisecondsTimeout);
```

The timeout version also waits for notification from the object (via a call to `Pulse`/`PulseAll`). However, this version times out after the number of milliseconds specified in the `millisecondsTimeout` parameter.

```
public static bool Wait(Object obj, TimeSpan timeout);
```

This second variation of a timeout version also waits for notification from the object (via a call to `Pulse`/`PulseAll`). However, this version uses a `TimeSpan` to indicate the timeout duration.

```
public static bool Wait(Object obj,
    millisecondsTimeout, bool exitContext);
```

This variation waits for the number of milliseconds in the `millisecondsTimeout` parameter. If `exitContext` is true, then the synchronization domain for the context (if in a synchronized context) is exited before the wait and reacquired.

```
public static bool Wait(Object obj,
    TimeSpan timeout, bool exitContext);
```

This version is just like the previous one, except that it uses a `TimeSpan` to specify the timeout period.

```
using System;
using System.IO;
using System.Threading;


public class Threading {
    public class UseMeToSignal {
    }

    public class ThreadObj1 {
        public ThreadObj1(UseMeToSignal umtsParam) {
            umts = umtsParam;
        }
        public void ThreadProc() {
            Console.WriteLine("Thread1- Acquiring Lock");
            Monitor.Enter(umts);
            Console.WriteLine("Thread1- release lock and Wait");
            Monitor.Wait(umts);
            Console.WriteLine("Thread1- Pulsing umts");
            Monitor.Pulse(umts);
            Console.WriteLine("Thread1- Releasing Lock");
            Monitor.Exit(umts);
        }
        public void StartThread() {
            ThreadStart ts;
            ts = new ThreadStart(this.ThreadProc);
            Thread thread = new Thread(ts);
            Console.WriteLine("Starting Thread1");
            thread.Start();
        }

        UseMeToSignal umts;
    }

    public class ThreadObj2 {
        public ThreadObj2(UseMeToSignal umtsParam) {
            umts = umtsParam;
        }

        public void ThreadProc() {
            Console.WriteLine("Inside Thread2- Acquiring Lock");
```

```
                    Monitor.Enter(umts);
                    Console.WriteLine("Inside Thread2- Pulsing umts");
                    Monitor.Pulse(umts);
                    Console.WriteLine("Inside Thread2- Releasing Lock");
                    Monitor.Exit(umts);
                }

            public void StartThread() {
                ThreadStart ts;

                ts = new ThreadStart(this.ThreadProc);
                Thread thread = new Thread(ts);
                Console.WriteLine("Starting Thread2");
                thread.Start();
            }
            UseMeToSignal umts;
        }

    public static void Main() {
        Console.WriteLine("Threading Client");
        UseMeToSignal umts = new UseMeToSignal();
        ThreadObj1 threadObj1 = new ThreadObj1(umts);
        threadObj1.StartThread();

        ThreadObj2 threadObj2 = new ThreadObj2(umts);
        threadObj2.StartThread();
    }
}
```

The previous example creates two separate threads that use a global CLR object to signal each other back and forth. The first thread starts and then waits for a signal from the other thread to continue. This functionality is useful when trying to coordinate reading and writing threads, for example.

Method-Level Locks

Sometimes placing a lock on an entire object is overkill. For example, if only one method needs to be synchronized, it's wasted effort for the runtime to lock every call. You may place the `MethodImpl` attribute on the method, passing the Synchronize flag. For example, if you wanted to have a single method in which only one thread could run, you would tack the following attribute on it:

```
using System.Runtime.InteropServices;
public class TestMethodLevelSync {
    [ MethodImpl(MethodImplOptions.Synchronized) ]
    public void OneAtATimePlease()
    {
        // Only one thread at a time will come in here...
    }
```

```
public void FreeForAll() {
    // Don't put any code in here
    //   that may not be accessed
    //   concurrently as there might be
    //   multiple threads at one time
    //   weaving their course through
    //   this method.
    }
}
```

This finer-grained method of thread synchronization is useful when you do not need to place the lock on the entire object at once.

INTEROPERABILITY

One of the backbones of Microsoft's strength within the industry is their attention to making sure software is backwards compatible. It would be great if we could sweep the table clean and start fresh each time a better technology was introduced. However, the fact is that there is much working software out there. The organizations that have invested time, effort, and money are not going to throw the investment away very easily. In that vein, the .NET platform bends over backwards to interoperate with older DLLs (COM or otherwise).This interoperability manifests itself as Platform Invoke (P/Invoke), COM callable wrappers, and runtime callable wrappers. Let's start with P/Invoke.

Platform Invoke

In terms of pure age and being time tested, plain-vanilla DLLs represent some of the denizen components of Windows development. Clearly, .NET developers are going to want to call into older DLLs from time to time. P/Invoke is available through the `System.Runtime.InteropServices` namespace. The key to calling from managed code into unmanaged DLLs is knowing the signature of the function call and using the `DllImportAttribute` attribute. To bind the client and the object, put the `[DllImport]` attribute preceding the file for which you want entry points. The following listing illustrates using the `DllImportAttribute` to interoperate with methods in the standard Kernel32.DLL and User32.DLL DLLs:

```
namespace DllInterop
{

    using System;
    using System.Runtime.InteropServices;

    class DllInterop
```

```
    {
        [DllImportAttribute("User32.dll")]
        public extern static int MessageBeep(uint type);
        [DllImportAttribute("User32.dll",
         EntryPoint = "MessageBeep")]
        public extern static int Win32MessageBeep(uint type);
        [DllImportAttribute("kernel32.dll")]
        public static extern uint GetLastError();
        [DllImportAttribute("user32.dll") ]
        public extern static uint MessageBox(int hwnd, String m,
            String c, uint flags);
        [DllImportAttribute("user32.dll",
        EntryPoint="MessageBoxW",
        ExactSpelling=true,
        CharSet=CharSet.Unicode)]
        public extern static uint UniCodeMessageBox(int hwnd,
            String m, String c, uint flags);

        static void Main(string[] args)
        {
            MessageBeep(0);
            Win32MessageBeep(0);
            MessageBox(0, "What's up Doc",
                "MessageBox", 1);
            UniCodeMessageBox(0,
                "We really mean it",
                "UnicodeMessageBox", 1);
            Console.WriteLine(GetLastError());
        }
    }
}
```

The previous example loads MessageBeep, MessageBox, and GetLastError from User32.DLL and Kernel32.DLL. DllImportAttribute is fairly flexible. At the very least, you need to give the file name in which you expect to see the entry point. For example, with the method MessageBeep, the runtime will load the User32.DLL file and search for the entry point named MessageBeep. Notice that there is not much type safety here. If you get the function signature wrong, the CLR gets confused and throws an exception.

The interoperation services let you alias your methods. The example defines a method named Win32MessageBeep and maps it to the MessageBeep entry point in User32.DLL. You may also ask for the entry point verbatim and define the character set. For example, the Win32 header files actually define two versions of MessageBox: MessageBoxA and MessageBoxW. MessageBoxA takes normal American National Standards Institute (ANSI) strings, whereas MessageBoxW uses wide character strings. The previous example defines a method named UnicodeMessageBox and maps the definition to the wide character version of MessageBox (MessageBoxW).

Interoperating with COM

If the only kind of legacy software out there consisted of plain old DLLs, we could stop the interoperation story right here. However, COM (even with all its warts) is the basis for tons of software out there. For the .NET framework to gain the kind of ground to make Microsoft shareholders happy, .NET needs to provide an interoperation path between COM and the CLR. Fortunately, there are two utilities for making interoperation between COM and the CLR very simple: TLBIMP.EXE and TLBEXP.EXE.

TLBIMP

TLBIMP's main purpose in life is to take COM type libraries as input and convert them into .NET assemblies with CLR type definitions corresponding to the COM type definitions. This is often named a runtime callable wrapper (RCW). Using TLBIMP is very straightforward. Just run it from the command line and include the COM type library as an input file. TLBIMP also has other command-line parameters for signing and versioning the assemblies.

The following listing shows some interface description language (IDL) describing a simple COM object with a single interface:

```
import "oaidl.idl";
import "ocidl.idl";
    [
        object,
        uuid(A60B4B2E-940B-439C-9B6E-2CEB64909E12),
        helpstring("IAppliedDotNetATLObj Interface"),
        pointer_default(unique)
    ]
    interface IAppliedDotNetATLObj : IUnknown
    {
        [helpstring("method Method1")]
        HRESULT Method1([in]short x,
                    [out, retval] long *plOut);
        [helpstring("method Method2")]
        HRESULT Method2([in]BSTR bstrIn);
        [propget, helpstring("property LongProperty")]
        HRESULT LongProperty([out, retval] long *pVal);
        [propput, helpstring("property LongProperty")]
        HRESULT LongProperty([in] long newVal);
        [propget, helpstring("property BSTRProperty")]
        HRESULT BSTRProperty([out, retval] BSTR *pVal);
        [propput, helpstring("property BSTRProperty")]
        HRESULT BSTRProperty([in] BSTR newVal);
    };
    [
        uuid(22A72A24-9C0A-4C32-9326-9E3E5148CD41),
        version(1.0),
        helpstring("AppliedDotNetATLSvr 1.0 Type Library")
    ]
```

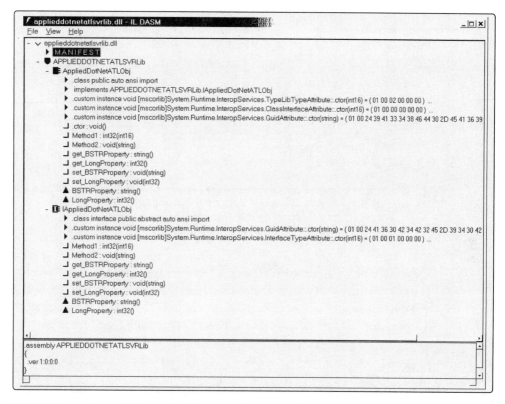

FIGURE 6-7   The .NET Assembly Metadata Resulting from Running the Type Library through TLBIMP.

```
library APPLIEDDOTNETATLSVRLib
{
    importlib("stdole32.tlb");
    importlib("stdole2.tlb");
    [
        uuid(9A348FD0-EA69-486A-ADB8-A6317A708079),
        helpstring("AppliedDotNetATLObj Class")
    ]
    coclass AppliedDotNetATLObj
    {
        [default] interface IAppliedDotNetATLObj;
    };
};
```

Given the IDL from the previous listing, TLBIMP generates an assembly. Figure 6-7 shows the assembly under the watchful eye of the ILDASM utility.

The following listing shows code using the assembly generated from the COM type library within a C# program:

```
using APPLIEDDOTNETATLSVRLib;
using System;
using System.IO;
using System.Reflection;

public class TestTLBIMP {
    public static void Main() {
        AppliedDotNetATLObj comObj;

        comObj = new AppliedDotNetATLObj();
        comObj.Method1(42);
        comObj.Method2("Hello");
        comObj.LongProperty = 343;
        long x = comObj.LongProperty;
        comObj.BSTRProperty = "What's up Doc?";
        string str = comObj.BSTRProperty;
    }
}
```

The command line for the previous program compile includes the assembly built from TLBIMP (which is how it may be referred to). At runtime, the CLR will generate an RCW when calling new to create the new objects. The CLR manages all the interface pointers and details such as QueryInterface, AddRef, and Release.

TLBEXP

TLBEXP accepts .NET type information (metadata) and creates a COM type library from it. For example, if you take the TYPETEST definition from the assembly's metadata and run it through TLBEXP, TLBEXP produces a type library containing the following definitions:

```
// Generated .IDL file (by the OLE/COM Object Viewer)
//
// typelib filename: <could not determine filename>
[
  uuid(38DB6B2F-6572-31F0-8F66-4A959D38D025),
  version(1.2),
  custom(90883F05-3D28-11D2-8F17-00A0C9A6186D, typetest,
    Version=1.2.1.21636, Culture=neutral,
    PublicKeyToken=8333ca23fd63b933)
]
library typetest
{
    // TLib :     // TLib : Common Language Runtime Library :
{BED7F4EA-1A96-11D2-8F08-00A0C9A6186D}
    importlib("mscorlib.tlb");
// TLib : OLE Automation : {00020430-0000-0000-C000-000000000046}
    importlib("stdole2.tlb");
// TLib : Common Language Runtime Execution
// Engine 1.0 Type Library : {5477469E-83B1-11D2-8B49-00A0C9B7C9C4}
```

```
    importlib("mscoree.tlb");
    // Forward declare all types defined in this typelib

    interface IFibbonaci;
typedef [uuid(2AB973E8-EB0B-3653-AF93-79F8CCA4B369),
    version(1.0)      ,
    custom(0F21F359-AB84-41E8-9A78-36D110E6D2F9,
    TypeTest.MonthType)]

    enum {
        MonthType_January = 0,
        MonthType_February = 1,
        MonthType_March = 2,
        MonthType_April = 3,
        MonthType_May = 4,
        MonthType_June = 5,
        MonthType_July = 6,
        MonthType_August = 7,
        MonthType_September = 8,
        MonthType_October = 9,
        MonthType_November = 10,
        MonthType_December = 11
    } MonthType;

typedef [uuid(60FE56EC-DEDD-3DEA-A26A-FF92EE94EC01),
    version(1.0)      ,
    custom(0F21F359-AB84-41E8-9A78-36D110E6D2F9,
    TypeTest.DayType)]

    enum {
        DayType_Monday = 0,
        DayType_Tuesday = 1,
        DayType_Wednesday = 2,
        DayType_Thursday = 3,
        DayType_Friday = 4,
        DayType_Saturday = 5,
        DayType_Sunday = 6
    } DayType;

typedef [uuid(4A211D25-4A26-3651-901E-6B03B7EAC3C4),
    version(1.0)      ,
    custom(0F21F359-AB84-41E8-9A78-36D110E6D2F9,
    TypeTest.Appointment)
]

    struct tagAppointment {
      MonthType month;
      DayType day;
    } Appointment;

    [
      odl,
      uuid(8124E89A-4E6B-391B-AED4-35E2F027D4B6),
```

```
        version(1.0),
        dual,
        oleautomation,
        custom(0F21F359-AB84-41E8-9A78-36D110E6D2F9,
            TypeTest.IFibbonaci)
    ]
    interface IFibbonaci : IDispatch {
        [id(0x60020000)]
        HRESULT Fibbonaci(
                    [in] long x,
                    [out, retval] long* pRetVal);
    };

    [
      uuid(075A818F-1101-30F2-8130-BC2D21AC3872),
      version(1.0),
      custom(0F21F359-AB84-41E8-9A78-36D110E6D2F9,
        TypeTest.SomeClass)
    ]
    coclass SomeClass {
        interface IManagedObject;
        [default] interface IDispatch;
        interface _Object;
    };
};
```

TLBEXP tries to get a representation as close to the metadata as possible. Unfortunately, the COM type information is not quite as rich as the .NET metadata. Whereas the .NET assembly is identified using a full strong name, a type library is identified using three elements: a type library identifier (TLBID), the version, and the locality ID (an LCID). Neither the name of the file containing the type information nor the friendly name defined within the library is part of the library's identity. The type information includes C-style enumerations (rather than pure .NET-style enumerations).

Using TLBEXP also generates version information from the assembly within the type library. Notice that the major and minor version numbers of an assembly are carried forward to the type library. However, assembly build numbers are left out. This means that two assemblies differing only in their build numbers always generate the same type library.

Once the types are in the COM type library, you need a way to activate the objects from COM. Of course, COM has its activation call `CoCreateInstance`, and it needs registry entries. A command-line utility named REGASM adds the correct COM registry settings for the CLR classes in an assembly. After using REGASM, the types listed in the type library are available to a COM application (as much as possible). You may call `CoCreateInstance` on any of the classes listed and obtain interface pointers to them. The CLR generates a COM callable wrapper (CCW).

WINDOWS FORMS

The Microsoft .NET initiative centers on the notion of Internet-based development. However, normal, double-clickable client applications will always be popular. You will probably always be able to write Windows-based applications using WndProcs and Petzoldian-style coding. If you are used to MFC, that works fine as well. If you are a Visual Basic developer, you are familiar with Visual Basic's forms-based approach to creating standalone applications. The .NET movement now brings the forms-based development model to the forefront. This technology is named *Windows forms*.

.NET Windows forms are built into the .NET base class library. You are not confined to using Visual Basic to get a forms-based development environment. You can use C#, Managed C++, or Visual Basic 7.0 (or any of the other .NET-compliant languages expected to emerge) to create Windows forms applications.

Underneath the hood, all Windows applications essentially work the same. Windows maintains a collection of Window classes (that is, windows whose behaviors are defined by WndProc functions). In the early days of Windows programming, the biggest task was to get about 80 lines of boilerplate code to work correctly, then gradually add event handlers to develop an application. MFC did away with requiring developers to carve out all their own WinMain and WndProc functions. Windows forms continues the trend of eliminating programming details, so you don't have to spend as much time writing grunge code.

Windows forms are very similar to standard Visual Basic forms-based development. Although SDK-style or MFC applications interact directly with the Windows API, Windows forms programming hides the boilerplate details in Windows programming. Like normal Windows applications, Windows forms respond to the usual events, such as mouse movements and menu selections, and they can also render within the client area. However, the syntax for managing these features is more abstract than the syntax in a program you write with the SDK or even with MFC and is closer to the syntax of Visual Basic programming.

Windows forms technology is useful for creating standard windows, creating multiple document interface (MDI) windows, dialog boxes, or surfaces for graphical routines. As with Visual Basic development, which uses a forms model of user-interface development, defining the user interface for a Windows form usually means placing controls on the form's client area. However, Windows forms can render pretty much anything you want on the drawing surface.

In addition to exposing a drawing surface and managing a collection of standard controls, Windows forms define their appearance through properties. For example, to move a Windows form on the screen programmatically, you set the Windows form's X property. Windows forms manage their behavior with methods, and they also respond to events to define their interaction with the user.

Windows forms are instances of classes running in the .NET framework or the CLR. Writing a Windows form application usually means instantiating an instance of the WinForm class, tweaking its properties, and setting up event handlers. Because a Windows form is a regular CLR-based class, which fully supports inheritance, you can build hierarchies of Windows forms classes in a standard, object-oriented way.

Right now, you can use Windows forms through C#, Managed C++, and Visual Basic.NET. Other languages will be following soon. These languages are equally adept at producing Windows forms applications. Following is a rundown of a basic Windows forms application.

The Form Class

The heart of a Windows forms application is a class derived from the CLR Form class. The Form class encapsulates all the underlying code necessary to display and run a Windows application. (The Windows denizens out there probably remember defining WndProcs, registering window classes, and spinning message loops.) The following listing shows a simple line drawing program written using C# and Windows forms:

```
namespace CSharpDraw {
    using System;
    using System.Drawing;
    using System.Drawing.Drawing2D;
    using System.Windows.Forms;

    public class Canvas : Form {
        int xAnchor, yAnchor;

        public Canvas () {
            SetStyle(ControlStyles.Opaque, true);
            Size = new Size(500, 500);
            Text = "CSharp Drawing";
            // add a button
            Button buttonClear = new Button();
            buttonClear.Size=new Size(100,50);
            buttonClear.Location=new Point(300,400);
            buttonClear.Text="Clear";
            buttonClear.Click += new EventHandler(Clear);
            this.Controls.Add(buttonClear);
        }


        //Fired when the Clear button is pressed
        private void Clear(object sender, EventArgs e) {
            this.Invalidate();
        }
```

```csharp
protected override void OnMouseDown(MouseEventArgs e) {
    Capture = true;
    base.OnMouseDown(e);
    xAnchor = e.X;
    yAnchor = e.Y;
    this.Invalidate();
}

protected override void OnMouseUp(MouseEventArgs e) {
    Capture = false;
}

protected override void OnMouseMove(MouseEventArgs e) {
    if(Capture) {
        Graphics g = CreateGraphics();
        Pen pen;
        pen = new Pen(Color.FromArgb(170, Color.Black), 3);
        g.DrawLine(pen, xAnchor, yAnchor, e.X, e.Y);
    }
}

protected override void OnPaint(PaintEventArgs e) {
    Graphics g = e.Graphics;
    e.Graphics.SmoothingMode = SmoothingMode.AntiAlias;
    g.FillRectangle(
        new SolidBrush(Color.FromArgb(250, Color.White)),
        ClientRectangle);
}

public static void Main() {
    Application.Run(new Canvas());
}
```

Any Windows forms application has to have at least one instance of a CLR-based form class. The Form class represents the various types of windows you see in an application. Underneath it all, a Windows form is a normal window—you just do not have to see all the details that would show up if you were programming using the raw Windows SDK. The Form class is useful for creating multiple document interface (MDI) windows, single document interface (SDI) windows, and dialog windows.

Visual Basic developers have had it easy for the last eight years or so. All that they needed to manage the status of a window was to manage the window's properties, such as size, background color, and caption. SDK developers have had to make low-level calls to the Windows API to do the same thing. Windows forms applications bring the simplicity of Visual Basic-style development to the CLR. All these form properties may be managed at design time through Visual Studio.NET or programmatically at runtime.

Handling Events

The main purpose for any Windows user interface program is to handle the various events that come into it. Normal events include mouse movement, mouse button presses, and key presses. Most normal events are handled by the Windows form by overriding a virtual function. Notice how the drawing program in the listing on pages 242 and 243 intercepts the mouse move, mouse button down, and mouse button up events by overriding the established OnMouseMove, OnMouseDown, and OnMouseUp functions on the Form class respectively.

A Windows forms application also handles button and control notifications. The drawing window places a button and wires it up to a handler. When the user presses the Clear button, the drawing form redirects control to the handler named Clear. The form class handles getting the event to the correct handler.

Graphics and Rendering

Windows forms programming is primarily user interface based, requiring you to draw on the screen. Windows forms define a well-established means of trapping the WM_PAINT message. The Form class contains a function named OnPaint that you can override. By overriding this function, you can intercept the drawing event and put whatever you want on the screen. Looking at the sample application source code, notice that the Paint event parameter includes a graphics object that resembles a device context from the SDK programming days. The graphics object includes methods for drawing lines, shapes, filling regions, and about anything else you might want to do on the screen. The great thing about Windows forms and C# is that you do not have to worry about managing the graphics device interface (GDI) styles of resources because the .NET framework does it for you.

CONCLUSION

In this chapter, we got a thorough idea of how the .NET runtime works. The .NET CLR is the component technology of the future. DLLs are a great way to distribute software given effective decoupling and versioning technologies. COM provided a great start in this direction by introducing extensible interface-based programming, but it did not go quite far enough. The CLR finishes the job. Components that play in the CLR game conform to rules that enable them to interoperate easily with other components following the same rules. From the people-oriented software perspective, the CLR is one of the strongest representations of universalization. No matter what language you choose to express your programs in, they generally come down to the same level—the CLR.

Building applications and components for the CLR involves creating and using assemblies, which are DLLs that include metadata describing the contents. In normal

Windows programming, the metadata was strongly encouraged but not strictly necessary. (Type information is necessary for COM+ because the interception layer uses it heavily.) There are several ways to write assemblies, but the two most common are to use Visual Studio.NET or the command line compilers and makefiles. (*CSC* is the C# compiler, *VBC* is the Visual Basic.NET compiler, and *CL* is the C++ compiler with managed extensions.) The biggest advantage of using the command-line compilers is flexibility, even though it may take a bit longer to get the build process working correctly. Visual Studio.NET provides convenience at the cost of flexibility. The .NET SDK includes a tool named ILDASM, which is useful for examining assemblies. Assemblies include version information and may be signed to ensure that clients are using the correct version.

For the most part, the .NET framework takes care of memory and resource leaks by introducing garbage collection. The downside of garbage collection is the lack of deterministic finalization. That is, you never know exactly when unused resources will be cleaned up. The CLR defines an interface, `IDisposable`, which adds a `Dispose` method to help clients get rid of your objects if the objects need to be released explicitly. This task might be required for objects that hold unmanaged resources.

Finally, the CLR universalizes the Windows client application by introducing a forms-based development paradigm at the runtime level. Visual Basic developers have been taking advantage of this software development model for years, consistently beating the C++ developers to the ship date. The forms-based environment is no longer confined to the Visual Basic runtime—any language and compiler that talk to the CLR can be used to create Windows forms applications.

ASP.NET Up Close

In the last six chapters, you have been introduced to a diverse C# CodeBase and some active server page (ASP) code sprinkled here and there. For example, in Chapter 4 we covered an application named *Managed Synergy,* primarily to show you how to apply C#. To do that, we had to throw in some ASP.NET in certain places. In this chapter (and Chapter 8), we discuss ASP.NET in more detail—what it is, how it works, and how to apply its more advanced features.

.NET is about to be released to the world at large. During the last few months of its beta period, its early adoption rate has been staggering. Judging from the feedback on the .NET lists and the size of the community that is growing up around it, .NET looks like it is going to be huge. As we have discussed so far, the .NET framework represents an implementation of several great modern software development ideas that have been a long time coming. These ideas include a Common Type System (CTS), a common runtime environment, the ability to really mix languages within a single application, and the ability to invoke methods over the Internet. These factors contribute to the new software paradigm coming down the road: people-oriented software. .NET comprises many facets, but one of the most important parts of .NET—the one that will almost certainly be a lynchpin in its success—is ASP.NET. ASP.NET ties together all three facets of people-oriented software: universalization, translation, and collaboration. Although a few of the modern Microsoft-based Web sites will probably continue using ISAPI extensions and classic ASP (and perhaps the Active Template Library server [ATL server]), most other Microsoft-based Web sites will be written using ASP.NET.

CONNECTIVE TISSUE

Most of us in the software industry these days agree that the computing world of the future will involve the Internet as the network of choice. How could it be any other way? The Internet is ubiquitous. The dream of the 1980s and 1990s was to get computers within a single office talking to one another. Now, local area networks (LANs) and companywide intranets are commonplace. The vision for the next decade is to get all the computers in the world talking to one another. Now that nearly everyone agrees on the protocol (Hypertext Transfer Protocol [HTTP] or HTTPS) and the bits to send across (Extensible Markup Language [XML] that is formatted using Simple Object Access Protocol [SOAP]), connecting Web sites programmatically can actually happen.

However, although the communication standards and protocols are currently being set up and agreed to, what is really going to kick the .NET vision into high gear is a decent way to implement the standards. At the heart of it all, Web sites are still going to be nodes on the Internet managing HTTP requests and responses. As developers, we need a structured way to intercept and respond to HTTP requests. This is what ASP.NET provides. ASP.NET is going to be one of the most important parts of .NET for bringing people-oriented software to life.

The Road to ASP

So that you can really understand ASP.NET, let's take a quick look at the metamorphosis the Web has gone through during the past few years. The Web really began to be popular around 1995 or so, and in that short time it has been transformed from a set of fancy marketing brochures into sites with full-fledged order-entry systems and other advanced features.

Classic ASP evolved as a way to more easily develop "dynamic" content—that is, to have the content of your Web site change at runtime. The first Web pages up on the Web were just hypertext markup language (HTML) pages that never changed—kind of like electronic brochures. People would sign on to a uniform resource locater (URL) somewhere, and their browsers would simply zoom in on some files in some directory on the remote computer. The browser on the client machine would download the HTML using HTTP and interpret it. Obviously, the next step was to make the content change based on various conditions (such as who is signed on, the content that is available at runtime, and the security context of the client). This is the origin of dynamic content.

The first dynamic Web sites were the result of the common gateway interface (CGI). CGI provides dynamic content by directly processing incoming HTTP requests and issuing responses in a custom process. The CGI process spits out customized HTML based on the requests coming in. One of the problems of CGI was the fact that each incoming HTTP request got a new process, creating a burden on the server. Creating a new process for each request was pretty expensive.

To reduce the burden of creating a new process for every request (on the Microsoft platform), Microsoft implemented a programming interface they named the Internet Services API (ISAPI). Instead of firing up a new process for each request, ISAPI fires up a new instance of an ISAPI dynamic link library (DLL), customized to spit out specific HTML. Of course, ISAPI DLLs were not the easiest things in the world to write. The next step in the evolution was ASPs (active server pages).

You can think of classic ASP as one big ISAPI DLL that Microsoft has already written for you. Classic ASP accepts and posts responses to HTTP requests. ASP mixes presentation (HTML) with scripting blocks so that you can control the content coming from an ASP page. ASP parses files with *.asp* extensions and does its best to emit the right kind of HTML. HTTP requests and responses are available as well-established objects you can get to easily from within the script blocks. (They are part of the component object model [COM] runtime context.)

CLASSIC ASP VERSUS ASP.NET

Classic ASP goes a long way toward simplifying Web programming. It is often much easier to write some HTML and mingle it with script than it is to write a new DLL from scratch. Still, classic ASP is not without its issues. First, ASP pages are often just an unstructured mass of code. Classic ASP is very much like the early days of Basic programming, when you could get something done quickly but the resulting code was often difficult to follow. The ASP object model has numerous intrinsic, or global, objects. For example, when writing script code to generate the content of an HTTP request, you send the content out to the client using the intrinsic Response object. For simple applications in which you can guarantee that only one client is involved in talking to your Web application, this isn't much of a problem. But how many Web applications can guarantee this? (The number is probably very close to zero—if it is not actually zero.) Because of the way ASP is structured with these intrinsic objects, managing the state of clients is a nightmare.

ASP.NET evolves classic ASP. For example, you still have the same intrinsic objects in ASP.NET and you can add scripting wherever you want it on the page. In fact, most ASP pages can easily be brought over and run as ASP.NET pages by renaming them with the *.aspx* extension.

ASP.NET brings a lot of new features to the table. First, ASP.NET pages are compiled into assemblies just like the other components within .NET, providing both performance and security benefits. Second, ASP.NET supports using any .NET language within it. No longer are you confined to using JavaScript or VB Script on your Web pages. You can now use more structured languages. ASP.NET lets you write the executable parts of your pages in C# or full-fledged Visual Basic.

ASP.NET brings with it a whole new programming model incorporating Web forms, server-side controls, data binding, and Web services. Web forms and server-side controls work by tailoring the markup language they spit out to match the client browser attached. Data binding formalizes exchanging data between controls at run-time (such as edit boxes and combo boxes) and data variables within the Web site program. Finally, Web services formalize the process of getting multiple computers talking to each other automatically using XML and HTTP (SOAP). ASP.NET is ripe for creating Web services in which a machine's software can reveal itself to the rest of the world as a SOAP server.

DEEMPHASIZING ISAPI

At the end of the day, writing a Web server is all about processing HTTP requests and delivering responses. ASP.NET is no different; its main purpose in life is to service HTTP requests and responses. In this vein, ASP.NET deemphasizes the ISAPI architecture that has been around for the last six years or so. ISAPI has not disappeared; it is just that ASP.NET prefers the common language runtime (CLR) to Internet information server's (IIS's) ISAPI/ASP architecture wherever possible.

ASP.NET works by dispatching HTTP requests to handler objects. That is, ASP.NET dispatches HTTP requests to those objects implementing a CLR interface named IHttpHandler. You can bind uniform resource identifier (URI) paths to classes for handling specific requests (see Chapter 8). InternetBaton (see Chapter 2) also uses this technique. For example, if someone submits a query for some information, you can map that URI to a specific class for handling that query. Incoming URIs that are not mapped to a specific handler class are swallowed by ASP.NET's default handler. Most of the time, the file specified in the URI is a basic ASPX file. Let's take a look at the core of an ASP.NET page.

ASP.NET: A COMMON LANGUAGE RUNTIME CITIZEN

ASP.NET improves on classic ASP by being a full-fledged CLR language. That is, ASP.NET files are compiled rather than simply interpreted like classic ASP. ASP.NET files are compiled on demand based on source code dependencies. ASP.NET compiles ASPX files once and caches the DLL in a well-established directory. If ASP.NET finds source code that is newer than the DLL, it compiles the new source code into a DLL and caches the DLL. ASP.NET is also superior as a deployment environment because you do not need to shut down your site to update the code. When new source code is added to the application, ASP.NET shadow-copies the old DLL to process existing requests using the preexisting DLL so that running processes may continue—you may upgrade the site without shutting it down.

System.Web.UI.Page

The core of every ASP.NET page is the `System.Web.UI.Page` class. Most ASP.NET pages work by extending this class. Nearly the whole user interface package for ASP.NET is wrapped up into `System.Web.UI.Page`. The following listing shows the `System.Web.UI.Page` class:

```
class Page : IHttpHandler, TemplateControl {
class Page : TemplateControl, IHttpHandler
{
    public Page(); // constructor
    public HttpApplicationState Application {get;}

    public Cache Cache {get;}
    public virtual string ClientID {get;}
    public string ClientTarget {get; set;}
    public virtual ControlCollection Controls {get;}
    public virtual bool EnableViewState {get; set;}
    public string ErrorPage {get; set;}
    public virtual string ID {get; set;}
    public bool IsPostBack {get;}
    public bool IsValid {get;}
    public virtual Control NamingContainer {get;}
    public virtual Page Page {get;}
    public virtual Control Parent {get;}
    public HttpRequest Request {get;}
    public HttpResponse Response {get;}
    public HttpServerUtility Server {get;}
    public HttpSessionState Session {virtual get;}
    public ISite Site {get; set;}
    public virtual string TemplateSourceDirectory {get;}
    public TraceContext Trace {get;}
    public virtual string UniqueID {get;}
    public IPrincipal User {get;}
    public ValidatorCollection Validators {get;}
    public virtual bool Visible {get; set;}
    public virtual void DataBind();
    public void DesignerInitialize();
    public virtual void Dispose();
    public virtual bool Equals(
        object obj
    ;
    public virtual Control FindControl(
        string id
    );
    public virtual int GetHashCode();
    public string GetPostBackClientEvent(
        Control control,
        string argument
    );
    public string GetPostBackClientHyperlink(
        Control control,
```

```
        string argument
    );
    public string GetPostBackEventReference(
        Control control
    );
    public Type GetType();
    public virtual int GetTypeHashCode();
    public virtual bool HasControls();
    public virtual void InstantiateIn(
        Control control
    );
    public bool IsClientScriptBlockRegistered(
        string key
    );
    public bool IsStartupScriptRegistered(
        string key
    );
    public UserControl LoadControl(
        string virtualPath
    );
    public ITemplate LoadTemplate(
        string virtualPath
    );
    public string MapPath(
        string virtualPath
    );
    public Control ParseControl(
        string content
    );
    public void RegisterArrayDeclaration(
        string arrayName,
        string arrayValue
    );
    public virtual void RegisterClientScriptBlock(
        string key,
        string script
    );
    public virtual void RegisterClientScriptFile(
        string key,
        string language,
        string filename
    );
    public virtual void RegisterHiddenField(
        string hiddenFieldName,
        string hiddenFieldInitialValue
    );
    public void RegisterOnSubmitStatement(
        string key,
        string script
    );
    public void RegisterRequiresPostBack(
        Control control
    ;
```

```
public virtual void RegisterRequiresRaiseEvent(
   IPostBackEventHandler control
);
public virtual void RegisterStartupScript(
    string key,
    string script
);
public void RenderControl(
    HtmlTextWriter writer
);
public string ResolveUrl(
    string relativeUrl
);
public void SetIntrinsics(
    HttpContext context
);
public void SetRenderMethodDelegate(
    RenderMethod renderMethod
);
public virtual string ToString();
public event EventHandler AbortTransaction;
public event EventHandler CommitTransaction;
public event EventHandler DataBinding;
public event EventHandler Disposed;
public event EventHandler Error;
public event EventHandler Init;
public event EventHandler Load;
public event EventHandler PreRender;
public event EventHandler Unload;
bool Buffer {set;}
protected bool ChildControlsCreated {get; set;}
int CodePage {set;}
string ContentType {set;}
protected HttpContext Context {get;}
string Culture {set;}
protected bool EnableViewStateMac {get; set;}
protected EventHandlerList Events {get;}
ArrayList FileDependencies {set;}
protected bool HasChildViewState {get;}
protected bool IsTrackingViewState {get;}
int LCID {set;}
string ResponseEncoding {set;}
protected bool SmartNavigation {get; set;}
protected virtual bool SupportAutoEvents {get;}
bool TraceEnabled {set;}
TraceMode TraceModeValue {set;}
TransactionOption TransactionMode {set;}
string UICulture {set;}
protected virtual StateBag ViewState {get;}
protected virtual bool ViewStateIgnoresCase {get;}
protected virtual void AddParsedSubObject(
    object obj
);
```

```
protected void AspCompatEndProcessRequest(
    IAsyncResult result
);
protected void BuildProfileTree(
    string parentId,
    bool calcViewState
);
protected void ClearChildViewState();
protected virtual void CreateChildControls();
protected virtual ControlCollection CreateControlCollection();
protected virtual HtmlTextWriter CreateHtmlTextWriter(
    TextWriter tw
);
protected LiteralControl CreateResourceBasedLiteralControl(
    int offset,
    int size,
    bool fAsciiOnly
);
protected virtual NameValueCollection DeterminePostBackMode();
protected virtual void EnsureChildControls();
protected virtual void Finalize();
public virtual Control FindControl(
    string id
);
protected virtual void FrameworkInitialize();
protected virtual void InitOutputCache(
  int duration,
  string varyByHeader,
  string varyByCustom,
  OutputCacheLocation location,
  string varyByParam
);
protected bool IsLiteralContent();
protected virtual object LoadPageStateFromPersistenceMedium();
protected virtual void LoadViewState(
    object savedState
);
protected object MemberwiseClone();
protected virtual void OnAbortTransaction(
    EventArgs e
);
protected virtual bool OnBubbleEvent(
    object source,
    EventArgs args
);
protected virtual void OnCommitTransaction(
    EventArgs e
);
protected virtual void OnDataBinding(
    EventArgs e
);
protected virtual void OnError(
    EventArgs e
```

```
    );
    protected virtual void OnInit(
       EventArgs e
    );
    protected virtual void OnLoad(
       EventArgs e
    );
    protected virtual void OnPreRender(
       EventArgs e
    );
    protected virtual void OnUnload(
       EventArgs e
    );
    protected void RaiseBubbleEvent(
       object source,
       EventArgs args
    );
    protected virtual void RaisePostBackEvent(
       IPostBackEventHandler sourceControl,
       string eventArgument
    );
    protected virtual void Render(
       HtmlTextWriter writer
    );
    protected virtual void RenderChildren(
       HtmlTextWriter writer
    );
    protected virtual void SavePageStateToPersistenceMedium(
       object viewState
    );
    protected virtual object SaveViewState();
    protected void SetStringResourcePointer(
        IntPtr stringResourcePointer,
        int maxResourceOffset
    );
    protected virtual void TrackViewState();
    protected virtual void Validate();
}
```

We discuss some of these properties and methods later in the chapter. For now, we are going to discuss how the class works. It is fairly large and contains pretty much everything needed to manage the HTTP protocol between the client browser and the Web server.

System.Web.UI.Page Fundamentals

`System.Web.UI.Page` implements the core ASP.NET interface named `IHttp-Handler`, enabling the `Page` class to receive HTTP requests and deliver responses. The `Page` class is from the `Control` class used for writing server-side controls. (We discuss the `Control` class later in this chapter.) This gives the `Page` class the ability to manage standard controls (like edit boxes and list boxes) and other user interface elements. The following listing shows an ASP.NET file that spits a bit of HTML out to the browser advertising the CLR type of the page. If the syntax looks a bit bizarre at first, do not worry. Later in this chapter, we discuss the specifics of mixing C# and ASP.NET code.

```
<%@ page language="C#" %>
<%
  // finding out the base type of the Web page
  string s;

  s = this.GetType().BaseType.ToString();

  // Send some text out to the browser
  this.Response.Write("<html>");
  this.Response.Write("<body>");
  this.Response.Write("Based on the following CLR Class:");
  this.Response.Write(s);
  this.Response.Write("</body>");
  this.Response.Write("</html>");
%>
```

Notice that the code in the previous listing is written with C# (indicated by the language directive at the top). When the page shows the type this, notice that the page reports the entire namespace: System.Web.UI.Page. Figure 7-1 shows the output to a browser.

The <% %> block markers specify a block of code and the language to use to execute the block. Notice that the structured C# code fits in with the rest of the page. In

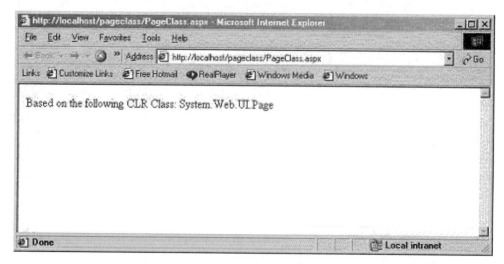

FIGURE 7-1   Output of the .ASPX File after Executing.

addition, notice that the base class is `System.Web.UI.Page`. The `Page` class includes a `Response` object suitable for spitting text out to the browser. The C# code that executes simply asks the page for its CLR type and spits that string out to the browser.

In classic ASP, the `Response` object was called an "intrinsic object"—a global variable. In ASP.NET, the `Response` object is moved into the CLR `Page` class, making it a bit easier to manage. You do not need to push all your markup language through the `Response` object. ASP.NET lets you include markup text as part of the page itself (just as in classic ASP). However, the ASP.NET model makes it easier to customize your output through the `Response` class as shown previously.

ASP.NET Connection Object Model

HTTP is basically a connectionless protocol. That is, the connection between the client and the Web server is not held. Unlike a connection-intensive protocol like distributed component object model (DCOM), clients connect to the server only for the duration of an HTTP request, meaning there needs to be some way of managing the connections within an application. ASP.NET's connection model is based on the `System.Web.Http.Context` class. ASP.NET generates one `HttpContext` object for each request serviced and passes it to HttpHandlers (of which `System.Web.UI.Page` is one). You can always get to the current `HttpContext` object because it is exposed as a static property of `HttpContext`: `HttpContext.Current`. You can use the `HttpContext` object to get information about the request and its relationship to your application. For example, `HttpContext` is useful for getting information about the HTTP request, as shown in the following listing. In addition, `HttpContext` manages the session state; you can get to the session state information through the `HttpContext` object via the `Session` property.

```
<%@ page language="C#" %>
<%
  string s;

  // Get The current context . . .
  HttpContext httpc = HttpContext.Current;

  // spit out some text . . .
  httpc.Response.Write("URL: ");
  // find out the URL of the current connection
  s = httpc.Request.RawUrl;
  httpc.Response.Output.WriteLine(s);
%>
```

The previous listing shows how to get the current connection state and query it for the current HTTP request and the URL used to get to the page. Figure 7-2 shows the output to the browser.

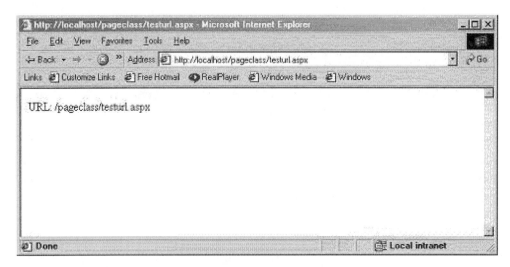

FIGURE 7-2   Output Advertising the Raw URL Used to Surf to the Page.

Mixing ASP.NET and C#

Take another peek at the previous listing. You may notice that the language directive at the top of the file immediately indicates the language of choice, in this case C#. (It could just as easily be Visual Basic.NET or some other CLR-compliant language.) The executable code is mixed in, bracketed by the <% and %> markers. This is often a convenient way to quickly mix executable CLR code with your HTML (or other markup language). Unfortunately, this technique can also create messy spaghetti code in your Web pages. ASP.NET supports *code behind the page*—mixing ASP code with executable code coming from another file. Basically, you write executable code using C# or Visual Basic (or some other CLR language) and insert it into the ASP page using a special directive.

To separate your executable code from the page layout, write a source code file containing your executable code and place it alongside your ASPX page. The following listing shows a C# class whose job it is to print out the date and time to any client connected to the server.

```
using System;
using System.Web.UI;

namespace AppliedDotNet
{
    public class CodeBehindPage : Page
    {
        public void PrintDate()
        {
```

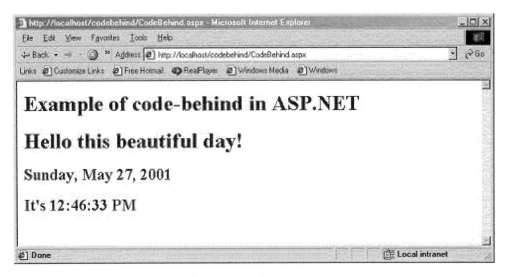

FIGURE 7-3 Output of Listings (pp. 258–260).

```
        String strDate;
        DateTime dateTime = DateTime.Today;
        strDate = dateTime.ToString( "D" );
        Response.Write(strDate);
    }

    public void PrintTime()
    {
        String strTime;
        DateTime dateTime = DateTime.Now;
        strTime = dateTime.ToString( "T" );
        Response.Write(strTime);
    }
  }
 }
}
```

Figure 7-3 shows the output of the previous listing and the next listing (pp. 258–260). Notice that the `CodeBehindPage` class derives from `System.Web.UI.Page`. The CLR `Page` class is the master class of ASP.NET that wraps up all the HTTP request/response functionality. Deriving from the `Page` class brings your ASP.NET page into the runtime. You can use all the functionality that comes with the runtime. The `Page` class also includes a `Response` object that can print formatted text out to the client. These two functions simply figure out the date and time using the CLR-sponsored classes and push the text stream out to the browser. The following listing shows the ASP page that uses the class:

```
<%@ Page language=C# src=CodeBehindPage.cs
Inherits=AppliedDotNet.CodeBehindPage %>
```

```
<html>
<body>
<h1>Example of code-behind in ASP.NET</h1>
<h1>Hello this beautiful day!</h1>
<h2><% PrintDate(); %></h2>
<h2>It's <%PrintTime();%></h2>
</body> </html>
```

One of the great advantages of ASP.NET is the ability to segregate the executable code from the presentation. The ASP.NET code-behind technique encourages this separation.

ASP.NET Configuration Files

Although ASP.NET still has a few ties to IIS, it tries to keep them to a minimum. ASP.NET adds the ability to configure Web applications through configuration files. After ASP.NET configures an application using the IIS metabase, ASP.NET looks to an application's configuration file to configure the application. (We already looked at configuration files in Chapters 5 and 6.) The ASP.NET configuration files include configuration information specific to ASP.NET.

ASP.NET configuration files are simply XML files named WEB.CONFIG. They can do a number of things, including mapping file extensions to custom handlers, registering custom extension modules, specifying how session state is implemented, and supporting user-defined element types (and corresponding parser objects).

Like normal CLR configuration files, ASP.NET configuration files include sections. The WEB.CONFIG file may contain several sections above and beyond the normal CLR configuration files:

- `<authentication>`: This section manages ASP.NET's authentication settings, including the default authentication code, the HTTP cookie to use for authentication, the password format, and the log-on user name and password.
- `<authorization>`: This section manages ASP.NET authorization settings, including allowing or disallowing access to a specific resource.
- `<httpModules>`: This section adds, removes, or clears HTTP modules within an application.
- `<customErrors>`: This section specifies custom error messages for an ASP.NET application, including specifying the default URL to direct a browser if an error occurs and whether custom errors are enabled, disabled, or shown only to remote clients.
- `<identity>`: This section controls the application identity of the Web application. Settings include specifying whether client impersonation is used on

each request and specifying the user name and password if client impersonation is set to *false*.

- `<pages>`: This section identifies page-specific configuration settings, such as
whether the URL resource uses response buffering, whether session state is
enabled, whether view state is enabled, whether page events are enabled, the
code-behind class the page inherits, and the virtual root location of the client-
side script libraries installed by ASP.NET.

- `<processModel>`: This section configures the ASP.NET process model settings on IIS Web server systems. Settings include whether the process model
is enabled, the number of minutes until ASP.NET launches a new worker
process to take the place of the current one, the idle time-out before ASP.NET
shuts down the worker process, the number of minutes allowed for the
worker process to shut down gracefully, the number of requests allowed
before ASP.NET automatically launches a new worker process to take the
place of the current one, the number of requests allowed in the queue before
ASP.NET launches a new worker process and reassigns the requests, the
maximum allowed memory size, which processors on a multiprocessor
server are eligible to run ASP.NET processes, and managing central processing unit (CPU) affinity.

- `<httpHandlers>`: This section maps incoming URL requests to classes
implementing `IHttpHandler`. The section adds, removes, or otherwise
clears HttpHandlers.

- `<sessionState>`: This section configures the session state `HttpModule`. This
includes setting the mode (session state turned off, session state stored in
process, session state stored in a remote server, or session state stored on a
box running SQL Server), whether to support clients without cookies, time-
out period for an idle session, the server name, and the SQL connection string.

- `<globalization>`: This section configures the globalization settings of an
application, including such items as the encoding of incoming requests, the
encoding of outgoing responses, ASPX file encoding, the default culture to
process incoming requests, and the default culture for user interface resources.

- `<compilation>`: This section contains all the compilation settings used by
ASP.NET. Settings include enabling debugging, the default language being
used on the page, the Visual Basic *Explicit* option, a time-out period for batch
compilation, whether to recompile resources before an application restarts,
and enabling the Visual Basic *Strict* compile option.

- `<trace>`: This section configures the ASP.NET trace service. Settings in this
section include enabling tracing, limiting the number of trace requests to
store on the server, and enabling trace output at the end of the page.

- `<browserCaps>`: This section configures the settings for the browser capabilities component.

Each section entry is associated with a specific value within the WEB.CONFIG file. (See Chapters 2 and 8 for examples of using configuration files.)

WEB FORMS

The new coding model for ASP.NET makes it easy to manage presentation (using HTML) and executable code—by either mixing the code into the Web page or writing separate code-behind pages. In addition, ASP.NET provides new server-side control abstractions for managing the right kind of HTML depending on the browser on the other end of the connection (so that you do not have to fiddle with the raw control tags). Combining all of this is the basis of Web forms. The Web forms model of programming makes it feel like you are building a local user interface (as you might in Visual Basic). However, in reality, it is a widely distributed user interface generated almost entirely by pushing HTML from the server to the client browser. We see an example of a Web forms application in the next chapter. The Web forms programming model brings with it the notion of custom server-side controls.

CUSTOM SERVER-SIDE CONTROLS

During the last five years, Web usage has increased phenomenally—both through regular Web surfing and e-commerce. Because of this, one of the most valuable assets consumers can provide for a company is their attention to the company's Web site. Naturally, companies want to create compelling, useful Web sites. Therefore Web users need sophisticated controls with which they can interact with the site.

Most browsers support standard controls such as push buttons and list boxes. However, the standard controls can take you only so far. Over the past few years, the primary way to enrich a Web page was to extend the browser. Several folks have taken a stab at that—notably with Java applets and ActiveX controls (and we focus on ActiveX controls here).

When the user hits a page containing an ActiveX control, the browser proceeds to download a binary file representing the ActiveX control's executable code. The browser calls `CoCreateInstance` on the object, negotiates some interfaces, and renders the control in the browser. Java applets work in a somewhat similar fashion.

Both of these approaches have some specific advantages. The most significant advantage is that you can provide much more natural and intuitive ways for the user and Web site to talk to one another.

A great example of extending the browser is a calendar control. Imagine you are signing on to a Web site set up to handle airline ticket bookings. When it comes down to actually selecting the date for travel, clients needs to give their travel dates to the Web site. It is possible the Web site could expose a text box so that the client can type in a complete date, such as *October 22, 2001*. A better way would be to have standard combo boxes for selecting the month, day, and year of travel. Imagine that the users can also pull up a calendar to select their dates. Ahhh! That is much more intuitive and even more convenient. They can just point at the date they want and click to select it.

Many sites out there display a calendar for selecting dates. However, invariably, the old standby controls—usually some combo boxes—are often right beside the calendar. What is going on? Why do users need both sets of controls?

Extending the Browser

The problem with extending the browser to enrich the user interface is that the browser has to support a technology to extend it. For example, if you want the browser to use an ActiveX control to interact with the site, that browser needs the infrastructure to support ActiveX controls. The browser requires a handful of COM interfaces for this. Likewise, any Web site using Java applets expects browsers to support the Java runtime.

Unfortunately, it is impossible to make sure every Web surfer out there uses the best browser available. It is difficult even to get people to agree on which browser is the best. It is also unrealistic to expect everybody to always use the very latest version of a particular browser. Most of us do not mind upgrading software every now and then, but there are many people out there who just hate it. The point is, there are diverse client browsers out there, and nobody seems to be able to enforce a standard.

It would not be so bad if the problem ended with browsers. However, during the last couple of years, numerous different devices—such as Internet cell phones, Windows CE machines, and handheld devices—are now able to browse Web sites. Now it is even more difficult to count on a specific kind of UI on the client end. If you make Java applets or ActiveX controls integral to your Web site, you cannot reach certain clients.

ASP.NET's answer to this dilemma is to move to the server the responsibility of rendering and managing custom controls.

Server-Side Rendering

In the Web client world, HTML is the common denominator. Almost every browser understands how to parse and display HTML. If you cannot enrich the user interface by extending the browser, why not have the server generate the correct kind of HTML to give a customized appearance to the user? These controls are called *Web forms* controls. Microsoft provides an established framework and protocol for generating a sophisticated user interface from the server.

Web forms controls are reusable in that they are independent of the Web pages using them and can be created, modified, and maintained separately from the pages.

The public fields, properties, and methods of a Web forms control can be accessed programmatically by the containing control or page. In addition, Web forms controls are
hierarchical and can inherit from, contain, and extend other controls. In short, Web
forms help "componentize" Web development (i.e., break apart Web user interfaces
into small modularized pieces) while simultaneously making it easier to reach a much
more diverse range of client devices.

Basically, a Web forms control is a component designed to work within the
ASP.NET page framework. It's a DLL written in a .NET CLR language that has the
proper hooks expected by the ASP.NET runtime. As ASP.NET parses a Web page, the
ASP.NET runtime may encounter one of these controls. When ASP.NET does
encounter a control, the ASP.NET runtime creates and initializes it. Like ActiveX controls, ASP.NET server-side custom controls expose properties, methods, and events.
However, remember that these components now live on the server (and are not
downloaded to the client on demand).

Control Life Cycle

A custom server-side control is much like a finite state machine. It has an established
life cycle and set of states in which it can exist. For example, the control can be in
a loading state, may be responding to a postback, or may be shutting down. The
`Control` class provides the methods and properties for managing a page execution
life cycle, including viewing state management, postback data handling, postback
event handling, and output rendering. Implementing a server-side control means
deriving from the `Control` class and overriding certain methods.

Knowing a page's execution life cycle is very useful for understanding how
server-side controls work. As a page is loaded, the ASP.NET runtime parses the page
and generates a `Page` class to execute. The `Page` class (which inherits from the
`Control` class) instantiates and populates a tree of server control instances. Once the
tree is created, the `Page` class begins an execution sequence that enables both
ASP.NET page code and server controls to participate in the request processing and
rendering of the page.

Following is a rundown of the individual control life cycle. The communication
protocol for a server-side control is divided between calls to established well-known
methods and various postback processing.

- Responding to a page request, the ASP.NET page first calls the control's
  `Init` function. Here's where any initial setup happens.
- The control now has an opportunity to set up its view state. View state information is not available during the control's `Init` call, so the control provides
  a function named `LoadViewState` explicitly for this purpose. A control

maintains its view state in a `Control.State` collection. The State methods allow you to programmatically restore internal state settings between page views.

- A page experiences something called a postback every once in a while. In addition to being activated as a result of a navigation request, ASP.NET pages can be activated as a result of a postback from a previously rendered instance of the same page on the client (for example, a registration form with multiple text fields that must be resubmitted and validated). Think of a postback as a chance to refresh. Controls have the opportunity to process data during a postback. That is, a control has the opportunity to process any incoming form data and update its object models and internal state appropriately. The visual and internal states of the control can automatically remain in sync. Postbacks are handled by the `IPostBackDataHandler` interface.

- Once a page has been activated, a control wants to know when it is being loaded. Controls have the opportunity to override the `OnLoad` method to perform any actions common to each incoming page request (such as setting up a database query or updating a timer on a page).

- A control may have to notify the client that data has changed. This is done during the postback change notification phase of the control. Controls fire appropriate change notification events during this phase in response to form and control value changes that occurred on the client between the previous and current postbacks to a page.

- Controls handle client actions that cause a postback during the postback event processing phase of the control. For example, a button server control could handle a postback from the client in response to being clicked by a user and then raise an appropriate `OnClick` event on the server.

- Controls have the opportunity to perform any last-minute update operations that must take place immediately before page/control state is saved and output rendered by overriding the control's `PreRender` function.

- A control has the opportunity to save its view state by overriding its `SaveViewState` method. A control's state information is automatically transferred from the `Control.State` collection into a string object immediately after the `SaveViewState` stage of execution. To prepare for this, controls can override the `SaveViewState` event to modify the state collection.

- Probably the most important function within a control is `Render`. Controls use the `Render` class to generate HTML output to the browser client. When it is time for an ASP.NET page to render itself, ASP.NET walks the entire list of controls instantiated on the pages, asking each one to render itself through the `Render` method.

- Controls need a chance to clean up after a page is unloaded. Controls override the `Dispose` method to perform any final cleanup work.

Reasons to Use a Custom Server-Side Control

We considered a specific scenario for using a custom server-side control. However, there are several other compelling reasons for using one. In addition to making the sophisticated user interface of your Web application workable for any number of client situations, you may want to use controls to partition your application into code and content. ASP.NET's programming model lets you separate HTML from executable code. By separating the presentation part and the logical part of your application, both parts can be developed in parallel and independently.

Custom server-side controls represent a great opportunity for encapsulating reusable code. Server-side controls can be designed to be completely self-contained so that a page developer can just drop an HTML tag onto a page.

Finally, custom server-side controls simplify the application programming model. By encapsulating functionality in a custom control, page developers can use that functionality by setting control properties and responding to events. ASP.NET custom server-side controls effectively handle the issue of getting a sophisticated user interface to work in a variety of settings.

WEB SERVICES AND ASP.NET

The coupe de grace brought by .NET (and ASP.NET especially) is support for programmable Web sites. In addition to simplifying the user interface aspect of Web development, ASP.NET's other huge contribution to the .NET platform is making it easy to produce Web services (which we have been discussing throughout this book).

During the short history of the Internet, there has always been a human interacting with Web sites, which has been a big boon to commerce in general. The Internet and the Web provide a whole new medium for research, information finding, advertising, and sales. However, this is only the tip of the iceberg.

There is a whole world of untapped resources, meaning that there is a whole world of problems to be solved—particularly those related to getting computers on the Web to talk to one another without human intervention and regardless of the type of computer platform being used. Sites with programmable services are called *Web services* in .NET parlance.

A Web service provides remote access to server functionality. For a number of years, those in both the COM camp and the Common Object Request Broker Architecture (CORBA) camp felt their particular component technology would revolutionize the Internet. The catch is that neither COM nor CORBA mixes very well with firewalls. The other problem is that neither protocol is ubiquitous between any two enterprises. Therefore although both these models are great for building software systems for the enterprise, they do not work between enterprises. Being able to programmatically contact another business and talk to it through the Internet has been stymied until now.

Although COM and CORBA are not viable Internet protocols, there is another protocol that everyone agrees on and is ubiquitous on the Internet—HTTP. In addition, XML has emerged as the de facto format for transmission. Together, XML and HTTP make up SOAP. SOAP makes writing programmatic Web sites possible.

In the .NET world, businesses will use Web services to expose programmatic interfaces to their data and business logic. Other businesses can then use those interfaces to communicate programmatically with the original business. Web services use HTTP and XML messaging to move data across firewalls—something that could not be done until recently. Because Web services are not tied to a particular component technology or object-calling convention, it does not matter which languages are used to write the programs and components. Microsoft puts the focus on interoperability, which will enable businesses of all natures to hook up through the Internet.

The idea of programmable Web sites is straightforward enough. Obviously, people have been getting information into Web sites (using browser interfaces). Web services allow computers to do the same thing. You just have to write your Web page correctly.

Web Methods and ASP.NET

When writing a Web forms application, the class you use derives from `System.Web.UI.Page`. When you write a Web service, the class you use derives from `System.Web.Services.WebService`. To add functionality to your Web service, your class includes methods marked with the `WebMethod` attribute. The beauty of ASP.NET is that it takes care of correctly mapping incoming HTTP requests onto calls on your object. (Technically, you can get by without using the `WebService` class. However, using `WebService` does give your application access to all of ASP.NET.)

Calling Web services from the client side is simple as well because the runtime provides proxy classes that wrap up the calls on the client side. A client-side proxy manages generating the right HTTP request to the server and parsing the response from the server.

Service Description Language and ASP.NET

Clients know the shape of the methods available on a Web service by reading its service description language (SDL). ASP.NET clients get a copy of a Web service's SDL by requesting the service's file (FOO.ASMX) and passing the SDL query string. At that point, ASP.NET uses reflection to generate an SDL file. The client code then uses the SDL to create a client-side proxy.

Invoking Web Methods

In addition to supporting Web service methods, ASP.NET supports invoking Web methods by one of three means: HTTP GET requests with parameters encoded within a query string, HTTP POST requests with parameters from input controls, and through a SOAP proxy (generated from a Web page's SDL).

OPTIMIZATIONS: ASP.NET CACHING

ASP.NET supports caching to reduce round trips to the server. ASP supports two forms of caching: output caching and data caching. Output caching improves server throughput. Data caching improves the performance on the client end.

Output Caching

When a Web page is accessed and a request is made, the server has to spend a bit of time producing the output. When a Web page's content does not change very much, it makes sense to cache the output so that the server does not have to regenerate it. This output caching is turned off by default, and Web pages need to turn it on specifically using the OutputCache directive. The OutputCache directive also controls the duration for which the output is cached in seconds.

Whenever an initial HTTP GET request is made for a cached page, the output for that page is cached. If an HTTP GET or HEAD request is made for the same page, ASP.NET satisfies the request from the contents of the cache (until the cached output expires). Very often, Web applications use query strings to look up data in a database and generate output. ASP.NET stores the query string, and the output cache compares query strings to verify a request's identity. HTTP POST requests are never cached—they are always generated explicitly.

Data Caching

In any distributed system, one of the most important optimizations you can make is to reduce the number of round trips between the client and the server. When developing Web pages, the fewer round trips your browser clients need to make back to the server, the better.

ASP.NET provides a full-featured cache engine that can be used by pages to store objects across HTTP requests. The CLR class System.Web.Caching.Cache provides this facility. The granddaddy of all Web page classes, System.Web.UI.Page, includes a property of type cache.

The cache is a simple database supporting a simple dictionary interface—very much like COM's property bags. When you want to cache values over a certain period of time, you put them in the cache. You can put almost whatever you want into the cache and, in addition, you have control over expiration of values.

MANAGING SESSION STATE

Building Web sites and Web services using HTTP is inherently different than building distributed systems using protocols such as DCOM. The DCOM is a connection-intensive protocol. It often makes sense to pay attention to state for the duration of a connection. That is, if a client connects to some server somewhere using DCOM, the server may usually expect that calls coming in over the same connection are always from the same client. Therefore the client can modify the state of the server several times over the course of a connection and may know that it is modifying the same state—this is not so with HTTP.

HTTP is light in terms of connections. That is, it does not maintain connections between requests. When you surf to a URL, your Web browser connects to the server and sends the request, and the server returns a response. That is the end of the connection—it gets torn down right away. The next time you surf to the same URL (e.g., by clicking on a link), the browser sets up a new connection, sends a new request, gets a new response, and then tears down that connection.

Because of its lightweight connection nature, HTTP is a stateless protocol, meaning the server has no automatic guarantee that a string of requests is from the same client (or even the same single browser instance). This is an issue for Web applications that need to maintain state across connections. Common types of state that are often shared include the contents of shopping carts and page scrolling (so that the previous page shows up in the same scrolling position when you hit the Back button). This sort of state management can be incredibly cumbersome to program by yourself, which is why transconnection state management is built into ASP.NET.

Web servers are constantly bombarded by incoming HTTP requests. Quite often an HTTP request will come in from one client and immediately be followed by a request from a completely different client.

ASP.NET makes managing state much easier. The state management facilities come for free. Classic ASP provides two facilities for maintaining state across requests, and they are based on application scope and session scope. Session-scoped objects are bound to a particular client Web application manager (WAM) and live for 20 minutes (by default) after the last request is received. Application-scoped objects are shared by all sessions in a WAM and live as long as at least one session is alive. Each WAM directory can have a `global.asa` file. ASP.NET provides session-management infrastructure with built-in session-state functionality. This built-in functionality serves four main functions:

- It helps you identify and classify requests coming from the same browser client into a logical application "session" on the server.
- It provides a place to store session-scoped data on the server for use across multiple HTTP requests.
- It raises session-lifetime management events (such as `OnSessionStart` and `OnSessionEnd`) so that you can manage the session in your application code.

- It automatically cleans up the session data if the same browser fails to revisit your application after a specified time-out period.

We discuss using ASP.NET's session-state management in more detail in Chapter 8.

CONCLUSION

You now have an overview of ASP.NET. Overall, the new .NET platform has a lot to offer the software developer, including an ecumenical type system, better type information, and an efficient compilation model, all of which truly tighten up the boundaries between components. Taking charge of all these great features is ASP.NET, which will most likely be .NET's "Killer App."

As we mentioned during our discussion of people-oriented software, the future of computing will undoubtedly involve getting machines to talk to one another over the Internet. The Internet is a ubiquitous network to which scores of people have access. Until now, there has not really been a way to use the Internet as a software platform. However, the technology is now in place to make that happen, and ASP.NET makes it that much easier to manage Web programming. ASP.NET keeps all the good features of classic ASP (in process performance, a well-established syntax, the ability to add executable blocks to your Web page) and improves on them (e.g., by providing a more granular HTTP request handling model, providing a compilation model for Web pages, and organizing the parts of a Web page into classes and making those classes available through the CLR type system). ASP.NET will undoubtedly be the tool of choice for most Web developers for the next five to ten years.

Applied ASP.NET

One of the main goals of people-oriented software (in general) and .NET (specifically) is to connect the entire globe's population. .NET puts the language wars aside by encouraging applications to run under a common runtime and share a Common Type System (CTS). C# (and Visual Basic.NET, as well as the other .NET languages slated to come out) provide a way to talk to the runtime (with more language options to follow, undoubtedly). Riding herd over these components is ASP.NET as a Web application development framework for the .NET platform.

Over the last few chapters, we have discussed generally how to use ASP.NET. For example, the InternetBaton and ManagedSynergy applications took advantage of ASP.NET. In this chapter, we take a closer look at the ins and outs of using ASP.NET by covering specific examples of ASP.NET's features, including server-side controls (hypertext markup language [HTML] controls and Web controls), Web forms, managing state, configuring ASP.NET, and setting up custom handlers.

USER INTERFACE CONTROLS AND THE WEB

In the mid 1990s, developers had to hand-code their controls tags into the HTML they were generating. They also had to write by hand all the code to handle the executable code for updating and managing the control's state. ASP.NET brings a declarative programming model for programming controls on Web pages. It provides two kinds of control abstractions that make it easier to deal with user interface controls on a Web page. These two kinds of controls are HTML controls (represented by classes derived from the CLR's `HTMLControl` class) and Web controls (represented by classes derived from the CLR's `WebControl` class). These abstractions improve the programming model and make developing a Web-based user interface much more straightforward.

Classic active server page (ASP) Web processing involves manually extracting form elements and managing HTML tags representing controls. ASP.NET introduces *server-side* controls to make managing the control tags more straightforward. Because HTTP is a connectionless protocol, managing control state can be a real headache. Server-side controls help solve this problem by retaining their state between postbacks, which keeps you from constantly having to write the HTML code regeneration by hand.

Classic ASP is all about mixing executable code with HTML so that a page is generated dynamically. Every time a request is submitted to the server, the server generates the appropriate HTML response. Unfortunately, this often ends up looking like early efforts at unstructured Basic programming from those cheap programming books that came out in the early 1980s. For example, to manage selections and show a selection box the user selected, you must write the `/selected` tag to only one of the selection items. Most pages do this by testing the `Request` object's query string to find out what the user selected and writing the HTML tag "`/selected`" next to the appropriate selection within the `option` tag.

Programming a page using server-side controls is rather like programming a desktop application. You can expect the state of a control to remain constant during the life of a desktop program. Server-side controls make the same thing happen on a Web page. The following listing shows how to use a couple of basic controls (buttons and combo boxes) on an ASP.NET page.

```
<%@ Page Language="C#" %>
<html>
<head>

<script runat=server>
  void CalcDistances(Object sender, EventArgs E)
  {
    String strDistance = "";
    if(Starting.Value == "Boston") {
        if(Destination.Value == "Fort Collins") {
           strDistance = "2000";
        } else if(Destination.Value == "Atlanta") {
           strDistance = "900";
        } else if(Destination.Value == "Santa Fe") {
           strDistance = "2100";
        } else if(Destination.Value == "Bellevue") {
           strDistance = "3000";
        }
    }
    if(Starting.Value == "Dallas") {
```

```
            if(Destination.Value == "Fort Collins") {
                strDistance = "800";
            } else if(Destination.Value == "Atlanta") {
                strDistance = "1300";
            } else if(Destination.Value == "Santa Fe") {
                strDistance = "350";
            } else if(Destination.Value == "Bellevue") {
                strDistance = "1000";
            }
        }
        if(Starting.Value == "Los Angeles") {
            if(Destination.Value == "Fort Collins") {
                strDistance = "1000";
            } else if(Destination.Value == "Atlanta") {
                strDistance = "2000";
            } else if(Destination.Value == "Santa Fe") {
                strDistance = "1000";
            } else if(Destination.Value == "Bellevue") {
                strDistance = "750";
            }
        }


        if(Starting.Value == "New York") {
            if(Destination.Value == "Fort Collins") {
                strDistance = "2000";
            } else if(Destination.Value == "Atlanta") {
                strDistance = "600";
            } else if(Destination.Value == "Santa Fe") {
                strDistance = "2000";
            } else if(Destination.Value == "Bellevue") {
                strDistance = "2900";
            }
        }
        Distances.InnerText = "From " + Starting.Value + " to " +
            Destination.Value + " " + strDistance + " miles";
    }

</script>
</head>
<body>
<form runat=server>
    Starting: <select ID="Starting" runat=server>
        <option>Boston</option>
        <option>Dallas</option>
        <option>Los Angeles</option>
        <option>New York</option>
        </select>

    Destination: <select ID="Destination" runat=server>
                <option>Fort Collins</option>
                <option>Atlanta</option>
                <option>Santa Fe</option>
```

```
        <option>Bellevue</option>
        </select>

    <input type=button value="Submit" runat=server
OnServerClick="CalcDistances" />
    <div id="Distances" runat=server />
  </form>
</body>
</html>
```

Selecting a source and a destination and pushing the Submit button causes the ASP.NET code to call the method `CalcDistances`, which renders a message to the browser indicating the approximate distance between the two cities. This ASP.NET code declares several standard controls on the Web page: a couple of selection controls (Starting and Destination) and a `Div` tag (Distances). They all run at the server. (Notice the `runat=server` attribute.) In addition, notice that you are able to access controls and their values within the server-side code block, which is very similar to desktop-type development. Figure 8-1 shows the Web page (from the previous code) in a browser.

Following is the HTML (generated by ASP.NET) that the browser sees in the previous code listing:

```
<html>
<head>
</head>
<body>
  <form name="ctrl2"
  method="post"
  action="ServerSideCtl.ASPX"
  id="ctrl2">
  <input type="hidden" name="__VIEWSTATE"
```

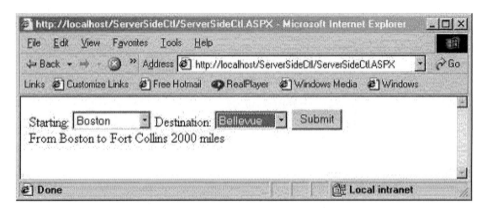

FIGURE 8-1   Output from Controls Code Listing (on pages 272–274).

```
value="dDwtMTY1ODQ0NTM4NDt0PDtsPDE8Mj47PjtsPHQ8O2w8MTw3Pjs+
O2w8dDxwPGw8aW5uZXJodG1sOz47bDxxGcm9tIEJvc3RvbiB0byBjAwMCBtaWxlczs+
Pjs7Pjs+Pjs+Pjs+j3F4G8i4EyG4DJ3ydQpOiYwJFEs=" />

    Starting: <select name="Starting" id="Starting">
    <option selected="selected" value="Boston">Boston</option>
    <option value="Dallas">Dallas</option>
    <option value="Los Angeles">Los Angeles</option>
    <option value="New York">New York</option>/select>
    Destination: <select name="Destination" id="Destination">
    <option selected="selected"
      value="Fort Collins">Fort Collins</option>
    <option value="Atlanta">Atlanta</option>
    <option value="Santa Fe">Santa Fe</option>
    <option value="Bellevue">Bellevue</option>
</select>

 <input onclick=
  "javascript:__doPostBack('ctrl7','')"
  name="ctrl7"
  type="button"
  value="Submit" />
  <div id="Distances">From Boston to Fort Collins 2000 miles</div>

  <input type="hidden" name="__EVENTTARGET" value="" />
  <input type="hidden" name="__EVENTARGUMENT" value="" />
  <script language="javascript">
<!--
    function __doPostBack(eventTarget, eventArgument) {
        var theform = document.ctrl2
        theform.__EVENTTARGET.value = eventTarget
        theform.__EVENTARGUMENT.value = eventArgument
        theform.submit()
    }
// -->
</script>

</form>
</body>
</html>
```

It is not as important to be able to follow the HTML code exactly as it is to marvel at how much the controls help abstract the details of getting an interactive user interface working across the Hypertext Transfer Protocol (HTTP). (Some of the code is generated specifically for use by ASP.NET, such as the VIEWSTATE code. The VIEWSTATE code is optional and exclusively for use by ASP.NET.) Before ASP.NET, these were the kinds of things you had to keep track of manually.

The common language runtime (CLR) includes two sets of control classes that further abstract the details of controls—HTML controls and Web controls. Let's discuss the difference between HTML controls and Web controls.

HTML Controls

ASP.NET's HTML controls are part of the CLR runtime classes, living in the namespace `System.Web.UI.HTMLControls`. They represent a direct translation to and from normal HTML control tags that cause controls (like push buttons and combo boxes) to appear on the browser end.

As we discussed, without an abstraction mechanism such as server-side controls, you would need to explicitly generate everything on the page by hand. HTML server controls run on the server and map directly to standard HTML tags supported by all browsers, thus allowing you to control the HTML elements on the Web page programmatically. Table 8-1 shows a rundown of the various HTML controls available within ASP.NET. All these controls derive from the CLR class `HTMLControl`.

The code in the previous listing uses HTML controls implicitly. For example, notice that retrieving the selected starting point is a matter of going to the Starting selection control and examining the Value property.

TABLE 8-1   HTML Controls and Their Functionality

Class	Functionality
`HtmlAnchor`	Programmatic access to the HTML `<a>` tag on the server
`HtmlButton`	Programmatic access to the HTML `<button>` tag on the server
`HtmlContainerControl`	Representative of the HTML server controls that must have a closing tag
`HtmlControl`	Representative of the HTML server controls in the Web forms page framework
`HtmlForm`	Programmatic access to the HTML `<form>` element on the server
`HtmlGenericControl`	Representative HTML server control tags not indicated by a specific .NET framework class
`HtmlImage`	Programmatic access to the HTML `<img>` element on the server
`HtmlInputButton`	Programmatic access to the HTML `<input type=button>`, `<input type=submit>`, and `<input type=reset>` elements on the server
`HtmlInputCheckBox`	Programmatic access to the HTML `<input type=checkbox>` element on the server
`HtmlInputControl`	Abstract base class representing functionality common to all HTML input controls, such as the `<input type=text>`, `<input type=submit>`, and `<input type=file>` elements
`HtmlInputFile`	Programmatic access to the HTML `<input type=file>` element on the server

TABLE 8-1   *(Continued)*

Class	Functionality
`HtmlInputHidden`	Programmatic access to the HTML `<input type=hidden>` element on the server
`HtmlInputImage`	Programmatic access to the HTML `<input type=image>` element on the server
`HtmlInputRadioButton`	Programmatic access to the HTML `<input type=radio>` element on the server
`HtmlInputText`	Programmatic access to the HTML `<input type=text>` and `<input type=password>` elements on the server
`HtmlSelect`	Programmatic access to the HTML `<select>` element on the server
`HtmlTable`	Programmatic access to the HTML `<table>` element on the server
`HtmlTableCell`	Programmatic access to individual HTML `<td>` and `<th>` elements enclosed within an `HtmlTableRow` control on the server
`HtmlTableCellCollection`	Collection for managing the table cells elements found within an `HtmlTable` server control
`HtmlTableRow`	Programmatic access to individual HTML `<tr>` elements enclosed within an `HtmlTable` control on the server
`HtmlTableRowCollection`	Collection for managing the table rows found within an `HtmlTable` server control
`HtmlTextArea`	Programmatic access to the HTML `<textarea>` element on the server

Web Controls

As with the `System.Web.UI.HTMLControls` namespace, The `System.Web.UI.WebControls` namespace contains a collection of CLR classes for managing Web server controls on a Web page. Web controls run on the server and include classes representing such controls as buttons and text boxes, as well as special-purpose controls such as calendars. By programming to Web controls, you affect the appearance of the Web page when it hits the browser. Web controls are more abstract than HTML controls and have rich functionality for managing the tags.

Programming using Web controls is rather like programming forms or dialog boxes, but the controls show up on the client's browser. Most HTML elements have corresponding Web controls classes. As a rule, the Web controls have a consistent programmatic interface (whereas the HTML controls can vary somewhat). The

Web controls classes often take the responsibility of interrogating the browser to find out whether they need to render themselves differently. The namespace, System. Web.UI.WebControls, also includes some controls (such as the CALENDAR and the DATAGRID control) with much higher-level functionality than an HTML primitive. The following listing shows a page similar to the one in the previous listing but incorporates Web controls.

```csharp
<%@ Page Language="C#" %>
  <script language="C#" runat="server">
  void Page_Load(Object Src, EventArgs E ) {
  }

   void CalcDistancesBtn_Click(Object sender, EventArgs E) {
     String strDistance = "";
     if(Starting.SelectedItem.Text == "Boston") {
        if(Destination.SelectedItem.Text == "Fort Collins") {
           strDistance = "2000";
        } else if(Destination.SelectedItem.Text == "Atlanta") {
           strDistance = "900";
        } else if(Destination.SelectedItem.Text == "Santa Fe") {
           strDistance = "2100";
        } else if(Destination.SelectedItem.Text == "Bellevue") {
           strDistance = "3000";
        }
     }
     if(Starting.SelectedItem.Text == "Dallas") {
        if(Destination.SelectedItem.Text == "Fort Collins") {
           strDistance = "800";
        } else if(Destination.SelectedItem.Text == "Atlanta") {
           strDistance = "1300";
        } else if(Destination.SelectedItem.Text == "Santa Fe") {
           strDistance = "350";
        } else if(Destination.SelectedItem.Text == "Bellevue") {
           strDistance = "1000";
        }
     }

     if(Starting.SelectedItem.Text == "Los Angeles") {
        if(Destination.SelectedItem.Text == "Fort Collins") {
           strDistance = "1000";
        } else if(Destination.SelectedItem.Text == "Atlanta") {
           strDistance = "2000";
        } else if(Destination.SelectedItem.Text == "Santa Fe") {
           strDistance = "1000";
        } else if(Destination.SelectedItem.Text == "Bellevue") {
           strDistance = "750";
        }
     }

     if(Starting.SelectedItem.Text == "New York") {
        if(Destination.SelectedItem.Text == "Fort Collins") {
```

```
                strDistance = "2000";
            } else if(Destination.SelectedItem.Text == "Atlanta") {
                strDistance = "600";
            } else if(Destination.SelectedItem.Text == "Santa Fe") {
                strDistance = "2000";
            } else if(Destination.SelectedItem.Text == "Bellevue") {
                strDistance = "2900";
            }
        }

        Distances.InnerText = "From "
          + Starting.SelectedItem.Text + " to " +
            Destination.SelectedItem.Text + " "
          + strDistance + " miles";
    }
</script>
<html>
<body>
  <form runat=server>
  From source:
  <asp:DropDownList id = "Starting" runat=server>
     <asp:ListItem > Boston </asp:ListItem>
     <asp:ListItem > Dallas </asp:ListItem>
     <asp:ListItem > Los Angeles </asp:ListItem>
     <asp:ListItem > New York </asp:ListItem>
  </asp:DropDownList>
  To destination:
  <asp:DropDownList id = "Destination" runat=server>
     <asp:ListItem > Fort Collins </asp:ListItem>
     <asp:ListItem > Atlanta </asp:ListItem>
     <asp:ListItem > Santa Fe </asp:ListItem>
     <asp:ListItem > Bellevue </asp:ListItem>
  </asp:DropDownList>

  <asp:Button id = "Calculate" Text = "Calculate"
   OnClick="CalcDistancesBtn_Click"
   runat = "server" />

  <br><br>
  <div id="Distances" runat=server />
  <asp:TextBox TextMode=MultiLine rows=3
                Text="Notes about trip" runat=server /><br/>
  </form>
</body>
</html>
```

The example in the previous listing illustrates using Web controls. Notice the `asp:` identifier immediately before each control type. This identifier distinguishes the control as an ASP.NET Web control. Notice that `DropDownList` exposes its contents through the `SelectedItem` property rather than the `Value` property (as does the `HTMLSelect` control from the listing on pages 272–274).

WEB FORMS AND VISUAL STUDIO.NET

The new programming model we have been driving at—in which server-side controls help manage the state of the user interface in the browser and simplify the conversation between the browser and server—leads to the next feature of ASP.NET: Web forms.

There are several ways of coding up Web forms. For example, you can easily open up Notepad, type out some ASP.NET code, and browse the code once in a while to make sure it appears as you want it to on the browser end. You might also write a C# assembly and link it to your ASPX file using the code-behind technique we discussed in Chapter 7. However, the easiest way to set up a Web forms application is through Visual Studio.NET.

As an example, we wrote a Web-based Tic-Tac-Toe game (*WebTacToe*) that two people can play. The example gives us a good chance to examine Web forms programming through Visual Studio.NET and then discuss issues such as managing session state and caching.

To play WebTacToe, a user surfs to the Web site and immediately sees a 9-square Tic-Tac-Toe board (Figure 8-2). The browser client can click each of the buttons to turn the state of the button from a blank to an *X* or an *O*.

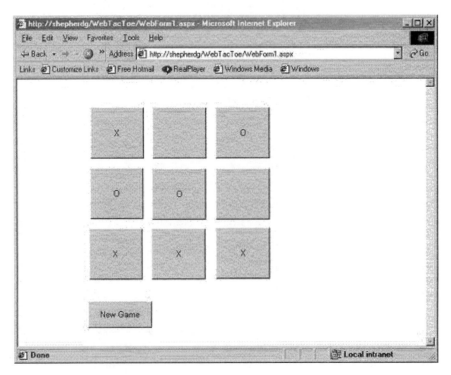

FIGURE 8-2   WebTacToe Playing Board.

Writing something like this in raw ASP would be complicated. Fortunately, ASP.NET uses structured object-oriented languages like C# to make things easier. The following shows the source code for `WebTacToe`.

```csharp
namespace WebTacToe
{
    using System;
    using System.Collections;
    using System.ComponentModel;
    using System.Data;
    using System.Drawing;
    using System.Web;
    using System.Web.SessionState;
    using System.Web.UI;
    using System.Web.UI.WebControls;
    using System.Web.UI.HtmlControls;

    public enum Player {
        XPlayer,
        Oplayer
    }
    public enum Mark {
        XMark,
        OMark,
        Blank
    }
    public enum Positions {
        TopLeft,
        TopCenter,
        TopRight,
        MiddleLeft,
        MiddleCenter,
        MiddleRight,
        BottomLeft,
        BottomCenter,
        BottomRight,
        Unknown
    }

    public struct BoardSpace {
        public BoardSpace(Mark markParam) {
            this.mark = markParam;
            this.button = null;
        }

        public void SetMark(Player player) {
            if(mark == Mark.Blank) {
                if(player == Player.XPlayer) {
                    mark = Mark.XMark;
                } else {
                    mark = Mark.OMark;
                }
            }
        }
    }
```

```
        public void Render() {
            switch(mark) {
                    case Mark.XMark:
                  button.Value = "X";
                  break;

               case Mark.OMark:
                  button.Value = "O";
                  break;

               default:
                  button.Value = " ";
                  break;
            }
        }

        public Mark mark;
        public System.Web.UI.HtmlControls.HtmlInputButton
                button;
    };

    public class Board {
        BoardSpace[,] boardSpaces;
        public Board() {
            boardSpaces = new BoardSpace[3,3];
            InitializeBoard();
        }

        public void InitializeSpace(int x, int y,  Mark mark) {
            boardSpaces[x, y] = new BoardSpace(mark);
        }

        public void SetButton(int x, int y,
            System.Web.UI.HtmlControls.HtmlInputButton
                    buttonParam) {

            boardSpaces[x, y].button = buttonParam;
        }

        public void InitializeBoard() {
            InitializeSpace(0, 0, Mark.Blank);
            InitializeSpace(1, 0, Mark.Blank);
            InitializeSpace(2, 0, Mark.Blank);
            InitializeSpace(0, 1, Mark.Blank);
            InitializeSpace(1, 1, Mark.Blank);
            InitializeSpace(2, 1, Mark.Blank);
            InitializeSpace(0, 2, Mark.Blank);
            InitializeSpace(1, 2, Mark.Blank);
            InitializeSpace(2, 2, Mark.Blank);
        }

        public void ClearBoard() {
            for(int i = 0; i < 3; i++) {
               for(int j = 0; j < 3; j++) {
```

```
                    boardSpaces[i, j].mark = Mark.Blank;
                }
            }
        }

        public void RenderBoard() {
            for(int i = 0; i < 3; i++) {
                for(int j = 0; j < 3; j++) {
                    boardSpaces[i, j].Render();
                }
            }
        }

        public void SetMark(int x, int y, Player player) {
                boardSpaces[x, y].SetMark(player);
        }

        public Mark GetMark(int x, int y) {
                return boardSpaces[x, y].mark;
        }
    }

    /// <summary>
    ///        Summary description for WebForm1.
    /// </summary>
    public class WebTacToeForm : System.Web.UI.Page
    {
        public System.Web.UI.HtmlControls.HtmlInputButton
            buttonCenterLeft;
        public System.Web.UI.HtmlControls.HtmlInputButton
            buttonUpperRight;
        public System.Web.UI.HtmlControls.HtmlInputButton
            buttonUpperCenter;
        public System.Web.UI.HtmlControls.HtmlInputButton
            buttonLowerLeft;
        public System.Web.UI.HtmlControls.HtmlInputButton
            buttonCenterRight;
        public System.Web.UI.HtmlControls.HtmlInputButton
            buttonUpperLeft;
        public System.Web.UI.HtmlControls.HtmlInputButton
            buttonCenterCenter;
        public System.Web.UI.HtmlControls.HtmlInputButton
            buttonLowerCenter;
        public System.Web.UI.HtmlControls.HtmlInputButton
            buttonLowerRight;
        public System.Web.UI.HtmlControls.HtmlInputButton
            buttonNewGame;

        // Member fields
            Player player;
        Board board;

        public void SetButtons() {
            board = (Board)Session["Board"];
```

```
        // top row...
        board.SetButton(0, 0, buttonUpperLeft);
        board.SetButton(0, 1, buttonUpperCenter);
        board.SetButton(0, 2, buttonUpperRight);

        board.SetButton(1, 0, buttonCenterLeft);
        board.SetButton(1, 1, buttonCenterCenter);
        board.SetButton(1, 2, buttonCenterRight);

        board.SetButton(2, 0, buttonLowerLeft);
        board.SetButton(2, 1, buttonLowerCenter);
        board.SetButton(2, 2, buttonLowerRight);
}

public Positions SetMark(Positions pos, Player player) {
    switch(pos) {
    case Positions.TopLeft:
        board.SetMark(0, 0, player);
        return Positions.TopLeft;

    case Positions.TopCenter:
        board.SetMark(0, 1, player);
        return Positions.MiddleLeft;

    case Positions.TopRight:
        board.SetMark(0, 2, player);
        return Positions.BottomLeft;

    case Positions.MiddleLeft:
        board.SetMark(1, 0, player);
        return Positions.TopCenter;

    case Positions.MiddleCenter:
        board.SetMark(1, 1, player);
        return Positions.MiddleCenter;

    case Positions.MiddleRight:
        board.SetMark(1, 2, player);
        return Positions.BottomCenter;
    case Positions.BottomLeft:
        board.SetMark(2, 0, player);
        return Positions.TopRight;

    case Positions.BottomCenter:
        board.SetMark(2, 1,player);
        return Positions.MiddleRight;

    case Positions.BottomRight:
        board.SetMark(2, 2, player);
        return Positions.BottomRight;
```

```
        default:
            return Positions.Unknown;
        };
}

public WebTacToeForm() {
    Page.Init += new System.EventHandler(Page_Init);
}


protected void Page_Init(object sender, EventArgs e) {
    //
    // CODEGEN: This call is required by
    //    the ASP.NET Windows Form Designer.
    //

    InitializeComponent();
    board = (Board)Session["Board"];
    player = (Player)Session["Player"];
    SetButtons();
    board.RenderBoard();
}

#region Web Form Designer generated code
/// <summary>
///     Required method for Designer
///    support - do not modify
///    the contents of this method with the code editor.
/// </summary>
private void InitializeComponent() {
    this.buttonCenterLeft.ServerClick += new
  System.EventHandler(this.buttonCenterLeft_ServerClick);

    this.buttonUpperRight.ServerClick += new
  System.EventHandler(this.buttonUpperRight_ServerClick);

    this.buttonUpperCenter.ServerClick += new
  System.EventHandler(this.buttonUpperCenter_ServerClick);

    this.buttonLowerCenter.ServerClick += new
  System.EventHandler(this.buttonLowerCenter_ServerClick);

    this.buttonLowerLeft.ServerClick += new
  System.EventHandler(this.buttonLowerLeft_ServerClick);

    this.buttonLowerRight.ServerClick += new
  System.EventHandler(this.buttonLowerRight_ServerClick);

    this.buttonCenterRight.ServerClick += new
  System.EventHandler(this.buttonCenterRight_ServerClick);

    this.buttonUpperLeft.ServerClick += new
  System.EventHandler(this.buttonUpperLeft_ServerClick);
```

```csharp
    this.buttonCenterCenter.ServerClick += new
  System.EventHandler(this.buttonCenterCenter_ServerClick);

    this.buttonNewGame.ServerClick += new
  System.EventHandler(this.buttonNewGame_ServerClick);

    this.Load += new
  System.EventHandler(this.Page_Load);

}
 #endregion

private void Page_Load(object sender,
                              System.EventArgs e)  {
}

protected void SwitchPlayer() {
    EvaluateGame();
    if (player == Player.XPlayer) {
       player = Player.OPlayer;
    } else {
       player = Player.XPlayer;
    }
     Session["Player"] = player;
}

protected void buttonUpperLeft_ServerClick(
        object sender, System.EventArgs e) {
     this.SetMark(Positions.TopLeft, player);
    board.RenderBoard();
    SwitchPlayer();
    Session["BoardSpaces"] = board;
}

protected void buttonUpperCenter_ServerClick(
        object sender, System.EventArgs e) {
    this.SetMark(Positions.TopCenter, player);
    board.RenderBoard();
    SwitchPlayer();
    Session["BoardSpaces"] = board;
}

protected void buttonUpperRight_ServerClick(
        object sender, System.EventArgs e) {
    this.SetMark(Positions.TopRight, player);
    board.RenderBoard();
    SwitchPlayer();
    Session["BoardSpaces"] = board;
}

protected void buttonCenterCenter_ServerClick(
        object sender, System.EventArgs e) {
    this.SetMark(Positions.MiddleCenter, player);
    board.RenderBoard();
```

```
            SwitchPlayer();
            Session["BoardSpaces"] = board;
        }

        protected void buttonCenterLeft_ServerClick(
                object sender, System.EventArgs e) {
            this.SetMark(Positions.MiddleLeft, player);
            board.RenderBoard();
            SwitchPlayer();
            Session["BoardSpaces"] = board;
        }

        protected void buttonCenterRight_ServerClick(
                object sender, System.EventArgs e) {
            this.SetMark(Positions.MiddleRight, player);
            board.RenderBoard();
            SwitchPlayer();
            Session["BoardSpaces"] = board;
        }

        protected void buttonLowerLeft_ServerClick(
                object sender, System.EventArgs e) {
            this.SetMark(Positions.BottomLeft, player);
            board.RenderBoard();
            SwitchPlayer();
            Session["BoardSpaces"] = board;
        }

        protected void buttonLowerCenter_ServerClick(
                object sender, System.EventArgs e) {
            this.SetMark(Positions.BottomCenter, player);
            board.RenderBoard();
            SwitchPlayer();
            Session["BoardSpaces"] = board;
        }

        protected void buttonLowerRight_ServerClick(
                object sender, System.EventArgs e) {
            this.SetMark(Positions.BottomRight, player);
            board.RenderBoard();
            SwitchPlayer();
            Session["BoardSpaces"] = board;
        }

        protected void buttonNewGame_ServerClick(
                object sender, System.EventArgs e) {
            board.ClearBoard();
            board.RenderBoard();
            player = Player.XPlayer;
            Session["Player"] = player;
            Session["BoardSpaces"] = board;
        }
    }

}
```

The WebTacToe listing includes the code necessary to manage a two-player Tic-Tac-Toe game whose user interface appears on a Web browser. The first player (always *X*) presses one of the nine buttons to mark a place on the Tic-Tac-Toe board. The internal state of the application then switches to the next player *(O)*, who presses a button to mark the space on the board. The state switches back to *X*.

Developing this application using Visual Studio.NET was positively trivial. Visual Studio.NET includes a forms-based development environment for ASP.NET. In fact, developing a Web forms application using Visual Studio.NET is almost like developing a standard Visual Basic desktop application. There is a canvas on which to drop controls and a toolbar from which to select controls to drop; double-clicking the control adds a handler.

One of the main reasons we display most of the listing is to show the superiority of ASP.NET over regular ASP. Regular ASP mixes presentation and executable code, but that's not the worst of it. What is worse is the fact that the executable code in a classic ASP page is scripting code, which has two disadvantages. The first is performance—scripting code is interpreted and always runs more slowly than native code. The second disadvantage is even more marked: scripting is typeless. Notice that the C# code in the WebTacToe listing uses well-defined structures to manage the Tic-Tac-Toe board. You cannot do this in a scripting language. There is simply no support. The old COM-style programming model for classic ASP involved using `IDispatch`, an inherently typeless interface. (Every parameter you pass through the methods has to be a `VARIANT`.) However, because ASP.NET is a CLR-compliant tool, you can easily mix whatever you want into your page. C# (and Visual Basic.NET) are excellent languages for defining types.

Therefore although developing the WebTacToe application from within Visual Studio.NET is pretty straightforward (and almost like traditional desktop-style development), there is one glaring issue—how to manage the state of the application and the sessions. If the state were kept around as a global variable, as it might be in a desktop application, the state of the game board would be lost between postbacks. Fortunately, ASP.NET provides a canned way for managing state between connections.

STATE MANAGEMENT FOR WEB APPLICATIONS

Managing the state of a desktop application is pretty straightforward compared to managing the state of a Web application. Inherently, desktop applications are encapsulated and stay connected to their data sources. They are like people you invite over to your house and allow to stay a while. You can sit down and have a conversation with them, and there is consistency from one minute to the next.

Web applications are different. They must be careful about how they manage state. A Web server serves many clients concurrently. That is, a client connects to the Web server, makes a request, and then leaves. Two seconds later, another client (or perhaps the same one) connects. If it is the same client, the session may be a chain of requests meant to fulfill a commerce order. If it is a different client, the Web application needs to be able to manage the information about the new client. To Web applications, having so many clients would be like you trying to hold a conversation with several people who come to your door one at a time, speak a single sentence, and then leave. The next ring of the doorbell could be the same person with the next sentence in the conversation, it could be a different person continuing an existing conversation, or it might even be a completely new person with a new story. You would have absolutely no idea who it would be. Pretty soon, you would have to start keeping a list of the people who visited you, what each one was talking about, and where each person was in each story.

There are several kinds of information a Web application has to manage during the course of its life: application state, session state, and control state. Application state is the data maintained on an application level and might include something like a database connection string or a uniform resource locator (URL). Session state is the per-session data that is stored for a given client interacting with the application. A great example of session state might be the items in a shopping cart. Finally, the control state is the state of individual controls on a form that need to maintain state for user-interface consistency.

ASP.NET provides facilities for managing application and session state. (Classic ASP does to some extent). These facilities include a pair of objects for managing application- and session-level state. Application state is the global application state that is normally stored once and then never modified. Session state is per-client state. ASP.NET generates a session ID when a client first accesses a page. The client becomes aware of the session ID through either an HTTP response, a client-side cookie, or a hidden field in a form—or it might be encoded in the URL. The session ID is the client's ticket to associate data with a single client between different connections. It allows the server to associate data with a particular request. Subsequent connections to the Web server by the same client are identified using the session ID. As we have already discussed, individual control state is more or less managed by ASP.NET's HTML controls or Web controls.

Application State

The idea behind application state is that it is global information an application needs. It is usually loaded when the application starts and then used by the individual pages during the life of the application. ASP.NET maintains a `System.Web.HTTPApplication` object that is accessible from the `System.Web.UI.Page` class.

The application state object is usually managed from within a file named GLOBAL.ASAX, which accompanies a typical Web application. The following listing shows the core of the GLOBAL.ASAX file used for Web-Tac-Toe:

```
public class Global : System.Web.HttpApplication {
   protected void Application_Start(Object sender, EventArgs e) {
                  // Initialize at the start of your app . . .
   }

   protected void Session_Start(Object sender, EventArgs e) {
                  // per session initialization

            Session["Player"] = Player.XPlayer;

            Board board = new Board();
            Session["Board"] = board;
   }

   protected void Application_BeginRequest(Object sender,
                  EventArgs e) {
            // Called at the beginning of each HTTP Request
   }

   protected void Application_EndRequest(Object sender,
                  EventArgs e) {
            // Called at the end of each HTTP Request
   }

   protected void Session_End(Object sender, EventArgs e) {
            // Called at the end of each session
   }

   protected void Application_End(Object sender,
                  EventArgs e) {
            // Called at the end of each Application
   }
}
```

It is usually a bad design technique to continually change and update global application state because you could severely hamper the performance of your application. However, *if* the global application state needs to be changed for some reason, ASP.NET provides the capability to lock and unlock it (`Application.Lock` and `Application.Unlock`).

Session State

The session state is used to store individual data for a user during a page interaction. It is identified by a unique session ID. The client usually finds out about the session ID because it becomes a cookie on the client side. Sometimes the session ID is encoded within the URL. Every instance of the page has a property named `Session` that represents the current `HttpSession` object. Session state is typically initialized in the `Session_Start` handler in GLOBAL.ASAX. (See the previous listing.)

The Session object includes a property bag into which you are able to place CLR-compliant objects. It is a dictionary (or map, if you will) relating String keys to the objects held. Notice that the entire game board is created and stored in the session state as part of the Session_Start method on page 290. If the game board were created during the constructor or initialization phase of the Web form, it would be newly recreated every time someone hit the session. It is important to draw the distinction between the *session* and the *application*. Remember, when a desktop application starts up, it is normally serving a single end user; any state being managed can endure for the life of the application if you want it to. Every time someone accesses the Web page, the runtime completely constructs a new Web form. In the case of WebTacToeForm, a new instance of the form is created every time someone hits the page (for example, by pushing any of the buttons or refreshing the page).

Therefore the game board is constructed as part of the session state and stored immediately. Notice that the initialization code for WebTacToeForm yanks the game board from the session state and starts using it. Also take a look at the method SwitchPlayers (which toggles between the *X* player and the *O* player). SwitchPlayers is called every time one of the buttons is pressed. Notice that SwitchPlayers also stores the game board back into the session state object. The next time the same client hits the Web page, the client gets a game board with the correct state. New clients get completely new game boards.

Session Configuration

For the most part, ASP.NET bridges the gap between sessions very well. You barely need to do anything but be aware that the support exists and know how to use it as described previously. However, there are times when you may want to configure the session state. ASP.NET is flexible enough to let you do this. For example, you may control the duration of a session before timing out and whether cookies are used to manage session IDs. All this happens within the sessionState section of WEB.CONFIG. Following is an example of a configuration file with some session state settings in it:

```
<configuration>

  <system.web>
  <sessionState inproc="false"
                server="StateServer"
                port="33333"
                cookieless="true"
                timeout="60"
  />

    <system.web>
</configuration>
```

There are a number of entries you can put into the `sessionState` section of the configuration file (Table 8-2).

The Web constantly generates an enormous amount of Internet traffic. As sites are forced to service more and more clients, most site administrators find themselves adding new boxes to the network to handle all the traffic. These clusters of servers are often known as *Web Farms* or *server farms*. The corollary of this is that a single session might be handled by multiple computers! Remember the houseguest example we discussed previously? Not only are you getting new guests in your house concurrently, some of these guests already started their conversations in another house. In short, managing state across multiple boxes is tricky and is something you have to do by hand using classic ASP. Fortunately, ASP.NET now handles the job of storing session state in a distinct process, which may be on a different machine. It can even be stored in a database. Making this happen is a matter of setting up the configuration file correctly using the WEB.CONFIG file.

TABLE 8-2   Entries for the sessionState Section of WEB.CONFIG

Attribute	Entry	Description
mode	`"Off"` == session state disabled `"InProc"` == session state stored locally `"StateServer"` == session state stored remotely `"SqlServer"` == session state stored in SQL Server	Specifies where to store the session state
cookieless	`"true"` == don't use cookies `"false"` == use cookies	Identifies session states with cookies
timeout	`Default` == 20	Number of minutes a session can be idle before the session is abandoned
connectionString	`"123.4.5.6:33333"` (This is an example. Your address may vary.)	Server name and port where session state is stored remotely; required when mode is set to `StateServer`
sqlConnection String	`"data source=123.4.5.6;user id=sa; password="` (This is an example. Your connection string may vary)	Connection string for an SQL Server; required when mode is set to `SqlServer`

CACHING

ASP.NET is chockfull of optimizations. For example, simply running under the CLR improves performance because intermediate language (IL) code is compiled into native machine code before it is run. No more scripting for running executable parts of your Web page (unless you want to, of course). One of the other optimizations made by ASP.NET is the ability to cache certain things. There are two main approaches to caching: output caching and data caching.

Output Caching

Generating HTML on the fly chews up clock cycles. If a Web page does not change very much, a great optimization would be to cache the generated HTML—this is exactly how ASP.NET's output caching works. Caching output is as simple as using the `<% OutputCache %>` directive. The following listing shows how to implement output caching in an ASP.NET file.

```
<%@ OutputCache Duration="60000" %>
<html>
  <script language="C#" runat="server">
    void Page_Load(Object sender, EventArgs e) {
          // Figure out the time this was cached
          String str;
          str = DateTime.Now.ToString("r");
          str += "  ";
          System.Threading.Thread.Sleep(15000);
          str += DateTime.Now.ToString("r");
          str += "  It took a while to generate the first time.";
          str += " Do a Refresh and see how fast the refresh is.";
          msg.Text = str;
    }
  </script>
  <body>
    <h3>Output Caching</font></h3>
    <p> <asp:label id="msg" runat="server"/>
  </body>
</html>
```

Figure 8-3 shows how the output appears in the browser.

The code in the previous listing simulates a lengthy page-output operation. Generating complex pages may involve database operations, connecting to servers, and so forth. When the data does not change very much, you get a lot of wasted clock cycles. Using the `OutputCache` directive solves this performance problem. If you were to hit the Refresh button on the page in the previous listing, you would notice how quickly the page came up compared to the first time.

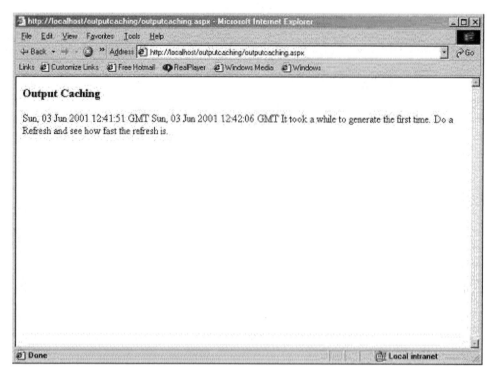

FIGURE 8-3   Results of Output Caching in the Browser.

Data Caching

The second kind of caching is data caching. Although Microsoft Chairman Bill Gates is a very rich and powerful man, the one thing he has not figured out how to do is increase the speed of light. This means that there is a time lag when you send data from one machine to the other. The net result of this is that round trips to the server are the single biggest performance bottleneck in Web development. You may be able to work around the bottleneck by somehow caching data in your application. The second bottleneck that you may encounter in your Web development is database contention, which may also be relieved using data caching. Finally, there may be other reasons for keeping data around between HTTP connections, requiring you to cache data. (Remember, HTTP is essentially a "stateless" protocol, meaning that another mechanism needs to be introduced to manage state between connections.)

ASP.NET comes with a robust cache mechanism for storing objects across HTTP requests. `System.Web.UI.Page` has a cache property. Like the session state, the cache relies on a simple dictionary interface for caching values. Each application instance creates its own cache. The easiest way to use the cache is to store values in your application using the dictionary interface, as shown in the following listing:

```
<%@ Page language=C# Debug="true" %>
<script runat=server>
  private string LastSource;
  private string LastDestination;

  void Page_Load() {
    if (!Page.IsPostBack) {
      LastSource = (string)Cache["LastSource"];
      if(LastSource == null) {
        LastSource = "";
      }
      LastDestination = (string)Cache["LastDestination"];
      if(LastDestination == null) {
        LastDestination = "";
      }
    }
  }
  void CalcDistances(Object sender, EventArgs E) {
    String strDistance = "";
    if(Starting.Value == "Boston") {
        if(Destination.Value == "Fort Collins") {
            strDistance = "2000";
        } else if(Destination.Value == "Atlanta") {
            strDistance = "900";
        } else if(Destination.Value == "Santa Fe") {
            strDistance = "2100";
        } else if(Destination.Value == "Bellevue") {
            strDistance = "3000";
        }
    }
    if(Starting.Value == "Dallas") {
        if(Destination.Value == "Fort Collins") {
            strDistance = "800";
        } else if(Destination.Value == "Atlanta") {
            strDistance = "1300";
        } else if(Destination.Value == "Santa Fe") {
            strDistance = "350";
        } else if(Destination.Value == "Bellevue") {
            strDistance = "1000";
        }
    }
    if(Starting.Value == "Los Angeles") {
        if(Destination.Value == "Fort Collins") {
            strDistance = "1000";
        } else if(Destination.Value == "Atlanta") {
            strDistance = "2000";
        } else if(Destination.Value == "Santa Fe") {
            strDistance = "1000";
        } else if(Destination.Value == "Bellevue") {
```

```
                strDistance = "750";
            }
        }

        if(Starting.Value == "New York") {
            if(Destination.Value == "Fort Collins") {
                strDistance = "2000";
            } else if(Destination.Value == "Atlanta") {
                strDistance = "600";
            } else if(Destination.Value == "Santa Fe") {
                strDistance = "2000";
            } else if(Destination.Value == "Bellevue") {
                strDistance = "2900";
            }
        }

        Distances.InnerText = "From " + Starting.Value + " to " +
            Destination.Value + " " + strDistance + " miles";

        string lastsrc = (string)Cache["LastSource"];
        string lastdest = (string)Cache["LastDestination"];

        LastCalc.InnerText = "Last calc was between " + lastsrc +
            " and " + lastdest;
        Cache["LastSource"] = Starting.Value;
        Cache["LastDestination"] = Destination.Value;
    }

</script>
<html>
<head>
</head>
<body>
  <form runat=server>
    Starting : <select ID="Starting" runat=server>
                  <option>Boston</option>
                  <option>Dallas</option>
                  <option>Los Angeles</option>
                  <option>New York</option>
                  </select>
    Destination: <select ID="Destination" runat=server>
                  <option>Fort Collins</option>
                  <option>Atlanta</option>
                  <option>Santa Fe</option>
                  <option>Bellevue</option>
                  </select>

    <input type=button value="Submit" runat=server
      OnServerClick="CalcDistances" />
    <div id="Distances" runat=server />
    <div id = "LastCalc" runat=server />
  </form>
</body>
</html>
```

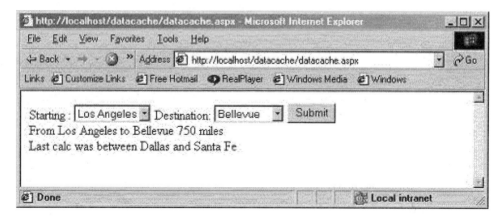

FIGURE 8-4   Internet Explorer Showing the Last Calculation.

The code in the previous listing shows how to use the page's `cache` property to store the names of the last cities checked between HTTP connections. Figure 8-4 shows Internet Explorer displaying the last two cities checked.

HTTP HANDLERS

In the last chapter, we briefly went over the architecture of ASP.NET. The heart of an ASP.NET application is the `System.Web.UI.Page` class, which implements `IHttpHandler`. In the absence of a specific handler for a specific URI, ASP.NET directs the request to be handled by the `Page` class. However, you may want to set up your own custom handlers from time to time to handle specific URIs or query strings. Setting up custom handlers for each request is simply setting up a class to implement `IHttpHandler` and mapping the request to the handler using the WEB.CONFIG file associated with the Web site. Following is the `IHttpHandler` interface defined in C#:

```
interface IHttpHandler {
   bool IsReusable();
   void ProcessRequest(HttpContext context);
};
```

The two functions of `IHttpHandler` are `IsReusable` and `ProcessRequest`. ASP.NET calls `IsReusable` to find out whether the handler can be recycled. `ProcessRequest` is where you put your response code. The following listing shows an implementation of `IHttpHandler` in C#:

```
using System.Web;
namespace AppliedDotNetHandlers {
   public class CSHandler : IHttpHandler {
      public void ProcessRequest(HttpContext context) {
         context.Response.Write("Hello World in CSharp!");
      }

      public bool IsReusable() {
            return true;
      }
   }
}
```

There is not much to this class. It simply takes the request/response context provided by ASP.NET for the particular request and says, "Hello World in CSharp!". You can include any markup code you want. You can also access the other properties of the connection context to do more specialized tasks. (For an example, look at the HTTP handlers listed in the InternetBaton application in Chapter 2. InternetBaton uses HTTP handlers effectively.)

Each Web site can have a WEB.CONFIG file associated with it. The <httpHandlers> block within the <configuration> block associates the incoming requests to an assembly implementing the handler. The following listing shows how to associate handlers to incoming requests.

```
<configuration>
   <httpHandlers>
      <add verb="*" path="CSHandler.aspx"
         type=" AppliedDotNetHandlers.CSHandler,CSHandler" />
   </httpHandlers>
</configuration>
```

This WEB.CONFIG file associates incoming requests to the handlers shown in the listing on page 297. For example, if you type the URL *http://localserver/CSHandler.aspx*, ASP.NET routes the request to the CSHandler class. You see "Hello World in CSharp!" appear in your browser.

CONCLUSION

This chapter provided an overview of how to apply ASP.NET in various situations. We have only scratched the surface here, and the topic of ASP programming could fill several entire books. Regardless, there's enough here to get a good feeling for what ASP.NET is all about. ASP.NET helps level the playing field for people-oriented software. For example, it supports detecting the client device and modifying its output to match the end device. This is enormously important for translation. Within people-oriented software, *translation* refers to the interoperability between platforms and systems; having the server do impedance matching on the browser enables translation.

ASP.NET makes it easy to write Web services as well, leading to *collaboration*. A Web site can expose its methods to become programmable. At that point, different Web sites can work together to fulfill a specific need of the end user.

Finally, because ASP.NET is built on the .NET runtime (the CLR), it leads to *universality* in its support of implementations. For example, most of the code in this chapter was written using C#, but it could easily have been written in Visual Basic.NET, managed C++, or any other language running under the CLR. In addition, ASP.NET is CLR, providing smooth integration between components. Gone is the overhead of COM, the ugliness of `IDispatch`, and the type ambiguity of scripting languages—which leads to a much more flexible environment for developing Web sites.

.NET Enterprise Servers

.NET ENTERPRISE SERVERS AND PEOPLE-ORIENTED SOFTWARE

Universalization

Universalization is not limited to the common language runtime (CLR). Although the CLR is dramatic in its capabilities and its multilanguage consolidation of development firepower, it is still a specific runtime environment for the code *you* develop. We need to go beyond this to leverage *already-developed* capabilities at a new level and to a greater degree. The CLR classes are an example of this at a lower level. The .NET enterprise servers provide an extensive array of capabilities that can be viewed as a larger, more generic, and comprehensive part of the universal runtime—defined by the complete set of services seamlessly available in a development and execution environment. These are exactly the types of services required to build real versions of the types of systems we have been discussing.

Collaboration

A basic aspect of collaboration is the capability to define and execute complex interactions that represent business transactions. Often these interactions involve separate application systems within the enterprise and across enterprise boundaries. The .NET enterprise servers provide a great deal of the building blocks for this type of interaction.

Translation

Inherent to interoperability is the translation of platform-specific formats in the context of method calls on Web services across platform boundaries. This extends as well to the translation of standard business documents to and from proprietary formats. BizTalk Server, in particular, includes a sophisticated set of translation capabilities put together to leverage standard technologies to minimize custom development while providing well-thought-out hook points to allow extensibility and custom development where necessary.

MAKING IT ALL WORK TOGETHER

It is one thing to talk of the next revolution in software for the Internet. It is quite another to seriously address the host of difficulties facing business analysts, software architects, designers, and developers seeking to develop actual large-scale business-to-consumer and business-to-business solutions. Following are some issues to consider:

- How do we represent business transactions in a way that facilitates the introduction and integration of trading partners?
- How do we define standard business documents so that they can be effectively processed and integrated with applications systems that have proprietary data formats?
- How do we translate documents from one format to another without incurring the costs and time delays of custom translation software development?
- How do we protect proprietary information, in both transmission and storage?
- How can we guarantee the effective and reliable execution of the business transactions?
- How do we track the dynamic status of transaction execution in a large-scale environment where many thousands of transactions are simultaneously active? These transactions have to be conducted reliably over a globally distributed processing framework, implying a need for asynchronous and disconnected processing models, combined with interactions involving long transaction lifetimes. Traditional two-phase commit transactional models are not practical for this type of problem. How do we meet the challenge of robustness and reliability given these constraints?
- How do we model the business processes in such a way that they are loosely coupled to the implementation and allow maximum flexibility and responsiveness to change—all while minimizing the amount of custom software development required?
- How can we apply such a model in a practical way to integrate existing software components of a variety of types from a variety of sources to leverage

the existing technology investment? How do we define and execute work-flows consisting of disparate system components? How do we manage the execution of such business processes?

- How do we effectively integrate our Web-based systems with multiple generations of legacy systems on foreign platforms?
- How do we do all of these things quickly in the face of extreme time-to-market competitive pressure?

Historically we have tried to address these issues by custom software development projects. These large, complicated, expensive, time-consuming undertakings have become dinosaurs in a world of extremely high time-to-market competitive pressure. In the current situation, by the time a large-scale custom development is completed, it is a legacy.

One of the closest analogues to the globally integrated cross-enterprise systems we are challenged with today is in the electronic data interchange (EDI) space. These systems historically provided solutions, of sorts, to some of these problems by custom development to support complex EDI standards, including things like forms creation applications, custom translation software, and custom communications applications. Security and connectivity issues were addressed by the use of expensive private value-added networks (VANs).

Proprietary application servers running on the VAN's hardware and custom client applications running on supported client platforms dealt with cross-platform issues, after a fashion. These types of systems were once the kings of this space, but they have eroded steadily in the face of the low-cost, ubiquitous global connectivity represented by the Internet, thin clients, and the search for increased responsiveness to changes in the global marketplace.

POINT OF CRITICAL SOLUTION MASS

A critical mass of standards consensus has emerged that addresses these issues based on the Web protocols, eXtensible Markup Language (XML) and related technologies, and application server products that are built on them. This situation has created an opportunity to realize significant gains in building these solutions. We have never before been in a better position to actually build these systems and reap the benefits of productivity made possible by finally integrating the Web-based systems with the core enterprise systems on a global scale across enterprise boundaries. This level of integration represents the next wave of productivity increases that technology can provide to global business.

The standards consensus around XML has allowed it to become the foundation of modern interoperability. In itself XML solves nothing, but it provides a basic alphabet for expressing the building blocks of solutions in a surprising variety of contexts.

A few examples include structured data exchange, schema definition of business documents, business process specification, remote object invocation, generic remote procedure call (RPC) protocol implementation, document translation technology, and asynchronous messaging.

Working somewhat from the bottom up, the rest of this chapter provides an overview of XML, Simple Object Access Protocol (SOAP), and two of the newer .NET enterprise servers—and how they address the challenges we will face during the next wave of Internet development known as *people-oriented software*. These application servers—BizTalk Server and Commerce Server—either heavily leverage these technologies or are built on them from the ground up.

BizTalk Server deserves special attention and therefore gets a special focus in this chapter. Perhaps more than any other of the larger services modeled under the universalization moniker, this server embodies the convergence of the standards-based approach to modern development with a full complement of tools for integration, translation, tracking, workflow, and delivery that are all built from the ground up on the XML technologies. It represents a huge step forward and will play a key role in process orchestration, integration, tracking, messaging, business document translation, and secure Internet delivery.

Although it may sound like it at times, this description is really not intended to be a wholesale approval and endorsement of Microsoft's implementations. Regardless, when you think about the full suite of capabilities represented by this convergence of standards and these server implementations, the end-to-end integration picture that emerges becomes quite compelling.

In Microsoft's vision, businesses present themselves to consumers on browsers, wireless phones, and personal digital assistants (PDAs) using ASP.NET, Internet Information Server (IIS), and Commerce Server. Web services are easily developed using .NET and exposed to trading partners and other consuming applications systems, and they provide services via SOAP based on XML and HyperText Transfer Protocol (HTTP). Sites are dynamically deployed using the .NET shadowing techniques to avoid file-in-use deployment conflicts, permitting zero-downtime upgrades.

Both Web methods and business-to-consumer site pages drop business documents into BizTalk Server, triggering the instantiation and execution of long-lived transactions in the form of "orchestration schedules." These execute in a managed and tracked framework, integrating with internal enterprise applications and foreign servers over the Internet and across enterprise boundaries. The BizTalk Messaging framework validates business documents using XML schemas, translates them using extensible style language transformation (XSLT), and delivers them with a variety of built-in integration components supporting standard Internet delivery and security protocols. The picture includes components to interoperate with corporate mainframes via queuing mechanisms, file system integration, and direct transaction integration using Host Integration Server.

.NET ENTERPRISE SERVERS AND .NET

It's important to understand the .NET moniker in a technology context and in a marketing context. The .NET platform as a technology generation focuses on the CLR, the .NET framework, ASP.NET, C#, Visual Basic.NET, and the new deployment technologies. The entire suite of Microsoft technology solutions is now being marketed under the .NET name as it was previously under the DNA label. The current generation of these servers is not built on the .NET framework. These servers are generally of the component object model (COM) technology generation, updated to leverage XML at about every conceivable point to make it easier to put together well-integrated solutions. A partial exception is BizTalk Server. Although built from the ground up on the XML technologies, it interfaces with the world using traditional methods of COM, file, and message queuing. This is a natural course of events and is a good thing, because these servers represent massive investments in research, development, and testing. We need to exploit these investments as the people-oriented software miner would, rather than reinvent these capabilities, so that we can deliver systems expeditiously. These are covered in this book because without capabilities like these, we cannot possibly deliver in Internet time the types of large-scale, globally distributed systems we need.

ROLE OF XML

Foundation of Modern Interoperability

The vision of a ubiquitous global network of interoperating services has been around for years, but there have been complications along the way. Distributed processing has largely been based on a synchronous RPC model, which in itself is fine, but the implementations have been very complex, binary based, and fairly closed natured. The major ones that naturally come to mind are distributed component object model (DCOM) and Common Object Request Broker Architecture (CORBA). In contrast to this arcane binary complexity is the refreshing simplicity of interoperability based on XML and the technologies built on it.

The idea of simple and lightweight being powerful—in contrast with feature-laden being powerful—characterizes what is happening with the Internet and the integration revolution that it is fueling. The Internet has always been powered by simple protocols. Text-based interactions are the rule of the day. XML is at once simple and powerful in that the structure is intuitively grasped and the text format is easy to use, yet the constructs allow the representation of an astounding diversity of information, both in type and semantics. A common developer reaction to learning the basics of XML is something along the lines of "Of course. Why didn't we do this before?"

By providing a simple way to represent data and structure, XML gives us the foundation of modern interoperability. Let's take a look at how this has transpired.

Structured Data Exchange

At the most fundamental level, XML provides a method of representing structure and data in a way that is easy to parse programmatically, reasonably readable to human eyes, and easily extensible with user-defined tags. Arbitrary types can be represented with the help of XML schema, and binary data can be encoded as part of the elements. These provide the basis for structured data exchange in the form of an XML document.

Business Document: XML

An XML document can represent a business document such as a purchase order, invoice, authorization, contract, or insurance policy. The document can be designed to be unambiguous and because the parts of an XML document conform to simple but strict "well-formed-ness" rules, standard parsers can be developed to provide fairly straightforward programmatic access to the document without extensive custom software development. In effect, the structure has been setup in a way that allows standard parsing and easy tag extensibility.

Business Document Specification: XML Schema

It is natural to try and standardize business documents to make it easier to develop and integrate software that processes them. We need a way not only to specify an easy-to-process document instance that is formed correctly for an XML parser but also to define the rules for determining whether the instance of a document meets the definition of a particular business document. In other words, we need to ensure, for example, not only that it is valid XML but also that it is a valid auto insurance policy.

XML originally provided this in the form of document type definitions (DTDs), but they suffer from the fact that they themselves are not in XML format, thus complicating parsing and tool development. DTDs also lack the ability to deal with namespaces—a significant limitation because it is unreasonable to expect that in the global business community, there will be no name collisions in business documents.

It would be even better if the way to represent the document schema were also an XML representation, which would further leverage the XML parser and keep you from having to use separate software to process schemas. The XML schema provides just this result.

Document Translation: XSLT

Enterprises do not all use the same formats for business documents. Even in an environment in which more people are agreeing on vertical market business document standards, we are a long way from a uniform definition—much less uniform adoption—of these standards. Most business data still resides in proprietary formats in proprietary systems on mainframes. To interact with these systems, document translation is a fundamentally required capability. Once you have structured data in XML modeling business documents in XML that are validated by schemas represented in XML, you are in a position to leverage XML technology as a solution to business document translation. Can the rules for document translation be represented in XML as well? It turns out that the answer is *yes,* in the form of XSLT. The name has its roots in style sheets, which fail to capture the powerful generality of its ability to represent, in XML format, a fairly arbitrary, template-based, pattern-matching transformation from XML to any text-based format. Because XML is a text-based format, XML-to-XML translation using XSLT is a natural foundation for a comprehensive document translation solution.

Business Process: XLANG

We can specify, validate, and translate documents using XML, but what good are valid documents if you cannot exchange them with trading partners? What if the business process interaction could itself be modeled using XML and standard software could be used to execute the interaction—like leveraging a parser? It can be, in what is called *XLANG.* XLANG is at the heart of BizTalk Server Orchestration, run by the XLANG execution engine.

Remote Object Invocation: SOAP

XML has been applied to the problem of remote object method invocation in SOAP. SOAP defines a remote procedure call mechanism and a serialization format that can run over various protocols. It typically runs over HTTP so that it can run through firewalls. Request and response packets are formatted in XML using elements to represent arguments and return values. The basic SOAP interchange is rather simple. The protocol makes no assumptions about transports, and the interaction is text-based. This simplicity and textual nature give it easy access to the wide range of platforms found on the Internet that need only support the basic Internet standards to allow interoperation.

Asynchronous Messaging: SOAP

The SOAP response message is optional. SOAP can be used as an asynchronous messaging protocol.

Description of Web Services: WSDL

The Web services description language (WSDL) uses XML to describe network services as endpoints operating on messages. These messages can represent documents or procedure calls.

We have discussed the fact that the simple XML standard can be applied to a variety of problems we face in Internet development. Let's consider the basics of XML itself.

Basics of XML

XML, or extensible markup language, defines a generic, text-based syntax for marking up documents with meaningful tags, providing a way to create standard, computer-readable documents. Unlike hypertext markup language (HTML), which has a fixed set of tags focused on rendering pages for human consumption, XML allows you to use any tag you like as long as it follows the rules for XML names. This characteristic makes it possible to define business documents of structured data with standard, agreed-on tags specific to the problem domain at hand.

XML is quite specific and unforgiving in its syntactical grammar, which paradoxically is one of its strengths. In XML, for example, each start tag must have a corresponding end tag, attribute values must be in quotes, and elements must be strictly nested (with no overlapping tags whatsoever). This characteristic makes it easier to develop software to manipulate XML, especially XML parsers.

Design Goals

The *XML Specification* (October 2000)[1] lists the following design goals:

1. XML shall be straightforwardly usable over the Internet.
2. XML shall support a wide variety of applications.
3. XML shall be compatible with standard generalized markup language (SGML).
4. It shall be easy to write programs that process XML documents.
5. The number of optional features in XML is to be kept to the absolute minimum, ideally zero.
6. XML documents should be human-legible and reasonably clear.
7. The XML design should be prepared quickly.
8. The design of XML shall be formal and concise.
9. XML documents shall be easy to create.
10. Terseness in XML markup is of minimal importance.

After reading these design goals, notice the emphasis on rules that simplify parser development, document validation, and writing software to manipulate XML. In one sense, SGML suffers from its flexibility. It requires a significant level of sophistication

---

[1] World Wide Web Consortium: *http://www.w3.org/TR/2000/REC-xml-20001006.*

to acquire the knowledge to use it effectively, but it can do most anything. Writing software to parse an arbitrary SGML document is a massive undertaking.

This is a general irony of our industry. Embracing flexibility, ostensibly to make things easier in the future, tends to result in the opposite. Flexibility often comes at the cost of complexity and adds a significant learning curve. This learning curve often consumes the benefits of the flexibility. In contrast, the well-defined, no-exceptions policy of XML serves us well.

Documents

An XML document is a tree consisting of a single element that may have zero or more "child" elements. The top element is called the *root element* or the *document element*. There can be only one root element.

Following is a very simple XML document:

```
<guitar color="blue">
    <manufacturer>Fender</manufacturer>
    <name>Stratocaster</name>
</guitar>
```

This document has a single root element—`guitar`—with a `color` attribute, and two child elements—`manufacturer` and `name`.

Documents should begin with the XML declaration. This is optional but desirable. The XML declaration describes the version of XML and the encoding of the document. Following is our document with an added XML declaration:

```
<?xml version="1.0" encoding="US-ASCII" ?>
<guitar color="blue">
    <manufacturer>Fender</manufacturer>
    <name>Stratocaster</name>
</guitar>
```

Elements

An *element* is text and markup bound by a start tag and an end tag. The *start tag* consists of an opening angle bracket (<) followed by an element name and optional attributes, and ends with a closing angle bracket (>). The *end tag* starts with </ and is followed by the name of the element the tag is ending and a closing angle bracket (>). XML element names are case sensitive.

Empty elements can be denoted as a start tag followed by an end tag or a special empty tag syntax—a tag starting with < and ending with />:

```
<name/>
```

In effect, the previous is the same as the following:

```
<name></name>
```

Attributes

Attributes are name-value pairs in the start tag of elements. You can use either single or double quotes around the value part.

There is obviously some ambiguity around whether you should represent data as an attribute or an element. It is up to you. Here are some things to keep in mind. First, elements can represent structured data because they can have child elements. Attributes cannot—their value is the single text string. Second, more than one element with the same name can be a child of an element. Only one attribute with a given name can be attached to a single element. The flexibility of elements lets you model a wide variety of things, whereas the limits of attributes give them a simplicity you may find helpful.

Well-Formed Documents

To say that an XML document is *well formed* means that it follows the rules of XML syntax. It does not mean that it makes sense or conforms to the semantic correctness standard for a domain—that is to say, is *valid*.

Validity

A *valid* XML document conforms to a schema that defines its semantic correctness. This could be an XML schema or a DTD.

Entity References

Because some characters are reserved for use in markup and could legitimately be part of the text, there is a need to represent them without confusing the parser. This is done by defining a markup to represent the characters. The convention is called an *entity reference*—it starts with an ampersand character (&) and ends with a semicolon (;).

There are five entity references defined by XML (Table 9-1). You can also add your own by using a DTD.

TABLE 9-1   Predefined XML Entity References

References	Definitions
&lt;	The "less than" character: <
&gt;	The "greater than" character: >
&amp;	The ampersand character: &
&quot;	The double quote character: "
&apos;	The single quote or apostrophe: '

CDATA Sections

There are situations in which you need to add text in an XML document that includes what would normally be considered markup, but you want to leave it unprocessed. Imagine, for example, that you wanted to write a Web service that allowed users to drop files to a central location on the Internet. Users could be notified via e-mail of new documents. Your Web service would have a method for depositing a document that included arguments providing the addressees of the e-mail. Perhaps you would like to allow the sender to customize the e-mail and supply the body as an argument in HTML format, but the HTML markup would confuse the XML parser and cause difficulties.

A scenario like this is perfect for a CDATA section. The parser ignores any character data in a CDATA section. A CDATA section starts with `<!CDATA[` and ends with `]]>`. Anything in between is treated as text and left unprocessed.

Processing Instructions

XML provides a way to communicate information to a downstream processing application in the form of *processing instructions*. A processing instruction is not eliminated by the parser and is available for the use of consuming applications. A processing instruction begins with `<?name`, where *name* is an XML name describing the instruction, and ends with `?>`. The text in between provides whatever further information is germane to the meaning the instruction intends to convey.

Comments

Comments can be placed in XML documents. They start with `<!–` and end with `–>`. Comments can appear anywhere except inside a tag or inside another comment. The parser may ignore the comments and strip them from the document.

Namespaces

Because XML allows you to define your own element names, it is likely that someone else will use one of them. XML namespaces provide a way to make your element and attribute names unique by attaching them to a unique identifier. The unique identifier is associated with a prefix, and the prefix is then used as part of the element name reference. By definition, uniform resource identifiers (URIs) are unique, so they are used as the unique identifier. Globally unique identifiers (GUIDs) can be used as well. Namespaces are frequently used to denote the set of tags agreed on for interoperability purposes.

The URI that provides the uniqueness does not actually have to point to a real resource, and there need not be a Web page corresponding to it. However, many people are under the misconception that these need to be real links. Therefore you might do what the World Wide Web Consortium (W3C) did—add stub Web pages with documentation for your URIs to deal with the stream of unnecessary notifications that they have broken links! The URIs used in namespaces are not accessed by the parser. They are simply unique identifiers.

The URI is associated with a prefix by using a special attribute in the element, of the form `xmlns:prefix="URI"`, where *prefix* is the prefix used and *URI* is the URI. For example:

```
<gt:Guitars xmlns:gt="http://www.myguitars.org/favorites/">
    <Name>Fred Thompson</Name>
<gt:Guitar>
<gt:Manufacturer>Hamer</gt:Manufacturer>
<gt:Name>Duotone</gt:Name>
</gt:Description>
Dual humbuckers and a piezo bridge pickup make this a highly versatile
instrument.
</gt:Description>
</gt:Guitar>
<gt:Guitar>
<gt:Manufacturer>Taylor</gt:Manufacturer>
<gt:Name>Grand Concert</gt:Name>
</gt:Description>An exceptional steel-string acoustic.</gt:Description>
</gt:Guitar>
</gt:Guitars>
```

In this example, the namespace prefix, `gt`, is bound to the URI `http://www.myguitars.org/favorites/` by the attribute `xmlns:gt="http://www.myguitars.org/favorites/"`. Therefore the Name element, denoted `gt:Name`, is in effect `http://www.myguitars.org/favorites/:Name` and is distinct from the other `Name` element in the document. Of course, this name could not be used in this literally resolved fashion, since the slash (/) is not a valid character for an XML name.

The scope of the namespace is the element where it is defined and all of its descendents, so this binding is in effect for all of the contents of the `gt:Guitars` element. The binding is to the URI, not to the prefix, so the following refer to the same element name:

```
<xyz:Guitars xmlns:gt="http://www.myguitars.org/favorites/">
...
</xyz:Guitars>
<gt:Guitars xmlns:gt="http://www.myguitars.org/favorites/">
...
</gt:Guitars>
```

You can also define a *default namespace* for any elements in scope, which do not have a prefix, by using the `xmlns` attribute without a prefix:

```
<gt:Guitars xmlns="http://www.myguitars.org/favorites/">
    <Name>Fred Thompson</Name>
</gt:Guitars>
```

In this case, the Name element is, by default, part of the gt namespace.

XPath

XPath is a language for document addressing. It is used by XPointer and XSLT to express queries used by XML processors to locate nodes. There are seven types of nodes from the point of view of XPath: the root node, attribute nodes, text nodes, processing instruction nodes, element nodes, namespace nodes, and comment nodes. When an XPath query is executed, the result is a set of one or more nodes. A wide variety of ways of describing the desired nodes and filtering the results are supported, including position, value, type, and content. XPath is an extensive and extremely powerful syntax.

XLink

XLink provides a way to place links in XML documents. It uses attributes as its syntax for creating links and describing the nature of the link. XLink uses the namespace URI http://www.w3.org/1999/xlink to indicate its set of tags, and this URI is conventionally bound to the xlink prefix. The attributes describe the type of link and the associated href. Behavioral information is provided by using the xlink:show and xlink:activate attributes. The xlink:show attribute suggests how the processor should render the resource, and xlink:activate suggests when the link should be followed. Relational information such as whether the link is parent/child, previous/next, customer/supplier, or any arbitrary relationship can be represented using the xlink:title and xlink:role attributes. These two attributes supply information about the nature of the link. The xlink:title attribute contains a short textual description. The xlink:role attribute contains a URI to a more complete description.

XPointer

XPointer provides a syntax to express a link to a *part* of another document. You can think of this as a more powerful version of how uniform resource locators (URLs) can identify a location within a document by use of a fragment identifier. For example, the following URL refers to the anchor named "fender" in the *guitars.html* document: *http://myserver.org/documents/guitars.html#fender*. A browser rendering this URL would display the document and scroll to the fender anchor.

XPointer extends this fragment identifier convention to allow the use of XPath queries as the content of the fragment identifier. This is done by providing the XPath expression as the argument to xpointer(). For example:

```
http://myserver.org/documents/guitars.xml#xpointer(
//stratocaster[position()=1])
```

This `xpointer` expression would look for the first `stratocaster` element in the target document.

Processing Models

The syntax rules of XML provide a basis for the development of standard software to process XML documents, which adds to productivity by allowing much of what would have formerly been custom code to be factored out and implemented for you. There are three basic processing models in use to work with XML documents. The three models are *memory tree* processing, *event-driven* processing, and processing based on *sequential navigation*.

Memory Tree

The document object model (DOM) embodies the memory tree model. When you use the DOM, you load an XML document into it. The parser implements the model, which reads the entire XML document into memory, parses it into nodes, and creates a live, searchable, modifiable representation of the document in tree form. You use the DOM method calls to search, read, and modify the content and serialize the document back to a file if desired.

The advantages of the DOM are simplicity of coding, easy searching, and ease of modification. The disadvantages include the memory storage requirements, which can be twice the size of the document, and associated resource usage. For very large documents the processing performance of the DOM could be inadequate for the overall system requirements. Some real-world business documents could be massive, in which case the DOM could become impractical.

Event-Driven

Event-driven processing means that instead of the entire document being loaded into memory, the processor reads the document and notifies the client application as it encounters items of interest in it. SAX, the Simple API for XML, is the dominant embodiment of this approach. To use SAX, you define and implement handlers for the items of interest. SAX calls your code when it encounters the item, and your code processes it. SAX is resource efficient because the entire document need not be loaded into memory.

Sequential Navigation Based

In sequential navigation processing, the document corresponds to the familiar file access model. You open a file, read lines from it, write lines to it, and close it. This type of model is implemented in the .NET CLR classes. This is a very familiar model to those versed in traditional programming and is rather easy to use. You open the XML document, read a node, test it to determine its type, and process accordingly. Sequential navigation provides the advantages of the notification-based model without the extra work of writing handlers. Depending on your background and bent of thinking, you may prefer this to the SAX approach.

SOAP

SOAP, the Simple Object Access Protocol, is built on XML and is a key technology to enable Web services to interoperate between disparate systems over the Internet. SOAP is the key enabling technology for people-oriented software's collaboration principle. It does not invent any new technology; it simply uses existing standards to provide a way to call code over the Internet and send asynchronous messages. SOAP defines a set of XML elements and semantics to achieve this as summarized by the SOAP specification:

> SOAP provides a simple and lightweight mechanism for exchanging structured and typed information between peers in a decentralized, distributed environment using XML.[2]

Description and Purpose

The original purpose of SOAP was to devise a way to call code over the Internet using XML as the RPC serialization format and HTTP as the transport protocol. This has expanded somewhat from the original synchronous request/response model to include the concept of asynchronous messaging without a response. In addition, SOAP no longer presumes HTTP as the transport protocol. Any reasonable transport could be used.

Maximized Interoperability

Because the protocol is defined in terms of XML documents, interoperability is greatly enhanced. It provides a protocol with a greater potential to work across vendors as easily, for example, as your Microsoft Web browser gets pages from a UNIX Web server. SOAP makes no assumptions about what is producing the XML document payloads that represent the calls and responses. The server could be calling COM code on a Windows 2000 machine, calling Java on UNIX, or invoking XSLT to transform the inbound XML request into an XML response. SOAP does not care. It earns high marks

---

[2] World Wide Web Consortium. *Simple Object Access Protocol (SOAP) 1.1:* May 8, 2000.

for simplicity, platform neutrality, and protocol neutrality, all of which are prerequisites for any hope of true convergence and large-scale interoperability.

Distributed Internet Computing RPC Mechanism

SOAP essentially serves as a network data representation (NDR) serialization format and a RPC protocol. As such it provides an XML-based replacement for proprietary marshalling formats such as DCOM NDR and CORBA common data representation (CDR). As a text-based format, it avoids many cross-platform representation issues.

Document Messaging Mechanism

The SOAP 1.1 specification includes the notion of SOAP messages being sent as asynchronous communication without expecting a synchronous response. This expands the utility of SOAP to situations that, for example, require very long-lived operations that would not make sense to implement as blocking calls.

Operation over the Internet through Firewalls

Even though any transport can be used for SOAP, we can expect that in the overwhelming majority of instances, HTTP will be the transport of choice—if for no other reasons than its ubiquity and its availability through firewalls.

Definition

A SOAP message consists of the SOAP envelope, optional headers, and the SOAP body (Figure 9-1). SOAP messages use an element view of the world, particularly in the message body.

SOAP Envelope

The SOAP envelope satisfies the XML requirement of a single, top-level element and encapsulates the entire SOAP payload. It uses the namespace URI `http://schemas.xmlsoap.org/soap/envelope/`, although this is not strictly required. This URI is typically bound to the SOAP-ENV prefix.

SOAP Headers

There is an optional `Header` element that, if present, must be the first immediate child of the envelope. This element can have multiple child elements, each element containing information of use to the object that will process the document. All of these must be qualified by a namespace. The header is designed to allow message extensions. In the example, the header is used to send information concerning the transaction in which the method call participates. Because headers can represent an

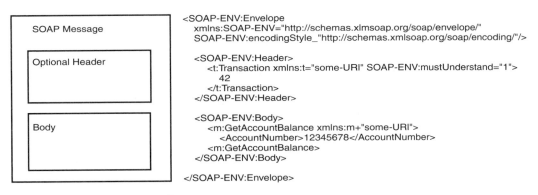

FIGURE 9-1 SOAP Message Format.

extension, which is possibly unknown to a recipient of the message, some mechanism is needed to tell the recipient whether the header information must be understood to correctly consume the message. This mechanism involves the `mustUnderstand` attribute. Its values are either *0* or *1*, with *1* meaning the header must be understood to proceed with processing.

SOAP Body

The `Body` element contains elements that define what the message represents. In our example, it represents calling the `GetAccountBalance` method with an account number argument.

Call and Response Pattern

When used for an RPC call and response pattern, one SOAP message is used to represent the call and another to represent the response. If HTTP is being used, the HTTP request and HTTP response implement the call and response, respectively.

Error returns are represented by using the SOAP `Fault` element in the body of the response message.

Data Types

Encoding of data types in SOAP is an important subject, the details of which are beyond the scope of this chapter. In summary, for simple types, SOAP uses the same data types as defined in the XML schema data types specification. The same is true for enumerations. Compound types corresponding to structs and arrays are supported. Arrays are represented as an ordered sequence of elements, with an attribute on the array element denoting the type of the contained elements. The name of the contained elements is not constrained. Structs are modeled similarly, with the members represented by elements. Each element name for a struct member must be unique.

Parts of the Implementation Problem

Many developers would love to escape the parts of their job that seem to have become largely integration work so that they can *write real code*. To these developers, the idea of writing code to process XML is an enticing temptation. With deep respect for this sentiment as hard-core developers ourselves, let's face it—the parser has already been written and should be used, not reinvented. The same thing should be said for the infrastructure that makes SOAP work. The SOAP specification describes the message formats and interchange protocol, not the operational infrastructure. A consideration of what needs to happen under the hood to make SOAP work might provide a level of appreciation for what is provided by a SOAP implementation. Naturally you want to avoid reinventing this type of plumbing. The parser, the extensible style language (XSL) processor, and the SOAP infrastructure should be seen architecturally, in people-oriented software terms, as services provided by the universal runtime.

First, on the client side, the capabilities of the server need to be discovered. Based on this discovery, the method call information has to be loaded and processed. Then the SOAP message has to be formatted. There is a significant amount of grunt-work code to marshal the arguments into XML format for transmission. Then the request document is sent to the server in a model using a synchronous call mechanism. If this were not supplied with an HTTP-type object available in your environment, you would need to create this as well.

On the server side, a listener needs to be implemented to field the SOAP request, parse it, instantiate the real server object, unmarshal the method arguments, and call the object's method. The code would further need to handle any errors in the call, format the SOAP response message, and return the message to the caller.

The client service layer would need to parse the SOAP response message, which includes error handling, and format a response for the original caller and return it.

Although rolling your own versions of all of these steps might seem attractive, we need to leverage what has already been done in these areas, as would the people-oriented software's miner People-Type.

Microsoft Implementations

SOAP SDK 1.0

The SOAP software development kit (SDK) 1.0 was a Microsoft Solution Developer Network (MSDN) sample application that provided an implementation to allow developers to begin to play with the technology using VisualStudio 6.0. The SOAP tool kit consisted of a remote object proxy engine, which handled SOAP message formatting and implemented the synchronous call model, and an ASP or ISAPI SOAP listener. It used SDL as the WSDL (Web services description language).

SOAP SDK 2.0

This version of the SOAP SDK uses WSDL at its core. It provides tools to easily expose dispatch-based COM interfaces as Web services and presents a dispatch-based COM interface to client consumers. On the server side, WSDL is used to describe the SOAP messages in a service, and Web services meta language (WSML) is used to associate the COM interface with the SOAP messages. WSML is specific to the Microsoft implementation.

VisualStudio .NET

By the time you are reading this, the VisualStudio .NET implementation and tool set should be the one recommended for production development. Web services built with VisualStudio .NET are bound to the open protocols. If you use C# or Visual Basic and ASP.NET, you get support for HTTP-Get, HTTP-Post, and SOAP protocols. If you use Active Template Library (ATL) server Web services, you get SOAP on top of HTTP.

BIZTALK SERVER ESSENTIALS: SOLVING THE EAI PROBLEM AND BEYOND

Previously in this chapter, we raised some questions about issues we must face if we are to build large-scale, interoperable, disparate systems communicating securely over the Internet. This section provides an overview of Microsoft's BizTalk Server 2000 product to show how its feature set addresses many of these problems. BizTalk Server could well be described as the Swiss army knife, adapter tool kit, and patch panel of business-to-business interoperability and enterprise application integration. It provides standards-based solutions to many of these problems in a customizable and extensible framework.

BizTalk Server consists of two major areas—BizTalk Orchestration and BizTalk Messaging. BizTalk Messaging provides a comprehensive framework for the exchange of business documents, including receipt, validation, translation, routing, tracking, encryption, secure delivery, and transport. BizTalk Orchestration provides an environment for modeling business processes and then implementing them in terms of the integration of software Legos and executing them in a tracked environment of long-lived transactions.

One interesting aspect of the design and implementation of the product is that BizTalk Messaging and Orchestration can operate in an integrated fashion or completely separately. BizTalk Orchestration does not depend on BizTalk Messaging, and Messaging does not depend on Orchestration. Orchestration can be used to define and execute long-lived business processes, composed of the interaction of reusable COM-based software components already in your development arsenal. If the services of BizTalk Messaging are appropriate to the solution, they can be utilized as a service, for example, to translate documents, encrypt them, and deliver them reliably.

If the solution does not call for a managed business process execution, or these functions are provided by existing services, BizTalk Messaging can be used without Orchestration to connect applications within the enterprise and communicate with trading partners.

BizTalk Orchestration

Much business productivity comes from understanding processes, analyzing them, and determining ways to streamline and automate them. This activity works in a process cycle of stepwise positive improvement, implying a dynamic environment of constant incremental change. These change cycles have historically involved large development efforts and significant cycle times to see productivity improvements. The cycle times need to decrease, but the resulting implementations typically have business logic baked into the software in ways that make a faster rate of responsive change difficult. Tools to allow the definition of business process in terms that are meaningful to business analysts who understand the problem domain are not sufficient—plenty of software allows you to model processes. What is desirable and highly useful is to be able to visually diagram these business processes and within the same environment to wire up the steps to real code implementations housed in reusable components.

The tool needs to model the realities of modern business processes, including asynchronous steps, parallelism in execution, long-lived operations, and results synchronization. The components that are being reused should have minimal interface requirements, following a dominant component interface standard. The binding of the components should leverage the existing work and also provide out-of-the-box implementations for core services. The services would need to support asynchronous operations and full-functioned messaging and communications services.

Orchestration is the term Microsoft has chosen to describe and market the ability in the BizTalk Server product to define business processes, bind them to code and service blocks, and manage their execution. *Workflow* was not considered the best term because it can conjure images of human interaction within messaging systems and is not sufficiently comprehensive to encompass the wide variety of business-to-business interactions that can be modeled and executed by BizTalk Orchestration. The concept of orchestration maps directly to people-oriented software's collaboration principle and to the conductor People-Type, which seeks to contribute by leading other components to perform together in an integrated way.

To reduce cycle time and allow more responsive change, the business logic steps need to be separated from the logic implementation. We have heard this in many contexts before. What is new here is a level of visibility and accessibility of the process to dynamic change by leveraging XML, COM, unified modeling language (UML), and Visio. Because the process definition describes the interaction of the participating components and this representation is XML based instead of hard-wired into the system implementation code, it can be revised more easily and changed more quickly.

One of the basic principles of reusability in engineering is the ability to factor commonality of function out of a design or implementation, and to implement it in such a way that it can operate in a loosely coupled fashion. COM has historically provided an excellent way to implement software components and connections between systems in a highly reusable and reasonably transparent way. Businesses have large investments in such software. Orchestration can make use of these Legos as blocks of processing in business process flows. The business process has been abstracted and separated from the implementation, and the execution of the process has been factored out into an execution engine based on XML representation.

One of the easiest ways to implement COM components is to use Windows scripting components, which use an XML format to describe the interface and methods supported by the component. The scripting component services provided in the operating system supply the COM machinery underneath, minimizing the amount of work to be done to make the component operational. Scripting components are fully supported as software Legos in BizTalk Orchestration.

BizTalk Orchestration Designer

The BizTalk Orchestration Designer tool embodies the definition and development environment for the business processes. The tool shows a two-sided design surface based on Visio, which allows the process designer to draw the business process as actions and decision steps. This is a dream tool for the conductor People-Type.

Figure 9-2 shows a fictitious example of a business process to generate an automobile insurance quote. The business process design is done using the flowchart shapes on the left side of the screen. UML users will immediately see a correspondence between the BizTalk Orchestration business process flowchart and the UML activity diagram.

The business process is designed, bound to software components that carry out the actions, and compiled into XLANG. XLANG is an XML representation of the business process bound to the components. The business process in this form is called a *schedule*.

The implementation shapes appear on the right side of the screen. Dropping one of them on the implementation surface starts a wizard corresponding to the

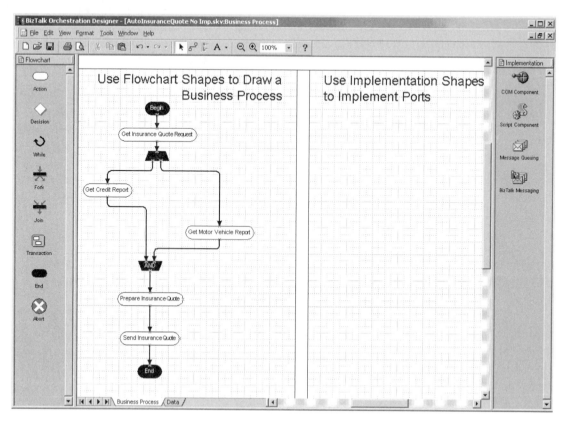

FIGURE 9-2   BizTalk Server Orchestration Designer Tool.

component type. The connection between the implementation and the business process shape is known as a *port*.

The communication between the steps is by means of this port, and the messages that pass through the ports are the content of the communication. Input arguments are passed in by an input message, and output results are returned in another message. Drawing the data flow connections between the message fields controls the flow of data between actions on the business process. This operation is done on the data flow diagram accessed by clicking the Data tab on the design surface.

Business Process Design

The business process shapes allow the process to define its beginning, its end, and the set of actions to perform along the way. Actions are linked to other actions, loops, and decision points. The processing flow can be split to model concurrency in execution, and the flow can be joined to model synchronization. Actions can be grouped into transactions. Each shape has properties that you set to configure its behavior in the process flow. Rules govern the behavior of *decision* shapes and *while* shapes.

Begin Shape

The *begin* shape defines the start of the business process and would be fairly uninteresting except that it is used to define the transaction behavior of the schedule.

Transactions are supported at essentially two levels in BizTalk Orchestration. First, you can consider the schedule as a whole as a transactional COM+ component. Second, you can define a group of actions in the schedule as a transaction using the transaction shape. Orchestration defines an identity property of the begin shape for you, a GUID that defines the version of the schedule. This changes every time you change and save the schedule.

Action Shape

The *action* shapes define the processing steps of the schedule. Actions are defined as message passing, so there are fundamentally two actions: sending a message and receiving a message. In this tool a synchronous method call is modeled as sending a message that also returns a message. This is modeled as a single *send message* action. The only property to set on an action is its name. The meaningful characteristics are defined when the action is linked to a port.

Decision Shape

The *decision* shape is how alternate paths of execution are expressed in the business process. One decision shape can model several alternative paths, as in a select or case statement in traditional programming. Each alternative path is represented by an inner box in the shape that you connect to the next action along that path. You add cases by using the Add Rule context menu. This adds an inner box to represent the case, with connection points to allow you to wire it up appropriately. You define a rule for each case. The rules are sequentially evaluated at runtime to determine the resulting execution path. These rules are expressed using VBScript in terms of the fields of the messages that are available in the schedule. The first rule that evaluates to *true* determines the execution path. If none are true, the Else path is followed.

While Shape

The *while* shape allows the modeling of a repeating action and uses a single rule to determine completion of the loop. Any rules defined for the decision shape are available to the while shape as well.

The properties allow you to control state persistence across loop iterations. This arcane-sounding property controls how the state of the messages used in each loop's iteration is persisted to the underlying XLANG database by the execution engine. You can persist either the state at the last iteration or a history of all the iterations. This affects the behavior of the transaction recovery mechanisms.

Fork Shape

The *fork* shape is how you model concurrency. It marks the start of parallel processing. The name is reminiscent of the C library `fork()` function that starts another process. There are no properties associated with the fork shape.

Join Shape

The *join* shape defines action synchronization. There is a single shape property that determines the type of synchronization—AND or OR. Up to 64 flows can enter a join; only one can exit. An OR join means that the execution proceeds beyond the join shape as soon as the first action wired to the input completes. An AND join waits for all connected input actions to complete before proceeding.

Transaction Shape

The *transaction* shape lets you group actions into a transaction grouping and apply transactional semantics to their execution. The idea is that all of the actions in the group will execute or all will fail. Reality is a bit more complicated. The actual effectiveness of the transaction semantics depends on the type of transaction and the good behavior of the components that implement the actions inside the transaction shape.

There are three kinds of transactions: short-lived, long-lived, and timed. *Short-lived transactions* are the Distributed Transaction Coordinator-style (DTC-style), two-phase commit transactions with which we are familiar. For this type of transaction to work properly, all of the participating implementation components need to follow the DTC rules using `SetComplete()` and `SetAbort()`. In other words, they are transactional scripts, transactional COM+ components, or transactional Microsoft Message Queues. *Long-lived transactions* have all of the atomicity, consistency, isolation, and durability (ACID) characteristics except isolation. They are defined to address the reality of business-to-business interactions that could take days or weeks—much longer than can be tolerated by transactions that lock down databases. *Timed transactions* allow you to declare that a certain operation must complete in a defined period of time.

To deal with the implications of error handling with long-lived transactions, two mechanisms are defined: *On Failure of Transaction* and *On Compensation of Transaction*. When defining properties for a transaction shape, you can add code for these. Adding code causes the tool to provide another page in the design surface for defining flows to be executed to handle the error.

On Failure of Transaction allows you to determine what should happen if the transaction fails and focuses on a single transaction. However, transactions can be composed, so how do you handle a case in which an inner transaction fails in a long-lived transaction? It cannot be rolled back.

On Compensation of Transaction is used to undo actions that cannot be rolled back by executing an action to reverse the effect of the completed inner transaction. This reversing action is called a *compensating action*. For example, a delivered e-mail cannot be unsent, but another e-mail can be sent to reverse the effect of the first message.

End Shape

The *end* shape marks a termination point of the schedule. There can be more than one end shape if your schedule includes any shapes that result in more than one flow on the page, such as a decision or fork.

Abort Shape

The *abort* shape is used within the transaction shape to explicitly trigger the abort of the transaction.

Port Implementation

After the business process is modeled on the left side using the process shapes, the process is wired to code by *implementing ports*. There are currently four implementation shapes: COM+ Component, Script Component, Message Queuing, and BizTalk Messaging.

When one of these shapes is put on the right side, the Orchestration Designer tool starts a Wizard to walk you through the binding process to the code. After the wizard completes, a port shape and an intermediate shape representing the port communication appear over the lines separating the two sides of the design surface. When you connect an action shape, another Wizard starts to complete the binding process by configuring the port communication.

COM+ Component

The COM+ Component shape is how you connect your action to a synchronous call to a method on a COM interface. The Script Component shape invokes the COM+ Component Binding Wizard. Here you supply the port name, provide the component instantiation rules, and select the class to use to instantiate a component instance. This can be selected from the installed classes the tool digs out of the registry or by entering a COM moniker. Then you select the methods involved from the list of methods supported by the component, which the tool extracted from the component's type library information. Last, you specify the security, transaction and state management characteristics, and error handling behavior.

When you connect an action to the port, the Method Communication Wizard starts. Here you define the direction of the synchronous method call, define message creation information, and select the message specification for the link. When finished, the description of two messages is done—one for input and one for output.

Script Component

The Script Component shape works like the COM+ Component shape, except it uses Windows Scripting Component (WSC) files instead of the registry to determine the methods. The Script Component shape invokes the Script Component Binding Wizard, which leads you through the steps of naming the port, identifying the type of instantiation desired, and binding to the script component file. You select the ones used in this interaction with the component. For each method, the tool defines messages to carry the data back and forth to the component. Finally you define security and transaction support characteristics to use.

When you connect an action to the port, the same Method Communication Wizard used with the COM+ component connection starts, and you supply the same information.

Message Queuing

The Message Queuing shape lets you bind the action of message I/O to a Microsoft Message Queue (MSMQ). You specify whether the action is reading a message from the queue or writing a message to the queue. You specify the queue path name, a static queue, or a queue to be created by the engine at runtime for the schedule instance. The received message can be in XML or a string. If it is a string, it is wrapped in XML by the schedule. All of the communication is XML based. Last, you specify the message type, which is checked against the MSMQ message label, and if necessary the root element name of the XML document.

When you connect an action shape on the left side to this port shape, the tool starts the XML Communication Wizard to take you through the steps to configure the port communication. The internal communication is defined in terms of XML documents.

BizTalk Messaging

The last implementation shape is BizTalk Messaging. This shape allows you to define the action in terms of BizTalk Messaging operations. The mapping of BizTalk Messaging operations to the send and receive semantics of the orchestration results in three possibilities.

First, you can send a document to a BizTalk Messaging channel. In this case you can specify the channel or you can indicate via the `data` page the message field and document from which the channel can be supplied at runtime. Second, you can receive a message through an HTTP URL. Third, you can configure the action to instantiate a schedule instance on receipt of a document by a BizTalk Messaging channel. This last technique is an important way that BizTalk Messaging and BizTalk Orchestration are integrated, and it is discussed in detail in Chapter 10. Figure 9-3 shows the design surface completed to include binding to implementation shapes.

Integration with Web Services

Any functionality wrapped in a COM interface or represented by the sending or arrival of a message in a message queue can be utilized in an orchestration schedule. For example, calls to Web service methods can be expressed as COM method calls. The SOAP tool kit includes a utility to generate such a COM wrapper to expose Web service calls via a COM interface.

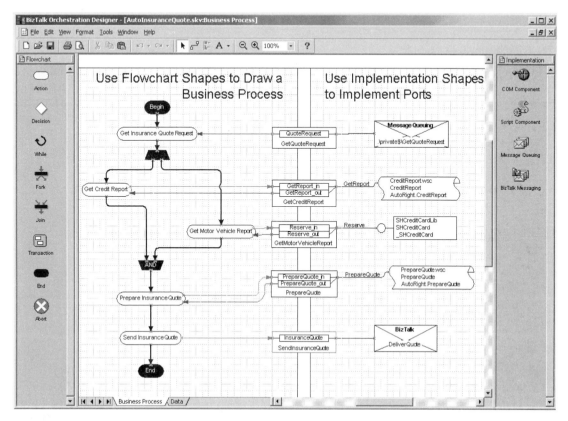

FIGURE 9-3   BizTalk Orchestration Wired to Implementation Ports.

Schedule Compilation

Once the business process is designed and bound to implementation, the schedule can be "compiled." The schedule compilation process is the translation of the actions, decisions, concurrency, and synchronization represented by the diagram into the XML representation XLANG. The schedule source is saved in a file with the extension *skv*, which is a Visio format file. The compilation process produces an SKX file, which is in XML format. The details of the format are beyond the scope of this book and are generally not necessary for developing effective schedules.

Schedule Instantiation and Execution

Now that a schedule is ready to execute, there are two ways to bring an instance to life and run it. The first way to instantiate an orchestration schedule is to call the Win32

API function `GetObject()`, passing it the name of the XLANG file to execute. The name is expressed in COM moniker format—`sked:`—a new type for orchestration schedules.

For example, the following call to `GetObject()` starts a schedule under the control of the business process execution engine:

```
' Code to start the XLANG schedule
Set oSked = GetObject
    ("sked://localhost/C:\SimpleHelix\Schedule\SpecialOrder.skx")
```

The second way to start a schedule instance is to configure a BizTalk Messaging port to start it (see Chapter 10).

BizTalk Messaging

BizTalk Messaging provides the infrastructure necessary to receive, transform, track, and deliver business documents. The framework makes extensive use of standards for document description, validation, transformation, encryption, and delivery, and provides a means of customization at key processing points. BizTalk Messaging can be used independently of BizTalk Orchestration.

Let's look at the overall architecture of BizTalk Messaging and then focus on the details. The architecture of BizTalk Server Messaging is built around the BizTalk Server Group, a group of one or more computers running the BizTalk Messaging Server, and SQL Server databases, which store the trading partner configuration information, the transformation rules, the delivery configuration, the queues of business documents, the administration data, and document tracking information. All of the servers in the BizTalk Server Group share the same set of databases and share the work of processing the documents.

Documents are submitted to BizTalk Messaging by means of the IInterchange interface. This can be called directly or by built-in receive functions. BizTalk determines a *channel* to execute based on the properties of the document and fires the channel. The channel controls the parsing, translation, and serialization of the document and routes the transformed document to a *port*. The port determines the transport used to deliver the document, destination, and security used on the document.

There are three SQL Server databases used to make BizTalk Messaging work: messaging management, tracking, and shared queue. The messaging management database contains all of the information describing the trading partners, documents, transformation rules, and integration and delivery machinery. The tracking database stores the information you select to record the history of messaging activity. The shared queue database is where the queues of documents are stored in the progress of their transformation and delivery.

Abstractions

BizTalk Messaging models the process of recognizing, processing, translating, and delivering documents using several abstractions.

Organizations

Organizations are simple names and identifiers used to denote the organizations involved in the exchange of documents.

Document Definitions

Document definitions provide a way to store and reference the properties of a business document. The definition includes the name, a reference to the document specification, and tracking settings. A *document specification* is an XML data-reduced (XDR) schema that describes the document. The reference is a Web Distributed Authoring and Versioning (WebDAV) reference. WebDAV allows you to represent folders and files with locking and version control using HTTP so that the schema can be anywhere on the Internet. The tracking settings let you control which fields are logged for this document type if logging is turned on in the channel.

Channels

A *channel* is an abstraction that provides a place to group settings used to decrypt, validate, translate, and route incoming documents to the proper destination. The channel's properties include name, comments, the source organization, the inbound and outbound document definition references, tracking settings, digital signature and decryption certificate verification settings, the map used to translate the document, logging settings, and delivery retry settings.

Ports

Messaging *ports* provide a structure to group the settings needed to control the transmission of the document to the destination organization or application. You set the port name and comments, the destination organization, transport configuration, and security configuration.

BizTalk Server 2000 suffers from unfortunate name overloading regarding the term *port*. Both BizTalk Orchestration and BizTalk Messaging use the term to refer to completely different things. The BizTalk Orchestration port is the binding of an orchestration action to an implementation. The BizTalk Messaging port, on the other hand, is an abstraction used to group and manage the settings for document delivery.

The security configuration for a port allows you to set the encoding, encryption, and digital signature to be used when the document is delivered.

Transports

The *transport* is the technology used to deliver the document. The transport configuration of a port allows you to specify a primary and secondary transport. For the primary transport, you can designate a service window. A service window is a span of time that the destination is expected to be available to receive messages.

A variety of transport types are provided out of the box. They include HTTP, HTTPS, Simple Mail Transfer Protocol (SMTP), Message Queuing, File, Loopback, and application integration component (AIC) (Table 9-2). Implementations for each of these except AIC are supplied out of the box. An AIC is used to provide a custom transport.

You might wonder why there is no File Transfer Protocol (FTP) support. It seems conspicuously absent from the list. We think this is because Microsoft originally planned to use WinInet's FTP support to supply this functionality, and there have been issues with WinInet on the server side. We expect that FTP will be supported in a future release. An easy alternative for the time being is to use a File transport type to write the document to your outbound FTP folder, from which your FTP software can deliver it.

TABLE 9-2   BizTalk Messaging Built-In Transport Types

Transport Type	Description
AIC	AIC delivers the document to the component for delivery. AICs are custom components you develop and register on the system.
HTTP	HTTP delivers the document using the built-in HTTP support. You supply the destination URL.
HTTPS	HTTPS delivers the document using the built-in HTTPS support. You supply the destination URL.
Loopback	Loopback is used with a synchronous Submit call to send the outbound document back to the sender.
Message Queuing	Message queuing delivers the document to the specified message queue. You supply the format name of the destination message queue.
File	The outbound document is written to the specified file. The path must exist. You can optionally include predefined variables in the file name that will be expanded to create unique file names. These include %datetime%, %document_name%, %server%, %uid%, and %tracking_id%.
SMTP	The SMTP transport type delivers the message using the SMTP protocol to the e-mail address you supply. You also supply a return address that is used as the From address in the outbound e-mail message.

Maps

A map is a set of rules for translating a document. The translation is done by mapping field-level information from the inbound document to the outbound document. XSLT is leveraged by BizTalk to accomplish the translation. The channel contains a map reference, which points to a map stored on a WebDAV server. Maps are created by using the document specification of the source and destination documents and the BizTalk Mapper tool.

Submitting Documents

There are three ways to submit a document to BizTalk Messaging: direct integration, a *file receive* function, and a *message queue receive* function. Direct integration is a COM call. The receive functions supply an active polling environment that watches a folder or queue for incoming items. These facilitate integration with file- and queue-based systems.

Direct Integration

To use direct integration, you create an instance of the IInterchange COM interface and call its Submit method. The arguments to the method allow you to control the routing behavior and whether the channel selection logic is executed.

File Receive Function

A *file receive function* is a feature of BizTalk Messaging that watches a folder for the appearance of files satisfying specified filter criteria. The file receive function reads any such files that appear in the folder and submits them to BizTalk Messaging. You create a new file receive function from the BizTalk Server Administration console (Figure 9-4) or programmatically using the object model.

The Add a File Receive Function dialog appears (Figure 9-5). You set the filter for the files the receive function will select and indicate the folder it should check. If you have installed any custom preprocessors, they will appear here in the Preprocessor drop-down list for your selection.

Message Queue Receive Function

A *message queue receive function* is a feature of BizTalk Messaging that watches a message queue for the appearance of a message. The message queue receive function reads any message that appears in the queue and submits it to BizTalk Messaging.

You create a new message queue receive function similarly to how you create the file receive function, from the BizTalk Server Administration console, or programmatically using the object model. No filter criteria can be applied to the messages in the queue. Any message that is written to the queue will be read and submitted. You can use a custom preprocessor if any are installed on your system.

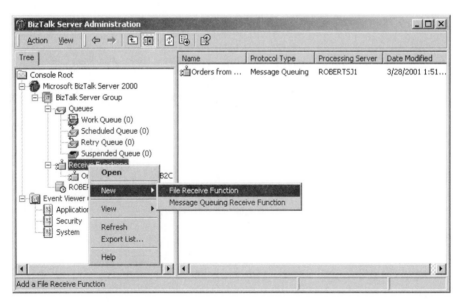

FIGURE 9-4   Creating a New File Receive Function.

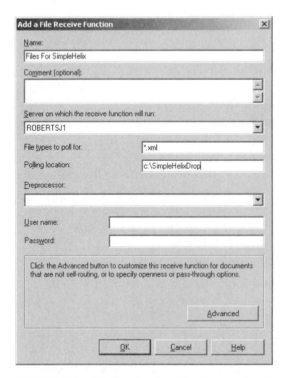

FIGURE 9-5   Configuring the File Receive Function.

Channel Firing

When a document is submitted to BizTalk Messaging, it goes through what we like to call *channel firing*. Based on the routing information in the document, the parameters to the Submit call, or the configuration of the receive function, BizTalk Messaging selects one or more channels to fire. For each channel it executes, it parses the inbound document, maps it to an outbound document format if needed, serializes it to its final form, and executes the port attached to the channel.

Translation

BizTalk Messaging translation provides a great example of leveraging the XML standards to provide a generic document translation framework. Translation, one of the basic principles of people-oriented software, is fundamental to modern interoperability.

The XML technology suite defines a standard way to translate from XML format into any text-based format, called *XSLT* (XSL transformation). Because XML is a text-based format, the XSLT can be used to translate documents from one XML format to another. Once documents are in a form of XML, maps can be created by XML manipulation tools to effect the transformation. The map is expressed in standard XSLT, so a standard XSLT processor can run it.

The translation problem is reduced and factored into two smaller problems: first, how to translate a source document into XML so that it can be run through the XSL transformation to produce a destination XML form, and second, how to translate the destination XML format into the final desired document format. BizTalk Server addresses the translation problem by splitting it into these three steps:

- **Parse:** Convert an incoming document into a XML version of itself.
- **Map:** Translate the document into an XML version of its destination document.
- **Serialize:** Convert an outbound document into the native version of itself.

Each of these steps is in a form that can be addressed by standard tools.

Instead of having to write custom code to do translation, you develop a description of the data and reuse the XML and XSL processing engines. These descriptions are called *document specifications*. BizTalk Server provides a tool to create document specifications—BizTalk Editor—and a tool to create translation maps—BizTalk Mapper. The editor and the mapper together are a dream tool for the people-oriented software linguist People-Type. BizTalk Messaging supplies standard parsers and serializers, but it allows you to supply your own in its extensibility model.

Extensibility Framework: BizTalk Hooks

Developers of any serious integration product know that it is impossible to envision all the functions for which the tool will be used and how the features of the tools will trans-

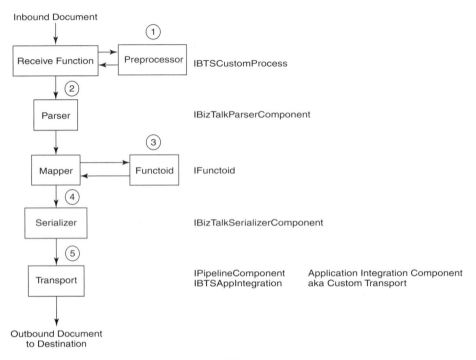

FIGURE 9-6   BizTalk Messaging Extensibility Framework.

late into real solutions. The usefulness of an environment can be greatly enhanced by careful selection of key processing points at which to provide the ability to inject custom code. The designers of BizTalk Server have done a good job of providing such facilities in the product. There are ways to hook in custom code at all of the major processing points along the path traveled by a document in BizTalk Messaging.

To understand these points, it helps to see them in the context of an overall flow of documents through BizTalk Messaging (Figure 9-6). The *receive function* notices that a document has arrived and submits it to BizTalk Messaging. BizTalk Messaging submits it to the installed parsers in the configuration order determined by the BizTalk Server Group settings.

The parser that recognizes the document does two things: (1) it translates the document into XML and (2) gathers the document fields that the server uses to select the channel or channels to fire. These include the inbound document's source and destination information and document type. The channel determines the mapping to be done based on its map settings. If a map is used, the server applies it using the XSL engine. Any functoids, which are part of the map, execute at this time. The document is now in the XML form of the destination document. The serializer converts it into the final form. The channel specifies a messaging port to use. The port specifies a transport, and the server gives the final document to the transport for delivery.

Custom Preprocessor

The first hook point is at the *receive function*. Using a receive function adds the flexibility to use a custom preprocessor. A custom preprocessor is a COM component you implement to modify the document on the way into BizTalk Messaging. It is connected to the receive function declaratively using the BizTalk Server Administration console. BizTalk passes the received document from the file folder or message queue to your custom preprocessor for transformation before submitting it to BizTalk Messaging. `IBTSCustomProcess` and `IBTSCustomProcessContext` are the interfaces to implement. In addition, `IBTSCustomProcess` implements two methods—`Execute` and `SetContext`.

BizTalk calls `Execute`, passing the document and other arguments to allow your custom preprocessor to discern the code page representation and determine whether the document is from a file or a message queue. `Execute` transforms the document and returns it in an output argument.

`SetContext` is called and passed an `IBTSCustomProcessContext` interface that in turn can be used to get the context information of the document's submission. This includes the channel, source, destination, document name, and associated information such as the arguments `to IInterchange::Submit`.

The custom preprocessor component must support the COM category ID `CATID_BIZTALK_CUSTOM_PROCESS`. You can find the definition of the category IDs in the file `bts_sdk_guids.h`. Supporting the category ID enables the tools to enumerate available custom preprocessors and make them available to the dialogs. The interfaces are dispatch based, so you can implement them using Visual Basic or Visual C++.

Custom Parser

After being submitted, the document is given to the parser. The parser's job is to convert the incoming document into XML and gather the document fields that are used to select the channel or channels to fire. Once the document is in XML, subsequent transformation is simplified. If the standard out-of-the-box parsers do not do the job for you, you can write your own custom parser. Your custom parser needs to implement the `IBizTalkParserComponent` interface and register under COM category ID `CATID_BIZTALK_PARSER`. The interface must be implemented using C++ because some arguments on the interface do not work with automation.

Custom Functoid

With the large variety of presupplied functoids, and especially with the provision of a scripting functoid in which you write script to do the mapping, you may never need to write your own functoid. Regardless, if you do, you can. Implement `IFunctoid` and support the category ID `CATID_MapEditFunctoids`. By supporting the category ID the mapper tool is able to find the functoids and present them for use in the functoid palette. This interface is fully automation compliant, so you can write the code using Visual Basic or Visual C++.

Custom Serializer

After being translated, the document is given to the serializer. The serializer's job is to convert the translated document into the final format. If the standard out-of-the-box serializers are insufficient, you can write your own custom serializer. Your custom serializer needs to implement the `IBizTalkSerializerComponent` interface and register under the COM category ID `CATID_BIZTALK_SERIALIZER`. The interface must be implemented using C++ for the same reason as a custom parser.

Custom Transport

Custom transports are a bit more interesting, and it is likely that if you implement any custom components, a custom transport will be among them. The official name of these components is application integration component (AIC). AIC is a good name because an AIC is the outbound connection of BizTalk Messaging to the outside world.

AICs enable custom postprocessing of documents flowing through BizTalk Messaging. Examples of custom transports could be legacy integration, a custom encryption or digital signature component, or a place to house existing proprietary translation code.

AICs need to support two COM category IDs to allow them to appear in the wizard dialogs and in the BizTalk Server Administration console. These are `CATID_BIZTALK_AIC` and `CATID_BIZTALK_COMPONENT`.

There are two possible interfaces—`IBTSAppIntegration` and `IPipelineComponent`—to choose from when writing an AIC. `IBTSAppIntegration` is the simpler of the two. You implement its single method, `ProcessMessage`, support the category IDs, and you are done. The server calls `ProcessMessage` to give your transport the document. There are two arguments to `ProcessMessage`—the input document and an output argument to allow you to return a value to the caller. Because BizTalk is primarily designed to operate asynchronously, you might be wondering why there is such an argument, because there is no one waiting on a synchronous call for an answer. It turns out that it is possible to submit a document to BizTalk Messaging synchronously. `IInterchange` supports a `SubmitSync` method as well as the `Submit` method we discussed. The value returned from `ProcessMessage` is returned to the caller of `SubmitSync`.

You can also allow setting of configuration information by supporting `IPipelineComponentAdmin`, which has two methods—`GetConfigData` and `Set ConfigData`. The argument to these methods is a dictionary object to allow the component to provide its properties and allow the client to set them. `GetConfigData` is called when the user activates the property page; `SetConfigData` is called when the data is saved. At runtime, the server calls `SetConfigData` to give you the most up-to-date configuration information; then it calls the `Execute` method on the `IPipelineComponent` interface.

The `Execute` method is where you write the code to handle document delivery. The first argument is the dictionary, and this is where you get the information needed to process the document. If you need to return a value to a synchronous caller, you can do so by setting a name-value pair in the dictionary.

Therefore the choice is a tradeoff between the features you need and the work that you are willing to do. If you can take the straightforward approach, use `IBTSAppIntegration`. If you need property-page configuration, use `IPipeline-Component` and `IPipelineComponentAdmin`.

You should register your transport to run as an out-of-process COM+ application. If you run inproc and fault, you can crash the BizTalk Messaging Server.

If your AIC is selected in a messaging port, at runtime the server creates an instance of the AIC and calls `QueryInterface` to see which of the interfaces it supports. It tries for `IBTSAppIntegration` first.

`IBTSAppIntegration` and `IPipelineComponent` can be implemented using Visual Basic or Visual C++.

BizTalk Development Tools

BizTalk Editor

The BizTalk Editor (Figure 9-7) is a reasonably well-featured tool used to create document specifications for the business documents you process with BizTalk Messaging. It can start from scratch, or it can import and create a schema from three sources: an XDR schema, a DTD (document type definition), or a well-formed XML instance. Document specifications can be saved to file or to WebDAV. The tool includes the ability to test your specification, create an XML instance based on your specification, and validate an XML instance against the specification.

BizTalk Mapper

The BizTalk Mapper tool (Figure 9-8) allows you to graphically construct the transformation rules used to translate documents. It operates on document specifications created by the BizTalk Editor. You connect fields in the source specification to fields

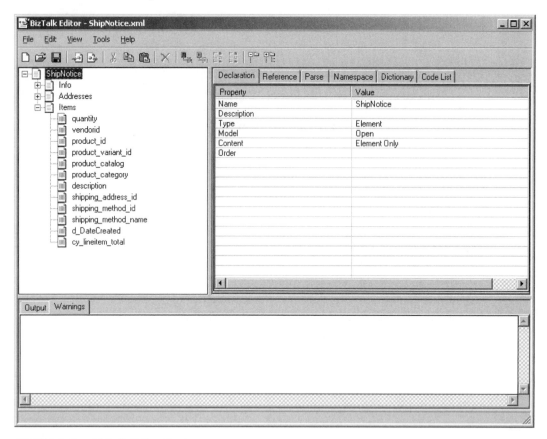

FIGURE 9-7   BizTalk Editor Tool.

in the destination specification. The mapper includes curiously named features called *functoids*. Functoids are blocks of processing that can be wired up to fields to house and apply transformation rules. The tool comes with a large arsenal of functoids that handle a surprising array of operations, including basic string operations, mathematical and logical operations, date/time operations, conversion and scientific calculations, and summation logic. There are even database access functoids that allow you to query databases and return information that is used to create the destination document fields. Advanced functoids allow you to control the iteration processing and include a scripting functoid you can use with your script to write special transformation logic. Because scripts can create and call COM components, the possibilities are far reaching. You can also write your own functoids and add them to the environment.

The tool compiles the map into XSL. The messaging channel uses the XSL to translate the document. The tool provides test facilities to try out your map by generating sample instances and executing the transform.

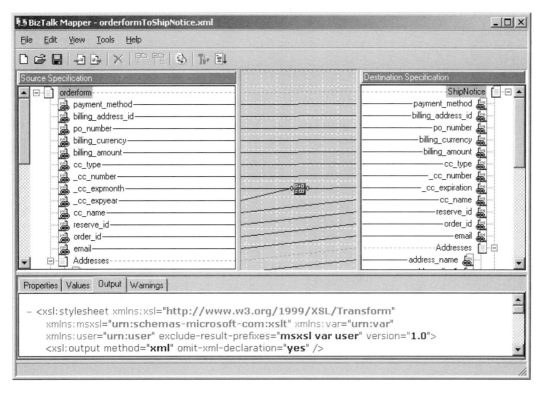

FIGURE 9-8   BizTalk Mapper Tool.

BizTalk Orchestration Designer

The BizTalk Orchestration Designer provides the framework for defining business processes and binding them to implementation code. (See the previous section, BizTalk Orchestration, for details.)

BizTalk Administration Tools

BizTalk Server Administration

The BizTalk Server Administration tool (Figure 9-9) is used to control the operation of the BizTalk Server Group. The tool shows the database queues used by BizTalk Messaging, the installed receive functions, and the messaging servers in the group. This is the tool you use to create and configure receive functions, monitor the work queues, and configure the work item processing of each messaging server.

These features are implemented using a Microsoft Management Console (MMC) framework with a snap-in for BizTalk. The console includes the Event Viewer for convenience.

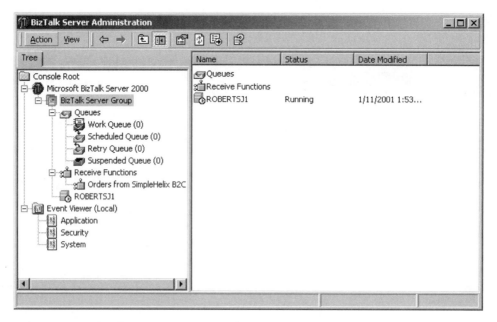

FIGURE 9-9   BizTalk Messaging Server Administration Tool.

BizTalk Messaging Manager

The BizTalk Messaging Manager (Figure 9-10) essentially serves as a front end to the databases that manage the messaging objects: organizations, document specifications, channels, messaging ports, envelopes, and distribution lists.

You can create new objects, search for and edit existing objects, and delete objects. Editing options walk you through wizards to set the properties. The tool ensures the data integrity of the objects. You should always use the supplied tools and the object model to manipulate the databases that house the messaging objects instead of directly manipulating the underlying SQL Server databases.

BizTalk Document Tracking

BizTalk uses a Web application to implement tracking. You can use it to construct queries and retrieve and view the status of messages moving through BizTalk Messaging.

BizTalk Messaging Object Model

BizTalk Messaging provides an easy-to-use object model to allow programmatic setup and configuration of the objects we have been discussing. You use the BizTalk-Config object to interact with BizTalk Messaging objects.

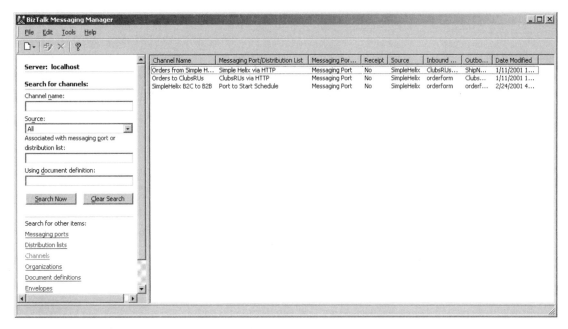

FIGURE 9-10   BizTalk Server Messaging Manager Tool.

To create an object, create an instance of the BizTalkConfig object and use it to create the object type you want. Then populate the object's properties, and call the object's `Create` method to write to the tables in the underlying database.

To modify an object, create an instance of the BizTalkConfig object and use it to create an instance of the object type you want to change. Then populate the object from the database records by calling the `Load` or `LoadByName` method. After you have populated the object, call its `Save` method to update the underlying database records.

Deleting an object is similar to modifying it. After populating the object with a `Load` or `LoadByName` call, call its `Remove` method to delete the underlying database records.

The properties of the BizTalkConfig object allow you to enumerate the current objects in the underlying administration database. These are returned as ActiveX data object (ADO) record sets and include organization, messaging ports, channels, documents, envelopes, port groups, and certificates.

Creating a BizTalkConfig Object

The following code creates a BizTalkConfig object and uses it to initialize objects for creating a channel, a messaging port, a document definition, and an organization. It could not be more straightforward.

```
' Create BTM objects
Set BTM = CreateObject("BizTalk.BizTalkConfig")
Set Channel = BTM.CreateChannel
Set Port = BTM.CreatePort
Set Document = BTM.CreateDocument
Set Organization = BTM.CreateOrganization
```

The creation of the actual underlying BizTalk Messaging objects is a matter of setting properties on the object and calling its `Create` method.

Creating an Organization

Organizations are created similarly. The following code listing shows an example. Notice that a reference to the organization is obtained by a call to `GetDefaultAlias`. This is used to set the properties on the channel and port that refer to the organizations involved.

```
' Create the Simple Helix organization
Organization.Clear
Organization.Name = "SimpleHelix"
SimpleHelixOrganizationHandle = Organization.Create
SimpleHelixOrganizationAliasHandle = Organization.GetDefaultAlias
```

Creating a Document

Following is an example of creating a document. The handle returned from the `Create` call is used later to set the document properties for the channel that uses this document. The document reference is a WebDAV reference.

```
' Create the orderform document definition
Document.Clear
Document.Name = "orderform"
Document.Reference ="http://robertsj1/BizTalkServerRepository/DocSpecs/
    SimpleHelix/orderform.xml"OrderFormDocumentHandle = Document.Create
```

Creating a Port

The following example sets up a messaging port using organization references which were obtained either from previous calls to create an organization or from enumerating the installed organizations:

```
' Create the port to ClubsRUs
Port.Clear
Port.Name = "ClubsRUs via HTTP"
Port.DestinationEndPoint.Organization = ClubsRUsOrganizationHandle
Port.DestinationEndPoint.Alias = ClubsRUsOrganizationAliasHandle
Port.PrimaryTransport.Type = BIZTALK_TRANSPORT_TYPE_HTTP
Port.PrimaryTransport.Address = "http://robertsj1/clubsrus/orderclubs.asp"
PortToClubsRUsPortHandle = Port.Create
```

Creating a Channel

Channel setup depends on the setup of the underlying objects, the channel references, the input and output documents, the port, and the end-point organization and alias.

```
' Create the Orders to ClubsRUs Channel
Channel.Clear
Channel.Name = "Orders to ClubsRUs"
Channel.InputDocument = OrderFormDocumentHandle
Channel.OutputDocument = ClubsRUsPODocumentHandle
Channel.MapReference = http://robertsj1/BizTalkServerRepository/
        Maps/SimpleHelix/orderformToClubsRUsPO.xml
Channel.Port = PortToClubsRUsPortHandle
Channel.SourceEndPoint.Organization = SimpleHelixOrganizationHandle
Channel.SourceEndPoint.Alias = SimpleHelixOrganizationAliasHandle
Channel.LoggingInfo.LogNativeInputDocument = 0
Channel.LoggingInfo.LogNativeOutputDocument = 0
Channel.LoggingInfo.LogXMLInputDocument = 0
Channel.LoggingInfo.LogXMLOutputDocument = 0
OrdersToClubsRUsChannelHandle = Channel.Create
```

Deleting an Object

The following code deletes a port:

```
Set BTM = CreateObject("BizTalk.BizTalkConfig")
Set objPort = BTM.CreatePort
' First load the object
objPort.LoadByName "Port "ClubsRUs via HTTP"
If Err.Number = 0 Then
        objPort.Remove
End If
```

Issues Addressed

Now that you have read a detailed overview of the features of BizTalk, we consider the issues we have addressed in a more general way.

Interoperability

General ease of integration is accomplished when a tool set and an execution framework are provided to connect disparate systems and components using standards while providing for custom code integration at key junctures in the framework's operation. BizTalk Server provides a sophisticated framework and tool set specifically targeted toward this problem. BizTalk Server Orchestration provides a generalized way to connect software components into a managed process execution. BizTalk Messaging provides an interconnection, translation, and secure delivery framework that makes general integration much easier.

Transport Protocols

BizTalk Messaging provides for standard transport protocol support out of the box. The messaging port can be connected declaratively to HTTP, HTTPS, MSMQ, or SMTP transport code.

Business Document Definitions (Schemas)

The BizTalk Editor supplies support for creating and testing XDR schemas from a variety of inputs. Schemas can be produced from a well-formed instance, DTD, or XDR schema. The document definitions are accessed at runtime from WebDAV, allowing flexible integration.

Business Document Validation

Business documents can be validated against schemas in two places in the BizTalk Server architecture: BizTalk Messaging and BizTalk Orchestration.

BizTalk Messaging validates incoming documents against the schema referenced in the document specification in the channel. If the validation fails, the error is logged into the event log, and the document moves to the suspended queue for reference.

BizTalk Orchestration optionally validates documents read from an MSMQ integration. You specify the message specification (which is the same as a document specification) in the XML Communication Wizard accessed from the orchestration port on the business process diagram.

Business Process Definition

BizTalk Orchestration provides a sophisticated environment for business process definition, with support for modeling actions, concurrency, synchronization, transaction behaviors, and logical branching and repetition constructs. In addition, the tools allow you to wire up the business process steps to a real implementation.

Business Document Translation

The combination of the design time tools, the BizTalk Editor, the BizTalk Mapper, and the runtime leveraging of XML and XSL provides a powerful standards-based document translation solution.

Integration with Legacy Systems, Internal Applications, and Cross Enterprise Applications

The integration capabilities of BizTalk Server are impressive. BizTalk Orchestration allows most any action that is exposed using COM to participate in the execution of a controlled business process. This includes BizTalk Messaging, MSMQ, any Windows scripting component, any COM transaction integrator (CTI) component to integrate with mainframes, any Web service callable from a COM wrapper, as well as any custom code packaged in COM components.

With its channel architecture, BizTalk Messaging directly models the basic distinction between EAI and interenterprise integration. Channel destinations can be to both organizations and applications.

BizTalk Messaging can pull in documents from the file system, message queuing, and direct COM call integration. It can send documents to file folders, message queues, Web servers, or custom integration components.

It is hard to imagine a more flexible situation.

Standards Support

BizTalk Server has rich support for standards. It is based on XML, XSL, and XDR schemas, and leverages HTTP, HTTPS, SMTP, and MSMQ. It can import DTDs, and supports encryption and digital signature standards.

Encryption and Secure Communications over the Internet

The need for encryption and secure communications is clear when we think of integrating the systems that run our businesses with other partner systems over the public Internet. Numerous types of proprietary information need to be transmitted over a communications system that is designed to have a greater degree of trust than that of a highly competitive business environment.

Although we use XML to improve the interoperability environment, we also open security issues. This was the concern of an engineering vice president of a company that is currently building a core enterprise system deeply integrated with Web technologies. This executive's reaction to the growing acceptance of XML was that because it is a text-based format instead of a binary one, it is extremely vulnerable to security problems and the exposure of proprietary information.

Any solution framework that seeks to be an enterprise-grade solution needs to provide an encryption and secure communications framework in a standards-based fashion that can be reasonably managed (Figure 9-11). BizTalk supports secure communications and encryption in its messaging infrastructure. BizTalk Messaging ports are abstractions used to group a set of properties that define how a document is delivered and where it travels. The messaging port is where the transport to be used is defined. The transport can be HTTPS, providing secure delivery over the Internet. Support for HTTPS is provided out of the box and is selected declaratively in the Messaging Port Wizard accessed from the BizTalk Messaging Manager.

Integration with proprietary secure transmission protocol implementations is possible because BizTalk provides a place to plug in your own transport component—an AIC. The Messaging Port Wizard also allows you to configure to digitally sign documents using installed certificates and encrypt them using public key encryption technology.

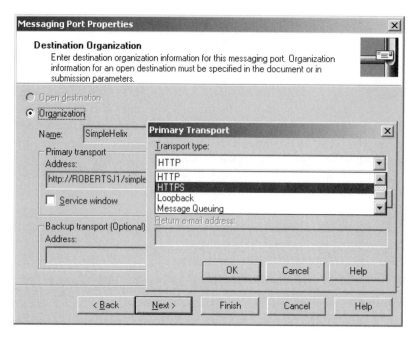

FIGURE 9-11   Selecting Secure Transport.

Management of the Execution of Business Processes

BizTalk provides the means to execute the business processes created by the Orchestration Designer tool in the form of the XLANG scheduler engine. The orchestration is modeled in XLANG, an XML representation of the business process interaction, and is called a *schedule.* The environment includes an engine to run the schedule, called the XLANG *scheduler engine,* and has hooks into COM to allow programmatic instantiation of schedules. BizTalk Messaging can also instantiate orchestration schedules using its application integration model.

Long-Lived Transactions

The relatively short-lived database transactions with which we are familiar are inadequate for solving the problem of large volumes of transactions that may need to live for days or longer. These transactions can involve multiple applications and organizations, can require considerable time to complete processing, and may depend on trading partners whose systems operate on limited availability schedules. The typical two-phase commit model just does not work. We cannot simply lock records and database resources for thousands of clients for days at a time.

BizTalk Server addresses this issue by its orchestration execution model. The

XLANG scheduler engine runs the schedule and can activate and deactivate it as necessary while it waits for the completion of external processing operations.

The process of deactivation and reactivation is called *dehydration and rehydration* in BizTalk lingo. In *dehydration,* the schedule instance state is persisted to an SQL Server database used by BizTalk. When a schedule is not performing any concurrent action and is simply waiting on a message and is not in a DTC transaction, it is a candidate for dehydration. *Rehydration* is the term Microsoft uses to describe the process of restoring the schedule instance to memory by reading the serialized version from the database and resuming the orchestration schedule. This scheme requires that all components implementing the interaction can be persisted. Because of the flexibility inherent in an environment in which any component can be made a part of a schedule, this is not true for all schedules.

Tracking of Business Transaction Status

BizTalk Messaging can track documents through the system and record the document contents at a selective field level. The status of documents can be queried through the Web-based administration tools.

Prepackaged Capabilities to Minimize Custom Development

The sophisticated set of capabilities and tools provided by BizTalk Server that has been presented is comprehensive, but perhaps the best example of the size of the prepackaged capability is the e-commerce example described Chapter 10. The business-to-business portion of the example uses BizTalk Server to implement order fulfillment with an outside vendor and is accomplished by a relatively small amount of scripting component development. The complicated features of long-lived process execution and management, document validation, document translation, document delivery, error reporting, retry after failure, and software integration were all done without writing code.

Extensible Design

The extensibility model in BizTalk Server is well designed, providing an opportunity to inject custom code at each key step in the process, from preprocessing through parsing, translation, serialization, transport, and correlation.

Architecture Issues with Current Implementation

There are a few architectural issues with BizTalk Server that should be noted.

Load Balancing
The BizTalk Messaging Server Group provides an environment in which work items are shared by any server in the group. Each of the BizTalk Messaging servers has mul-

tiple threads that are polling for work based on the settings for the server. You can control the frequency with which the scheduler gets work and the number of worker threads per processor on the property page for the server in the BizTalk Server Administration tool. However, there is no active load balancing in operation. As an example, let's say there are 15 work items in the shared queue database. There is no mechanism to prevent one of the servers from taking 13 of the available 15 items and another server taking the other 2.

Server Affinity

The current BizTalk Orchestration implementation handles the correlation of messages in such a way that the same orchestration server that sent the message needs to receive the response to allow the schedule instance to operate properly.

COMMERCE SERVER ESSENTIALS

A common pattern of any industry's development is a movement from custom work to common parts, to standardization of subassemblies, to standardization of construction techniques. The software industry is no different; it is just in the early stages of this process cycle compared with, for example, the power industry, architecture, building construction, or the auto industry. First is custom development, followed closely by software parts to provide reusability at some level of abstraction. Initially the commonality is in the form of lower-level functions, which gradually appear as aggregates comprising greater and greater functionality.

In time, what was a custom application is factored into components, which can then be assembled into a tool set for building applications. Some components become features in a base framework, runtime, or operating system. Examples include low-level runtime classes and libraries, as well as larger packages such as component services, load balancing services, transaction services, and Web servers. Others are put together into products that package common functionality to be used to build custom applications as a natural outgrowth of this process.

Commerce Server provides such a framework to accelerate the development of Web-based business-to-consumer applications. It is a prebuilt platform for building business-to-consumer Internet sites. It is a good example of people-oriented software's universal runtime concept.

Commerce Server Architecture

Commerce Server is built on a three-tier architecture (Figure 9-12). At the bottom level is the data layer, containing the schemas. The data used by the higher-level components is stored here and includes profiles, catalogs, ads, promotions, and the data warehouse.

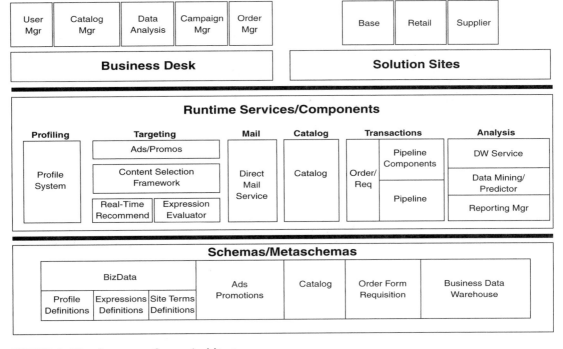

FIGURE 9-12 Commerce Server Architecture.

The next level contains the runtime components. These components provide the core commerce services and are where the action is on a running Web site. The services are grouped into features for profiling, targeting, mail, catalog operations, transactions, and analysis.

The top layer contains two main categories of tools: the business desk and the solution sites. The business desk provides the user interface to allow a business analyst to manage the commerce site. The business desk is designed for a businessperson's use, not a developer's. The business desk is Web based and is a framework for housing business management modules; it includes more than 20 such modules to support typical business operations. Developers can extend the business desk by using the SDK for module development. Objects are provided for validation, security, and navigation.

The solution sites seek to decrease time to market for e-commerce site development by providing tested, scalable, sites that embody real-world examples of how to use the Commerce Server objects in a coordinated fashion to quickly bring a site online. The intention is to allow you to add graphics and then deploy. There are three solution sites in the product: a retail commerce site, a supplier site, and a base site that includes all the basic plumbing so that you can start your site with all of the commerce features available.

Continuous Improvement Cycle

The parts of Commerce Server are designed to support the ongoing improvement of your e-commerce site by means of a continuous cycle of site management. The cycle starts with collection of data concerning how customers use your site. As the customers browse your site, search the catalogs, and place orders, the site collects usage data. This data is called a *click history* and allows you to find out things such as the path the customers took through your site, which URL referred the user, which ads the users saw, and which catalog items they viewed. When a customer makes a purchase, the transaction history is captured. All of this information, which is stored in log files and the Commerce Server databases, can be imported into the data warehouse.

To analyze the information in the data warehouse, a set of predefined reports is available in the Business Desk. About 40 reports are supplied and cover a broad range of areas such as ad placement effectiveness, reach and frequency, sales reports, Web usage, browser and operating system types, distinct user statistics, general site activity, and troubleshooting.

Based on your analysis of the site usage, you revise the site to improve it. The targeting and personalization systems can be used to define content based on profile properties or to extrapolate where you lack sufficient information for explicit targeting. The changed site is monitored and the data captured for analysis, completing the cycle.

Business Processing Pipelines

Business processing pipelines allow you to model a business process in a series of steps. These steps are executed in order when the pipeline is executed. A pipeline consists of stages, which consist of components implemented as transacted COM+ objects. The stages operate on a data object being passed through the pipeline, reading or writing to the object. Examples of uses of pipelines include content selection, order processing, and event processing.

The Pipeline Editor is a developer tool for graphically creating pipelines (Figure 9-13). It makes pipeline configuration (PCF) files that contain data representing what the object does.

Six Commerce Server objects can run pipelines: `MtsPipeline`, `MtsTxPipeline`, `PooledPipeline`, `PooledTxPipeline`, `OrderGroup`, and `OrderPipeline`. To execute a pipeline, you instantiate the object you are using to execute the pipeline and feed it the PCF file using the `LoadPipe` method. This way, you can execute pipelines from ASP pages. The pipelines use COM+ object pooling to enhance performance.

Profile System

Commerce Server's profile system lets you store information about entities you want to track. This sounds a bit generic because the profile capability is quite generic. The

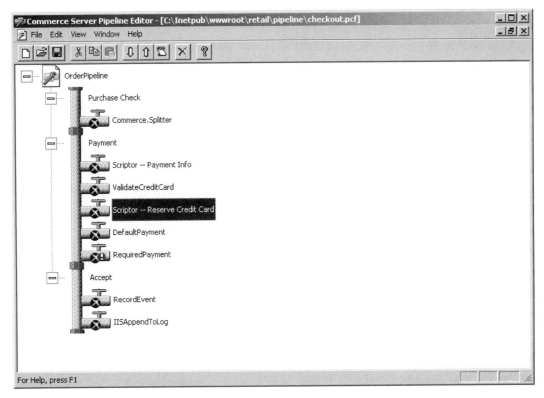

FIGURE 9-13   Commerce Server Pipeline Editor.

core idea is that when operating a commerce site, you collect information about the use of the site in a way that allows it to be analyzed and used to improve the site. The improvement might be minor changes you make to the site's appearance or dynamic changes to the content based on the measured behavior of users. This type of activity is most easily understood in terms of user profiles, which are used to store information about what particular users do on the site. Commerce Server generalizes the concept of *profile* to include any entity of interest.

From an architectural point of view, code that tracks usage has been written to operate on generic profiles. This abstracts the collection code from the storage technology. The second need for abstraction involves which data is collected and how these properties map to the underlying fields in the store. Commerce Server provides facilities to define profiles, control the information collected in a profile, and map this information onto the fields of the data store. The data store can be the active directory, an SQL Server database, or any OLE DB data store.

Because the collected information is stored in profiles with known definitions, the business analysis subsystem can operate on this level also.

Commerce Server comes with profile definitions for users, addresses, purchase orders, organizations, and target contexts.

Targeting System

The combined profiling and targeting system forms the heart of the product's ability to enable you to personalize the site and target users and sets of users. The key idea is to be able to identify a business-based condition and having identified it, to tailor the content delivered to the client based on the condition.

To support this, the targeting system includes the content selection framework, which uses pipelines to determine the content to deliver. The content selection framework allows the selection algorithm to be customized. The targeting system also includes add-in modules to the Business Desk to manage the delivery of advertisements and promotions, using the facilities of the catalog system and the profiling system.

At design time, using the Business Desk, you create expressions to identify conditions using the expression builder user interface. The expressions are in terms of properties of profiles you want to target. Because the profiling system is not limited to users, you can target based on other objects, such as companies or anonymous users. These expressions are saved in an SQL Server database for use by the expression evaluator. This component can be used in your ASP and is used by the content selection framework.

You can specify ranges such as the qualifying products for discounts or varying discounts based on user category, and control the amount of product on which customers can get a discount. Discounts can be expressed as a percentage off or a certain amount of money off.

Sometimes there may not enough property information available to target content. In this case, the Predictor subsystem can fill in the information gaps in the profile using information mined from the data warehouse.

The targeting system also includes a direct mail service to manage an e-mail campaign and send e-mail advertisements to a targeted group of users.

Product Catalog System

Commerce Server includes a set of components that implement a full-featured catalog system. The Business Desk provides a management interface into these features. Product catalogs can be exported and imported in XML or comma-delimited value format. User-defined product types are supported. Full-text and property-based searches are supported, and searches can be carried out in multiple catalogs. The catalog system is fully integrated with the other components of Commerce Server. Catalog information is integrated with the data warehouse via SQL Server's Data Transfer Service (DTS).

The Catalog Designer tool allows the management of the catalog schema and its product categories and properties. The catalog schema is sophisticated and capable of representing multiple levels of product categories and product variants. The Catalog Editor tool lets you create and manage the catalogs themselves and allows you to import and export catalogs. As many as one million products can be accommodated in the catalog system. Pricing can be done by product category—products get their prices according to their category.

Business Analytics System

Commerce Server includes an extensive data warehousing and business analytics subsystem that completes the data capture and analysis circle. The two main parts of this part of the product are the data warehouse and the business analytics.

The business analytics arena is more comprehensive than just Web usage, hits, and click streams. The broad problem now is the need to consider all facets of your business and include all of that data in the scope of analysis tools to provide a 360-degree view of your business. Commerce Server makes progress in this area in large part by leveraging SQL Server features; it provides a way to understand users, sales, and marketing, as well as a scalable mechanism to import the information into the data warehouse.

Once data is in the warehouse, you must be able to correlate different data—such as user activity and product sales. This information can be used to, for example, send targeted mail to new users about the last week of a product discount and show them targeted ads the next time they visit based on the content selection framework.

The data warehouse component tracks every transaction on the system. Every click, addition, and browsing of an item in a catalog is captured and recorded in the data warehouse. The data warehouse leverages SQL Server DTS and the SQL Server scheduler to get import data for analysis. There are custom actions in the DTS tailored to import data from Commerce Server, which knows the warehouse schemas and the Commerce Server schemas. In addition to the Web log import process, there are three more processes to import information from the product catalog, the user profile, and the transaction activity.

For example, the Web logs are a data source for the warehouse. The Web log import process knows how to import Web logs, the schema of the source, how to transform the source and load it into the data warehouse, and the warehouse schemas used. The logs are parsed and processed through an inference engine to produce summaries of activity that are stored in the warehouse for analysis. The log, which is in W3C Extended Web Log file format, is analyzed to sequence the hits and make inferences about the user, establish what a page request is, and infer a user session. There is nothing in the Web logs that establishes what a page request or a user is, so this inference capability is vital.

The data warehouse is the basis for building the models of the prediction sub-system. In this way, the models are not generic but are based on your business. This characteristic allows the predictive models to change as your site changes.

The programmatic interface to the data warehouse is open. An OLE DB ADO interface is provided. The business analytics allow a business manager to gain insight into how the Web site is performing by providing reports to mine the data warehouse. This information can be used to fine tune the targeting system to make the site more effective. The standard reports that are supplied out of the box are focused on e-commerce and go beyond Web behavior to correlate behaviors from a business point of view. For example, instead of just analyzing click streams, you can correlate Web browsing and purchasing behavior. The analytics system gains performance and scalability by leveraging SQL Server's capabilities. The reports leverage office Web controls, particularly the Pivot Table and the Pivot Chart controls.

The analysis infrastructure is built on report objects. These objects consist of ASP code and COM components that can render an ASP page with the Pivot Table and Pivot Chart controls. The definitions for the reports are stored in the data warehouse, and the schema for the definitions is open and customizable.

There are two categories of reports: dynamic and static. Dynamic reports are designed to provide a live report that can be manipulated for further analysis. They use the Pivot Table and Pivot Chart controls to render multidimensional data structures in the online analytical processing (OLAP) services. Static reports are rendered in HTML and are typically used for large reports—larger than ones you might want to analyze dynamically on screen and would prefer to print instead.

Solution Sites

Commerce Server includes *solution sites.* Solution sites focus on reducing time to market for e-commerce Web site development. The basic idea of the solution sites is to provide a data-driven site to which you add graphics and your product catalog and rapidly bring up a business-to-consumer site. Naturally the reality is not quite as instant as Microsoft might suggest, but a large part of the framework and operations are in fact in place and ready to customize. Three solution sites ship with the product—Blank, Retail and Supplier. Blank is essentially a core template that includes all of the Commerce Server resources and jump-starts your development of a custom site. For example, global.asa creates Commerce Server objects and initializes them for use by the site pages by extracting them from the Application object.

Retail is a retail e-commerce site and includes catalog browsing, shopping basket management, transactions, profiling, and data warehousing. Consumers can edit their profiles, place orders, and view order status and history. Order progress updates are included.

Microsoft claims it has designed and tested the solution sites for production viability in stress and scalability. They embody coding best practices in the use of the Commerce Server capabilities.

The solution sites are shipped as packages. Packages place the entire site in a file for easier deployment. A utility is provided with the product to package and unpackage the site. The files that contain the packaged site are known as packager/unpackager files, or *Pup files;* they have a *.pup* extension.

The solution sites are based on traditional ASP and ADO. Microsoft also offers the Reference Architecture for Commerce: Business to Consumer. The reference architecture is based on XML content and XSL to target the client device. It also includes the core features of a retail commerce site: the shopping basket, credit card processing, catalog browsing, and order history.

SUPPLIER ENABLEMENT TOOL KIT

As of the time of this writing, an add-on feature to Commerce Server called the Supplier Enablement Tool Kit is in technology preview. The kit is a set of objects, ASP pages, BizTalk Messaging channels, BizTalk AICs, and Business Desk add-in modules that make it easier for a supplier to do the tasks necessary to start participating in a business-to-business marketplace.

Features include the ability to publish catalogs in standard catalog formats such as cXML and xCBL, the ability to convert Commerce Server catalogs into cXML and xCBL, and the support of supplier-managed catalogs. Also included is support for receiving and processing business-level orders.

Supplier-managed catalogs, also known as *remote baskets, punch-out, tap-out, Web tap,* and *roundtrip,* allow you to control how your products are presented on a marketplace Web site by defining a protocol to allow the marketplace Web site to call your site to supply the presentation and selection of your products. It tries to help suppliers avoid being considered merely a price and a stock-keeping unit (SKU) on a marketplace Web site—and help them emphasize real value-added differentiators such as quality of service.

The tool kit leverages the translation facilities of BizTalk Server Messaging to convert the catalogs and involves a change in the Commerce Server catalog structure to make this feasible.

Despite the marketing literature emphasizing the fact that BizTalk's translation framework can map from anything to anything, in practical terms it is quite possible to define or encounter XML-based file formats that are quite difficult to translate. This is not really an issue with BizTalk because it simply leverages XSLT to do the mapping. The creation of document specifications for some documents can be quite challenging. One of the design tradeoffs is weighing the simplicity of processing against the flexible variety of format. For example, a catalog is much more translatable if it does not include categories within categories.

INTEGRATION POINTS

This section discusses key integration points between BizTalk Server and the other .NET enterprise servers. Most of these integrations are rather straightforward. The following code listings provide simple examples. There are more extensive samples included with the BizTalk product.

Internet Information Server to BizTalk Server Orchestration

The focus here is how to start a BizTalk Orchestration schedule from IIS. It is very simple—just use `GetObject` from ASP to instantiate an instance of the schedule:

```
' Code to start the XLANG schedule
Set oSked = GetObject
("sked://localhost/C:\SimpleHelix\Schedule\SpecialOrder.skx")
```

Internet Information Server to BizTalk Server Messaging

Integration of IIS to BizTalk Server Messaging is also fairly straightforward. You extract the document from the intrinsic ASP `Request` object and submit it to BizTalk Messaging using one of the three submission methods. In each case the request's byte array needs to be converted to UNICODE format. These code listings enlist the help of a `Stream` object to accomplish this.

From HTTP Request to BizTalk Messaging via Direct Integration

The following code gets the bytes from the request, writes them into a `stream` object, reads them out as UNICODE, and sends them asynchronously to BizTalk Messaging using `IInterchange::Submit`:

```
<%
Dim objBTS, BIZTALK_OPENNESS_TYPE_NOTOPEN, objADO

if Request.totalBytes = 0 then
    Response.Write "No Data Posted From Simple Helix BizTalk Server. "
    Err.Raise vbObjectError+ 101,,"No Data Posted From Simple Helix BizTalk
                        Server."
    Response.End
end if

Set objADO = CreateObject("ADODB.Stream")
objADO.Open
objADO.Type = 1
```

```
objADO.Write Request.BinaryRead(Request.TotalBytes)
objADO.Position = 0
objADO.Type = 2

BIZTALK_OPENNESS_TYPE_NOTOPEN = 1
Set objBTS = Server.CreateObject("BizTalk.Interchange")
objBTS.Submit BIZTALK_OPENNESS_TYPE_NOTOPEN, objADO.ReadText, , , , , , _
"Orders from Simple Helix"
Set objBTS = Nothing
%>
```

From HTTP Request to BizTalk Messaging via Message Queuing Receive Function

Using message queuing is slightly more complicated. You need to use the MSMQ objects to put the message in a queue. BizTalk Orchestration requires the message queue to be transactional. This code creates the queue and a transaction dispenser at application startup. It also assumes that a BizTalk Messaging MSMQ receive function has been configured to watch the queue. Following is code from `global.asa`:

```
<SCRIPT LANGUAGE=VBScript RUNAT=Server>

Const MQ_SEND_ACCESS = 2
Const MQ_DENY_NONE = 0

Sub Application_OnStart
    Dim ShipNoticeQueue
    Dim QueueInfo
    Dim MSMQTxDisp
    Dim MSMQName

    Set QueueInfo = Server.CreateObject("MSMQ.MSMQQueueInfo")
    Set MSMQTxDisp = Server.CreateObject("MSMQ.MSMQTransactionDispenser")
    Set ShipNoticeQueue = Server.CreateObject("MSMQ.MSMQQueue")

    MSMQName = "DIRECT=OS:.\private$\SHShipNoticeIn"
    QueueInfo.FormatName = MSMQName
    Set ShipNoticeQueue = QueueInfo.Open(MQ_SEND_ACCESS, MQ_DENY_NONE)

    Set Application("MSMQTxDisp") = MSMQTxDisp
    Set Application("ShipNoticeQueue") = ShipNoticeQueue
End Sub

Sub Application_OnEnd
    Dim ShipNoticeQueue
    Set ShipNoticeQueue = Application("ShipNoticeQueue")
    ShipNoticeQueue.close
End Sub

</SCRIPT>
```

Following is code to receive the message and put it in the queue for the BizTalk Messaging MSMQ receive function:

```
<%
Dim ShipNoticeQueue
Dim QueueMsg
Dim MSMQTx
Dim MSMQTxDisp

if Request.totalBytes = 0 then
    Response.Write "No Data Posted From BizTalk Server."
    Response.End
end if

'Create Stream object to convert Byte Array Into UNICODE String
Set objADO = CreateObject("ADODB.Stream")
objADO.Open
objADO.Type = 1
objADO.Write Request.BinaryRead(Request.TotalBytes)
objADO.Position = 0
objADO.Type = 2
objADO.CharSet = "us-ascii"

'Create required MSMQ objects
Set QueueMsg = Server.CreateObject("MSMQ.MSMQMessage")

QueueMsg.Label = "ShipNotice"
QueueMsg.Body = objADO.ReadText
Set MSMQTxDisp = Application("MSMQTxDisp")
Set MSMQTx = MSMQTxDisp.BeginTransaction
set ShipNoticeQueue = Application("ShipNoticeQueue")
QueueMsg.Send ShipNoticeQueue,MSMQTx
MSMQTx.Commit

Set MSMQTX = Nothing
Set QueueMsg = Nothing
%>
```

From HTTP Request to BizTalk Messaging via File Receive Function

The following code uses the file system object to write the document to a folder. It assumes that a BizTalk Messaging file receive function has been configured to pick up the file and submit it to the channel selection process.

```
<%
Const ForWriting = 2
Dim DropPath
Dim fso, ts
DropPath = "c:\InsuranceDocDrop\XMLAuto.xml"
Set fso = Server.CreateObject("Scripting.FileSystemObject")
Set ts = fso.OpenTextFile(DropPath, ForWriting, True)
```

```
ts.Write Request.Form
ts.Close
%>
```

Commerce Server to BizTalk Server

Integration to BizTalk Server Messaging

Although direct integration can be used (i.e., getting an instance of IInterchange and calling its `Submit` method), it is not recommended. It works, but it does not allow for a more loosely coupled architecture. Because the implementation is apartment threaded, it does not scale well. A preferred method is to use a receive function. You configure an MSMQ receive function or a file receive function and drop the output from Commerce Server into the queue or directory.

Integration to BizTalk Server Orchestration

In the example in Chapter 10, the business-to-consumer site produces an order form XML document that contains a special order. The question is how to integrate this with the instantiation of an instance of a BizTalk Orchestration schedule.

One option would be for the business-to-consumer site to instantiate the orchestration schedule itself by a GetObject API call to instantiate the schedule directly, but this is not a good idea. It requires that the BizTalk BPOActivation COM+ components be installed on the business-to-consumer machine. It would be much better to have a more loosely coupled situation. Alternatively, we could have the business-to-consumer site write the XML order form document to a Microsoft Message Queue on the BizTalk Server machine. Then the business-to-consumer machine has no BizTalk dependencies. Regardless, just putting the message in a queue does not start an orchestration schedule.

One way of solving this would be to write a simple adapter application that would watch the queue and, when a message arrived, it would instantiate an instance of the orchestration schedule using GetObject with the `sked:` moniker; it would then put the message in the message queue where the schedule expected to find it. This orchestration schedule would begin with an action connected to a message queue port, configured to receive messages from the queue (Figure 9-14).

The newly instantiated schedule begins by waiting for a message to appear in the SHOrderOut queue, as shown by the MSMQ implementation shape shown in the upper right of the orchestration schedule snippet in Figure 9-15.

Using your own adapter application is certainly workable but is not really necessary. Maybe you think that we can configure a BizTalk Server receive function to watch the message queue and submit the document to the BizTalk Server, but this means the document is submitted to BizTalk Messaging. How do we get BizTalk Messaging to start an orchestration schedule?

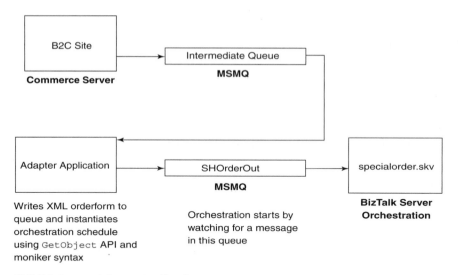

FIGURE 9-14   Adapter Application.

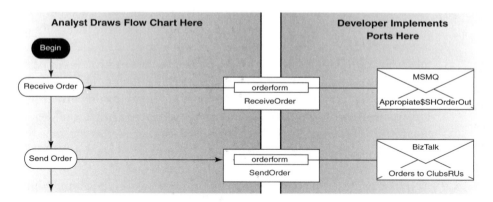

FIGURE 9-15   Orchestration Schedule Starts.

As it turns out, this is not an unusual scenario. You do not need to write an adapter application. We describe it from front to back, but you set it up back to front. This is generally a good idea anyway when working with BizTalk.

An MSMQ receive function is setup to watch a queue, configured to send to a known BizTalk Messaging channel. When a message is dropped into the queue, the receive function reads it out of the queue and submits it to the BizTalk channel.

The channel connects to a BizTalk Messaging port. This port is configured to send to an application. The destination application is a new XLANG schedule. The properties of the destination application specify an SKV file containing the XLANG schedule to create and an orchestration port name within the schedule to receive the payload. This port name needs to be the first port at the beginning of the schedule and is connected to the BizTalk Messaging implementation shape in the Visio-based Orchestration Designer tool. The BizTalk Messaging Binding Wizard pops up when this shape connection is made, and the communication direction is set to receive.

Given this setup, when a message is put into the queue, the receive function reads it from the queue and submits it to BizTalk Messaging using the specified channel. This channel's port is wired to instantiate the specified orchestration schedule and gives the message passing through the channel to the orchestration port that is denoted in the port properties. The orchestration schedule is then running, and the receive action in the orchestration flow has the message. In this configuration, there is an implied queue that receives the message and presents it to the newly activated orchestration schedule. This is how the message gets into the schedule.

CONCLUSION

It turns out that the .NET servers marketing name is more appropriate than it first appeared. The .NET servers provide a powerful illustration of the universalization, collaboration, and translation principles we have been using throughout the book as fundamental to this new type of software development. If we are impressed by the XML support classes in the CLR and how we can write *little* code to read and write a *single* XML document, how much more should we be impressed by an environment in which we can describe, receive, validate, translate, and reliably transport *classes* of XML documents *without writing code*?

A pertinent measure of reuse potency answers the question, "What is the leverage level of the primitives I'm using?" In the case of the .NET servers, the leverage is much higher than with the CLR. By the time you are mining the CLR, you are already at the point of writing custom code and are at a lower level of reuse leverage of a universal runtime. The .NET servers provide an essential set of capabilities required to bring real, people-oriented systems to life.

Applied .NET Enterprise Servers: Order Fulfillment with an Outside Vendor

As an example of building systems using the .NET enterprise servers , this chapter presents a case study of a business-to-consumer site using Commerce Server with business-to-business order fulfillment powered by BizTalk Server. In people-oriented software terms, it provides an example of *universalization* in mining the rich capabilities of these .NET servers, *collaboration* in the orchestration of processes across enterprise boundaries, and *translation* in the transformation of business documents to accommodate the expectations of the cooperating systems.

This chapter's case study focuses on the e-commerce site of Simple Helix, a fictitious company that sells golf clubs and accessories to consumers. Table 10-1 shows Simple Helix's Web site features and which parts of the .NET server technologies were used to provide them. This table provides a glimpse of the remarkable capabilities available for mining.

Commerce Server provides the framework for the Web site, and BizTalk Server is used to provide order fulfillment with the outside vendor ClubsRUs. Commerce Server provides the framework for log-in, catalog browsing, and order pipeline processing. The order pipeline processing ends with a Simple Helix order form that needs to be turned into goods that are delivered to the customer. For this to happen, many steps need to be coordinated involving Simple Helix, the external vendor, the customer, and the customer's credit card company. All of these interactions are managed by a BizTalk Server Orchestration schedule.

The order form must be translated into a purchase order format expected by the external vendor system and be delivered over the Internet. The customer needs to be

TABLE 10-1   Miner's Roadmap to Simple Helix Features

Simple Helix Feature	.NET Server Solution
Log-in	Commerce Server Retail Solution Site
Browse catalog	Commerce Server Retail Solution Site
Shopping basket	Commerce Server Retail Solution Site
Check-out	Commerce Server Retail Solution Site
Reserve credit card amount	Custom component added to Commerce Server order-processing pipeline
Translate order to vendor system format	BizTalk Orchestration and Messaging
Send order to vendor system using standard Internet protocols	BizTalk Messaging HTTP transport
Notify customer of order placement	BizTalk Orchestration and custom Windows scripting component
Maintain order fulfillment status	BizTalk Orchestration and custom Windows scripting component updating Commerce Server database
Provide order status to customer on demand	Commerce Server Retail Solution Site
Receive ship notice from outside vendor system using standard Internet protocols	Internet information server, message queuing, BizTalk Orchestration
Charge credit card	BizTalk Orchestration and custom Windows scripting component
Notify customer of order shipped	BizTalk Orchestration and custom Windows scripting component
Coordinate overall order fulfillment execution	BizTalk Orchestration Engine

notified of the order's status at key points in the process. The Web site database needs to be updated with the correct status of the order. Some actions can proceed in parallel, for example, ClubsRUs order processing and Simple Helix site database updating. Others must happen in a certain order. The entire process could take days depending on how long it takes the external vendor to deliver the goods.

The external vendor receives the purchase order and turns it into a ship notice, which it sends back to Simple Helix over the Internet. Simple Helix receives the ship notice and attempts to charge the customer's credit card. Based on the results of the attempt, either a charge failure or an order shipped notification is sent to the customer, and the e-commerce site database state for the order is updated accordingly.

ORDER PROCESSING PIPELINE

Simple Helix leverages the check-out pipeline from the Retail solution site as the order processing pipeline (Figure 10-1). A component has been added to the pipeline's payment stage; it approves credit card payment to reserve the order amount on the credit card. This component appears as *Scriptor—Reserve Credit Card*. The credit card is not charged until the outside vendor ships the product, which is indicated by receipt of a ship notice. These steps are handled by the BizTalk Server Orchestration.

BUSINESS PROCESS DEFINITION

A sequence diagram in Figure 10-2 shows the high-level interactions between the entities involved in the purchase transaction. The consumer places an order to Simple Helix. In response, Simple Helix reserves the payment amount with the credit card service, sends the order to ClubsRUs (the external fulfillment vendor), and notifies the consumer that the order has been placed. When the order is shipped, ClubsRUs sends

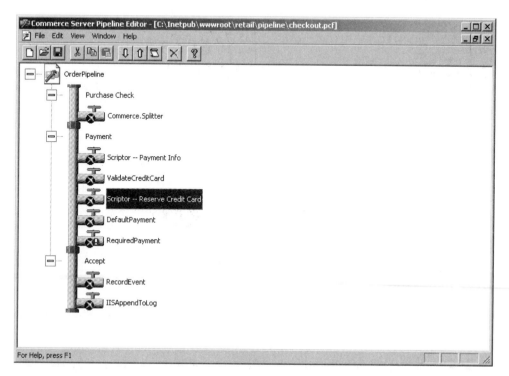

FIGURE 10-1 Simple Helix Commerce Server Order Processing Pipeline.

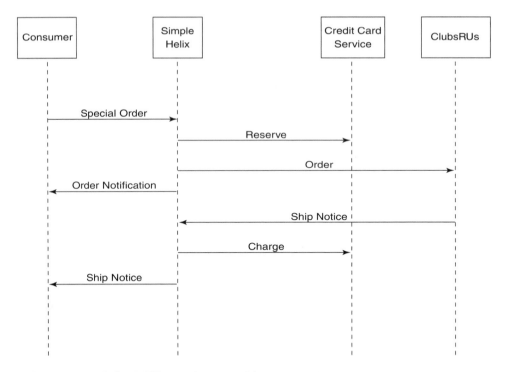

FIGURE 10-2   Order Fulfillment Sequence Diagram.

a ship notice to Simple Helix. In response, Simple Helix charges the consumer's credit card for the purchase and notifies the consumer of shipment.

The behavior of Simple Helix in the Figure 10-2 sequence diagram can be modeled fairly directly in a BizTalk Server Orchestration schedule, using the shapes in the Orchestration Designer tool (Figure 10-3). The sending of the messages maps to the action shapes on the design surface. The arrows show the sequence of the actions. Because the schedule views the interaction from the perspective of Simple Helix, it turns out looking like a serial sequence of events. In fact, certain events are simultaneous—the external vendor is processing the order while Simple Helix is notifying the consumer.

PORT IMPLEMENTATIONS

After the business process has been modeled, you implement the solution by connecting components to the actions. The two main steps of implementation are (1) describing the implementation component and (2) specifying the data flow. The Binding Wizard for each implementation shape type handles the first task, and the eXtensible Markup Language (XML) Communication Wizard handles the second.

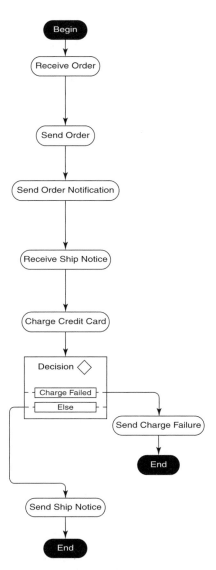

FIGURE 10-3 Order Fulfillment Business Process Diagram.

There are four implementation shapes in the tool—a component object model (COM) component, a Windows scripting component, a message queuing shape, and a BizTalk Messaging shape. When you drag and drop one of these shapes on the design surface, the tool starts the Binding Wizard to walk you through the process of wiring up a software Lego to the business process action (Figure 10-4). The connection is called an *implementation port,* which has nothing to do with a BizTalk Messaging port. This unfortunate terminology usage can cause confusion.

FIGURE 10-4   BizTalk Messaging Binding Wizard.

In this case study, we use the BizTalk Messaging shape, the Microsoft Message Queuing (MSMQ) shape, and the Script Components shape. The first action, Receive Order, is connected to a BizTalk shape. The Binding Wizard walks you through the creation of the port. Our case study involves the creation of a new port.

Actions in a BizTalk Orchestration schedule consist of sending or receiving a message. For each port implementation, you specify whether the action is sending or receiving. The first step in the schedule is to receive an order, so the communication Direction is *Receive* (Figure 10-5).

In other words, a BizTalk Messaging channel and port combination presents an order message to the orchestration schedule. A common scenario is that the arrival of a message triggers the instantiation of an orchestration schedule to handle it. (This scenario was described in Chapter 9 in the discussion of the integration of Commerce Server to BizTalk Server Orchestration.) To achieve this activation (Figure 10-6), the BizTalk *Messaging* port properties must be configured on the Destination Application pane to start a new schedule. Because we selected *Receive*, the next Binding Wizard pane asks whether we have configured the BizTalk Messaging channel accordingly.

Technically, this configuration is in the BizTalk Messaging *port*, but we can deal with this discrepancy in the wizard screen. Figure 10-7 shows what the screen looks like when accessed from the BizTalk Messaging Manager tool. The configuration information includes the schedule moniker and orchestration port name. The schedule moniker specifies the location of the XLANG schedule file (SKV file) that contains the XLANG schedule, and the port name is the same name we supply in the first pane

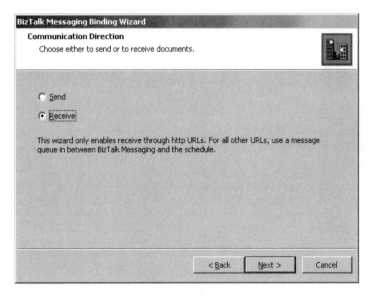

FIGURE 10-5   Binding Wizard Communication Direction.

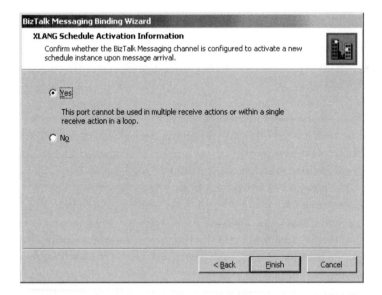

FIGURE 10-6   Binding Wizard XLANG Activation.

of the BizTalk Binding Wizard. You do not have to configure the messaging port properties at the time of the schedule shape implementation. It just has to be set up before you run the schedule.

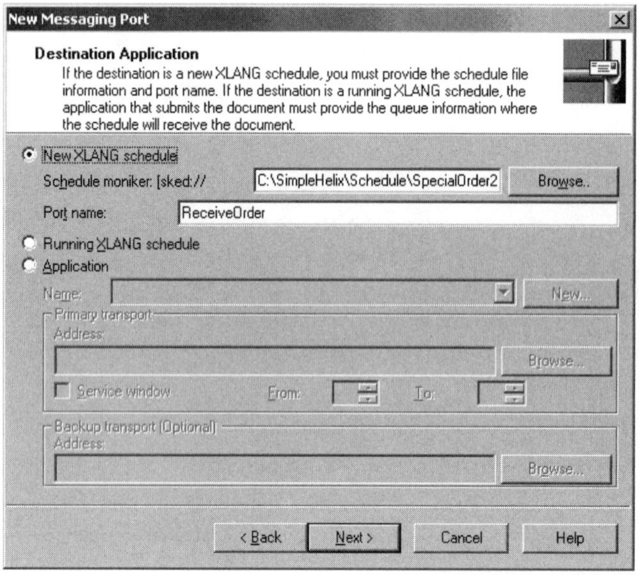

FIGURE 10-7   Binding Wizard Destination Application.

When you click the Finish button, the tool draws the port on the design surface. The next step is to connect the port to the action, which you do by connecting the action shape anchor point to the port shape. When you do, the tool starts the XML Communication Wizard (Figure 10-8). All of the data flow in a schedule is handled by XML. In this case, we have already indicated that we are receiving, so the only thing to consider is providing information to allow the XLANG scheduler to decide whether to deactivate the schedule if no message is immediately available. The default of zero means the message is expected immediately. The schedule is never dehydrated if this value is 180 or less.

The next step is to provide information about the message that will be received (Figure 10-9). We tell the Wizard to create a new message and name it *orderform*. This name will appear on the port connection in the tool and identifies the message on the Data Flow tab of the tool. Next we specify the format of the data as XML or string (Figure 10-10). The engine works only with XML. The message can be a non-XML string but if it is, we tell the engine so that it can wrap it in XML internally.

This technique of using a BizTalk Messaging port to receive a message implies a queue under the hood. The engine uses the information we supply next to check that the message in this queue is the expected one. It checks the string entered against the message label and against the root element of the message if the message is in XML format (Figure 10-11). Finally, the engine can validate the received message against a schema (Figure 10-12). BizTalk Messaging also validates messages against a schema,

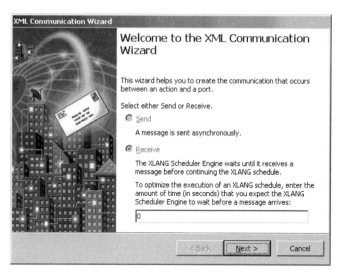

FIGURE 10-8 XML Communication Wizard.

but this is a separate validation. Remember that orchestration can be used completely without BizTalk Messaging.

From the screen in Figure 10-12 you can create a schema. If you press the Create button, the BizTalk Editor is invoked to help you. Pressing the Finish button completes the XML message wiring to the port. We have now

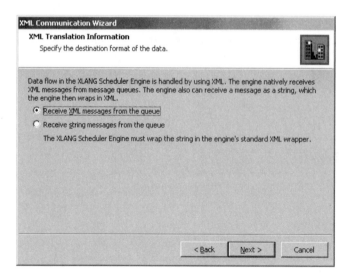

FIGURE 10-10   XML Translation Information.

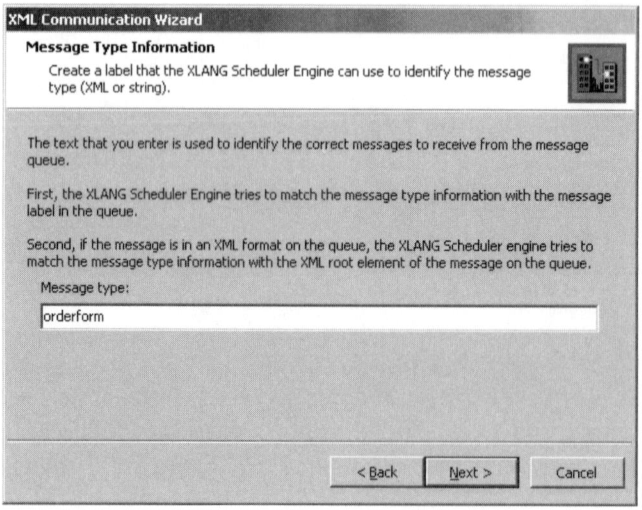

FIGURE 10-11   Message Type Information.

finished implementation of the first action. The resulting schedule is shown in Figure 10-13. The rest of the actions are implemented in a similar way. The entire orchestration design surface is shown in Figure 10-14.

Rather than discuss all of the wizard details for each step, which you can do by opening the schedule in the design tool by clicking on the shapes, we describe the entire flow at the runtime interaction level.

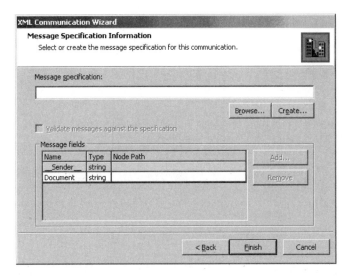

FIGURE 10-12   Message Specification Information.

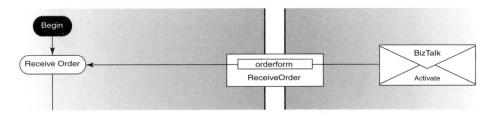

FIGURE 10-13   First Implementation Port.

INTEGRATION WITH BUSINESS-TO-CONSUMER SITE

The business-to-consumer site drops an order into the SHOrderOut message queue. A BizTalk Messaging MSMQ *receive* function is configured to watch for messages in this queue. When the message appears, the receive function reads the message from the queue and submits it to the BizTalk Messaging channel specified in the receive function. This channel, called *SimpleHelix B2C to B2B* (business-to-consumer to business-to-business), is connected to the messaging port called *Port to Start Schedule*. This port is configured to start an instance of the orchestration schedule, represented by the file `specialorder2.skv`, and present the message to the orchestration port named `ReceiveOrder`.

ReceiveOrder gives the message to the SendOrder action, which passes it to BizTalk Messaging for delivery to the external supplier. The implementation port specifies the BizTalk Messaging channel destination. In this case, we specify a static channel, meaning the channel is specified at design time. It is also possible to specify

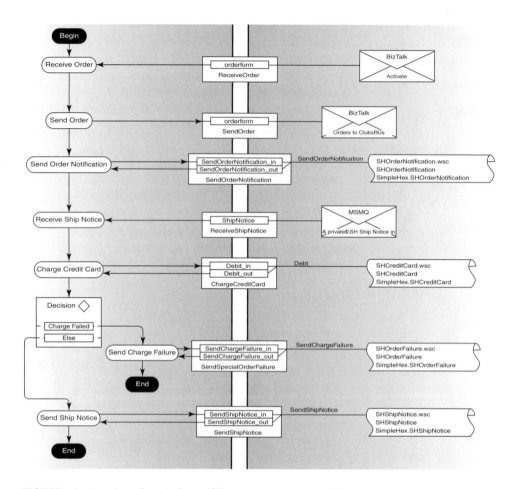

FIGURE 10-14   Complete Order Fulfillment Orchestration Diagram.

the channel at runtime by specifying the use of a dynamic channel and getting the channel name from a message field.

Order Translation to Outside Vendor Format

The channel used is called *Order to ClubsRUs*. The incoming document needs to be validated, and ClubsRUs expects to receive documents in the form of ClubsRUs purchase orders. The orderform document received from Commerce Server needs to be translated into a ClubsRUs purchase order and delivered to ClubsRUs.

The channel validates the incoming document against the inbound document definition designated in the channel. The inbound document definition name is *orderform* and refers to a document schema, orderform.xml, accessible at runtime via Web

Distributed Authoring and Versioning (WebDAV). This schema was created using the BizTalk Editor tool. The outbound document definition, ClubsRUsPO, was also created by this tool and stored in the WebDAV repository in the file ClubsRUsPO.xml. The document specifications are located in the WebDAV repository under C:\ Program Files\Microsoft BizTalk Server\BizTalkServerRepository\DocSpecs\ SimpleHelix.

To wire up the translation, we specified the outbound document specification and a translation map. Because the inbound and outbound schemas are not the same, BizTalk wants a map to use to translate from one to the other. The map was created using the BizTalk Mapper tool and is called *orderformToClubsRUsPO.xml.* BizTalk Messaging applies the map using extensible style language transformation (XSLT) and produces a ClubsRUsPO as a result.

Delivery to Outside Vendor's BizTalk Server

The *Order to ClubsRUs* channel is connected via HyperText Transfer Protocol (HTTP) to the messaging port called *ClubsRUs.* The port specifies the transport as HTTP and the destination uniform resource locator (URL). After translating the document, BizTalk Messaging uses the built-in HTTP transport to deliver the message to the URL, *http://server/ClubsRUs/OrderClubs.asp.*

Commerce Site Status Update and Consumer Notification

After sending the order to the external vendor for fulfillment, the schedule moves to the Send Order Notification action. This step updates the commerce site order status in the site database and notifies the consumer via e-mail that the order has been placed. These actions are packaged inside a Windows scripting component.

The scripting component has a `SendOrderNotification` method that encapsulates this functionality, and the schedule is configured to create an instance of this component and synchronously call this method. How do you pass the information from the schedule message to the arguments of the method call?

The Scripting Component Binding Wizard interrogates the type library information in the component and uses it to connect to a method call. At design time, when a method is selected, the tool creates messages representing the input and output arguments to the method. It uses the name of the method followed by `_In` and `_Out` to denote the input and output arguments. Our component takes a single argument, the orderform. The orchestration data page contains a flow (Figure 10-15) to connect the orderform document field to the document field in the `SendOrderNotification_ In` message. This gets the document into the method call.

The scripting component processes the XML document using the document object model (DOM) and calls helper routines to update the site database and send an e-mail message to the consumer at the address included in the message, formatted

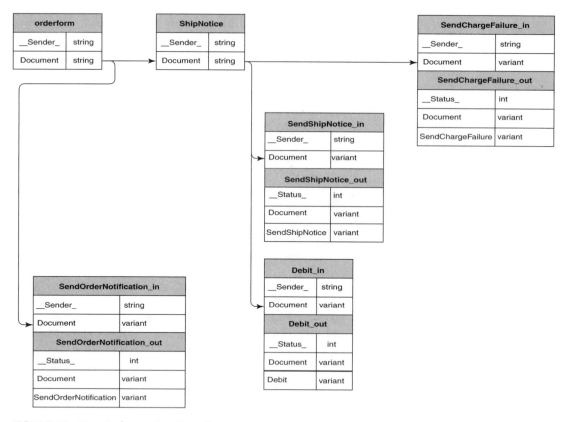

FIGURE 10-15   Orchestration Data Flow.

with order details from the order form fields. The schedule now proceeds to the Receive Ship Notice action, where it waits for a message to appear in the SHShipNoticeIn queue.

Outside Vendor BizTalk Processing

The active server page (ASP) on the supplier site extracts the order from the Response object, converts the content, and submits it to the supplier's BizTalk Server Messaging using a channel called *Orders from Simple Helix*. This channel expects to receive a ClubsRUsPO.xml document specification. The channel converts the ClubsRUsPO document into a shipping notice using the map ClubsRUsPOToShipNotice.xml. The shipping notice document is defined by the document specification ShipNotice.xml in the DocSpecs in the repository.

The supplier channel Orders from Simple Helix is connected to a port called *Simple Helix via HTTP*. This port uses BizTalk Server's built-in HTTP transport to send the shipping notice back to Simple Helix using a faceless Web site page, ShipNotice.asp. This simulates the supplier actions of accepting the order and fulfilling it, shipping the order to the consumer, and sending the ship notice to Simple Helix.

ShipNotice.asp extracts the message from the response object and drops it into the message queue SHShipNoticeIn. Message queues used with orchestration schedules are transactional queues.

Ship Notice Handling

The orchestration schedule's Receive Ship Notice action is watching this queue. The schedule activates when the ship notice arrives in the queue, and the schedule reads the notice. The port defines the message expected, and the data flow connects it to the message used in the next step, Charge Credit Card.

Charge Credit Card

The ship notice lets Simple Helix know that the order has been shipped, so the next step in the schedule is to charge the consumer's credit card and update the commerce site database accordingly. These operations are encapsulated in the SHCreditCard Windows scripting component. The Charge Credit Card action instantiates the SHCreditCardLib COM component and calls its `Debit` method. This is a synchronous call. The `Debit` method follows a similar pattern to that used by the `SendOrderNotification` call. The scripting component is passed to the ship notice XML. It uses the DOM to extract the arguments needed to call the functions it uses internally to charge the credit card and update the database. In the new world order, this would be a .NET credit card service. In this example the functionality is simulated by a COM component.

The last shape on the schedule represents a decision based on the outcome of the credit card charge. The funds were reserved in the commerce site payment pipeline before the orchestration schedule was started, but it is still possible that the charge may fail. There are a variety of ways that failures can be handled in this architecture and like any error handling, the choices involve both functional tradeoffs and style choices. One choice would be to fail the schedule based on an error HRESULT from the scripting component call. This can be configured in the Binding Wizard for the scripting component. We did not choose this because we wanted the schedule to clearly show the flow and invoke the proper notification action. Transaction support in the schedule could have also been used. Using the decision shape gave us the level of clarity and control we wanted.

The decision shape provides a way of expressing alternate execution paths. Although this decision shows two paths, multiple paths are possible. For each alternate path, you define a rule, which is written as a script expression. If the expression evaluates to *true*, the schedule follows the connected path of execution. The expression is written in terms of the fields of the messages that are present in the schedule. For example, in this case the rule named Charge Failed is expressed as `Debit_out.Debit = ""`.

When you implement a port that calls a COM component or Windows scripting component, the tool represents the inputs and outputs of the call as fields on messages. There are two messages—one for the input arguments and one for the output arguments. In this orchestration schedule there is a message named `Debit_out`, which represents the output from the call to the scripting component that wraps a credit card service. `Debit_out.Debit` represents the return value from the call to the Debit function. This particular component uses a convention of returning a transaction ID as a string, and an empty one indicates failure.

If the charge fails, the schedule moves to the Send Charge Failure action. If it succeeds, the schedule executes the Send Ship Notice action. Scripting components are used to implement these actions as well. The SHOrderFailure component implements a `SendChargeFailure` method that updates the site database and notifies the consumer.

The `SendShipNotice` method of the SHShipNotice component does the same things for the success case. It updates the site state and notifies the consumer that the special order has been shipped and the credit card has been charged. The schedule ends after the completion of either of the alternate execution paths.

CONCLUSION

This chapter described a fairly realistic scenario of an e-commerce site with order fulfillment using an outside vendor. Very little code development was necessary. Most of the key capabilities were mined from Commerce Server and BizTalk Server and constructed and configured declaratively.

This example reveals a compelling implementation of people-oriented software's universalization, collaboration, and translation principles in action. It is an example of high-powered, high-level leverage of functionality, such as managed execution of separate logic implementations as a coordinated schedule, translation of documents to various formats, security features of an e-commerce site, catalog browsing, order placement, order status tracking and notification, order fulfillment, standard Internet protocol transfer of documents, long-lived operations, and credit-card processing.

The .NET enterprise servers complete the picture for real-world development by providing true horsepower behind the global interoperability tool set we find in the .NET framework.

Index

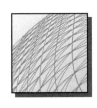

Note: Italicized page locators indicate figures or tables.